True Gospel Revealed anew by Jesus

Volume IV

Second Edition

Received by: James E. Padgett

Original Editor: Dr. John Paul Gibson

Current Editor: Geoff Cutler

Published July 2014.

True Gospel Revealed anew by Jesus

Volume IV

This is the Second Edition: 2014

This volume was initially published in 1972 as "True Gospel Revealed anew by Jesus" by the F. C. N. B., Inc.

It is believed that Victor Summers, acting as president, put all these messages into the public domain on December 25th 1984.

July 2014, Bayview, NSW, Australia.

Editor: Geoffrey John Cutler.

I.S.B.N. : 978-1-291-96086-0

Other Divine Love related publications
By Geoff Cutler.

A Gospel of Truth and Light to Mankind. Published November 2011. This is the full set of Padgett Messages arranged in date order. It contains the contents of the four volumes known as the *"True Gospel revealed anew by Jesus"*, Volumes I to IV. This is the most up to date of various similar publications, in that the most recent date research is as per this book. Available at Lulu only. A very large hard cover book (11 inch by 9 inch) of over 700 pages.

Judas of Kerioth. Conversations with Judas Iscariot. Published December 2012. This is a 600 page book (9 inch by 6 inch) of communications from Judas. It contains many previously unknown details about the life of Jesus of Nazareth. Available at Lulu and Amazon.

Is Reincarnation an Illusion? Published March 2011. 191 pages. This is an original work based on ten years research into the subject, and drawing on many sources in order to evaluate all the issues that lead people to believe that reincarnation is true. Available at Lulu and Amazon.

Getting the Hell out of here. What happens after you die? Published March 2011. This is a small book of 45 pages summarizing the fascinating details of life after death. It draws on many sources, but particularly the Padgett Messages and the Judas Messages. Available at Lulu.

Many of these have pdf or Kindle eBook versions available either free, or at a nominal cost. Check the new-birth.net web site for details.

Introduction to Volume IV Second Edition

By Geoff Cutler

This was the fourth volume of Padgett messages produced by Rev. John Paul Gibson, and it was first published in 1972, forty nine years after the death of James Padgett. In publishing these messages initially the date of the message was ignored, but as the years rolled on and further Volumes and editions were produced, dates started to be attached to some messages. James Padgett maintained a diary that indicated who communicated and a short summary of their message. When this diary surfaced around the year 2000, efforts began to date each published message and those published on web sites could now be dated and indeed be indexed and read in date order.

In recent years a significant number of new publications have appeared, by various editors, many of them using the now freely available dates of the messages. As one of the people deeply involved in matching the often terse summary in the daily dairy, with these published messages, I am familiar with the benefit offered by reading the messages in the very sequence in which they were received. However I have also recently become aware of the difficulty in correctly absorbing this material, when one is required to read some 1250 communications, to cover all the subjects fully.

The benefit of these original publications lay in the fact that messages were collated together on a topic particularly in Volumes I and II, and it is far easier for a reader to absorb these new spiritual concepts, particularly as one is able to read in sequence messages that may have been received years apart. In this edition dates have been added where known.

There are 52 messages in Volume IV which are repeated in earlier volumes. Every instance of a duplicate is slightly different, indicating it was re-transcribed from the original, and not simply copied. The number of duplicates may appear higher to the reader as every instance is flagged, and hence each duplicate is flagged twice at some stage. Within this Volume eleven messages were repeated, and in order to reduce the size of the volume, the second instance has been removed. I do feel that it is important to publish the most accurate of these repeated messages, on a word by word basis. This of course means that the resultant message that has been used is not exactly the same as any of the originals from which it was derived. In each case, a footnote to that effect has been included here. Footnotes from earlier editions are also included. As Reverend Dr. John Paul Gibson himself used footnotes, each footnote is marked (J.P.G.) or (G.J.C.) to indicate which editor is responsible. The details of these duplicates are set out in some detail on my web site – www.new-birth.net.

While I respect the desire by this last publisher (of the First Edition) to never change a single comma in their publication, publishing standards have moved on considerably since that time. One simply no longer uses capitalization for emphasis, as an example. It is in the interests of readability that I have adopted modern standards of typography. Where a word has fallen into disuse, I have added its current equivalent in () brackets, rather than changing the word. I certainly have punctuated extensively, creating smaller sentences where in some cases the sentences were almost unreadable.

In the process of discovering the dates of the messages, it became apparent that Dr. Stone particularly, and to a lesser extent Rev. John Paul Gibson had concealed the names of many of James Padgett's legal acquaintances who came through as spirits in darkness. This was a very sensible approach at that time, but now that it is 100 years later it is more useful to see the spiritual progression of these individuals over time. Accordingly in every case where I have been able to discover the real name of the spirit, that has now been used. Similarly where additional detail regarding "preachers" was in the diary, this too has been added as background.

This content was first published in Kindle eBook format in December 2013.

Geoff Cutler. Bayview, NSW, Australia.

July 2014

James E. Padgett

JAMES E. PADGETT

Mr. James E. Padgett was born August 25th, 1852, in Washington, D.C. and attended the Polytechnic Academy Institute at Newmarket, Virginia. In 1880 he was admitted to the bar in Washington, D.C. and thereafter he practiced law for 43 years until his death on March 17th, 1923. During his student years, he became friendly with Professor Joseph Salyards, an instructor at the Academy who, after his death in 1885, wrote him many interesting messages. His wife, Helen, died on the 14th February 1914, and was the first to write him from the spirit world. Padgett never practiced the gift of mediumship as a means of earning money. He was dedicated wholly to the reception of the great messages signed by Jesus and his many disciples.

Introduction by Rev. John Paul Gibson

I first heard about *Messages From Jesus and Celestials*[1] from a total stranger at lunch in a New York City restaurant, which was just after I was discharged from the United States Coast Guard in 1945. Since the conversation during lunch led to spiritual subjects, the above book was mentioned, that was received by Mr. James E. Padgett through automatic writing. I knew a great deal about automatic writing and could receive messages from some of my loved ones in the spirit world. I became quite anxious to obtain a copy as soon as possible, because I was planning to leave for California. So the good Doctor Arnet that I was talking with offered me a copy, and I could have it by calling at his office. This I was happy to do.

In California I had considerable opportunity to study the messages that were written by Jesus of Nazareth and other Celestial writers. And the new prayer by Jesus became very important to me, as it filled my soul with greater love than I have ever felt before; but there was a small part that seemed to bother me whenever I would repeat the prayer, where it said: *"Even though the world believes that One is Thy equal and a part of Thy Godhead."*

I decided to write to Dr. Stone about my feeling in this part of the prayer, and received a beautiful reply, stating his own feeling about this part also, in view of what has been written about the Godhead by St. Luke.[2]

This started my friendship and correspondence with Dr. Stone that continued through the years until his sleep on January 6th, 1967, to continue with his work in the Spirit World. I performed the burial and interment services for my friend a few days later. However, our thoughts on the correction for this part of the prayer were the same.

But it wasn't until September 26th, 1965, that our wishes for the correction of the prayer were fulfilled, when the second instrument selected by Jesus to continue with the writing where Mr. Padgett stopped with his work upon earth, which fulfills his second coming on the material plane, received the corrected prayer as is now printed in this volume, as well as Vol. III of the True Gospel Revealed Anew by Jesus.

Mr. Padgett began to receive spiritual communications from his

---

[1] This was one of the titles used to publish these volumes. In fact it was the title first used in the 1956 third edition of Volume I. It was also used on the First Edition of Volume II in 1950. (G.J.C.)

[2] See Vol I (5th Ed.) page 72. (J.P.G.)

wife Helen only a few months after her passing into spirit. The loss was so great that with a friend they visited a medium in Washington who advised him that if he would pick up a pencil his wife would try to write through him, since he had the gift of automatic writing. The first writings were received about the middle of 1914, but it was not until Mr. Padgett received the Divine Love of the Father that Jesus was able to write his formal messages that are printed in Vols. I and II of the True Gospel Revealed Anew by Jesus.

As disclosed in this and other volumes, there were present during his communications a Mr. Morgan, an old friend, as well as Dr. Leslie R. Stone With the help of Mr. Padgett, Mr. Morgan also received the gift of automatic writing, and Mr. Padgett wrote through him a few days after his passing into the Spirit World.

Jesus has written that he selected Mr. Morgan and Dr. Stone to perform special work in behalf of the Kingdom, but that their work would be different from that of Mr. Padgett. Since Dr. Stone was the last surviving instrument of the original three, he became the custodian of all the writings that were received by Mr. Padgett, as well as those received by Mr. Morgan. Mr. Padgett willed his writings to Mr. Morgan and Mr. Morgan willed both writings to Dr. Stone, who in turn transferred everything to the Leslie R. Stone Foundation, that was organized and incorporated to honor Dr. Stone, who had preserved the writings of both Mr. Padgett and Mr. Morgan as well as his close association with Mr. Padgett and the plans that they made to put his material into print. This Dr. Stone was able to do in printing Vols. I and II with the help of his many friends, both living and some now in the Spirit World.

Jesus, our Leader, proposed the name of Leslie R. Stone Foundation, but the incorporation was not quite suitable for a church organization to be on the par with all other churches. Several names were suggested and we finally had approved by Jesus the Foundation Church of the New Birth, Inc., and all the material in Dr. Stone's possession was transferred to the church corporation. Since the editor was responsible for forming both corporations, and later found no need to pay taxes on the Stone Foundation, with the approval of Jesus of Nazareth, our Leader, the Stone Foundation was dissolved. And the Foundation Church of the New Birth, INC. obtained a tax-exempt status, on a par with all churches in America, that took five years of hard work by the Trustees of the Church of the New Birth. Dr. Stone lived long enough to see that the original plan that was received by Mr. Padgett was fulfilled. And Volume III also became a reality with the continued effort of the editor to transcribe many valuable writings for man to benefit by, that were approved by Jesus, to be placed into print. And the editor will continue to transcribe additional material to fill this volume and perhaps another.[3]

Since this volume is a personal tribute to honor Dr. Stone, there are many beautiful messages from his soulmate, Mary Kennedy, on soulmate love and her spiritual progress into the Celestial Heavens that could encourage many a mortal while still on earth to seek and obtain the Divine Love of the Father to live in the Celestial Heavens.

Editor of the First Edition

Rev. Dr. John Paul Gibson, D.D.

---

[3] Had more care been taken in the selection of messages, and the duplications not occurred, almost one whole physical volume could have been avoided, which would have been a considerable saving on publication costs. Many of the originals of the handwritten messages still exist, but they are not all stored in one location, being currently in four separate locations in the U.S.A. It has proved very difficult to obtain even scannings of all the material, and to date not all have been scanned. Sadly it is also apparent that some have been lost over the years due to poor storage. (G.J.C.)

Table of Contents

Table of Contents

Table of Contents

Table of Contents

Table of Contents

Celestial Spirits 145

Jesus

What men should believe in order to again become the perfect man

Helen Padgett

Affirming that Jesus wrote on what men should do to become the

perfect man

Jesus

The things material that men pray for are answered by God by using

spirits for that purpose

The master stresses the importance of the work yet to be done and

assures Mr. Padgett of his help in times of need

Helen Padgett

Urges Mr. Padgett to remain in a condition of Love for the sake of the

work to be done

Jesus

Gives advice for Mr. Padgett to help a medium into a knowledge of

the Divine Truths

The importance of the work set before Mr. Padgett. The necessity of

getting into condition to do this work

Helen Padgett

Confirmation that Jesus wrote about getting in condition to do the

work

Jesus

Accepts suggestion from Mr. Padgett to write on the soul, that is,

when he is better able to do so. Jesus also informs Mr. Padgett that

Mr. Morgan's work will not be the same as his

How the Divine Love may be called upon and used in the healing of

our physical bodies

Helen Padgett

Confirms that the healing forces of Divine Love had been utilized in

Mr. Morgan's behalf

Jesus

Informs Mr. Padgett that his soul has had a great inflowing of Divine

Love

Table of Contents

Table of Contents

Table of Contents

Table of Contents

Ben Robinson

Jesus

Edwin Forrest

Messages

Jesus selects Dr. Stone

October 14th, 1914.

I am here, Jesus.

I know that the Doctor is anxious to hear from him who selected him to do a work of great importance for the Heavenly Father and the establishing of the Kingdom of God. I and all the disciples and the inhabitants of the Celestial Heavens are deeply grateful for the work so rewarding and beneficial to his soul as that which Dr. Stone, my selectee, has so faithfully and conscientiously carried out. The Doctor need have no undue fears for the eventual fate or future of my gospel, which will be given to all mankind. The assignment which I have selected him to do has been very largely executed by my faithful friend and disciple, and he shall have his reward. Later I shall come and explain what is to be done, but the main thing at present is to continue along the path now being followed.

So be of good cheer and pray and pray, and pray again for the Love which the Father so gladly bestows upon His children who seek it in earnest longing of soul, and I will say good night and may you both enjoy the full Love and blessings of the Heavenly Father,

Jesus of Nazareth.

Talks by Dr. Leslie R. Stone to unseen guests

Dr. Leslie R. Stone's daily talks to unseen guests began in 1915 or just shortly after Mr. Padgett received the gift of automatic writing when the requests were made from the spirit side of life for knowledge of the truths that were being received by Mr. James E. Padgett from Jesus as well as other Celestial writers on the New Birth so that they may also progress to the Celestial Heavens. In these talks Dr. Stone creates a desire in these dark or undeveloped spirits to follow the bright spirits so that they may be shown the brighter side of their spiritual life, and progress even to the Celestial Heavens where these bright spirits live. One of Dr. Stone's talks begins as follows:

My dear brothers and sisters. I am now going to give you a talk as revealed by Jesus and Celestials Spirits on the Great Truths that are known to be facts by these High Spirits, and are so desirous to enlighten you in your progress to the Celestial Heavens.

We are all created by the Heavenly Father and therefore we are all His children and in that sense we are all brothers and sisters. These High Spirits are anxious to come to you and tell you of their personal experience and progression after they entered the spirit world, and are so desirous to tell you how they progressed from the lower spheres into the Celestial Heavens.

You may never of had the opportunity of seeing these bright spirits who are anxious for you to see them. You who are in the lower spheres might say; if it is their desire for me to progress into higher spheres why did not they come to me before? Well, the answer is, you have never made the favorable condition possible, so that they could make the contact with you to permit you to see them in their glory and beauty.

To bring into operation this law of rapport, you have to make the favorable condition so this law of rapport will come into operation, for these spirits are controlled by law as immutable as the law itself. You have the power to make the necessary conditions and the high spirits will do their part. To begin, if you will send out a sincere and earnest desire to the Heavenly Father, He will send one of His bright spirits to you and show you the way to the Celestial Heavens, only then will the barriers between you and the Celestial Spirits be dissolved and the law of rapport, will be made and you will see the bright spirits. And when you do this, then go with these bright spirits and they will tell you of their personal experiences and how they made their progression from the lower spheres into the Celestial Heavens.

At the end of my talk, I will pray to the Heavenly Father, that He may send to you the Divine Spirits to help you to progress out of sour present condition, and permit you to see them.

(John 3:3-4&5) Except a man be born again, he cannot see the Kingdom of God. Nicodemus saith unto him. How can a man be born when he is old? Can he enter the second time into his mother's womb, and be born? Jesus answered; Verily, verily, I say unto thee. Except a man be born of water and of the Spirit, he cannot enter into the Kingdom of God.

In one of Jesus' messages that was written through Mr. Padgett,[4] Jesus says:

"It is the inflowing of the Divine Love into the soul and the disappearing of all that tends to sin and error transforming the soul into the Divine Nature of the Father and unity with Him."

---

[4] This would appear to be the message in Volume II: "Jesus is not God, but was sent by the Father to lead men to His favor and Love. He is the Way, the Truth and the Life." (4th Ed.) page 3. (G.J.C.)

There is only one way to obtain this Great Free Gift—of Divine Love—into the soul. You must pray for it with the faith that causes the soul energies to become so active in its longings going out to the Father with such intensity to cause the soul to be opened up for the inflowing of this Great Gift of Divine Love, that transforms the soul into the Divine Nature of the Father.

When you are praying for this Love and you haven't the Faith, then ask the Father to give you this faith, and when He does, your soul longings will become a thing of real living existence in its intensity and your soul will open up and the love will come in, and remove the causes of your suffering.

I know that the Orthodox Churches have been teaching all down the centuries that if you go to hell where you find darkness and suffering, then there you will have to suffer for all eternity, and you will have to give up all hope to progress out of this deplorable condition. Well, there are many millions now in the spirit world, who have given up all hope and believe their darkness and suffering is for all eternity, because of this terrible belief while on earth, because it is not true.

The Heavenly Father is not an angry, wrathful God, waiting for the penalties to be paid and never have an ending. He is a God of Infinite Love who smiles upon us in our weakness and always ready to help us and fill our souls with His Divine Love. His Divine Love reaches down into the lowest hells as well as into the highest heavens and no spirit will be deprived of His Love, if that spirit will only pray for this Great Free Gift of the Father, and with that Faith that makes the soul longings a thing of real living existence for its inflowing. And I repeat again, if the spirit has not sufficient faith and soul longings, then he should pray to the Father to give him that faith, and when that faith comes into the soul, the soul's longings will become so real and intense in its longings that will cause the soul to open up and the Divine Love will come in, and remove all those memories of things done on earth. The sins of omission as well as commission that causes so much suffering and unhappiness.

So when you pray to God for forgiveness, you are really praying for His Divine Love to enter into your soul. This Love as it enters the soul displaces and removes all that tends to sin or error, and as the Scriptures say, you become a new creature, born again, born from above, for it is the New Birth that Jesus taught and explained to Nicodemus, as it is written in the Scriptures. This Divine Love, as it fills the soul, does not change the law of compensation "as you have sown, so shall ye also reap." But it does change your soul. When this love fills your soul, you have invoked the Greatest Law in all the Universe, for it is the Greatest Attribute of God and all other laws have to give place to it, for it is subject to no law except the law of its ownship.

All spirits suffering under the Law of Compensation find in their memories every act and deed of their earth life. They keep their own records, not an angry wrathful God keeping their records. When their conscience becomes awakened, only then do they become their own judge and executioner. Their conscience tells them they have violated God's laws of harmony and until they get into harmony with His Laws they suffer the inharmony which causes the suffering. As I have already said, they need the New Birth. When this Divine Love enters the soul, it radiates through the spirit body and there comes to that body a radiance of glory and beauty and wonderful feeling of joy and happiness beyond mortal conception as the spirit rises into a beautiful sphere, where there are spirits who have obtained the same degree of the Divine Love that the spirit has, who has just entered the sphere, that was open to it.

All souls are subjects of the Father's creation, but no soul, at its creation was ever created with the Divine Love, but only with the natural human love. When men say or believe that they are created with the Divine Love or as some say that they have a Divine spark within them, which they can develop by following moral precepts, and renunciation of sin and error, turning from the evil and seeking the good and pure, and etc. (stet)

This belief was taught before Jesus made his advent on earth. Many spirits had made their progress by developing their natural love, free from the perversions of this natural love and reached the Kingdom of God—and became the perfect natural man of the sixth sphere. These spirits are wonderfully happy and beautiful spirits and have become like the first parents before their fall.

However, these spirits in the sixth sphere are in a condition of stagnation because of the purifying process that they have passed through. Many of these spirits are stagnated in this sphere for many centuries and will continue to be so, unless they are willing to listen and take the advice of the Celestial Spirits who come from a much higher sphere, known as the Celestial Heavens, where Jesus lives, and these Celestial Spirits often visit the Kingdom of the Perfect Natural Man to let them know that they have the privilege of progressing into a higher and a more beautiful heaven, than the one in which they now live. But, so many of these Natural Love Spirits are so satisfied with their own surroundings that they refuse to believe that there is a better place or more beautiful than the one they live in. The spirits who have their Natural Love developed to a pure state and have been stagnating for many centuries, find that their souls become hungry for something more and "They know not what." It is only then that the Celestial Spirits are able to tell them—what that great something is—The Divine Love of the Father.

This Great Divine Love which they never understand and did not pray for, was explained to them by the Celestial Spirits and encouraged them to pray to the Father for the inflowing into the soul longing of the real living existence of the Divine Love of the Father. And when these Natural Love Spirits are willing to accept this truth and pray for this Great Free Gift of Divine Love, only then will their progress into the Celestial Heavens be assured.

In Volume II, of the True Gospel Revealed Anew by Jesus, there is a message written by a spirit whose name is Saleeba, a beautiful Egyptian Princess, that was living at the time in the Kingdom of the Perfect Natural Love for many centuries. And on one occasion she saw some of the Celestial Spirits that were writing through Mr. Padgett, and asked permission to write, which was granted and she wrote that she wanted to know why these spirits were so much brighter than she was, and wanted to know how they obtained their glory and beauty. She recognized that though she was a very bright spirit, but she was not as bright as they were in comparison. Like pale moonbeam as compared to the brightness of the mid-day sun. This Princess, after asking questions of Mr. Padgett was told to go with the Celestial Spirits who would instruct her in what she needed to know about the Higher Love which was greater than what she possessed of the Natural Love in the pure state. Which is the Divine Love that is the Greatest Attribute of the Heavenly Father and is separate and distinct from the natural love, even in its purest state, for it is that Love that is the very essence and substance of the Father, while the Natural Love that she possessed in a pure state was not.

Saleeba took the advice of the Celestials and has now advanced to the Celestial Heavens. She wrote through Mr. Padgett some time later and said, that she was now writing her friends in the Sixth Sphere and telling them all about what great happiness she experienced after obtaining the Greater Love in her soul, and urged her friends to pray to the Father for this Great Love.

The soul progress of those spirits who at one time were in darkness and through prayer to the Father advanced to the Kingdom of the Perfect Natural Man by developing their Natural Love free from the perversions, by exercising a mighty will to love those who despitefully use you and living up to moral precepts and renunciation of sin and error, they find it is a long experience of expiation. It has taken centuries for many of these spirits who are now living in this Kingdom of the Sixth Sphere of the Perfect Natural Man. And since it has taken them so long to reach this sphere, they become stagnated as a result of the purifying process that they passed through.

With what has already been explained to you, you can realize how important it is to learn about Jesus teachings: "The Way the Truth and the Life" and through prayer obtaining the Higher Love, the Divine Love, that when possessed by the soul you partake of the essence and substance of the Father which transforms the soul from the merely natural man into the Divine Nature of the Father. So that when you become in full possession of this Divine Love you have obtained this Great Free Gift and are "Born Again," as Jesus told Nicodemus. Because this love comes from God by His Holy Spirit which is that part of His active energy held most sacred. Holy and Merciful, for it conveys into the receptive soul "His Divine Love" and transforms the soul from the human and natural man into the Divine Nature of the Father. And as you obtain this love in increased abundance, sin and error must decrease. For sin and error cannot fill the same part of the soul at the same time.

Jesus taught: "*Seek ye first the Kingdom of Heaven and all these things will be added unto you.*" Then love to God and fellowman will follow as naturally as the dew falls from Heaven without effort or sacrifice. Jesus also taught that when you obtain the Divine Love in that abundance to enable you to enter the Celestial Heavens, you have then partaken of the Divine Love to that degree that makes you a part of His Divine Nature and there will come to you the consciousness of knowing that this Immortal Love of the Father has given to you that Immortality and the certainty that the decree "dying thou shall die never and cannot be pronounced upon you." This is the Immortality that Jesus brought to light, when he told Nicodemus, you must be born again. Which is the New Birth. And to become Immortal you must know what is immortal and possess it. God is the source of Immortality and unless we seek that source by obtaining this Immortal Love of the Father, we cannot have the consciousness of knowing we are Immortal.

Only as we obtain the Father's Divine Love in sufficient quantity, will there come to us, throughout all eternity, as we obtain His Love in increased abundance, we will never cease to progress nearer and nearer to the Fountainhead of the Father's Great Soul. Increasing in glory and beauty and joy and happiness for all eternity. Should we not thank Him with all our hearts and souls for having bestowed upon us His children such a great privilege?

Jesus taught that only by the New Birth and by obtaining the Divine Love into the soul in sufficient abundance can there come to us the consciousness and certainty of immortal life. And again when Jesus spoke about the parable which refers to those who were invited to the wedding feast and that they must have on the wedding garment. This means of course they must have obtained the New Birth or have had the Divine Love born into their souls in that abundance to qualify them to enter the Celestial Kingdom. Those who refuse this Great Gift—The Divine Love which Jesus made known, will suffer the doom of the second death.

When Jesus said: "Work while it is day, for the night cometh when no man can work." He meant that while the Celestial Kingdom is open for spirits to enter therein we must work, for when this Kingdom is closed the work and the Angelic laborers will cease, and man and spirits be left to an eternity in the spirit spheres.

Jesus and the Celestials are constantly working in the spirit spheres. When this Kingdom is closed then the Kingdom of the Perfect Natural Man will be the only Kingdom that will be open to all spirits who have refused to seek the inflowing of the Divine Love into their souls that is necessary to obtain, to have the consciousness and certainty of immortality that Jesus brought to light when he told Nicodemus "you must be born again."

Jesus also taught in His messages that God's spirit and His laws are constantly working upon all mortals and spirits. His laws being perfect, and in time all the hells will be emptied and all the spirits from these hells will finally progress not by the mere fiat of God, but by the spirits seeking to free their souls from all sin and error, and eventually progress to the Kingdom of the Perfect Natural man. This also includes those spirits that have refused the New Birth and wish to stay in the sixth sphere and be happy with the Natural Love and further stagnation.

Whether these spirits will live for all eternity only God knows. But there is one memory that may last as eternity rolls on, and that is that they neglected to seek for that higher love—Divine Love—and if they should become unhappy, which is possible, since changes do take place in the spirit world, just as they do on earth. God in His Love and Mercy may allow their souls to disintegrate into the elements of which they were first created. Jesus, who possesses the Father's Divine Love in such exceeding abundance, and greater than any other of the Celestial Spirits, and has a closer communion with the Father, says: that he does not know what the future destiny will be for the Perfect Natural Man.

However, God does know that immortality is certain for those that have obtained the New Birth and a great uncertainty for those that have not.

Very often before giving my talks I read an important message from the "True Gospel Revealed Anew by Jesus," and then I explain the message. Because the Father's Love is so great and broad and deep that it reaches down into the lowest hells as well as into the Highest Heavens and no mortal or spirit will be deprived of the Father's Divine Love if they will only pray for it with all the earnest longings of their soul and when they obtain this love, their darkness and suffering will leave them and they will progress into the bright spheres.

And after I have referred again to the law of rapport and how all spirits can make the favorable condition to see these bright spirits and obtain their help. I then direct all spirits present to send out all the longings of their souls that God will send the bright spirits to them and if they will do it right now, then the barriers between them and these bright spirits will dissolve and you will see them, and they will be very happy to let you know of their personal experience and how they made their progress to the Celestial Heavens.

After I have done this, I have the wonderful experience of seeing most beautiful lights from the many high spirits. These lights seem to surround me and envelop my whole body and the wonderful feeling that comes to me from these spirits I can hardly express in words. These Celestial Spirits circle around me for some time, then I realize without any doubt that these Divine Spirits were present, and then I tell all spirits who are present, the bright spirits are now here and I tell them to look earnestly around until they see them and then go with them, and they will receive help that they so badly are in need and that they will be shown the way to the Celestial Heavens. I then extend my arms to all spirits present and radiate the wonderful love and power and pray to the Heavenly Father to bless them and fill their souls with His Great Divine Love in abundance.

Dr. Leslie R. Stone

Dr. Leslie R. Stone spoke almost every day to mortals and spirits since 1915, or just shortly after Mr. James E. Padgett received the gift of automatic writing and Jesus selection of him to do this kind of work, when the request was made from the spirit side of life for more knowledge of the truths that were being received from Jesus as well as other Celestials writers on the New Birth, so that the souls in the Spirit World may also obtain the Divine Love of the Father and progress into the Celestial Heavens; and these talks continued until his passing into the Spirit World on January 6th, 1967.

Rev. John Paul Gibson.

In Memoriam

It is with the sincerest regret and grief that we, the Trustees, announce that Dr. Leslie Rippon Stone, our beloved President of the Foundation Church of the New Birth, passed over into the Spirit World on January 6th, 1967, as the within writings were in the process of proof. Surely, he is now with his soulmate, Mary Kennedy, and with his family, relatives and friends, to live in happiness and Love, in the mansions of the Lord forever, Amen.

Dr. Stone died at the age of 90, in Washington, D. C., his home for over 50 years and which he loved like his own homeland. He was a man of great courage and convictions, believed implicitly in the truth of the writings from Jesus and the Celestial Spirits and in the visits to the Spirit World which he spoke of having made in the past, and of the Divine Love which he and his soulmate, Mary Kennedy, had for each other, the one in mortal life, the other as a Celestial Spirit.

Dr. Stone backed up his love and faith in the daily acts of his life, kind, loving and generous to all, despite his all too modest means, and sought each day to serve the Lord by preaching and teaching the "good news" of the Father's Love, to whomsoever would listen in the city of his choice. He held on to his beliefs with a tenacity and conviction and faith comparable to the early Christian martyrs in Rome, and deprived himself of food and necessities so that the Messages from Jesus and the Celestial World would be printed and brought to the attention of mankind.

His great faith was finally rewarded, after many years of tribulation, by the founding of the Church of the New Birth, and the successive publication of Volumes I, II and III of the True Gospel Revealed Anew by Jesus. His passing leaves an irreplaceable gap of love and devotion among the trustees, members and friends of the Church of the New Birth, a love and devotion we surely need now more than ever before. May he continue to love and help us from his new abode in the great beyond, with his Mary at his side, and with Jesus to point the way.

THE TRUSTEES

Dr. Leslie R. Stone

Dr. Leslie Rippon Stone was born November 10th, 1876 at 9 Wellington Street Aldershot Hants England. Attended the schools in England and learned the trade of his father as a Saddler. After coming to America he attended the Nurses Training School of the Buffalo State Hospital and graduated June 16th 1908 as a male nurse. And obtained a

Healing Arts license in the District of Columbia. Became a citizen of the United States on December 7th 1910. He met Mr. James E. Padgett through Church of the New Birth, Inc in 1958.[5] Dr Stone edited two volumes of the True Gospel Revealed Anew by Jesus before his death on January 6th, 1967.

John states the great importance of Jesus' message in selecting his friend Dr. Stone to also perform a great work in behalf of the Kingdom

October 3rd, 1915.

I am here, John.

I came merely to say that you have received from the Master a communication which has more importance than you at this time appreciate. I am referring more particularly to that part of it which states that your friend (Dr. Stone) has been selected for a work which is of great importance. I know how important that work will be, and he will be impressed at it and will probably hesitate to undertake it, but he must not falter for he will be given all the power that will be necessary for him to have in order to do what shall be required of him. You both are highly favored in being selected for these missions and you must not let doubt as to your being selected or as to the Master writing to you or as to your having the power conferred on you which will enable you to do the work.

I am interested in both of you, and you must recollect that, while you are both weak and unimportant mortals, yet you have behind and sustaining you the great power of the celestial world, with Jesus as the leader. What a wonderful thing this is! Why when we were selected as mortals, to become the disciples of the Master we never had such power to sustain us, because Jesus himself was not then as powerful as he is now, and he had not then formed the celestial spheres with all the powers that now exist there.

So I say there is no reason why you two should not be greater in your works than were any of us who worked with the Master while he was on earth or who worked afterwards as long as we remained mortals. Do not think that this is improbable, for it will come true; and while you may doubt, considering the fact that you are weak mortals with all the deficiencies of mortals, yet you must remember this one fact and that is, that so far as you are personally concerned, you are not of importance in

---

[5] There is an obvious error here, and it is presumably simply the rather abridged death notice that has been reprinted here. But Dr. Stone did not meet James Padgett only in 1958, via the church that he founded. He was in fact a regular attendee during the period 1914 to 1923 when the messages were being received. (G.J.C.)

doing the work, but as mediums and instruments through which it will be done, you are of the greatest importance to the plans and designs of these higher spirits—of more importance than any other mortals at this time. So there is no reason to flatter yourselves because of the great powers that will be given to you, and of the importance that you will be to the salvation of mankind, but you may congratulate yourself that you have been selected from all humanity to do this work. And further, remember this, that as a result of your doing this work you will receive such an abundance of the Divine Love, and come in such close association with the celestial spirits, that you will probably find yourselves in that condition of soul development as will enable you to enter those spheres where your soulmates may be living at the time, without having to go through the experiences of the lower spheres.

I will not write more tonight as your power has been greatly called on by the messages which you have received. So with all my love for you both, I am

Your brother in Christ,
John[6]

Affirms that John wrote on the selection of Mr. Padgett, Dr. Stone and Eugene Morgan to work for the Kingdom

February 6th, 1917.

I am here, Helen.

I will write now, for I want to add my testimony to that of Mary and Mrs. Stone as to the truth of the fact that John actually wrote the message that you received.

Of course, you have been told this many times before, and you certainly had no reason to doubt, and I did not think it necessary that you should have the additional assurance, but John has been present most of the evening and heard your conversation and also that part in which you spoke of Mr. Morgan's doubts, and he felt that you should be again assured of the fact of your selections; and what he said to you and the Doctor also applies to Mr. Morgan.

My dear, if you and the Doctor could have seen the great glory that was with John when he made the announcement, you would never again—and I mean all three of you—doubt the fact. The work is before you, and no other at this time can do it, and you all must consider this the great object of your efforts during the few years that will be yours on earth. There is no mistake, and the reality of the mission is so certain

---

[6] This message is a composite of two, being published twice in Volume IV. In this edition only one instance is included. (G.J.C.)

that when you shall have done your work and seen the results when you come to the spirit land you will wonder that you ever could have doubted.

Your own true and loving
Helen

Urges that Mr. Padgett, Dr. Stone and Eugene Morgan never doubt that they have been chosen to work for the Kingdom

February 6th, 1917.

I am here, Priscilla Stone (Dr. Stone's Mother).

I am not going to write much, but I must say to my boy that I heard what John said to him, and that it is of such great importance to him now and hereafter that I must assure him that it was John who really wrote. He was almost glorified as he announced the great truth of your selection, and I do not want my boy, or you either, to doubt this fact ever again. It is all so wonderful that I might doubt myself had I not seen the writer and heard the authentic words that he uttered. So, believe with all your hearts, and let your principal object in life for the future be the performance of this work.

I cannot write more now, for I am so very happy at the new assurance that has been given you. So, with my love, I will say good night.

Mrs. Stone.[7]

The soulmates shed tears of joy to hear that Mr. Padgett, Dr. Stone and Mr. Morgan were favored by Jesus

March 23rd, 1916.

I am here, Mary.

I am here and I want to write to my soulmate and I know that you will let me do so. Helen said she would make you take the pencil and told me to get ready and catch hold and as soon as you did so, and you may depend on it that I was right here and grabbed the pencil as soon as I could.

Well, it has been so long since I wrote him that I was hungry to do so. I know that he writes me and that I make him realize that I am with him, but that doesn't satisfy me altogether for you know that when you love a person you just have to tell them. It really gives relief, and

---

[7] This message is a composite of two, being published twice in Volume IV. In this edition only one instance is included. (G.J.C.)

besides I know that he likes to have me tell him.

Well, I suppose he will not think it anything new when I say that I love him with all my heart and soul but nevertheless I must tell him for I do.

If I could only write to him as your sweetheart does to you, it would not occasion so much anxiety for then I could spread it out and not have to wait to bunch it all together. But it keeps and I don't lose any of it. Tell him that I am progressing very rapidly now and will soon get into a sphere where Helen tells me I will find so much more happiness, and that the more Love of the Father that I get, the more I will love my soulmate. I am with him a great deal as I have told him before. I try my best to help him.

He is developing in his soul also and I am glad. I must tell him what a love feast we three had last night. I mean Helen and Clara and I.

When we heard Jesus say that Mr. Morgan had been selected by Jesus and would be given the great Love of the Father and knowing that you and my dear had already been selected, we just hugged one another and shed tears of joy for to us who know what a wonderful spirit the Master is and especially having seen the great display of his glory, we thought how fortunate we were in having soulmates who had been so favored by Jesus and the Father.

You cannot appreciate what it means to us for you don't know conditions here and what power and Love exists not only in the Celestial Heavens but in the spirit heavens.

Oh, I tell you that if we were mortals and you were our husbands on earth, we should have such a pride as might condemn us to do penance.

You must all believe what has been told you as to the work which you are to do and thank the Father for the great opportunity that will be given you to do so much good to mankind and to develop your own soul, for we know that if you do the work we will not be separated very long.

I am so happy tonight I could not talk about anything else and Leslie must pardon me for not having written about other things. Soon I will come to him and tell him about my home here, and what he may expect when he comes over.

I have written him a long letter and I must stop. So with my sisterly love for you and my soulmate love to him,

I will say good night.

His Mary.

John, as Mr. Padgett's guardian angel will go wherever Mr. Padgett will go to enable him to perform his work in protecting and enlightening Mr. Padgett

March 15th, 1917.

I am here, John.

I was with you tonight at the séance and heard what the medium[8] said, and saw that as she delivered the various messages, she was being dictated to by spirits of a very low order of development, and that they enjoyed very much the deception that they were practicing upon the medium and upon the hearers.

These spirits are not the kind that you should have the association of, and while your band was present and prevented any of these spirits from getting in rapport with you, or from affecting you by their influence, yet it does you no good to mingle with such spirits.

The medium believes that the spirits who came to her are really the relatives of, or spirits interested in the people in the audience, but as a fact, these spirits are mostly impostors who have gotten possession of the medium and use her for their own enjoyment. When she attempted to describe the spirits present, she was not only imposed upon, but the spirits whom she saw, as she said, were not the spirits whom the sitters might suppose them to be.

But there were some of these spirits whom she saw really were the ones that she described them to be, and were interested in the people to whom they came, but they were of the earth plane, having very little development.

When she attempted to tell you of your condition and want of spiritual development in the knowledge of the truth, she was dictated to by some of the fraudulent spirits, who did not know the truth and who were not in condition themselves to read your condition of spiritual development and took you to be one of the usual visitors at their séances, and, hence, caused the medium to commit the error that she did.

The spirits who she says came to you were not your grandparents, for you must know that none of your spirit band manifested themselves, and the ones that she saw and said were interested in you, were some of the spirits who are with her very often, trying to deceive the people.

The medium has the powers of seeing and hearing the things of the spirit world to some extent, and is generally honest in her attempts

---

[8] This message was received by Mr. Padgett after Mr. Padgett and Dr. Stone had attended a séance of Dr. Bruen in Washington D.C. (J.P.G.)

to convey what she receives, but sometimes she exercises her own thoughts and fabricates the message that she delivers.

It is a pity that such a condition of affairs should exist, but it is a truth and will continue so long as these spirits of deception are given the opportunity to manifest themselves.

And I will further say that while Dr. Stone had around him a number of his spirit friends, yet they did not manifest themselves, and the Indians that the medium described were not in any way connected with the Doctor. Of course at these séances there are always a number of Indians present who delight in manifesting themselves to the medium, but tonight none of these Indians formed any part of the Doctor's guides or band, and he must not believe that he has around him these howling Indians, for there is nothing in common between him and such spirits, and he is too well protected for these spirits to form any rapport with him.

While at times the Doctor may do some good to some of these wandering spirits who attend these séances yet, as a general thing, they are not helped by him, for the most of the spirits who attend such séances do not come there for assistance, but for enjoyment or, if they are thoughtful and anxious spirits, to communicate with their friends.

His work does not lie in the séance room, when great numbers of spirits of all kinds and conditions congregate, but in the quiet of his own room, or as he walks the streets, or in the church meetings where spiritual truths are taught, and where people of some soul development assemble. He has around him many of these spirits who are earnestly seeking for light and relief from their sufferings, and if he, in these moments of quietness or when he is where the spiritual atmosphere prevails, will let his thoughts go out to these spirits of darkness, and his mind formulate and project the advice and knowledge which he has of spiritual things, he will do much good and help many spirits toward progression.

Of course, the mediums of the kind that you visited tonight, have a work to do, and notwithstanding all the undesirable conditions that surround them, they do some good both to spirits and mortals, and they should be encouraged and helped to understand the possibilities that are theirs; but this does not mean that you and the Doctor, who have often gotten into the association of a very different and higher order of spirits, and having before you a work of a different character from that of these mediums, should not seek such places and encounter the retarding influences that are always present, in order to do the good that you can do.

I realize that this may seem unkind to these mediums, but what I state is a fact, and is not stated for the purpose of decrying the work of these mediums, but only to show you that such places for you to

15

frequent, as your work is not there, but is as I have above stated.

You will comprehend the purport of my message, and it is not necessary to write more upon the subject, but understand this, that in order to do your work most effectively, it is meant that you go not where these low and vicious, or merely dark spirits congregate and seek control of the mediums, and of the sitters as well, but on the contrary, demand that these dark spirits shall come to you where the influences are more helpful and seek your help, and you need not fear that they will not come, for, as a fact, they are with you whenever they get the opportunity, when possible. Every mortal for his own work and in his own place.

Well, I was there, because, as I have told you, I am your especially appointed guardian to direct in your soul development, and it is not a waste of time or a descending to places that you may think I should not attend to do this work of looking after you, and accompanying you in your visitations to séances or churches or wherever .you may happen to be. You are the instrument that we are using to do our great and vital work for the salvation of mankind, and I can do greater work to help and protect that instrument. Because I come to the earth plane and engage in this work, I am no less the John of the Celestial Heavens.

And what I have said in reference to you applies to the Doctor for James was with him, protecting and looking after him, and doing the work that, as the Doctor's special guardian, he takes delight in doing.

We are Celestial Spirits of the highest order, but that fact does not prevent us from realizing the necessity of the salvation of man, and even though we have to come to earth to bring about this salvation in work and association with spirits of the earth plane, yet it is a labor of love, and humility is the touchstone that brings to us happiness in our work.

No, we are with you often and in close association and we would not be fellow workers with the Master, if for one moment we should have the feeling that because of our high estate, we should not come into rapport and helpful association with sinful mortals; and so long as the Father requires His great truths to be taught, and men's souls to be Saved from the effects of the great fall and made angels of Divinity, our work will continue.

But some time our work on earth as well as in the spirit spheres will cease, and then our homes in the Celestial Heavens will be our only places of labor and love. The kingdom will be completed, the doors of the Heavenly Kingdom closed and the angelic hosts be separated from the spiritual and perfect man. Such is the decree.

And as the Father desires all men to become at-one with Him in His Divinity of Love, we must work until the day of the great consummation of the kingdom arrives, and the spirits who have not on the wedding garment shall suffer the doom of the second death.

And when Jesus said "Work while it is day for the night cometh when no man can work", he meant that while the kingdom is open for men to enter we must work, for when its doors shall be closed the work of the angelic laborers must cease, and man and spirits be left to an eternity in the spiritual spheres.

And so we work, and so you must work until the time of the (great) separation, and as the Master said, the wheat and the tares must be permitted to grow together until the great time of the harvest, so must the soul with only the natural love and that with the Divine Love be permitted to mingle together until the reaping of the harvesting shall take place. And until then, we must mingle and work and pray without ceasing.

Well, my brother, I have written enough for tonight and will stop, but do not misunderstand what I have said in reference to the mediums of the séances. They have work to do, and they must do it, and not be discouraged. You have a work to do, and you must do it in the way that we have pointed out, and the work that you can do they cannot, and hence, you must do your assigned work, and that alone.

So with my love, and the Blessings of the Father, I will say good night.

Your brother in Christ,
John.[9]

John heard the manner of conversation that Mr. Padgett had with Dr. Stone and approves the idea

April 30th, 1917.

I am here, John.

I merely want to say that you are in a better condition tonight than you have been, and I should like to write you a message but it is too late.

I heard your conversation tonight, and was much interested in it. You and your friend (Dr. Leslie Stone) have the right idea as to the manner in which the truths are to be made known to the world by preachers and others who may become believers in these truths and feel the call to make the same known.

The great qualification will be the possession of the Divine Love. If this is wanting the teacher has not that which is absolutely necessary to make his teachings a success. In good time all these things will be

---

[9] This message is a composite of three, being published in Volume I and Volume II and in Volume IV. (G.J.C.)

explained to you.

So have faith that you will be placed in condition to do the work that is named. Good night.

Your brother in Christ,
John.

Helen relinquished part of her message to permit Dr. Stone's soulmate, Mary Kennedy, to express her love and happiness in the work that he was performing with the dark spirits

April 26th, 1915.

I am here, Helen.

Let me write, [10] for I have been waiting so long for the opportunity to send a message to my soulmate and let him know that I am so happy, not only because of love that I possess in my soul but because he has a great deal of this abounding love.

I am with him very often as he knows and I am so glad for him that I can impress upon him my presence and love. We are all very much gratified that he is progressing so much in his soul and realize that he is progressing in the right way to a position here when he comes over to enjoy the bliss that is outside the spheres of darkness. Many spirits attend him in his serious talks to mortals of the truths of the spirit world as he knows them and the effect that they have on the spirits who listen to him and think of what he tells them. He must continue in this work for he hardly knows or realizes the vast number of spirits who surround him and anxious to hear of those things that show the way to a new life.

Now to be a little more personal I must tell him that when he talks in this way, I feel that he will surely be mine without the long wait that comes to many spirits who do not know the way and has not the longings for this Love as he has. Surely God is good and loves his children and we should thank Him with all the gratitude of our souls, and never cease to render unto Him the expression of our gratitude. There are many spirits present tonight and for a fact are always present with him

---

[10] This message is clearly dated as 1919 in Volume IV, yet there are a great many earlier dated messages from Mary Kennedy herself, which begs the question: "Why in 1919, if that date is correct, is she unable to communicate directly with James Padgett?" It frankly suggests the date is wrong, or something is very seriously awry with James Padgett's mediumistic condition. The diary entry recorded against Helen on April 26th 1919 does not indicate that Mary Kennedy wrote through Helen. There are three other entries for Helen on Apr. 26th, but none of those appear to match either. Mary Kennedy's messages were frequently not recorded in the daily diary, and there are no entries for Apr. 26th. This message is most likely prior to or around April 5th, 1915, which is the first recorded message from Mary Kennedy. Indeed this message has a clue as to its date, because it says Mary is in the Fifth Spirit Sphere, meaning it is definitely in 1915. (G.J.C.)

for they learn that he has in him that which enables him to receive the impression of the spirits who are so anxious to meet with their loved ones on earth. This is a wonderful gift, and if men could only know that it is as interesting to spirits as it is to mortals they would realize how blessed the man is who has a soul in unionism with the spirit world.

I will not write more now, but only say that he must continue to proclaim the truths of God and not be disappointed when men do not heed or are indifferent, for in the end the seed that he sows will bear fruit and he will see the results of his work when he comes to the spirit world.

With my love and everlasting longings for him. I will subscribe myself his loving -

Mary.

As early as January 1915 before Mary Kennedy could write her own message and be able to control the mind and hand of the instrument, she was permitted to dictate her thoughts of love to Mrs. Helen Padgett who wrote through her husband Mr. James E. Padgett the following:

Tell Leslie that he is so very dear to her that he must not let his thoughts of love wander away from her towards any other person upon earth or in the spirit world, that she loved him so long and only recently has she had the opportunity to let him know in a way that he could understand, that she feels as if she must just let her whole heart burst upon him with its great fountain of love for him. She is not able to express to him the extent or intensity of this love but she does love him to the full limit of her capacity. When he lies down at night or when he awakens in the morning, she is with him trying to flood his soul with her love and happiness.

Mrs. Helen Padgett further says, that Mary Kennedy will not be content to have Leslie think that her love is not his for it is to its fullness and tell him, he must believe her and that she is with him nearly all the time, trying to help him and make him feel her presence. She is not so far away that she cannot know at all times what his feelings are, and when he gets lonely and wants her love and help, he must try to become in rapport with her, even when he is alone in his room and thinks that no one is with him. She is his now and will be through all eternity. Only love like hers can last when disappointments and troubles come and when they do come then her love grows stronger, sweeter and he must feel it more as he feels the need of it. She is not now trying to make him believe that she is only waiting for him to come over in order that he may know that she loves him with all her heart and soul, but she loves him in that way while he is on earth beset by all the cares that come to

19

him. He must love her more and more each day and he will find that his happiness will increase as this love grows. Tell him she is in the fifth sphere and is preparing a home which will be so beautiful that he will be more surprised than he will be at the beauties of the spirit plane where she is, for her home in addition to having the beauties that are in that sphere will have her love permeating it.

She also has another love for him to become more intense and pure but which draws her nearer to her Father of Love. This is the greatest of all Love and she so wants him to let his heart become filled with it also. It is his, if he will only seek for it and believe that the Father is ready to give it to him, for He is not only ready but anxious. And she further says: Tell my dear Leslie to pray to God and ask that this Love may be given to him and fill his soul, for if he does, he will receive it, and when he does he will not only love God supremely, but will love his true soulmate with a purer and sweeter love than he can conceive of. And when he does that he will find that his happiness will be so great and joyful that the little cares and troubles of his earth life will not be able to mar that happiness or make him to wish for any other kind. Because I am his and he is mine and when he realizes that, he will know what soulmate love means.

We are not for each other for a limited time only, but for all eternity. And even eternity will not be too long in the enjoyment of our mutual love. Oh, he is, my own true soulmate and sweetheart and I am so happy in that knowledge that my cup of joy seems to be full and running over. Let him think of me as being close by his side all the time sharing his joys and sympathizing with him in all his sorrow and he will feel that he is not alone. Tell him to try to become a true lover of God and the truths of His teachings by His son, our brother and helper Jesus. I am a firm believer in these truths and know that they are true and I want my dear soulmate to believe with me for in that belief is found the great happiness which I tell you of. So Leslie dear—goodbye for now.

Mrs. Helen Padgett in her writing through Mr. James E. Padgett makes further comments:

Well, she loves him with a very pure and steadfast love, she is a lovely spirit and one who is filled with the Love of her Father, and she is worthy of all the love that any man can give her. I am very fond of her and see a great deal of her. She is so gentle and loving and tender and is loved by many spirits to whom she has administered consolation and help.

Well sweetheart I must stop for tonight. Good night, with all my love.

Your own true

20

Helen.

A joint message from Helen and Mary expressing their happiness that the Master will be with Dr. Stone with all his love and power

September 28th, 1915.

I am here, Helen.

What a wonderful, happy night we have all had—you and Dr. Stone in the mortal life, and all of us spirits in the spirit life. For I must tell you that your room has been filled with spirits of all spheres and conditions.

Your reading of those messages accompanied by the power of the Divine Love caused such an emotion among the spirits here as I have never before seen since I have been writing to you. And best of all the Master was with us, and his great love and glory seemed to fill the whole room and all our souls as well. I tell you sweetheart, that heaven has been with us tonight and Dr. Stone must not wonder that he felt the great power and influence which he speaks of, because never before has he been surrounded by such a host of Celestial spirits as were with you all tonight. Not the least interested and happy was his own sweet Mary and her happiness was really beyond what I can tell you of. She was filled with love for him and with the Divine Love, and her love was glowing to him in great beams of light and joy.

She wants to write a little although she says that she is too full of the emotion which has taken possession of her to write very much.

Mary now writes:

My dear soulmate, I am with you in all my love and longings, and you must believe that I am your own true soulmate, happy in the knowledge that you love me in return for all the great love of my soul which I send to you without one iota of reservation you have my love and my great desires that you may be happy and contented in the knowledge that your Mary is all your own and not another's. She is with you so very much and tries to comfort and keep you from everything that will make you unhappy. Many times when things look a little dark she comes to you with her love and whispers words of cheer, and tickles your ear to let you know she is with you.

I am glad that your soul is open to the influence of not only the Divine Love of the Father, but to the love of the Master, for he loves you more than you can imagine, and is also with you very often, for he sees that you are in condition to become a follower of him, and that you will also be able to do his work in conjunction with your friend who writes. He is so gracious and loving and so wants you to learn of him and help spread his truths as he sees that you may do. I believe that he will soon write to you and tell you the way in which you may become his disciple also; for he sees that your soul is longing for the great Love of the Father, which will make you a power also in making known the truths of God to mortals.

I do not know just what you shall do, but I know that you will have a mission to perform and that the Master will be with you in all his love and power, blessing you until your life shall become a great peace and happiness.

Oh, my dear Leslie, to think that you too will have such a special friend and loving savior; and that our souls will have the possibility of becoming one in the great Love of the Father, even while you are on earth. I must not write more tonight but I must say that this night has been to me one of the happiest and soul loving in all my spirit life. So think of me and write me a long letter tonight, and tell me of your love to me, and of your great desire to have me close to you.

Good night,
Mary

Helen writes:

Well, you can see what love can do. She loves him and the Master loves him and we all love him.

What a happy meeting for us all. I must not write more tonight, but only say to you and to him too—pray more to the Father for His Love, and for faith, and believe.

I am yours forever in love.
Helen

First message for Dr. Leslie R. Stone from Mary Kennedy, his soulmate via Helen Padgett

January 23rd, 1915.

I am here, Helen.

Well, sweetheart, as Dr. Stone wants so much to hear from his soulmate Mary, and she is here and is so very anxious to write him, I will tell you what she says, as follows:

She wants Leslie to know that he is so very dear to her, that he must not let his thoughts of love wander from her to any other person either on earth or in the spirit land. Then she has loved him so long, and only recently has she had the opportunity to let him know in a way that he could understand, that she feels as if she must just let her whole heart burst upon him with its great fountain of love for him.

She is not able to express to him the extent or intensity of her love, but she does love him to the full limit of her capacity. And when he lies down at night or when he awakens in the morning, she is with him trying to flood his soul with her love and happiness.

She will not be content to ever have him think that her love is not his, for it is, to its full; and tell him that he must believe her, and that she is with him nearly all the time, trying to help him and make him feel her presence. She is not so very far away that she cannot know at all times what his feelings are, and when he gets lonely and wants her help. He must try and come in rapport with her even when he is alone in his room and thinks that no one is with him. She is his own now and will be through all eternity.

Only love like hers can last when disappointments and troubles come; and when they do come then her love grows stronger and sweeter; and he will feel it more as he feels the need of it. She is not now trying to make him believe that she is only waiting for him to come over in order that he may know that she loves him with all her heart and soul, but she loves him in that way while he is on earth beset by all the cares that come to him. He must love her more and more each day, and he will find that his happiness will increase as this love grows.

Tell him that she is in the fifth (spirit) sphere and is preparing a home for him which will be so bountiful that he will be more surprised than he will be at the beauties of the spirit plane where she is, for her home in addition to having the beauties that are in that plane, will have her love permeating it.

She has another love which not only helps her love for him to become more intense and pure; but which draws her nearer to the Father of Love. This is the greatest of all Loves, and she wants him to let his heart become filled with it also. It is his if he will only seek for it, and believe that the Father is ready to give it to him, for he is not only ready but anxious. Tell my dear Leslie to pray to God, and ask that this Love may be given to him and fill his soul; for if he does, he will receive it, and when he does he will not only love God supremely, but will love his true soulmate with a purer and sweeter love than he can conceive of, and when he does that, he will find that his happiness will be so great and joyful that the little cares and troubles of his earthly life, will not be able to mar that happiness or make him wish for any other kind. I am his and he is mine, and when he realizes that he will know what "soulmate" means. We are not for each other for a time only, but for all Eternity; and even Eternity will not be too long for the enjoyment of our mutual love.

Oh, he is my own true soulmate, and I am so happy in that

knowledge that my cup of joy seems to be full and running over. Let him think of me as being close by his side all the time, sharing his joys and sympathizing with him in all his sorrows, and he will feel that he is not alone. Tell him also to try and become a true lover of God, and the truths of the teachings of his son, Jesus of Nazareth, our brother and helper. I am a firm believer in these things and know that they are true; and I want my dear soulmate to believe with me, for in that belief is found the happiness which I tell him of.

I must stop now—so say goodbye; and rest in the belief, that no matter what troubles or cares may come, whether you love me all the time or not, I will love you now and always with my whole heart and soul, and will wait with all the patience possible for your coming. So, Leslie dear, goodbye.[11]

Mrs. Padgett further writes: Well, she loves him with a very pure and steadfast love—not so demonstrative as Rose's love for the Judge (Judge Syrick) but so deep and pure. She is a lovely spirit and one who is filled with the Love of her Father, and one who is worthy of all the love that any man can give her. I am very fond of her and see a great deal of her. She is so gentle and loving and tender, and is so loved by many spirits to whom she has administered consolation and help.

Helen.

After a lapse of time, this is the second message written by Mary Kennedy

September 7th, 1915.

I am here, Mary Kennedy.

I am so glad for the opportunity to write to my dear soulmate as it has been a long time since I wrote to him, and told him of my love and happiness.

He is dearer to me than ever, and while he cannot hear me tell him so, yet every day I am with him and try to breathe into his ear the expressions of the great love which I have for him. I wish that he had the power to write as you have, for if he had, I believe that I would monopolize all his time in telling him how much I love him, and how I long for the time to come when I can have him all to myself. He, I know, cannot realize what a love like mine is, but thank God in the not far distant future I will be able to enfold him in my arms, and tell him with

---

[11] This message started Dr. Stone on the way to praying with all the intensity of his soul longings going out to the Father to fill his soul with His Divine Love. And as he has written that he felt this Love with its warm glow burning in his soul in response to prayer. (J.P.G.)

all the feelings and warmth of my soul how much I love him and how dear he is to me.

I am with him nearly all the time, trying to cheer him and make him feel that he is not alone in his struggles in life, and that my love for him is so great, and with and in him all the time. When he prays, I pray with him, and when he is happy I am happy too. But when he is unhappy I am not unhappy but sympathize with him, and exert myself to make him realize the great love that I have for him and that I am near him.

His sorrows are only temporary and my love is eternal—and my love means his happiness as well as mine. So tell him to believe with all his heart that his Mary is with him and will be with him in all his times of sorrow and joy, and will try to interpenetrate his soul with her own burning and pure love, which is all his and which can never be given to another.

I read his letters, which he writes at night, and for every expression of love which they contain I have a responsive answer, only more intense and more longing. Tell him not to stop writing to me for I can see what he writes; and tell him also that he must believe that my answers are all that he would have them to be and more too.

I must not trespass longer on your indulgence but only wish to say that I love my dear Leslie with all my heart and soul, and will so love him until time and eternity shall be no more. Oh, how I wish that I could have him see me face to face, and hear my voice telling him of my great love, and that he is mine and I am his.

So kind friend, I thank you and will give way to your wife to resume.[12]

Mrs. Padgett resumes:

Well, sweetheart, isn't she a dear, loving soulmate?

It does me so much good to hear her tell her love to the Doctor, and see her eyes and whole being aflame with love to him.

First message received from Helen, wife of Mr. Padgett, for Dr. Stone

December 30th, 1914.

I am here, Helen.

Dr. Stone is a different man. He has considerable spiritual development, and is an earnest seeker of the higher things of the spirit

---

[12] This letter I have read many times as it always brings me such happiness and love and I feel her pure love burning in my soul. (Dr. L. R. Stone.)

world, and has had a considerable experience in these matters.

He is not right when he ascribes the inflowing of God's Love to any vibrations of spiritual forces, other than the pure and only love of God. His Love is not a mere vibration, but an actual existing Love, which has its source only in the fountainhead of His Love, no other force or thing enters into it—only pure and everlasting Love which emanates from the Father. So tell Dr. Stone that he must believe that God is an infinite actual being who loves him as a father, and not some mere vibratory love or power moving through the universe without a fixed and predetermined plan for the happiness of mankind.

I hope he will soon see that if he wishes to obtain the greatest happiness on earth as well as in the heavens, he will come to believe that God is his real, personal Father, with all the love that a Father—the only one—can have for his child.

He can obtain the happiness, resulting from the possession of this Love, only by prayer to the Father, and belief in the actual existence of the Father, and His desire to bestow this love in answer to such prayer. He must let this Love of God into his soul and believe that it is there. When he gets it though he will know it and he will not need any further proof than the happiness that will come to him by its mere possession.

Tell him to pray for its inflowing, and not wait until he can understand how such a thing can be, and he will get it.

I am much interested in him for I see that he has a longing to know the truth, and to obtain all the happiness that may be found in the spirit world.

Let his thoughts about the movements and operations of the astral body, as it is called, and the vibrations necessary to bring one into harmony with the higher things of this world (spirit world) be taken from his consideration, and let his whole thoughts and aspirations centre upon the great love which the Father has for him.

He will then soon learn that in order to get this great happiness of which I speak is not depending upon any knowledge of the laws which govern vibrations or astral bodies, or anything else which merely are useful in carrying out certain operations of God's laws in His spiritual kingdom.

He must believe, as I say, if he wants to succeed in finding that which is far more desirable than anything which the mere acquisition of the knowledge of the laws governing the inter-communication between the spiritual and the material world can give him.

I am so much interested in his spiritual welfare, that I almost feel that I must come to him personally and try to impress upon him with all my powers, the necessity of his trying to get this great happiness in the way that I have indicated. So be sure to tell him that he must pray to God for an inflowing of His love and believe that God is able to fill his soul with this love, and let all the desires as to why these things can be, pass from him for the time being.

I know his soulmate and she is a beautiful spirit living in the same sphere with me. When I heard you talking today, I immediately tried to find her and succeeded. She knows that he is her soulmate, and she is so anxious to get into communication with him, for she says that he is very dear to her, and she wants him to obtain this great love, which will enable him to come to her direct when he comes over, so he will not have to have an experience of expiation in the earth plane. She says tell him that he is her true soulmate and that he must believe it to be so, for she has known it for some time, and has been with him many times when he has felt downhearted and needed help. She will now be with him very often, and she only hopes that she may in some way cause him to feel that she is, and realize that he is not alone in his earth life.

She never knew him on earth. She says that her home was in England, not very far from where he lived, and that her name is Mary Kennedy. She was the daughter of a very prosperous businessman, and has been a spirit only for about ten years.

She is not only waiting for him to come over, but is trying to prepare a home for them both, that will show him how much she loves him, and how much she has thought of him for several years past. I never knew her until today, but she seems to be a very lovely spirit and one of entire sincerity. So tell him that here is another reason why he should strive to obtain this love of God in his soul, that I have above all things tried so very earnestly to impress upon him the necessity of obtaining.

So tell him further that from now on he will have a beautiful spirit to enter into all his joys, and to sympathize with him in all his sorrows—which I hope may be few.

I must stop now for I have tired my darling Ned. You must pardon me for having taken up so much time in writing about Dr. Stone but I could not help it as I saw that he is almost ready to let God's love come into his soul and make him a happy man.

Helen.

Doctor Stone writes on the great impression this first message had on him

Before receiving this message from Helen, I have to confess I had no knowledge of the great importance of obtaining the New Birth that Jesus told Nicodemus. *"Except a man be born again, he cannot enter the Kingdom of God."*

I was introduced to Mr. Padgett about the middle of September, 1914, by Arthur Colburn, a good friend of mine in Takoma Park,

27

Maryland, where I had just learned about his spiritual gift of automatic writing.

This first message from Helen made a great impression on me, and when I reached home with a copy of this message that was given to me by Mr. Padgett, I read several times and felt an intense longing for the New Birth, as I prayed with all the longings of my heart and soul, with such intensity going out to the Father that caused my soul to open up and let the Divine Love come in, in such great abundance, that it seemed as if my whole soul was being melted by this warm glow of Divine Love, and I shed tears of joy and happiness that came to me beyond all conception that was mine. It was then I realized that the mere natural love even when it is developed in its purest state is separate and distinct from the Divine Love. After this experience I realized without the slightest doubt that my dear brother and friend, Padgett, was receiving the great truths from Jesus and other celestials. And as Jesus has written since that he will never come again in the flesh, but he has come again in the form of his revelations that contain many of the vital truths that he taught and lost sight of after his early followers died. St. Luke[13] wrote about the leaders and the hierarchy of the churches, as the additions and emasculations and interpretations were made in the original writings of those who declared the truths as they heard them from the Master and the decreasing want of comprehension of spiritual things and the growing wisdom of their finite minds and intellects, caused them to conceive a plan of the part of God for man's salvation and as the recopying continued the thoughts of those who copied, or dictated the same, became more centered on this plan, and so the copies were gathered together and considered, and no doubt efforts to have some agreement in the declaration of this plan; and as the new copies were made, they were constructed with the view of showing forth this agreement.

The Bible has changed and perverted the plan of God for the salvation of man, and has substituted a plan that arose from the limited wisdom of those whose attempted to convince mankind that they had a knowledge of God and of His designs as to the creation and destiny of man.

The Bible contains many truths to enable man to reach the Kingdom of Heaven, provided they are correctly understood and applied, but there are so many things taught therein as truths which are just the opposite of truth, and do not comprehend the will of God, with respect to man, and this makes it difficult for men to discern and apply the truths and the destinies that must be theirs according as they follow and obey that will or not do so.

---

[13] This is in a message from Luke on page 138 of Volume I (5th Ed.) (J.P.G.)

In closing, I wish to say that after reading and studying the many vital truths contained in the Messages from Jesus and celestials that I am convinced without the slightest doubt that these messages I have just referred to are the greatest and most important truths that have ever been given to the world since Jesus taught them nearly 2,000 years ago. Dr. L. R. Stone.

Writes that Dr. Stone is progressing in his soul development and in his rapport with the spirits of the higher spheres

January 8th, 1917.

I am here, James.

I want to say a few words to you and the Dr. for as you know I am especially interested in him as his guardian and spiritual helper. I of course do not have the opportunity to write him as often as I should desire, but yet I am with him very much trying to help him in his soul developing and in his spiritual understanding of the heavenly things that Luke has just written of, and I am glad to inform him that he is progressing in his soul development, and in his rapport with the spirits of the higher spheres.

I am with him frequently as he tells others of the Divine Love, and the other truths pertaining to the spirit world, and sometimes I suggest to him thoughts, which I see may be beneficial to his hearers. He may think that sometimes the thoughts that he conveys to those with whom he talks are thrown to the winds and leave no impression on the minds of his hearers, and sometimes this is true, but I must tell him here, that in many cases they take root, at least, for the time being, and cause these hearers to think and wonder if there can be any truth in what they hear, and as to how they may learn more of the things that are told them. He is doing a good work in this way, and must continue to do so, for there is no telling when a word or idea dropped into the mind of other people, may find lodgment, and grow into greater and wider thoughts, and cause serious inquiries as to the truth.

What he says has this advantage over what is generally taught as to religious matters, and that is that his thoughts as he expresses them are new and not objectionable to reason, and as a consequence—the hearers wonder how the thoughts could have arisen and give to their consideration more attention than they otherwise would do. All the world is ready for the truth that will satisfy the soul and liberate the mind from creeds and unreasonable beliefs, and whenever anyone speaks such truth it is heard no matter what its source, the anxious soul will grasp it, and often meditate over it.

He must keep up his courage and belief in his spirit friends, who are behind and with him, helping him in this part of his work, for it is a part but not the important part. Have faith and let his soul reach out more and more for the great love of which he speaks and believes in, and he will realize in the not far distant future a power that he little conceives of. He must know this also, that he is being prepared and developed for the great work which he has to do, that will help very largely to make certain and convincing the truths that you are receiving in the messages. He must have patience and he will not be disappointed, for the powers that are with him are great enough to carry forward the great work which is set before him to do. Even now they could fill him with the power which will be his, but the time is not yet in the order of the plan which has been determined on for the forwarding of the work that must be done. I am pleased that I could write this tonight, as I feel that though he has much faith, yet he must also have encouragement based on what will be his as the time comes for helping humanity.

Love is the great thing, and he who teaches the way to that love is a great instrument in the work of the Father, and his position of a good and faithful servant, will be one that even angels may envy. This is not extravagance, but actual truth, and I know that when he shall have finished his work, and come to his spirit home, he will realize that what I have said is a faint representation of the actual fact. I must not write more tonight. With my love to you both, and the promise of continuous help, I will say, good night.

Your brother in Christ,
James.

Is pleased with the progress of Dr. Leslie R. Stone who is his special charge to guide and wants him to trust him

May 13th, 1917.

I am here, James, Apostle of Jesus.

I have heard you read the messages, and I have listened to your conversation and I am much pleased that you both enjoyed the messages so much, for if you had not had the soul development that is yours, you would not have been able to understand the purport of the messages as you did.

It is a wonderful message of truth, and if men could only understand what its real significance is, they would soon renounce not only their sins and evil thoughts, but their belief in the false creeds that cause them to neglect the true way to the Kingdom of God, that many of them, even though they may not receive the Divine Love that is so necessary to lead them along the way to the Celestial Heavens.

I am glad that this great knowledge has come to you both and that you are on the way to this greater and grander kingdom where are men who are men no longer, but are angels of the divine nature that the Master has to such a degree of perfection.

Well, I want to say a few words to my special charge (Dr. Leslie R. Stone) tonight and he must believe me and trust in me as his special angel; I would desire to inform him that his soul is developing more and more each day, and that we are all well pleased at his progress. Soon he will be in that condition that he will not have to wait until he gets into the spiritual world in order to have some of the Celestial Heaven in his soul, and with it that happiness and peace that comes only to those who possess the Divine Love in a degree that many spirits of that soul development don't have. He is pursuing the right course and he must not let doubt enter his mind or soul, for he is, in truth, one of the redeemed of this love that he has been so often told is waiting for him without limitation.

I am with him very often, trying to help and influence his thoughts for good of the Divine, and he must continue to pray and believe; and I, James, his own true friend and guide, assure him that he will not be disappointed.

Life on earth, at the most, is short and fleeting, and his work is one that only he can do. His is not the gift that another may have, but is his all alone and in a short time now, it will be developed in him, and he will be informed of just what his work will be. He is now doing a good work but its results he has no conception of, for there are many spirits who a short time ago were in darkness, and now are in light and much happiness, who give to him the credit of being the one who started them on their progress to light and happiness.

So tell him to have courage and faith and he will not be forsaken or left to the influence of evil or depraved spirits who are so very numerous in the earth plane at all times trying to influence mortals to become as sinful and depraved as they themselves are.

I will not write more, as I feel that he would like to hear from some others who are present. But tell him that I as well as many others of the higher spirits love him and are with him very much and pray to the Father to shower upon him the blessings of the Divine Love.

So with my love to you both, I will say good night and God bless you,

Your brother in Christ,
James.

Confirms the writing of James

May 13th, 1917.

31

I am here, Mary Kennedy.

I am here and I will not let my dear boy (Dr. Stone) be disappointed, for he is just itching to hear from me and had almost given up hope of doing so; but he must know that I would not leave without hearing from me in some way. Well, I am truly glad that I can write to him once again for it does me as much good to write to him as I know it does him to hear from me, and especially when we are both so anxious to know just how the other is; you must know, of course, how he is, but he can only surmise how I am except as to one thing, and that he knows, and that is that I love him with all my heart and soul.

I am progressing all the time and love him the more that I receive this Divine Love in my soul; yet I do not cease to want to be with him as much as the performance of my work will permit, even though I have to leave the sphere of much grandeur and beauty and come down to the dark plane which offers such a contrast. But love makes all things beautiful and our eyes are closed very largely to the unpleasant things when our hearts are so full of love.

I have recently read some of the letters that have been written him and it gave me great happiness to know that he received them and enjoyed them, and I want to say that they were true and were written by the spirits who professed to write them. This I will tell him, that he may not doubt, for he senses that his soulmate would not tell him an untruth. I am with him very often trying to help him, as he knows, and there are other spirits with him also; and I must tell him that James takes a special interest in him and is doing everything to help develop him in the way that will enable him to do the work which lies before him. He must not think that there is no special work for him to do, for there is, and while he is now doing a work in helping the dark spirits, yet this is not the work. I wish I could tell him now what it is, but that is the matter that is in the keeping and control of the other higher spirits and I would not disclose their plans even for my sweetheart, which I would like to do.

Well, I must not write more now, for your wife says that you are tired and must not write more tonight. So with my love to him and sisterly love to you, I will say good night.

Your sister in Christ,
Mary.[14]

First formal message from Dr. Stone's father, William Stone

November 14th, 1915.

---

[14] This message is a composite of two, being published twice in Volume IV. In this edition the second instance as not been included. (G.J.C.)

32

I am here, William Stone.

I am the father of the Doctor and I want to tell him that I am with him very often trying to help him, and make his material affairs become more successful. I am also with him in his soul aspirations, for I can see that he is more in the way to learn the truth of the life in the spirit world, and of the destiny of mortals after they become spirits. So if he will at times give me a loving anxious thought I will be able to come into closer rapport with him and impress him more consciously as to what I think is wise for him to do or not do.

He may be surprised that I am here, but I have been present on several occasions, when his soulmate and his mother and your wife have written to him, and have observed the effect upon him of the communications as given and received.

While his soulmate is with him so very much, and is closer to him than any of us, yet his mother and I have a great interest in him and love him very much.

I am his guardian angel and have looked after him ever since I entered the spirit world and became imposed with the duty of looking after him. I only wish to tell him this tonight. I am very happy and am in the fifth sphere and expect to soon get into the seventh sphere where his mother is, but I am afraid that before I do so, she will leave for the Celestial and so I will have to strive again to reach her. I have nothing further now to say tonight.

Well, his brother is in the condition that his mother told him, and is suffering a great deal, but he will soon see the light and get relief. Some of your band who seem to love his mother so much are working with him, and he seems to be interested in them, and believe that they are really trying to help him.

I would prefer if he wait until I come again as this is my first attempt at writing, and I want to be in condition to answer any question that he may ask without confusion. So tell him that I will come again and will be willing to answer his questions.

So, bidding you good night, I will leave you both my love and best wishes.

His Father,
William Stone.

First formal message from the mother of Dr. Leslie R. Stone

January 1st, 1915.

I am here, mother.

I am the mother of your friend, and want to tell him how glad I am that I can be with him and make known to him my presence and the fact that though his mother is a spirit, yet she can be with him and feel for him all the love which she had for her boy while on earth. He must not doubt that his mother is here, for she is, and has been with him many times when you were writing and has sent him some tokens of her love through his soulmate, Mary.

Why, Leslie, she, I mean your Mary, was a little English girl, and when on earth did not live many miles from your home, and if it had been intended you two could easily have met when you were very young. But of course you might not have known of the fact that you were soulmates.

I want to tell you now, that Mary is a real, existing spirit who was once a little English girl, and is all beauty and goodness, and is waiting here for you to come to her and when you do you will not find some shadowy unsubstantial thing of air, but a real live, beautiful spirit, with form and features perfect and well defined, and full of animation and pink roses on her cheeks, and hair all dark and glossy, and blue eyes, and mouth like cupids, and teeth as you would say like ivory. She is not a very demure little girl either, but is full of life and love and happiness. I tell you all this that you may form some idea of her, and be able to see her, to some extent, in your mind's eyes as you mortals say. And more than all, she is so pure and good, and is loved by every spirit with whom she comes in contact.

I will not write much more tonight, but merely add that my prayers for you go out to the Father, and my faith that he will look after and preserve you for the better things not only of the spirit life, but of the earth life, is without a bit of doubting.

I must not write more tonight.

But in concluding, I must say that you have with you all the love and blessings of a mother who loved you so much on earth. So think of me sometimes.

Your own dear and loving mother,
Priscilla Stone.

Priscilla Stone and Sister Kate wrote a message of love to Leslie R. Stone

November 23rd, 1915.

I am here, mother.

I want to say one word to my son before you stop writing, as I feel so much love for him tonight and am so anxious to let him know that I am with him and feel that he is my dear loving boy, whom his mother is so much interested in and so thankful to God that he has found the way to the Father's love.

Oh, my boy, if you could only know the happiness that you have given your mother by having sought and found this love of the Father, you will also thank God, that you had the opportunity to make your mother so happy.

I am your own dear mother, and will always love you and pray to the Father for you and for your happiness and well being of your soul. Your sisters are here too, and they are among the redeemed, and enjoy the happiness which the Divine Love gives to them, and they want me to tell you that they are happy too, because you have found the great love and mercy of the Father.

So press forward in your soul development and you will find a wonderful happiness and love, not only on earth, but when you come to us as well. Your Mary loves you too as you know, and her love for you is something wonderful and beyond what we can tell you, and beyond your comprehension.

I will not trespass longer tonight as your friend is tired and should not write much more, but I must say that I am so glad that you met him, and have the benefit of his knowledge and experience of these higher things of the spirit world.

Be always friends and you will both realize a wonderful outflowing of love from the higher spirits, and from the Father, and also from Jesus, who is the most wonderful and loving spirit in all the Celestial Heavens.

I will stop now and in doing so, give you all my love and blessings of a mother whose love is without limit.

Your loving mother,
Priscilla Stone.

I want to tell my brother that he must not leave until I tell him that I love him too, and am praying for him with all my heart, and am with him very often trying to help him. So he must believe me and love me too.

I can't write more—but I love him.
Good night,
Sister Kate.

Priscilla Stone, Mother of Leslie R. Stone, has advanced to First Celestial Sphere

January 10th, 1916.

I am here, mother.

I am here, the mother of the dear boy, and I want to tell him that I am exceedingly happy in my new home, as I am now in the First

Celestial Sphere of which he has heard a great deal, and what he has heard is all true and more besides. I cannot attempt to tell him at this time, what a glorious home I have, and how the good Father has provided for my happiness everything that the heart and soul can wish for. This is the result of that Divine Love which he talks so much about, and which he has to some extent, and which I know will be his in an abundant degree, even before he comes to the spirit world. There is no conception of what the power of this great Love can do to make mortals and spirits both happy, and the mortal who learns the way to possess it is blessed above every other mortal of your earth life.

But he must not think that because I am so happy and so much nearer the fountainhead of the Father's Love, that I am not still interested in him, and loving him with all my heart for it is a fact that the more of this great Love that I receive into my soul, the more love flows from me to him, and the more my efforts are to have him get into his soul this Divine Love, and the knowledge that he is an accepted child of the Father and is an heir to the great kingdom which Jesus is now establishing in these Celestial Spheres.

Well, I must not write very much tonight as it is late but I do want him to know that I and all of his folks who are in these higher spheres are trying to help him, and make him feel the influence of our love and blessing. So tell him to believe in his mother and in the Master with all his heart and soul. His father is also very happy and is progressing and I know is endeavoring with all his faith to progress to my sphere, and get with me, and then we will be one in actual living as well as in the knowledge that we are one and always have been.

So with all my love, I will say good night, and thanking you I will leave my love for my boy and the prayer of a mother that he may continue in the favor of God and in the progress of his soul.

His mother,
Priscilla Stone.[15]

Regards the work of both Mr. Padgett and her son very important and mentions the great love of the Master for both

February 17th, 1916.

I am here, mother.

---

[15] This message is another curious one from a date perspective, in that it would seem to be very noteworthy as a message, yet it's simply not in the daily diary, but is clearly date marked in the first edition of Volume IV. Even though Helen has an entry for that same date, no mention is made of this communication. (G.J.C.)

I am here and I want to say just a word to my son as I have not written him for some time, and you know how much a mother's love means.

I only want to say that I am with him so very often with my love and mother's longings for his happiness and prosperity. He, I know, has a great deal of the Father's Love in his soul and that brings him so much nearer to me and causes me the happiness which the knowledge gives me that he will when he comes over become one of us in our consciousness of immortality. Oh! I tell you that this knowledge is a thing more precious to me than I can express, for it shows me that he, my boy, is very dear to the Father and to his elder brother, Jesus, the glorious one and the most loving one. Why if I could only tell you of the love of the Master for you both, you would never more doubt that you are his chosen ones for the great work which lies ahead of you, and which even more is resulting in the salvation of many.

He may not know that he is helping you in your work among the dark spirits, but he is, and very frequently when you two are sitting together and talking about the great Love of the Father and the fact that these poor spirits can be helped by the higher spirits, these dark ones hear you and many times they believe enough in you to cause them to seek our help and thereby learn the way to light. It makes me so happy because I know for each of these spirits that are rescued from their darkness and suffering there comes to you an additional blessing from the Father, and increased love from all the spirits who love to linger around you.

So, tell my boy, that what I say is true, and he must realize that while he cannot communicate to these spirits as you do, yet, he has helped many of these spirits with his conversation and the love which he had in his soul and which these spirits sense when they come in close contact with him as they frequently do.

We are all very happy and are waiting for the day of our uniting, which will be in God's own time, but not now, he has a work to do on earth and until that work is done he will not come to us, and that is more real than apparent. His little soulmate certainly loves him, and at times we all tease her but she seems to rather enjoy it, and she does. His father and sisters send their love and want him to know that they are with him very much. So, thanking you for your kindness—I will say with all my love and blessings for you both,

His mother,
Priscilla Stone.

Expresses her great love for her son and reports on progress of his father and sister and his soulmate Mary

March 6th, 1916.

I am here, mother.

I am here, the mother of the boy who is sitting close to you. I am so glad that I have the opportunity to write to him, for, while it has really not been a great while since I wrote him, yet, it seems so to me, and I have so much love for him, and desire so much to tell him so. I am very happy both on account of my own condition, and because I see that there is developing in his soul the great love of the Father in greater and greater abundance. He may not realize this to the full extent, but it is true and I am able to see it and rejoice that it is so.

His father is also very happy, and is progressing and is now in condition to soon make sure his coming to me, where we can be together, without any necessary separation. His father says—that he is with his son quite often and is trying to encourage him, and cause him to believe that his earthly affairs will continue to grow better as they will.

His sisters are here and also send their love and want him to know that they are very happy, notwithstanding that they see that another brother on earth is not in that condition of soul development, that they so earnestly pray for, but they have great hope that at some time very soon he will have an awakening, that will cause him to turn his thoughts to the higher things of life, and seek the love of the Father, which is waiting for him to ask for.

While we all feel the great want of spirit progression that our brother lacks, and that he is not very happy and is doing those things that tend to turn him away from the things that would make him happy, and more in accord with the Will of the Father, and also that he really suffers at times because of his soul condition, yet, we are not really unhappy, because we know it is only for a season, and that sooner or later our prayers and influence will have their effect, and he will realize that there is something more to live for, as well as die for, than the mere material things of earth.

Well, I do not know that I should write more tonight especially as there is a girl[16] here who is very impatient to write, and who is almost selfish in her desires to tell her Leslie as she calls him, that she loves him more and more.

So thanking you I will say good night.

With all my love to my son, and thanks to you I will say—

I am his mother.

---

[16] The little girl referred to is my soulmate, Mary Kennedy. (Dr. S.)

The little girl referred to above is my soulmate, Mary Kennedy, who will now write:

Well, I am not a selfish girl if my mother-in-law says so. You know what an awful reputation mother-in-laws have for interfering between the daughter-in-law and the son who thinks more of his wife, than he does of his mother. But this is not the case in the present instance for his mother loves me as much as she does him, and is glad when I can come to him, and tell him how much I love him.

Well, tell him I do love him, and intend to tell him so every time I get the opportunity, even if he does get tired of listening to me. I am very happy and realize that he is coming closer to me every day, and that his soul is expanding with the Father's love. Oh! How splendid it will be when the time comes when I shall have him with me.

I wonder sometimes if he will become dissatisfied at the contrast in his condition now, and when he comes over. I mean that now he has no one to say to him what he shall do, or when he shall go out, and when come in, but when he comes with me, I will stick to him so close that he will not be able to move about without my being with him, but, I am willing to take the chance, and I don't believe that I will be disappointed. So, tell him he had better take all the advantage possible of his present liberty for when he comes to me, he will surely become my captive, and I may be a hard mistress, so far as restricting the freedom of his movements.

Well, now to be a little serious. I am trying my best to help and encourage him in his earthly desire, and in succeeding in his business affairs, and I believe that he soon will find that success will come to him. We are all with him a great deal, and we also pray for him very much, and I know the Father hears our prayers, and will in His own good time answer them.

Besides this, the Master is with him also and sheds over him his influence, and says that he is to be an instrument for doing his work, when the time becomes ripe, which he says will not be very long now. What this means neither you nor he can appreciate as can we spirits, who know so well what the Master is in his power and love. It makes me happy beyond expression to know that Jesus has selected my soulmate for one of his disciples to do this great work, for in knowing this I realize that Leslie will have around and in him during his earth life an influence and love that not many mortals will have the benefit of.

I am so glad that I can write to you tonight, for you understand that we can only slip in at times when these higher spirits are not communicating their truths.

I love him with all my heart, and I so long for him to have him see me, as he will sometime for I am trying to make myself visible to him in some of the visions which he has.

And so is your Helen (Mr. Padgett's wife) trying to bring about this end, for she loves me so very much and wants me to be happy, when I might not be. So, thanking you, I will say—tell my dear that I am his own loving,
Mary.

I (Leslie R Stone) then asked—which brother my mother referred to who was lacking in soul development and then the following was written by my mother through Mr. Padgett. "I have heard what Leslie said, and I mean the brother in Canada,[17] who has become a soldier. I refer to him because it may be that he will sooner use the opportunity of turning his thoughts to God, while on earth, and this opportunity is a very vital thing to his soul condition, that will comfort him when he comes over." I then asked my mother to write his name, but conditions were not favorable through the intervention of undesirable spirits, who wanted to write. Leslie R. Stone.

Again expresses her great love for her son and is very happy to see his soul development in the Love of the Father as well as the love of his soulmate Mary

October 13th, 1916.

I am here, mother (of Leslie.) I am here, the dear boy's mother, and I want so much to write him. When I heard of him speak of his boyhood days my heart went out to him with such love and yearning, that I just had to make the effort to tell you that I wanted to write, and I am so happy that you heard me and gave me the opportunity.

I am so very happy and as I listen to him talk about the Love in his soul and tell of the experiences that he has when that Love is working in his soul, for I realize that as he receives this Love, he comes nearer to me, and feels my love which is surrounding him, and trying to steal into his heart, it is his mother's flavored with the Divine Love, which I have in my heart and soul, and as it goes out to him I know that he must feel it, and realize a happiness that was never his before.

I love my boy more than I can tell him. I loved him with a mother's love on earth but now I love him, not only with a mother's love, but with one that surpasses all love which any mortal mother can have.

I desire him to know that I am progressing and that I know that

---

[17] This is my brother, Harold Stone, of Toronto, Canada, passed over 1964, who is a soldier fighting in the French trenches. (Dr. L. R. Stone)

immortality is mine, and that the Celestial Kingdom is mine, where only the great all-enveloping Love of the Father is.

I am so happy when I see that he realizes to an extent this Love, and that his faith is growing day by day, and also that the sins and errors which were once his are leaving him, and in their place is coming this great Love, that only those to whom God has called and bestowed His Love knows what it means.

I will not write of other things tonight for I am so filled with love, that I cannot think of things that are not connected with it, but I will say though; that his father is also progressing and in a short time I hope will be with me.

Tell him to remember that he has the love of many high spirits around him trying to influence him and turn his thoughts more and more to the Father and to His wonderful Love and goodness.

I will not forget to say that there is also with him the love of his soulmate and such a very beautiful and pure love it is, such as no mortal can understand but, yet as real as the heavens, and as deep as the sea. Yes, and as everlasting as eternity. I could not possibly have a more beautiful or desirable daughter than is his Mary, and he must believe that she is an actual existing spirit who is with him quite often knowing that he is hers forever and that some day she will have him with her.

God bless my boy and keep him from all harm and unhappiness is the earnest prayer of his mother.

Mother.

Mr. Padgett and I were conversing on things spiritual, and I referred to my boyhood days, and then Mr. Padgett heard the voice of my mother and told him she wanted to write me. Mr. Padgett then took up the pencil, and this is copy of letter:

From Mary Kennedy—October 13th, 1916.

You heard me and I am thankful. I will only say that what his mother said about my deep love for him is true. I know that I have told him many times that I love him, but I wanted his mother to tell him also, for he knows and can realize that his mother was and is a real being, and there must not come to him any shadows or thought as to her being a real spirit, and I thought that if she would only tell him that I am real as she is, that he would conceive of me in his soul's eye of faith as being like his mother. This is what I wanted to say, and I am so happy that I can say it. Good night my dear friend,

Mary, soulmate of the Doctor.

From Mary Kennedy, written immediately after my dear mother, who also spoke to Mr. Padgett that she wanted to write, and was heard and received clairaudiently by Mr. Padgett the request that she wanted to write. Message was written automatically as usual. And Mr. Padgett and I felt a wonderful love present. Leslie R. Stone

Writes on his trip into the spirit world

December 16th, 1916.

I am here, the mother of Dr. Stone.

And I want to write just a few lines for it does one so much good to tell him of my love and my nearness to him. I want him to believe without doubt that what Mary wrote him as to his coming to the spirit world in his spirit body, and meeting us is true. For he did come, and to his mother's eyes he was more beautiful than he appears in his physical body, and why not? When I remember that his soul shone through his spirit body, and we could see that he had much of the Father's Love in his soul.

I was so happy that I could not help shedding tears, and I took him in my arms and hugged and kissed him as I once did on earth, and he kissed me in return and said he was so very happy, and that he now knew that what his mother had written him about his still being alive, and his own loving mother was all true, and he told me of his love for me, and he longed at times to have me with him, and feel the inflowing of my love. He really met his father and sisters and brothers who all happened to be present, though some of them could not stay very long, for they were just not suited to remain with us, but their love had drawn them to him and they were benefited by meeting him.

Of course, it is needless to say that Mary was there but like the good and loving girl that she is, she stood back until his family had embraced him and told him of their gladness, and then she came to him in all her love and in the purity of her feelings, threw herself into his arms and cried great big tears of joy, and wept as if her very heart would break for gladness, and he looked at her and put her from him, and looked again, and then embraced her with all the strength of his love, and cried too. It was a happy time and we left them to themselves, and they were truly lovers and became oblivious to everything but themselves.

I cannot express my great happiness and the beauty of the scene, for I had never before seen a spirit, and the spirit of a mortal meet in the spirit world, and there were many others looking on in wonderment and appreciation of the evidence of love, but they soon recognized that they should not longer stay, and left.

He stayed with her a long time, and Mary said he did not want to return to earth again, but she told him it was not time yet to remain with her, and she promised that he should come again. It is all so wonderful that I can scarcely realize that it was not a dream, but I know it was not, for I felt his arms around me, and his kisses upon my cheek, and his tears upon my face. Oh, how good the Father is to those who love Him and long for the happiness which only He can give. I must not write more now, and thanking you I will say—with all the love for my boy a fond good night.

Your sister in Christ,
Priscilla Stone.

Explains the great joy living in the Father's Kingdom that she wants her son to know a great deal about

November 20th, 1916.

I am here, mother.

I would like to say a word to my son, if you will permit, for I so much enjoy telling him of my presence and love. Of course he knows that I am with him quite often, yet my presence realized in that way, I mean by the impressions that I give him, is not as satisfactory as conveying my thoughts to him by a written message.

I wish to tell him that I am progressing and very happy and know only the joy that my living in the Father's kingdom gives to me. If I could only make him understand for just a little moment what this happiness means to me, and what it may mean to him, he would strive with all his power of will and longing of his soul to get the love in more and more abundance. Yet I feel that even without this one glimpse of what I speak of he is quite happy at times and is trying to progress in this love.

I do not feel that I should write longer tonight as you have written considerable already, and I thank you for your kindness. I will stop now and say, but the little sweetheart says:—tell him that she is here too and loves him, and wants him to love her and to believe that she is his affinity notwithstanding what the woman said to him tonight.[18] She has her affinity too, and it is not that unspiritual husband that she is living with. So tell my boy to love me, and think of me as I do of him. Good night,

---

[18] I had attended a circle where there was a well known medium, and the medium asked me - "if I associated much with the girls." I replied "very little." And a lady sitting on my left said: "Perhaps I had not found my affinity." I did not give any satisfactory answer, but my soulmate was present with me at the time, and gave me the signal of her presence, which she often does, and is doing so while I am writing this postscript, and I can feel her love and influence very strong, and my mother is giving me the signal of her presence also, and their love and influence always give me so much happiness. (Dr. L. R. Stone)

43

Your sister in Christ.

Second message from William Stone, father of Leslie R. Stone

November 23rd, 1915.

I am here, your loving father.

I am the father of that boy, and I want to say to him that I am happy too, as well as his mother but not as happy as she is. I am not in her high sphere, but I am striving to get there and enjoy her home. Leslie, my son, I am also happy that you are trying to follow the steps of the Master and in your love for the Father, and in your soul aspirations.

Believe in this truth, and you will not be disappointed, and when the great day of reunion comes you will find more love waiting for you than you ever thought possible for a spirit to receive. So trust in God and follow the teachings of the Master, I know the importance of this, as one who was ignorant when on earth and now have learned only since coming into the spirit world.

God Bless that dear Mother of yours! If it had not been for her teachings after she came into the spirit world, I probably would be an easy going spirit, as I was a man, enjoying the happiness which my good nature and love of things generally gave me. But when your mother came over, and I saw that she had a Love which I had not, and which I must get in order to be with her, and when she told me how much she loved me, I sought for the same kind of Love which she had. And with her help and the help of the Father's Holy Spirit, I obtained this Love and am now very happy, for it is this love which alone may make it possible for me to be with her where she is. But I am not yet with her, as her soul condition is above mine for me to be able to share her home. She is so beautiful and good that I am not satisfied to live away from her and I am trying with all my soul's desire to be together with her, through prayer to the Father for this Divine Love, the one possession that can make me worthy of her.

So Leslie believe what we say to you and trust in God and you will be happy.

Your loving father,
William Stone.[19]

---

[19] This message is a composite of two, being published in Volume I and Volume IV. (G.J.C.)

Makes considerable effort to help her children on earth even to follow them on the battle field, also tells of her progress in the Celestial Heavens

April 19th, 1917.

I am here, mother of Leslie. I came to say that I am much pleased for this opportunity to write to him once more.

Of course I have been with him a great deal and he has felt my presence, but it is so much more satisfactory to write him and tell him in words of my love and solicitude for his welfare. I am now in a higher sphere of the Celestial Heavens and correspondingly happy and I find that as this great love comes to me it seems that I love him with a greater intensity. I wish that I could describe the glories of my new home so that he might have some idea of what the heavens constitute in which his mother now lives and what it means. He has heard described some of the spiritual spheres which transcend all conceptions. But those descriptions are very inadequate to convey the true portrayal of what the heaven which is mine contains.

But I am also happy in that his father has also progressed and is so much happier and has so much more of the love in his soul. We are in the earth plane a great deal of the time trying to help his sisters and brothers who have their many troubles and moments of unhappiness and if we could only get in rapport with them like we can with Leslie, they would be much happier. But as it is they do believe in our presence as their true loving parents and are conscious of us sometimes when they need our help. But this they cannot understand and their thoughts do not often turn to us and as a consequence we are not able to get as close to them as we desire.

The girls are more interested in earthly matters than in those pertaining to the spirit world, and are very largely absorbed in the war and its possibilities. Well, this is quite natural, but yet if they could only know that the other things such as the spirit are more important and if they would only turn their thoughts more to the spirit world and think of their parents more often, they would receive an influence and help that would add so much to their happiness even though they could not understand its source.

As you know we are controlled by law and no matter how great our desires may be to come in closer contact with our children and cause them a greater happiness but if they do not want to respond to our feelings, they can prevent our doing so. Of course they do not understand what possibilities are theirs and what a little thing keeps them from us or rather permitting our influence to come to them as it otherwise would. Let them have a real yearning for our presence or a wish that they could have us with them and it will lift the veil that keeps us from making our presence conscious to their souls perceptions.

We are hoping though that someday or rather someway they will have an awakening so that we may come closer together. Tell Leslie to write them to think more about their mother and send out a desire that they could have her with them and then I will be with them and they will know that it is true although they may not realize the fact.

Yes, I sometimes visit the scenes of battles and it is also possible that I do not stay very long, except at some time when I have the opportunity to help some poor spirit who has suddenly found himself in the spirit world and is in great confusion and apparently all alone. I am also with my son who is in the army and try so hard to reach his consciousness, but with very little success and while I do not know when he may be called to battle and suffer the dissolution of life, yet I am with him waiting to help him should the end of life come to him. My love draws me to him and my love will keep me with him until he either becomes a spirit or returns to his home.[20]

Oh! What a terrible thing is war and if mortals would only understand what it means to the individual spirit, they would try to bring an end to its ravages and destruction.

I have written considerably and must stop. But I wish to say that Leslie's father is also here now and sends his love and blessings and wants him to know that the signal which he spoke of is the one that his father uses to notify him of his presence. Also tell Leslie to continue to pray and believe for in doing so, his prayers ascend to the real living and loving Father and his beliefs are of the truth of the great truth—that leads to God and redemption and immortality.

Thanking you I will say—good night.
Priscilla Stone,
Mother of Dr. Stone.

Gives a report on his son's work and spiritual development in his great mission selected by the Master

March 23rd, 1916.

I am here, father.

I desire to write just a line, before my son leaves. I am his father and I want him to know that I have not forgotten to take advantage of

---

[20] Dr. Stone has written: That his brother Harold did survive the battle although he was injured, but returned to his home and family in Toronto, Canada and lived until he was 80 years old. (J.P.G.)

any opportunity to write that may arise.

His mother is here too, and she sends her love to him and desires to say that she heard the message which Mary wrote him, and that she is the happiest little angel in all the spirit world. And we are all happy and know that what has been told him is true. He must not doubt even though he cannot now realize the possibility of performing this great mission of which he has been called by the Master. In time he will be instructed and will have sufficient power given him to do this work.

I say we are all happy because of this great favor. Your mother says that she is thankful beyond all expression—that her prayers have been answered so surprisingly—that she never for one moment imagined that her boy would have been made the instrument in doing this work—that she only prayed—that he might receive this Divine Love and become at-one with the Father. And when this other surprising favor came to him, she realized that God was very good to her beyond all conception.

Tell my boy that he must believe and try his best to perform this work, that I am sure that a way will be opened up by which he will be enabled to do this duty, for now it is a duty.

I am very happy and the more I progress the greater my happiness becomes and the goodness of the Father appears.

His sisters are very happy too and rejoice with us all.

Last night I was not present at the wonderful séance which his soulmate speaks of, but I know that it must have been impressive beyond conception, and I must say that I have never seen Mary so happy as she has been since then.

Well, I will not write more tonight.

I thank you and with love and esteem,

I am, his father,

William Stone.

Both Helen and Mary write this message and Mary has progressed to the First Celestial Sphere which is confirmed by Helen

May 6th, 1916.

I am here, your Helen.

And I merely want to say that I have been listening to the talk between you and Dr. Stone, and I think that you both have been enlightened as well as entertained by the message. It undoubtedly contains truths that are pregnant with ideas and thoughts that will cause many men to wonder and change the conceptions of many of their beliefs.

47

Well, who do you think is here now like a hen on a griddle, so afraid that she will not have the chance to tell the Dr. that she has another secret and he must know it; and she says just let her say one little word. So I suppose she will have to have her way.

Mary:

Well, Dr., I am here, as you may be surprised to know, if you have forgotten my last secret, but I don't believe that you have. I want to say I am in a happier condition than I have ever been, for I am now in the Celestial Spheres where I know that happiness is so much greater than ever before. So you must believe me when I tell you that my love is so very much more abundant, and that you are dearer to me than ever before. So try to realize what I mean, and imagine that you are with me, even for a little while, and then you will be happier too. I have said what I wanted to and must stop.

Helen:

Well, she feels better and says if she could go to sleep she would sleep better now.

Yes, I am here again. Mary means that she is in a condition that is full of the love of the Celestial Spheres, that are higher than the one in which she was when she last wrote you. She is in the first Celestial Sphere, but she feels that as she progresses the other spheres are so much more filled with the love that she speaks of.

Her expression of being near the celestial spheres may be misleading, but the truth is that her home is in the first celestial and she is very near the second and will probably be there in a short time. I have told you the exact fact and you must believe what I say.

Well sweetheart, I will not write more.

So with all my love, I am your own true and loving,

Helen.

Is so happy that Dr. Stone now has a photograph of her

March 24th, 1920.

I am here, Mary.

Let me write, as I am very anxious to say a word to my beloved. I listened to his mother as she wrote on the photographs, and felt that while what she said was true and must be believed, yet I could not feel satisfied until I could write him of the happiness that I have in the knowledge that he has a picture of me, though not a satisfactory one, so far as I am concerned.[21] But, yet, he has one, and will not now have to depend entirely upon his imagination to conceive what his soulmate may look like! If I could only have appeared to him as I really am, or to an extent, at least, that he could see without any inconvenience, I would feel so much happier and the more satisfied.

I love him so much that I could not restrain myself from writing, and I asked Helen to impress you to take the pencil in hand and give me the opportunity; and as she is in such rapport with you, I knew that she could succeed in causing you to do as I wished. I am very grateful, and can only repay you by throwing around you my best influence, and helping you whenever possible.

Oh, the wonder of it all, and how thankful I am to the Father that one little insignificant spirit such as I am, viewing all the hosts of spirits by whom we are surrounded, can enjoy such a blessing! Tell him that he must try to appreciate our privilege also, for it is the cause of a happiness that very few, comparatively, possess.

I am now in the Celestial Spheres, higher than he can imagine, and yet I have these pleasures of joy and bliss, to come to him and tell him of my love, and enjoy his presence. What a wonderful thing the soulmate love is! And how it makes a spirit who possesses the Divine Love happier, in that it has a knowledge that this love of ours is not inconsistent with the Father's Love, and is the object of the approbation of the real, true Father. So you see, He is not a jealous God, as so many believe, but is anxious that all His children shall love and enjoy those things that He has provided for them, the least of which is not the soulmate love.

You have been very kind, and I will not write more now, only to say how much I love him and want him to be happy. Helen is here and says she will write you and tell you of her love, and the things that await you when you come to the spirit world.

Your sister in Christ,
Mary Kennedy.

---

[21] This photograph is displayed in the next section. (G.J.C.)

Soulmate Love

Dr. Leslie R. Stone with soulmate Mary Kennedy.

Wants him to know that God's Love has flowed into his soul in great abundance

June 21st, 1917.

I am here, William Stone.

I want to say just a word to my son. I have been with him a great deal of late, observing the presence of the Divine Love in his soul. I am justified in telling him that this Love at times has flowed into his soul in great abundance, and as John said, all the powers of the spirit world could not have prevented it from doing so. He must realize that earnest prayer and the longings of his soul are the only meditations between him and the Father and that this response is of that nature that in order for him to be conscious of it, it is not necessary for some spirit to tell him. No, only he, and God, knows where the Love comes from and no spirit can possibly get between that God and the mortal soul. Of course we can see the effect of the possession of that Love by the soul of the mortal and spirit as well, but when it comes only he can sense it. God is his only bestower and He alone can direct the Holy Spirit. I write thus, because I want to implant firmly in my son's mind and consciousness the fact that this Love needs no help from spirits to bring him its presence.

My Father is always waiting to bestow the Love even though He, the substance, may not be present in His soul form; but His Love is never absent and never fails to respond. I am happier than I can express over the fact that my boy has the opportunity to come into a knowledge of the way in which this Love can be obtained and the further fact that his soul consciousness has been so developed that he can sense its bestowal.

We are all present tonight and are praising and thanking the Father for His goodness and mercy and our prayers are ascending to Him for a greater and greater bestowal of this Love.

While we are not unhappy over the fact that if our other children would turn their thoughts to this Love and seek for it, we would be able to rejoice with a greater joy. We realize that life on earth is short and that very soon all our children will be with us and then they will learn the truth and turn their thoughts to things spiritual, and that we will be able to help them without the interference of the flesh, and the allurements of the world; but how much better it would be if they would only start on their progress while they are surrounded by the temptations of the flesh. We are praying for them and constantly trying to impress them with our love and thoughts of things spiritual; and have a lively hope that before they come to us the awakening may come to them.

I am progressing and the fact that my son sends us loving thoughts and attracts to him spirits of the high Celestial Spheres help us all so much for we get the benefit of the truths that they convey and the wonderful atmosphere of Love and the Divine Love that they bring with them.

I will not write more. All send their love and blessings, good night.

Your friend in Christ,
William Stone.

Is very happy to hear them discuss the Divine Love of the Father

I am here, Leslie's mother.

I hope you will pardon my intrusion and I feel confident that you will when you understand how anxious I am to write him a few lines. I know that it gives you pleasure when you have a communication of love from your dear one and I want to assure you that it makes me equally happy when we have the opportunity to communicate in this very satisfactory way. And here let me say that I continually thank God that he has opened this means in which we can tell our dear children the truths of existence in the spirit world and the fact that we are with them so often and love them so much.

I have listened to your conversation tonight with great pleasure, and here let me say that many other spirits have been present and listened intently, and I cannot tell you the joy I experienced in realizing that my boy and you too are understanding the Divine Love of the Father, and its effect upon your souls.

The spirit who just wrote was a spirit who seemed to be very much in earnest and evidently a very intellectual one, and his inquiring was made in seriousness and he seemed very much gratified that he could go with the Professor and have the benefit of the conversation to which the Professor invited him. So this is another demonstration that you mortals can do a work that we spirits cannot always do, and you should feel so thankful to the Father that you both have this great power bestowed upon you to help spirits where even other spirits are unable to give help. Praise the Father for His love and goodness to you both.

Tell my boy that his mother is very happy and is progressing all the time and that the more of this Love that she receives from the Father the more she loves her dear son. It is all so wonderful that sometimes I wonder that there can be such a loving Father who thinks so much of His disobedient children.

I have been with him a great deal of late trying to help him with my influence and love, and making him happy in his thoughts for now my rapport with him has grown so great I can come into his thoughts and experience and influence him into the way of peace, or rather into feeling of peace, and I do so, he may rest assured.

I must not intrude longer, as you have written enough for tonight. But I must tell him that his father is progressing also and I hope that very soon now we will be together in our home of the soul, as I used to sing when on earth. When I fell in love with his father, I thought him a very handsome man and so he was, but now his handsomeness has turned into beauty, and the beauty that only a soul filled with the Father's Love can develop.

His sisters have been here tonight and Kate says that she wishes that her brother would get married, as that is the proper life for him during the short earthly life that will be his. She doesn't mean that he will not live the ordinary life but that life at the longest is short.

Mary says she has heard what I have said, or rather just written, and if it is for her soulmate's happiness on earth she will not object, because she knows that if he should marry his soul will be hers. She is a dear little angel and we all love her so very much.

Well, I must stop now. So with my love I will say good night.

His loving mother,

Priscilla Stone.

Is grateful for the messages received by Mr. Padgett from the Celestials to permit her faster spiritual progression

June 16th, 1917.

I am here, mother of Leslie.

Let me write a line, as I am anxious to contribute my encouragement to what John has said, and I know that what he told you as to the powers that are working in this matter is all true.

While we do not pay much attention to time, yet in the present case time is essential, and every day is important in the furtherance of the work, and we know this to a greater extent than you possibly can. Do the best and the most that you can, until the time comes for you to have the surroundings that are so desirable to make the work easier of performance. You have the love of many high spirits and their powers are not to be underestimated.

You may think it strange that I write in this way, but you must understand that while I am not of those who inhabit the high Celestial Heavens, yet I am interested in the work, for I know what it means. The truths to be conveyed to you have saved me from the slow progression of the soul without the Divine Love, and have also lifted my boy from the darkness of ignorance and false beliefs into the knowledge of the truth and the salvation of his soul; and what they have done for him they will do for all mortals who receive the light and pray for the Love. And you can see that this Love is so great and of such a nature that we who have it to a degree want every one of our brother mortals to know the way to obtain it.

So do not think that I, just because I am of little importance among the high spirits of the Celestial Heavens, may not help a little for I can and am endeavoring to do so. Tell my boy that his mother loves him with all her heart and soul, and is praying for him, and that she knows, as regards his prayers, it does not depend upon the help of spirits to bring a response, for the Father answers directly and sends His Holy Spirit to bring to him the response. Oh, how I love the Father, and how His Love makes me happy and gives me a peace that only He can confer.

We are all present tonight with our love and influence and prayers. I must not write more now. So believe that I am a spirit who loves her boy with a true love that no earthly mother can know. Good night.

Your sister in Christ,
Mrs. Stone.

Explains conditions of those that are suddenly forced into the spirit world as a result of war, and the great effort to contact his children on earth

I am here, William Stone.

I am here and want to write a few lines. I am Mr. Stone and I have been present for some time listening to your conversation and enjoying the same, for whenever you talk in such a way as to show us that you are progressing in your knowledge of the truths it makes us all feel very thankful and satisfied at the wonderful privilege that you both have had bestowed upon you. All my family here tonight are very anxious that our son shall know that we are with him so often trying to help him.

I am progressing all the time and feel that the love never fails to bring to us not only happiness but a continual progress towards not only the higher spheres but also towards the fountainhead of the wonderful love.

I am also interested in our other children who are on earth and hoping that some time or something will come into their lives to turn their thoughts more to the life in the spirit world, and cause them to be dissatisfied with their condition of security in their old beliefs that they have nothing to do but rest upon the workings of the blood of Jesus and all the other means that have been promised by preachers for their future happiness as they have believed.

The last letter my son wrote was received by them and I am sorry to say did not make much impression on them although in some of the thoughts that were contained in the letter they found some things that aroused at least their curiosity.

My advice is that my son will continue to call their attention to these truths, for while they may consider that he is deranged in these matters yet after awhile something may happen in their lives when they may look upon some things that he may write them as being worthy of their consideration.

The subject of spiritualism is now agitating the English people to a greater degree than heretofore and many persons with whom they may come in contact will discuss the knowledge of the truth of the communication with the spirit world, and I am expecting that from this source their interest with the subject may be incited and finally lead them to investigate the subject.

Well, the truth of spiritualism will become more readily known and people will seek to know more about it, and when once they become interested the probability is they will continue in their pursuits of the truths until they will be willing to search in every manner possible that may lead to the acquiring of increased knowledge. I am with my children very often and see what their condition of mind is and try to impress them with my presence but so far they have not realized the fact of my presence.

They have been to a séance lately and have been a little surprised at some things that they heard others talk about but they are not willing to ascribe the things to the real cause of the manifestations, but I have hopes that their experience may lead to further investigation.

I sometimes go to the front where the battles are being fought and observe the entrance of many spirits into the spirit world and how sad it is that so many come totally ignorant of what they may expect and consequently are not fitted for the experience that comes to them.

I will not write further and only wish that I could write to the other children as I do to my son.

So tell my boy to persevere in his efforts to help both mortals and spirits, and he is helping both although he may think that his success with the mortals is not very satisfactory, but he must continue in his work and efforts to let them know the truth.

We all send our love and pray to God to bless him and keep him in His Love and faith and happiness.

Good night.

Your friend and brother in Christ,

William Stone.

Is happy that Jesus selected his son, Leslie, to perform special work in behalf of the Kingdom and he must not doubt

October 3rd, 1915[22]

I am his father.

And I want him to know that I have not forgotten to take advantage of every opportunity to write whenever I am permitted to do

---

[22] There is more than one instance of this topic, but this date seems the most likely. (G.J.C.)

so.

His mother is here, too, and she sends her love to him and desires to say that she has heard the message which Mary wrote him and that she is the happiest little angel in all the spirit world.

And we are all happy and know that what has been told him is true. He must not doubt, even though he cannot now realize the opportunity of performing this great mission of which he has been called by the Master. In time he will be instructed and will have sufficient knowledge given him to do this work.

I say we are all happy, because of this great favor, and your mother says that she is thankful, so very much, and all her prayers expressed have been so surprisingly answered, that she never for one moment imagined that her boy would have been made the instrument in doing this work, that she also prayed that he might receive the Divine Love and become at-one with the Father, and when this other surprising favor came to him she realized that God was good to her beyond all conception.

Tell my boy he must believe and try his best to perform this work that I am sure a way will be opened up by which he will be enabled to do this duty, for now it is a duty.

William Stone.

Writes that only the Father's Love is important tonight for her soulmate, Leslie

April 5th, 1915.[23]

I am here, Mary Kennedy.

You have had some spirits tonight who are no doubt thankful that they could write to you, but they do not know what it is to love you and enjoy your company as do some others, of whom I am one, and strange as it may seem, that while you knew them on earth and you did not know me, and yet I am closer to you and that dear boy who is waiting for a word from me, than any of these other spirits are, or can be.

Helen thought it wise to let these spirits write tonight as they were so anxious, and wanted so very much to let you know that they had not forgotten you. I do not refer to that fraudulent spirit who came and thought that he was telling you something that would give you a great surprise, but let me tell you that he was caught as the law sometimes catches the fraudulent ones of earth; but he was not caught by the law, but by love, for if you could have heard how Helen told him of the great

---

[23] This date is printed in the first edition of volume IV, but there is no entry in the diary for this date. (G.J.C.)

Love of the Father and how much he needed it, and how it was waiting for him, and how happy it would make him, you would not regret that he came to you and wrote.

Well, he is one of so very many who know nothing of this Love, and who need it so much. He is now thinking, and I hope that he may be benefited.

Well, I will say a few words to Leslie, for I feel rather serious tonight, and want to tell him that he must not let his faith lessen, or any doubt come to him of the truth of this Great Love, or of the fact that I am his own true soulmate, and love him with all the love of a soul that has much of the Father's Love.

We are here in great numbers tonight, trying to impress you both with our love, and praying to the Father to bestow it upon you, I mean His Love, in great abundance.

Sometimes as you know, I am quite jolly, and as some of the sedate spirits may say, frivolous, but tonight I do not feel that way, for the love is with me in such degree, that I feel I must get closer to my dear in all its seriousness. He is so very dear to me, and I am so anxious that he get into a condition of soul exaltation that I do not feel that even my soulmate love should intervene. Let the Father's Love, alone, be his tonight.

I am with him, as he knows, and am happy when I can come to him. So tell him to pray more and believe, and he will find a wonderful happiness come to him.

I will not write more now, as Helen says that you are tired.

So with my love to him, and best wishes to you, I am,

Mary.

Is happy when she is permitted to write to Leslie

November 23rd, 1915.

I am here, Mary Kennedy.

Your wife did not mention my name and so I thought that I would tell you myself, for I am of much importance to my dear as any of them that she mentioned. I wanted to tell him that I am right here and close to him, and won't let even his mother take my place, though I love her very much and she loves me, but she knows that I am entitled to the first place, and that I won't let anyone take my place.

I am with him nearly all the time, trying to help and comfort him, and make him have good thoughts, and wish for me. So he will understand when you read this to him that I intend that he shall know that I am with him and won't let him forget me even if he wanted to, which I don't believe.

I was with you on Friday night, but I did not write or say anything, as his mother and grandmother and sisters and brothers were so anxious to communicate with him; but now, while I am here and have the opportunity which is mine by right of love, I intend to be first to write him. He must not think I am a bit jealous, for I am not; but you know that when a sweetheart has a chance to write to her soulmate, she is going to do it or try very hard. They can write too, but they must wait until I get through, and then they can tell him whatever they wish. So tell him to love and think of me and wish that I may be with him very often.

I am progressing in my soul development and I am very happy; and the only thing that when he is around makes me happier is to have him with me, but that will not be very soon, for he has a work to do before he comes over, and he will have to wait until he does that work.

I am so glad, though, that he has this work, and as he is doing it and helping others, he will also help himself, so that when he does come over he and I will not be separated for a very long time.

I suppose I have written enough under the circumstances, and should let others write, but I certainly wish that I could have one evening when I could take my time, and tell him of a great many things that I want him to know. So tell him that I am not stopping because I want to, but because decency requires it.

He is my own true love, and I love him with all my heart, and sometime he will know what this means.

So with all my love for him and my sister's love for you, I will stop.

His own true,
Mary.

Answers the call of her soulmate Leslie

Yes, I am here, Mary Kennedy.

Leslie loves me, how can I stay away when he calls me.

Of course, I would respond, for he is my own dear soulmate and when his love calls me I must respond and shake that hand of yours and let you know that I am here.

I was afraid that you would not write anymore and I tried to impress you to write and so did your wife (Helen) for she knew how much I wanted to do so.

I will come whenever he calls and I will not take more time.

So with all my love, I am his own

His loving,
Mary.

Lived in England near the Stone family

December 8th, 1917.

I am here, George W. Smith.

I am a spirit who lived in England and knew the family of your friend (Dr. Stone) and have met them in the spirit world and have seen them write to him and call him their son, and as I am permitted to write, I thought that I would say a few words. I am not in such an exalted position as my friends and have with me some darkness and suffering though I am progressing and learning of the way which they tell me I must pursue in order to get rid of my present conditions. Mrs. Stone has been a very angel of goodness to me and has so patiently tried to show me the way to truth and to the love that has made an angel of her. What a glorious and beautiful spirit she is and how fortunate her son is to have such a mother who loves him so much as I have heard her often say.

Well, I merely want to say that I have heard the conversation between you and my brother and have believed with interest in what he said about writing to my sisters and telling them some of the spiritual truths that have been written to him by our mother and others.

Well, I will not write more but I have learned that the prayers of you mortals do help the darkened spirits very much and wish that your friend and you would pray for me. Heaven is ahead of me they tell me and I want so much to get there. Good night.

George W. Smith.

Urges Leslie to write his sisters on earth regarding spiritual communication

November 22nd, 1915.

I am here, Kate Stone.

Let me write a few words as I have not written you for a long time and in view of the fact that I have been present so often when other spirits have written and have never sought the opportunity to write. I feel that I am not intruding by sending a short message, especially as your wife says just go ahead and write as long as you feel inclined to do so.

Well, I merely want to say that I have heard the conversation between you and my brother and have believed with interest to what he said about writing to my sisters and telling them some of the spiritual truths that have been written to him by our mother and others.

I am with my sisters quite often and try to impress upon them but do not succeed very well, for the reason that mother has explained and I am so much disappointed for they need to know that I am with them and so much desire to get close to them and have them feel my influence.

They are as Leslie says. They are very orthodox and are loath to believe anything that is not in accord with their understanding of the Bible teachings, and I realize the difficulty in convincing them or even opening up their minds to a reception of the truth that is so important for them to know.

But I shall be with them when they receive his communication and will try to influence them so that they will at least give it a serious reading and if possible will open the way to a closer rapport. If they would believe one little bit that I was with them and let one longing for my presence flow to me I would so much be encouraged in the hope that a possible rapport might be made with them.

I love them so much and so want them to feel my love, of course they would not consciously do so yet they could have a feeling that I was with them with an influence such as love only brings.

Tell him to not fail to write as he expressed his intentions of doing and to add to his letter that their Kate loves them with all the love that a redeemed child of the Father can and does possess, that they are so very dear to her and that her prayers are constantly ascending to the Father for their awakening to the truth and their happiness.

I am so glad that I could write tonight and I thank you so much.

With my love to my brother and kind regards to you, I will say good night,

His sister,
Kate.

Describes the difference between the soulmate love and the mother's love for her son

I am here, Mary.

I am very anxious to tell that little boy sitting opposite you that his Mary is here and loves him just as much as ever, and that she does take delight in tickling his ear to let him know she doesn't intend to be forgotten.

So, I thank you very much for listening to my impressions, as I am so anxious to just say that he must love me with his whole heart and soul, as I do him.

I am so glad that he is progressing in his knowledge of things spiritual, and that when the time comes for him to come over, he will not feel like a stranger in a strange land, as Judge Syrick said, but will know that he is among friends, the chiefest among whom will be his Mary.

I won't let even his mother claim that privilege, although she loves him very much and is here now, and sends her love to him and wants him to know that she was with him this morning, and cast on him all her love and influence. "He realized it and I was happy that he could realize the presence of such love." This is what his mother says.

Well, tell him I was there too, and my love was flowing towards him as well as that of his mother, but there was no conflict in our love, for we both love him more than he can conceive of. The only difference is that my love is one that will grow and last through all eternity, while that of his mother will not last through all eternity, as she will have to give it to her soulmate when the time comes for a separation between him and her. This does not mean that his mother will not always love him, but that another will be first in her love, while he will always be first in my love, for he is my soulmate, and no love can come between us, even the Divine Love of the Father will not do that, but it will only make our love for each other the stronger.

Well, as he said, you will commence to think that I will write all night, but he slanders me for I would not be so unkind to put you to such an ordeal.[24]

So thanking you I will say, that I love you as a sister, and him - well, I suppose I will have to say as a real true soulmate; and if he doesn't be a good boy and love me, I will not let him know again how much I love him.

So my dear friend I will say good night,

Mary

The soulmate of Leslie, the bad boy.

Intends to take the spirit of Dr. Stone out of the body to show him where she is living in the same way that Helen did with Mr. Padgett

July 3rd, 1916.

I am here, Mary.

I want very much to write as I have been waiting for some time to send my dear Leslie (Stone) a communication, and I have been so disappointed because it seemed to me that conditions would never present themselves that would enable me to tell of my love and desires. But now that I am writing again, I hope that you will not think me selfish

---

[24] While Mr. Padgett was receiving the message from my soulmate, I jokingly said - "Mary will write all night if you will let her." It was then that she referred to my remark.
This shows that "spirits like a little fun as well as mortals even if they have reached the higher spheres."
Mr. Padgett was much amused at her reply and we both had a hearty laugh, and have no doubts that the spirits present did also. (Dr. L. R. Stone)

if I should write a little longer than seems to be reasonable.

Well, I was present the other night when you came to us in your spirit form, and what Helen told you is all true, but she did not tell you the whole truth for if she had, she would have told you that I greeted you also, and that you said I was very beautiful and that Leslie had no conception of what a lovely sweetheart he had, and that if he could only see me and be with me he would never want to return to earth again. And I told you to tell him that I was his, and no one else's, and that I was waiting for him to come, and that I was going to try to bring him to these spheres of love just as Helen did you, and I am going to do it, too.

Of course, I have never had any experience of this kind, but Helen says that she will show me the way and that very soon. And now I desire to tell him that he must not be surprised if some night before very long he finds himself with me and enjoying my love and happiness.

But Helen says that if he does come she will meet him also and tell him some things that will cause him to think that I do not love him so much; but I don't care if she does so that I have him with me.

He must believe in what I here write, for it is true and we will have all the enjoyment that I can possibly promise, and I know that then I will be so real to him that he will never thereafter have to wonder what kind of looking girl his soulmate is. He may not recollect any more, than you do, his experience, but yet there will remain with him in his memory some conception of what his Mary looks like, so that she will be real to him as your Helen is to you.

Oh, what a glorious thought that I can have him with me in his actual spirit presence, and talk to him and have him talk to me! Won't that be heaven for us both! But I must not get into such rhapsody for if I do I may forget some other things that I desire to say.

Tell him that I am with him so very much and that when he thinks I am giving him the signal I am really doing so, and that when he does not receive the signal I am frequently with him. And tell him, too, that as I progress in my soul development and get more of the divine love in my soul, the more I love him, and try to make him realize it, and that now as I am in the celestial heavens, I know that he will not be left in the lower spheres, for I could not be perfectly happy without him, and that God is too good to deprive me of his companionship.

What a wonderful thing is love, and I mean not only the love of the Father but the lesser love of the soulmate when it knows that it's soulmate on earth returns that love; but of course, the mortal soulmate can never love as does the soulmate in the higher spheres. I am so very happy tonight that I could write for a long time yet, but I must not, though I will add a postscript.

I am with his mother very much, and love her very dearly, because she loves her son so much, and we often talk about the time when he will come to us and be one of the family of redeemed spirits, and when his home and my home shall be the same. His mother is a very beautiful spirit and knows only love, and while she loves all her children on earth yet she feels closer to him because he gives her the opportunity to come to him and he responds to her thoughts of love and happiness.

His father is also much interested and is with him very much, trying to help him and turn his thoughts to the higher things of life on earth as well as here and is now here telling me that I must let him know that he, the father, is so very happy that his son's longings and aspirations are so often given to those thoughts that will enable him to progress to the delights that come only with the divine love of the Father.

Well, I must stop now or you will think that I am very selfish and I do not want you to think that, for you know I love you as a sister and want you to believe that I am a good little spirit, even if I do love more than some spirits who don't know so much about love.

So I will say good night, but tell my dear one to prepare to have his spirit carried away some night to fields of bliss and beauty that very few mortals visit.

So goodbye. Your own true friend and sister,
Mary Kennedy.

Confirms Mary's plan

July 3rd, 1916.

I am here, your own true and loving Helen.

You have received quite a letter from Mary tonight, and she was so glad that she could write you for she wanted to let the Doctor know that she intends to carry his spirit with her and enjoy his presence as I did yours. I will assist her and she will succeed, and the Doctor will be carried to the sphere to which his soul development will enable him to enter which I think will be the third, for he has much development and is in possession of much of the love.

Well, I see that you do not feel like writing much tonight, and I will not try to write longer, and only say that I love you with all my heart and soul. So love me and give me my kiss.

Good night,
Your own true loving,
Helen.

Succeeds in bringing her soulmate, Leslie, into the third sphere, although upon his return he did not remember the travel he made into the spirit world

December 13th, 1916.

I am here, Mary.

Let me write just a line and I will feel better, for I am so anxious to tell the Doctor that he is such a dear boy, and needs me more than he thinks. Of course this is in a kind of humorous vein, but still humor sometimes contains much truth.

Helen says that I might write a short letter, and I know that when she says so you will have to submit, but I know that you want to favor me anyhow. I understand from what he has said to you that he has no recollection of his experience, and I am very sorry for if he could only recall just a little of what he saw and felt when he was with me he would never doubt for a moment that I am his true soulmate, and that his heaven is all that he has had described him.

It was a very happy night for me and for him too if I may judge from what he said. He did not want to return and said—that there was no special reason for his returning and that he was so happy with me that he felt justified in requesting that he may be permitted to stay with me, but I reminded him that could not be as he had been chosen to do a work among mortals, and that until that was finished he could not come to the spirit and remain, but I promised that he should come again as a visitor, and that his happiness would be just as great as he was then experiencing and that possibly he might at some time be able to recall some of the experiences of his visit.

Well I had him with me and we were in the third sphere, where everything was so suited to our love feast, and we were happy, I must tell you. He met his father and mother and sisters, and some other spirits who were interested in him, and they were all so happy to have him with them, especially was his mother very happy for she took him in her arms and kissed him and cried for very joy.

They stayed with us for a little while but soon saw that we were anxious to be alone, and they left with their blessings. But Helen said—that she did not intend to leave, for fear that I should get in such a condition that I would forget that he was still a mortal, and do something that might prevent his return to his body. She said—I was not responsible and that she thought too much of the Doctor to leave him alone with such a lovesick and foolish girl as I was, and asked him if I was not right, and if he did not think it best for her to stay, and he said—that of course he appreciated her anxiety on his account, and he knew that she did not want anything to happen to him, but that he was quite a brave man, and was willing to run the risk of being left alone with me, and then she gave me a kiss and hug and left us.

I would like to tell you of some of the things he said and did, but I have not the time tonight but only say it was a time of happiness and bliss and a forerunner of what is in store for us when he comes over never to return to the body.

I will come soon and try the experiment again, and I suppose again, for the joys of our being together are so great that I know that I will not be able to resist the temptations of having him with me. Helen says—that I must stop as you are tired. So thanking you, and with my love to Leslie, and in the hope that he will soon be with me again, I will say good night.

Your loving sister,
Mary.[25]

Spiritual help given to Dr. Stone in his healing prayer for the sick

April 4th, 1918.

I am here, Mary Kennedy.

I want to tell Leslie that Dr. Campbell is a wonderful spirit and they say a real physician who knows pretty much the condition of the sick. I am so glad that he came to my dear with his help, and I cannot tell him how glad I am and was when the Doctor told him the other night of the great powers that could come to him in certain conditions, so tell Leslie that he must follow the Doctor's advice and then he will see wonderful displays of the powers that come from the healing spirits that have been with Leslie a great deal for the past four days, while he attended the sick woman and I was trying my little might to help him though he did not need me for he had some very powerful spirit doctors with him. I realized it is a great thing to help the distressed, yet it is a greater thing to love you, for the sick may get well and must die at sometime and disappear from his recollections, yet, his Mary can never die again and will always be a part, not only of his recollections but of his very being.

I will not write more tonight as there are many spirits here who

---

[25] The day following the information received from Mr. Padgett that his Helen and my soulmate Mary were going to try and take me out of the body as they had written about three weeks before. I felt a wonderful influence of love that seemed to take possession of my whole being, and it lasted for three days and made me feel so happy.
Mr. Padgett had a similar experience after going to the spirit world in the third sphere a few months previous to my experience, and said that he felt much love present in his soul after the event. (Dr. L. R. Stone)

want to write and some of them will, so tell him to remember me in love and believe that I am with him almost constantly and loving him. But yet I am so selfish that I must come back to myself and tell him that in all his thoughts in reference to these matters of which I have just written, he must not forget me, for while it is a great thing to relieve the sick, yet as I have written, it is a great thing to love his Mary.

With all my love I must stop and say good night.

Mary.

Pleased with the help given to her brother Leslie R. Stone by Dr. Campbell

April 4th, 1918.

I am here, Kate Stone.

I am here and want to write a line. I am the sister of Leslie and I desire to tell him that I have been with him quite often during the last three or four days. He may be somewhat surprised to learn that I have been present with Dr. Campbell while he has been watching the effect of his medicine upon the kidneys of my brother and of course was much interested for as you may know it is a new experience for us who are with him as it is for him, and he must not doubt what Dr. Campbell prescribed for him and has given his attention to the effect of the medicine so that as he says he may be able to give him advice as to what shall be done if anything else is necessary.

I am pleased that Leslie can have the benefit of the help of Dr. Campbell for I know that his advice is based upon his actual knowledge of conditions and not merely guesswork. And as I and the other spirit friends of my brother desire that he become a well man spiritually and also desire that he become well physically and remain so, and the Doctor's advice is that Leslie must become free from any trouble with his kidneys and also will become strong otherwise. I cannot tell him how thankful we are that he has such a good adviser as to his physical condition. We, as we know, are anxious that he become perfectly whole in his physical and spiritual condition and the combination of the two states of well being makes for him a condition that will bring to him much material enjoyment and spiritual happiness. When we come to think of the wonders of these things, we cannot keep from being agreeably surprised, and I want to tell him that I know of no other mortals who are enjoying the advantages of having such unusual and believable help. We are very happy and progressing all the time and are doing a work that is very helpful to mortals. Our work is largely with mortals in the way of attempting to impress them with spiritual thoughts, and of course we are especially with our brothers and sisters, but this is not our only work for the spirits in darkness are also the objects of our efforts and endeavors to help out of the sufferings.

All send their love and earnest wishes for his progress in his soul development which of course means a greater inflowing of the love.

I will not write more now. So good night.

With much love,

His sister Kate.

Wrote of his son's experience in his first travel into the spirit world where he met his family there

December 28th, 1916.

I am here, father.

I desire to write a few lines to my son as I see that he is in a condition that makes any communication from us very desirable to him. I want to tell him that I am very happy and am progressing very rapidly and will soon, I hope, be with his mother when my happiness will be complete for my love for her is so very great that I am happy beyond desire when I am with her. This is a reality, and I know for I am with her at times, and feel the certainty of the truth of what I say. She is very happy also, and so are his sisters, who are here now, and who are with him so often and who would like to come in closer contact with his brothers and sisters of earth, if they would only believe that their spirit sisters so desire to make their presence felt. But their want of belief and of desire to have their spirit sisters with them prevent a rapport being made, which is necessary for the enjoyment of the close communion that I speak of.

Tell my son that I enjoyed his visit a few nights ago and was sorry when he had to return to his body. We were all there and talked with him, and made him realize what beautiful homes we have, and the wonderful happiness that is ours. This is not mere imagination, or tale of magic, for he was actually with us, and saw and felt our spirit bodies and also experienced the atmosphere of love that he ran into. Of course his soulmate, had him most of the time of his visit to herself, but she was very generous and told us to enjoy his presence to our hearts content, but, of course, we understood and withdrew.

I imagine that he may not quite believe all that he saw, but I want to assure him, with all the love of a father, that it is a fact, and that sometime I hope he may have a recollection of some of his experiences, and I know that he will.

Well, I must not write more now, except to say, that he must continue to pray and believe in the divine love of the Father, for I can assure him that it is the one grand thing that makes angels of spirits; and soon I hope to be one of the angels, as his mother now is. So with my love I will say good night,

William Stone.

Under Jesus' direction helped to correct Mr. Padgett's digestive organs, as a result of his prayer to the Father for help

February 15th, 1915.

I am here, White Eagle.

You are much better. The Master helped you very much last night. I manipulated you as he directed, and your digestive organs are now doing their work. Your prayer to the Father was answered. He heard you as Jesus told you He would if you would pray in faith. You had the faith and the cure came. So it is with everything in life, only pray and believe and you will receive the answer. You are certainly blessed, and I wonder as do all of us, at your faith; but thank God you are the one that the Master has selected, and you will be in condition soon to do his work as he desires.

Yes, you are right. He is the only one that can help you in time of trouble. Only continue in your faith and you will realize that he is your Father and your helper. Jesus says that your faith is wonderful, and that you will be able to do many things that will help mankind. Only be true to him and you will never be forsaken.

No, you need not use any more medicine now, the work is done, and medicine is no longer necessary. Well, he (Dr Stone) may help you some in starting your various muscles and nerves to get into activity, but even his treatment is not necessary now. When God heals He heals effectively, and no other help is needed.

You are commencing to get that Great Love in your soul now, and soon you will be filled, and then your happiness will be complete, that is it will be of such a character that the worries of life will not make you unhappy.

Yes, he (Jesus) was present and he directed my movements. He is the all-powerful one. His knowledge is without limit, and he is so full of love, that when he tries to impress you, you cannot resist the influence of that love. So be more prayerful and you will become possessed of that Love to a degree that will make you love all mankind as well as God. Well, I am telling you what the Master tells us, and he knows. You had better not eat promiscuously yet, give the digestive organs a chance to get back their full strength.

So good night.

69

White Eagle.[26]

This photograph of White Eagle was published in Volume III without any comment as to how it was obtained.

White Eagle

Further comment accompanying this photograph reads as follows:

White Eagle is a powerful Indian and has often used his great healing powers to restore Mr. James E. Padgett to good health. He wrote often as he had considerable Divine Love in his soul that made him a bright and beautiful spirit.

Says that she was not very wise when on earth but now knows the wonderful things that come to her with the inflowing of the Father's Love

June 6th, 1916.

I am here, Kate Stone.

Let me write just a line or two, for while so much love is present I want to enjoy it and tell my brother that Mr. Morgan is not the only one on earth who has a mother and sisters and soulmate's love.

I have not written often to him, but have been present many, many times when others were writing their messages of love, and while I

---

[26] This message is a composite of two, being published in Volume III and Volume IV. (G.J.C.)

was not writing I was impressing him with my love and I know that he felt it, for I could see his emotions, and the return of his soul love to me as he received mine.

Of course, the sister's love is not so great or of the same quality as the soulmate's, or even that of the mother's, yet it is a love that is all pure and unselfish, and carries with it the influences that can come only from a soul that has received the purification and great joy of the Father's Love.

I do love my brother, as we all do and I try so hard and so often to cause him to realize that my poor little sister's love is flowing to him in all its fullness.

I know that he has a great deal of not only the natural love, but also of the Divine Love as well, and if he could only know how happy it makes us to realize that he possesses this Divine Love, and is constantly seeking for more, he will try all the harder to get more of it. We can see his soul condition, and to us it is just as naked and open to our soul's vision as is the souls of spirits one to another, and nothing can be hid from us.

So you see from what I say that he cannot pretend to love his soulmate, for she knows exactly what love he has in his heart for her, and when he tells her that he loves her she knows to just what extent, and so with the rest of us.

All of us are very happy and constantly progressing in our soul development and in happiness, and while this is so, we do not forget him, or our brothers and sisters on earth; but I am sorry to say that they do not know of this Divine Love, and we are trying so hard to impress them with the knowledge of its existence, and the fact that it is waiting for them; but we know that some day they will have an awakening and receive it, for we do not think it possible that such love as ours can be with them so constantly, seeking to influence them, and not in the end bring to them a consciousness that the other love is waiting for them, and we have a great deal of faith, and the Master tells us our prayers will be answered, and he knows. What a precious brother and friend he is, and how he seems to love you and your friends.

When mother and father and the rest of the family here get together, we often wonder and try to understand why the Master should have selected you as the recipient of his love to such an extent, and for his disciple to do the great work that must be done for the salvation of mankind.

Oh, we are all so thankful and happy that such a thing has come to you, and you, my dear, dear brother, must try to appreciate what it means to you and to others.

The Master is with you quite often and when you and your friends get together he comes to you, and casts upon you his love and blessings, and also come many high and wonderful spirits with their love and influences of happiness and peace.

So listen to your sister, who was not very wise on earth, but who now knows the wonderful things that come to her with the inflowing of the Father's Love.

When she tells you to pray more and let your faith increase, and when doubts come to you, turn your thoughts to the Father and ask His help and blessings, and they will come to you, and you will know it. And love will become a part of your very existence, and the happiness that you will receive will be only a forecast of what is waiting for you when you become one of us in our glorious homes in the skies.

I must not write more now, but in closing will say that we all love you, and are all with you, and pray to the Father that His Love and Blessings may come to you in increasing streams of purity, and joy also, which only He can give.

With all my love, I am your own dear and loving sister,
Kate.[27]

Is happy to see his son's wonderful development in his soul

November 4th, 1915.

I am here, Leslie's father.

I will write a few words also, for I know my son will enjoy a short writing from me tonight. I have been with him a great deal, as you may think, and am so very much pleased to realize that he has made a wonderful development in his soul, and that he is nearer the Father's Divinity than he has ever been before. I will not tell him of our condition, for he must know that we are very happy, and one of the reasons for our happiness is the fact that he not only knows the way to this Love, but is striving to obtain it, or rather, to increase his possession of it, for he has much of it already, and he is conscious of that fact.

I was present a few nights ago when his mother wrote him, and I cannot tell him of the great happiness we all had—a happiness that no reunion on earth could ever have given.

I will come soon and write him a letter in reference to the War, for while my thoughts are given more to the great truths that make angels of men, yet I have been somewhat interested in the progress of the War, as my people, I mean my friends and citizens of England, are very much in the War, and many of them have paid the price of their patriotism and sacrifice, and are now in the Spirit World. But this I will

---

[27] This is to me a wonderful and most beautiful message and gives me much happiness and consolation. (Dr. L. R. Stone)

say now, that the spirits who have been closely watching the events of the War and its progress, and who have visited the directing minds of the various contending nations, and also the people of these nations, say that the end of the war will soon come, and all the bloodshed that mortals expect will not take place.

I will not write more now, but will repeat what has been said to you both so often: "Watch yourselves and pray to the Father with all the longings of your souls."

With my love I will say,

The doctor's father,

William Stone.

Makes reference as did John Padgett to the depressing influence which Richard the Third brought with him

November 6th, 1916.

I am here, Kate Stone.

Let me say just a word, for I want to tell you that this wicked spirit (Richard the Third) has left[28] and his depressing influence has gone with him, and we feel better, as well as do you. I will not write much. I merely wanted to tell you this, and to say that your band are here and are exerting their peaceful influences.

I am very happy and I want you to be, and also I desire my brother to enjoy the feeling brought to him by his loved ones, of whom I am one and a dear one.

I would like to write him a long letter tonight, but you have been too much drawn on for me to do so. But tell him that I love him, and that we all rejoice at the great blessing that has been recently bestowed upon him by the Master and John and others, and I want to tell him that he must believe and trust in these good and higher spirits who are so very loving and kind to him. We all love him so much, and I not the least, although I suppose his Mary thinks that she has more love than any of us - and she is right. So with my love and prayers I will say good night.

His own loving sister,

Kate.

Kate Stone and family always respond when the call comes that Leslie needs help

I am here, Kate Stone.

Let me write a line for I desire to tell my brother that I have been

---

[28] The message from Richard the Third has not been published. (G.J.C.)

with him so very often and the difficulties that have come to him at times in reference to his material affairs.

If he only knew what happiness I experience when I realize the results of his longings for the love he would know how much I love him, and how I rejoice when I see the transformation of the Divine Love and his progressing as he is doing.

This love is all so wonderful that it is impossible for me to tell him what it means to a soul that has the consciousness of its existence as I have, and how as it fills my soul I become the more desirous that it shall fill his also.

We, and I mean his parents and sisters, and, of course his Mary are with him whenever we feel that he wants us, for his desires in this particular come to us as the electric fluid fills the wire when the receiving end calls for its coming from the sending end. We always respond and even though we may not be present with him, yet, our rapport is now so perfect that whenever his desires for us ascend from his heart, we never fail to sense the same and respond, and as we come to him, we bring all our love and happiness with us, and try to make him realize the influence of the same.

There are no limitations such as we had on earth to prevent our coming, and space is as it were non-existent, and we are with him "in the twinkling of an eye" in all our love and sympathy. What a wonderful provision of the Father this all is! And how the great enemy of mortals as most men call it, I mean death enables us to come so close to our mortal friends when they call for us. Death as I just heard him quote is a friend of all mortals and the great friend of spirits, for when it comes the mortal is no longer bound by the bands of the limitations of the physical but becomes as a free bird of the air, or rather, as the stars that shoot from their courses, because we spirits have it with a greater velocity than do the shooting stars especially when love calls us.

I felt in the mood of writing as I have tonight as my soul is filled with love for my brother, and I want him to know that it is a truth, and that nothing can keep me and my love from him but he himself, and knowing this he must realize that I am always so happy when he calls for me, even if it be only a wish unexpressed or the longings of a sigh.

We are all progressing and happy beyond expression and at the same time have our wishes that his sisters and brothers may know the great truth, that we, whom they suppose to be away off either in heaven or hell, are at times very close to them, so close that even the whisper of their passing thoughts cannot escape our hearing; and if they could only know this, and would think of us at times when their thoughts may be taken from their earthly affairs, how we would come to them and throw around them our love, and make them feel our presence. But they do not believe that we can be with them (and throw around them our love and make them feel our presence) and especially that they can call us as I have written.

We all hope though that someday their eyes may be opened to the light and that they will consciously realize that parents and sisters are not dead, but are really living the true and immortal life.

Well, this is what I wanted to say tonight and I hope that it may do Leslie some good, and I know it will—for love has never yet failed of its mission when it has found a receptive soul. Of course he knows many things in connection with spirit life, and among them that there are different kinds of love, and that some are because of their very nature deeper and more intense than others, but nevertheless the love of a mere sister, as I am, who has the Love of the Father in her soul is beyond all conception to mortals.

I will not write more now and am thankful that I could write.

Good night and God bless you both is the earnest and sincere prayer of—Kate.

Mr. Padgett and Dr. Stone go to a Presbyterian church for the New Year's Eve service

December 31st, 1916.

I am here, Helen.

Well, we are here in great numbers and all wish you and the Doctor a very Happy New Year, and one that will bring to you not only prosperity and happiness in your material affairs, but also a great and abundant inflowing of the divine love of the Father, which will bring you a happiness that no earthly prosperity can possibly bring. We were with you tonight at the (New Year's Eve) church services and tried to throw around you our influence of love and peace—the peace that passeth all understanding—and when this peace came to you as it did to a degree, we all rejoiced.

The Master was present, for there were many souls there that were longing for this love, although they associated it with Jesus in the way that they believed it came from him as the fountainhead; but notwithstanding this error, their souls were right and the Holy Spirit responded, and the Love was present and many a worshipper felt its influence.

I suppose that you and the Doctor would like to know who were present, and I should like to tell you but to do so would require more paper and more time than you have at your disposal tonight. But this I will say, that in addition to the Master there were present your special guardians. I mean John and James, and also Mary and the Doctor's parents and sisters, and your parents and of course myself. We all felt that as this is the night that brings into your lives a new year, with the great possibilities that will be yours, we should become a little human and bring to you our love and wishes, and the fact that there are surrounding you the spirits of those who once loved you so much when they lived on earth and had nothing more than faith. Now they come to you with knowledge, and with some of them the knowledge that they are angels, and redeemed children of the Father, and inhabitants of His celestial kingdom—the kingdom which Jesus has been and is establishing for the eternal homes of all who may receive the new birth.

If you could have seen all the glorious spirits that were present, and the love and beauty that surrounded you, you would have thanked God with all the powers of your soul that you were so blessed, and we all said and prayed to the Father—"God bless you", and what it meant only we knew, though you could receive its benefits.

Well, I am happy, and Mary is happy and all the spirits who love you so much, are happy. What a blessed thing the love of the Father is! As the preacher said, this Love makes your soul a new thing, not as a new creation only, but in the important element of being new in quality and consistency. I hope that you may continue to increase in your realization of the abundance of this love that will surely be yours, if you continue to pray to the Father in earnest and longing desire.

I will not write more tonight except to say, that Mary wants to tell the Doctor that as the hours go by she feels that she is getting closer and closer to him in the holy love that is theirs, and that can never be taken from them. She is anxious that he feel this growing love and increased rapport, and that some day she may become as real to him in his conscious recollections, as he is to her. So repeating our wish that you both may have a Happy New Year, with increasing love and joy as the year grows older, I will say with all my heart's love, good night. We both want our kisses.

Your own true and loving,
Helen.

Is very happy to see the inflowing of Divine Love into Leslie's soul and sorry that she cannot reach her other children on earth

I am here, mother Priscilla Stone.

I am here and want to write a line to my son, for I have been listening to your conversation and saw that his soul has more of the Divine Love than he realizes or is conscious of, for I am so happy when I come to him and find that the Love is possessing him and at times when it is so active I am enabled to get in very close rapport with him and to have the influence of my love enter into his feelings; for when I say my love I do not mean my mere mother's love but also the love that flows from me because of my possession of this Divine Love.

Well, quite a number of spirits have been present tonight listening to your conversation and they have enjoyed the thoughts that you have both expressed and are so pleased as they are that you comprehend some of the divine truth that is so much increasing with you. How we pray for you and send our longings to the Father for a greater inflowing of the Love into your souls.

I have recently been with my other children on earth and when I compare the great difference in my ability to get in contact with them and with my son it makes me so sorry that their conditions are such as to keep me from them.

How strange as you might say that with one of my children, and I love them all very dearly, I can come in with closeness and with the others I cannot enter into their feelings and longings. Yet it just illustrates of the experience, and I may say of the Divine Love with some mortals it can find a lodgment in their souls and with others it cannot for their conditions are as if there were an adamantine wall separating them from the inflowing of that Love. But we pray and try to impress our mortal children with our thoughts of what the truth is and the necessity for them seeking these truths and we believe that our prayers will be answered for we know that the Father is always ready and willing to bestow that Love and only their false beliefs or their idle thoughts prevent them from receiving that bestowal.

Tell my boy not to cease in his endeavors to bring to the knowledge of his brothers and sisters the existence of this Love, and that upon themselves depends its inflowing into their souls.

We are all very happy and progressing more and more towards the fountainhead of this Love, and we know that it is of real existence and is waiting for us all without limit.

I will not write more now and am thankful that I can say these few words to my dear boy. We are with him very often trying to help him and we also never cease praying for him.

So good night and God bless you both,
His loving mother.

Tells of her spiritual progress and her Great Love of the Father; and confirms his visit to Eleanor Meads, age 15, now in the spirit world, to help her again as he did when she was still on earth

December 10th, 1917.

I am here, his mother, Priscilla Stone.

I am here, the mother of Leslie, and very much desire to write a few lines, as I feel that he would like to hear from me and receive an expression of my love. Well, in the first place, I desire to tell him that I am progressing and am in a sphere that is so beautiful and full of the Father's love that for me to attempt to describe it, would result only in failure. But when I tell him that my happiness is so very great that even I, at a very recent time, when in what I thought was the acme (The highest point, as of achievement or development) of happiness, had no conception of what happiness meant as compared to what I now possess.

All this is so wonderful to me, that it is difficult even for a soul that is filled with this Love to conceive what the Love of the Father in its fullness can be. And the great thing of wonderment is that as we progress we realize that it is impossible to comprehend the heights and depths of this great Love. When on earth and I read that "God is Love" I had not a faint idea even of what the expression meant, for, as you must know, my conception of love was based largely on what I knew or thought the human love was, such as my love for my children, which was to me the greatest expression of love. But, as I say, this love is not even a faint shadow of what the Love of the Father is: and the great beauty of it all is that, while this Divine Love is always the same, yet in seeking and obtaining it I find that more and more is waiting for me. We know of no cessation of progress and are never satisfied, yet never unhappy, because we realize that we are not the possessor of it in all its fullness. No, our happiness is in proportion to the amount of love that we possess, and for the time that love is sufficient for our complete happiness. I do not know that mortals can fully understand this, because, as you may know, when mortals are seeking the natural love of another and desire more and more of it, and they are happy in its possession, yet at the same time they have some pain or unhappiness, because they do not have all the love that their desires ask for.

Well, this is not the condition of us who have and seek this divine love, for it, of itself, seems to have the quality of causing complete, perfect happiness, without taking from us the desire and longings for more. I doubt that any of your philosophers can explain this apparent inconsistency, because they have nothing on earth to which they can make a comparison. A mortal who is satisfied with the love that he may have on earth has not the longings for more, and when he has the longings, he is not wholly happy in the enjoyment of that which he possesses.

And the same principle applies to the possession and longings of mortals for everything else of the natural or material. Ambitions for fame and power and position and the accumulation of wealth, and the love of a woman or man, are all subject to this law of the accompaniment of pain and unhappiness. So you may in a short way understand what great qualities the divine love has in its operations, and how it differs from the mere natural love.

Well, my boy will think I am somewhat of a philosopher and have changed from my course of thought while on earth. And so I have, but he must not be surprised to know that as I receive the great love in my soul in increased abundance there comes with it a knowledge of law and principles and the relationship of things that I have never studied or attempted to acquire by study. And this is one of the surprising results of the obtaining of this divine love. It seems to have in it, as a part of its qualities, knowledge and wisdom and understanding that is not dependent upon the mind or intellect of the natural man, but which is a part of the mind of the soul that is developed as the soul is developed in love.

I thought I would write in this way tonight, that Leslie may, in a faint way, comprehend what the progress of his mother means and comprehends. With love there can be no ignorance, for love is, of itself, wisdom and knowledge and understanding. And from all this you will see that the mortals whose ambition is that when they get into the spirit world they will have the opportunity to pursue the studies which they loved on earth, and that during all the long eternity there will be no cessation of opportunity to gratify their ambition. I say, you will see that these mortals will find themselves very poor indeed as compared with those whose ambition is to obtain the divine love, which brings with it all these things, and others greater and beyond conception of knowledge that these mortals can possibly have.

Well, I will not write further on this subject tonight, but some time, if it pleases you, I will come and write my boy a regular thesis upon some spiritual truth that may interest him very much.

I heard him tell of his experience of a few nights ago, in going out of his body,[29] and wondering if it were really true. Well, it was true. He left his body, and he may be a little surprised to know that the great desire of that young spirit to have him come to her and tell her again of some of the things that he had told her on earth was the cause of his leaving his body. Her desires were so great that they actually drew his spirit to her. What he saw, he saw with his spirit eyes, and the persons who appeared to him were actually present; and the young spirit heard his conversation, and in it found some relief.

She brought with her to the spirit world some of the thoughts that he had conveyed to her during his earth life; and having the experience of not finding what she had been taught, when on earth, that

---

[29] Mrs. Stone confirms Leslie's astral flight to help in the spirit world in the same way that he tried to do when the spirit was a mortal in order to help Eleanor Meads. (J.P.G.)

she would find in the spirit world, she became disappointed and doubtful, and then recalled what Leslie had told her, and with these memories came the desire that he should come and repeat to her these explanations that he had made to her of the truths and condition of the spirit world.

She is now very much better, and is seeking for the truth, or rather a corroboration of the truth that she learned from him. I was present, as he thought, and when he left her I went with her and took her in my care, and have been trying to help her into the light and to a longing for this love. She is so young and her soul so susceptible to the influence of love, without being bound very much by erroneous beliefs that were taught her, she will, I know, soon become convinced of the true way to happiness and redemption. And her grandmother, who loves this young spirit so much, was with her and heard what Leslie said, and, of course, was shocked and grieved that he should try to teach the child such blasphemous things; and she shed tears and was very unhappy and wanted her child to go with her and not listen to what he said or was saying. But just here we interfered to a certain extent, and caused them to separate, and induced the grandmother to leave the child for awhile, though she did not want to do so.

And when Leslie said that he assisted her to a lower plane, he actually did so, for while she is a woman of a kindly nature, and a somewhat Christian character, as she understands, yet she is not fitted for the plane on which the scene related took place. And here let me say that the young spirit and her grandmother, because of the great law of attraction, are not suited to the same plane, and this grieves the grandmother very much, and also the child. But the regeneration of the child will, no doubt, have a great effect upon the grandmother, and when the time comes, that is after the child has learned the truth and received some of the love and goes to her grandmother to show her beauty and tell of her experience, we will go to the grandmother, also, and attempt to explain to her these truths and the error of her belief.

Well, I have written enough, and your wife says that I had better stop now. So with my love I will say good night,

His mother,

Priscilla Stone.

Confirms that Dr. Stone's mother wrote

June 16th, 1917.

I am here, your own true and loving Helen.

Well, dear, you have had some beautiful messages tonight and in them was much love, and I was glad that you received these messages.

Tell Doctor that his mother actually wrote and that she is here now and says that she will accompany him alone and remain with him until he goes to sleep. Her love for him seems to be great tonight. And dear Prof. Salyards also wrote in his loving and sympathetic way. What a wonderful spirit he is in his deference to the female spirits and he sees only love and beauty in all.

The last spirit who wrote, I am not acquainted with, but I have no doubt that she is who she represents herself to be. At any rate, she is quite a beautiful spirit but does not know what the Divine Love means and went with the Doctor's sister, who will tell her. For Kate is a very beautiful spirit with much of the love in her soul and seems so full of desire to let all know what this love is. She is doing a wonderful work among the dark spirits and is one of the busiest of the spirits who attend on your evenings when the dark spirits come for help. And I must also say that she is so joyful in the fact that the Doctor has found the way that will lead him to the Celestial Heavens.

And there is another one present whom I must not neglect to mention, and I could not if I wanted to, for she says now Helen if you love me tell Leslie that I am here and want only to say that I love him as he knows. She is progressing in her soul development very rapidly and I tell her that she is commencing to look real beautiful and if the Doctor could only see her he would think so too. And she says that it does not matter whether she is beautiful or not if she could only make herself visible to the Doctor he would not look to see whether she was beautiful or not because she would look at him with such eyes of love that he wouldn't see anything but her eyes.

Well, dear, you must not write more. Keep up your courage and believe what has been told you for you will not be disappointed. Tomorrow night the Master desires to finish his message. So with my love to you both I will say good night.

Your own true and loving—Helen.

Dr. Stone's mother helped her grandfather to progress out of darkness

I am here, Leslie W. Winfield.

I am a spirit whom as a man you never knew for I died many years ago in England. I was the grandfather of Dr. Stone's mother and have been in the earth plane as they call it all the long intervening years since my coming here. But recently I have come in contact with his mother who is such a beautiful and heavenly spirit. She did not know me until I told her who I was and then she remembered having heard of me and then she commenced to tell me of her beautiful home and the reason for being a bright spirit and that if I would follow her advice I would and could become bright and happy also.

I wondered at all she said to me and concluded that I would try to follow her advice and I have been trying and find that new sensations have come to me, and that some of my dark conditions are leaving me. All the long years that I have been a spirit in ignorance of the way that she told me of and I found that I was gradually getting into a better condition as the time went by, but the change was very slow and I thought it was natural, and hence, felt contented but hopeful and now when I know of this other way I wonder that I was never told of this new way to light.

But the spirits in their condition were much like myself and were contented in the same belief that I had.

How strange though that these bright spirits never came to us before. Of course, many times have I seen these spirits but I was not interested in them and did not think that they were spirits such as I was and shunned them.

It is all so wonderful now that I know. I am glad that I could write this, for it helps me. I must stop and say good night.

Leslie W. Winfield.[30]

Praises the work of both Mr. Padgett and her son, Leslie R. Stone, and thanks the Heavenly Father for bringing her son to the knowledge of this Love

I am here, Priscilla Stone.

I desire to write a few lines tonight if agreeable to you as I so much want to tell my son that I have been with him a great deal of late trying to make him happy and to assist him in turning his thoughts to things spiritual and to the Father's Love which makes us all so happy and draws us so near to the presence of the Father.

I have been able to get in quite close rapport with him not only in a physical sense but in his soul qualities and have enjoyed the presence of the Love in his soul as well as that in my own, and he must understand that the love that I possess is a part of the same love that he possesses both having the qualities of the Divine and the very Substance of the Father and partakes of immortality. It is a wonderful and consoling thought and fact to know that what binds our souls together is this great love that comes direct from the Father without stint or limit except as only our want of longing and faith prevents its coming. Of course in the earth life he cannot receive this love to such a great degree as I have it in

---

[30] This message is important, for it shows that dark spirits in the lower spheres under favorable conditions can visualize the bright spirits, but like my great grandfather refused to obtain help in their progress from the bright spirits and shunned them. (Dr. L. Stone)

the spirit life but it is the same love and to him it is just as freely given as to me.

What a happy mother I am to have a son whom I know is bound to me by a tie that has an eternity of existence that can never be severed.

I thank the Father so much for His goodness and His mercy in bringing my son to a knowledge of this love and the way of making it his own. Well, I have also been interested in the conversation between you and my son, and I want to tell you that the Doctor is a wonderful spirit with a great amount of the Father's Love in his soul and who is devoted to the work of doing good to others whenever the opportunity arises, and especially is he interested in you both for he realizes the work that you have been chosen to do and knows that it is the greatest work upon mortals since the Master came to fulfill the great mission that the Father bestowed upon him. This may seem extravagant to you and you may hesitate to believe fully what I say, but this I want to tell you that my assertion is based upon what I have heard the Master declare and what the others of the high spirits of the Celestial Heavens have said and what they are working to accomplish.

You are both a blessed pair of mortals and should never cease to thank the Father and love the Master for the great opportunities together with the gift that has been bestowed upon you. Only have faith and pray and work and the certainty and truth of your mission will come to you some day in such convincing force that you will never again doubt.

Well, I will only say that we all are very happy and enjoy so much the atmosphere of love and joy that comes to you so frequently.

You have at times a visitation of the joy of the Celestial Heavens and your souls at times as I can see respond to the love and influences that surround you. Your father and sisters are present tonight and send their love and you may rest assured that the other dear one is also here in all her love and wants me to say that her love is like a sunshine of a summer evening that becomes the more beautiful and mellow as the twilight comes and soothes the soul of man as he meditates upon the wonders of the Father as displayed in the glories of the heavens. When his soulmate sees the Father's Love flowing into the soul of her one dear soulmate she then offers her thanks that such is his condition and privilege.

I will not write more now and will only say to him watch and pray, for with watching and praying his soul will be able to realize the wonderful greatness and all-embracing qualities of the Great Love.

Good night and may the Father bless you both,

His mother,

Priscilla.

Writes about the beautiful spirits present tonight in such great numbers that no dark spirit could stand to be present in the same atmosphere

I am here, Priscilla Stone.

Let me say just a word for I am so filled with the Father's Love tonight, and there are so many spirits around you both who have this love to such a degree, that their souls have been transformed into the Divine Nature of the Father that causes their happiness unspeakable. This influence of love cannot be around you without your soul's realizing its presence, and when you both say that you feel the wonderful power present tonight, you are stating a fact and a truth. It would hardly be possible for you to be in the presence or atmosphere of so much love without being conscious of its existence for your souls are open to this influence, and because there is so much of the love itself, that it would be impossible for the love in greater qualities, without you knowing the fact by your own soul perceptions. You must remember that this love is one and indivisible and that the smallest amount of it in a human soul is linked with the greater amount in all the fullness as it flows from the Fountainhead of the Father.

Well, I am happy and we are all happy, because we feel a greater nearness to you both than ever before, and this fact must convince you that the possibilities of our becoming more at-one with one another, that is our spirits with you two mortals, is without limit. As has been said, this love has a wideness that is beyond all the conceptions of mortals or even with us spirits though we have our homes in the highest Celestial Heavens.

We are so glad that so much of this love has come into your souls never to depart, even though it may not at all times be so active or sensible to your consciousness or experience. The staying power of this love is the thing that even we spirits are amazed, and cannot fully comprehend. But it is never absent from the soul when once received by it, and this you must remember in all your hours of discouragement and lessening of faith.

Well, I wanted to write this much tonight that my son may know that this love is a reality, and not only that, but that he has some of it, and it will always be his, and has no limit to the possibility of its growth in the soul. And I must tell him this also that the Master, the most perfect in love of all the Celestial spirits, has been present shedding around the influence of his love and the peace that can only come from the presence of this Divine Love when the soul of the mortal is susceptible to its influence.

And besides, many other spirits are present and here I want to tell you a fact that you may not know, and that is—such a flood of this love is present that none of the dark spirits or even those of more natural love development are present and cannot be for the power of this love is such they could not endure its presence. No, this is a night when only those who have been transformed are present and heaven itself is here without the influence of those things that make the place like a heaven. This may impress you but it is a fact, and how blessed you are that while you cannot go to the heaven of which we tell you so much about, yet, for the moment that heaven came to you and the peace that passeth all understanding is here for you to possess.

Well, I must not write more. But I so wanted my boy to know the things that I have written.

Pray more and let your longings go to the Father with greater intensity and in the quietness of your rooms meditate upon his love and goodness and you will find an at-oneness with Him that you have never felt and cannot until you have the experience conceived of. So love the Father and have faith and you will not be disappointed not only in the hereafter but in your life as mortals.

Good night and may the Father bless you both,

His mother,

Who loves him as only a mother who possesses this Great Love can love a son who has come so close to her by reason of the Love that is in his own soul.

Priscilla Stone.

Writes that both of Dr. Stone's parents are now living in the Celestial Heavens

June 10th, 1920.

I am here, Mary.

Let me write a few lines to my dear one, as you disappointed me when he was last here. I thought that certainly you were going to let me write and when you did not I just couldn't help telling Helen that you were real mean, but you know I did not mean it for you have been very kind to both the Doctor and myself. So I hope you will not feel bad because of what I said. You see, we are not very different here from what we were on earth when something interferes with our love-making.

I noticed also a side remark of Helen and I want to say that she was only jealous of me or very antagonistic for me to write. Of course, she did not know what I was going to write about and I will prove it.

Well, the Doctor knows how much I love him and I know how much he loves me, and it is not always necessary to write of this, but thinking of my messages, I believe I do always say something of love and

I am glad of it.

But last night when he was with you I wanted to say something else and I will tell you now what it is. I know that he is much interested in the progress of his own folks and their happiness. I wanted to tell him that his father and sisters are in the Celestial Spheres and know to the extent that this makes their certainty of immortality and a home in the Father's house that can never be taken from them. His father has been so very earnest in his prayers and longings for the Love that it came to him in such abundance that he found himself an inhabitant of the Celestial Spheres where his mother is, and Kate is with them. So that now we are all safe in the shelter of the Father's Love, and know that forever and ever we will abide in the Heavens of the Father. We are all so glad, that we had a regular old-fashioned love feast and praised God for His goodness and mercy.

I have been with Leslie a great deal lately and feel that he, too, is getting more of this Love in his soul, and if he could fully realize what it means he would feel like shouting as the old Methodists sometimes do. I sometimes wonder at what all this means, and why we should be privilege to possess this Love and have the corresponding happiness; and this I know, that no matter how much men are disappointed in the earth life or spirits in the spirit world, the Father never disappoints them who long for the Love that is free for all, but how few realize what this freedom means. Only those whose Love from God enters and takes possession of the soul can have a possible realization of what God's free Love means. I am so glad that day by day this knowledge is coming to my soulmate. And when I say knowledge I mean something more than a mere intellectual knowledge. This latter of course is necessary, but it is not the knowledge that comes to the soul.

Tell the Doctor to pray more and more, and believe with all his soul that there is no limit to the inflowing of the Divine Love to become his. I have written enough for tonight and notwithstanding Helen's remarks, I am going to tell him that I love him with all my heart and soul, and will never leave him until the time comes for him to join me, and not then, of course.

I thank you very much for permitting me to write tonight, and you must believe that I love you as a sister, and would not for all the world call you hard names or make you feel that I am not your true, loving sister. His parents send their love to him and the assurance that they are helping him with all their powers and love. Good night and God bless you both, and in the end lead you to one of the glorious mansions that are waiting for you.

Your true friend and the only true love of the Doctor.

Mary.

Writes that she is both hungry and thirsty for Dr. Stone's love

I am here, Mary.

Let me say one word and I will be satisfied, for I so long to tell Leslie that I am hungry and thirsty for his love. He may think it strange that I should say this, because as I write him I have so much of the Divine Love of the Father. But a stranger thing than this is, that while the Father's Love is all-sufficient to make me happy and contented, yet when we have in us the soulmate love, and know it, this love must have its full enjoyment, and our desire to make it known to our mortal soulmates does not take from us one iota of the Divine Love, but rather when we possess this latter Love to a great degree it causes us to have more longings and desire for the exercise of this lower love to a great degree. He may not understand this, but the Father is so loving and unselfish that He will not permit the Divine Love to satisfy us, so that the soulmate love will have no existence in our souls, but further, our souls will have longings and desires for the return of this love by our soulmates of earth.

Leslie will understand and feel that I am his in all the truth and beauty of my love, and that in loving him so much I do not in the slightest degree reflect upon the sufficiency of the Divine Love. How wonderful it all is; and from this he can realize how poor the spirit is who has neither the Father's Love nor the soulmate love. Well, I merely wanted to say this, and to encourage him to believe in his soulmate and her love.

I will soon come and write him a longer letter. Good night,

His loving,

Mary.

Writes that Celestial Spirits are proud to know Dr. Stone

I am here, Mary.

Let me tell you just one thing—Helen says I may, and I of course want to, and I will not trespass very long.

You know I don't get the opportunity to write so often as Helen does, although I have just as much desire to do so as she has, and when the opportunity comes my way I am not as modest as I should be in taking advantage of it.

But I know you sympathize with me, for you can see how much good it does me, and I believe it does the Doctor also.

Well, I suppose the first word you expect me to say is that I love him with all my heart and soul, but I will not do that, though I have said it—haven't I? Well let it go and I am glad of it.

I am with him so often that if he could see me I am afraid that he would get tired of me and so you see there is some advantage in being invisible, but how I wish that sometime I could be visible to him that he might know just what kind of looking sweetheart he has. But this is of minor importance as compared to the fact that he is my soulmate, and that our loves are linked together for all eternity, and that only a comparative few years separate us from each other.

I am very happy in my new home, and I am so anxious to tell him of it, and try to describe some of its glories, but I cannot do so tonight.

Well, he must continue to believe in me and in my love, and that he is to me the dearest being in all God's universe, and that no one else of all the myriads of men or spirits, can take his place now or ever.

I see that he is quite happy and that makes me happy, and I must tell him this—that while there is none that loves him just as I do, yet there are many high spirits, as well as his own folks, who are with him very much trying to help him with their love and influence. It seems so strange to many spirits here that such things should be, and it is wonderful when I tell you that very few of the spirits of the spiritual spheres have the celestial spirits with them as he does, and thence these spirits of the spirit spheres look upon him as a kind of important mortal whose company it is well to cultivate, and many of them are with him also.

Thank God, that he is able to have such associates as these celestial spirits, with their wonderful love and influence. God is love, and His love goes out to mortals just to the degree that they open up their souls to its inflowing, and my dear has his soul very much opened up, and the love is coming to him all the time. I must not write more now, and I thank you for permitting me to write.

So give him my love, and remember that I am your sister in love, and pray for you both, with all the earnestness and faith that I possess.

Good night,
Mary.[31]

Has progressed into the same sphere that is inhabited by Mrs. Helen Padgett

I am here, Mary.

You must not be surprised that I can come to write, for if you could realize that it has been a long time since I wrote, you would excuse my intruding and say: -

Mary, you are entirely welcome to say a few words to the Doctor though he may not deserve them.

---

[31] This is a wonderfully beautiful letter and gives me so much happiness and joy. (Dr. L. R. Stone)

Besides Helen says that as I have been such a faithful attendant on my soulmate she thinks I am entitled to write, and says that I shall do so although she (Mr. Padgett's wife) intended to write you (Mr. Padgett) a long letter tonight.

But she loves me and thinks a great deal of the Doctor and says that a few words from me may make us both happy. So I know that you will be glad to have me write.

Well, I know if he heard what I have just written, the thing that he would say is—that the first thing I am going to tell him is—how much I love him, but I am not, for I know now that I don't have to tell him as I am so entwined in his heart that he knows it without my telling him, but I somehow must whisper that I do love him. Ain't I a weak little girl? If he should say so I would feel real hurt.

Well, I am with him so often that I know he realized the fact and can tell when I tickle his ear that I am with him, and I am.

But I have something else to tell him which I know will please him very much, and that is that I am progressing so very rapidly that I am in a higher sphere and hope to work with Helen, and she tells me that I will, as I am so filled with the Father's Love, that it has made me so bright and glorious that my home will be where she is.

I cannot tell him how happy I am, and how much more love I have in my soul, and how much more love I have for him. This heaven is wonderfully beautiful and glorious, and my home is beyond all description. I wish I could describe it to him, for then he might get some faint idea of what is in store for him in the future when we shall become one in our purified love.

Oh, how thankful I am to the Father that he is on the way and that the love is in his soul, and more is waiting to enter.

He knows the way and at the most it cannot be very long after he comes over until we will be together.

Heaven is more than he or any mortal can conceive of, and even if he were without a soulmate he would be happy beyond all concept, but when he has his soulmate with him as he will have, then the happiness that will come to him will be more than any but a celestial can endure.

I am so happy that I can tell him this, and I know that he will be happy in my happiness. He must try to think of me as I now am, and if I can I will come to him in vision, so that he may get some idea of what I am.

I will not write more tonight, and in closing will say that I thank you with my sister's love to you and my soulmate love to him. I will say good night.

Your sister in Christ,
Mary.

89

Tells of Leslie's friend Plummer's progress out of darkness

March 15th, 1917.

I am here, Leslie's father.

Well, what do you think of Plummer? He is just as he wrote you and we are somewhat surprised at his progress. He is a very enthusiastic spirit, and knows that he has found the way, he never ceases praying except when he is at work, even then he prays. I have been much interested in him, as you may suppose because he came to me for help and instructions, and we naturally have an interest in those that we are called upon to help, and especially is this true when we are successful in our efforts. But while he has progressed into the light and is rid of much of his sufferings, yet he is not in that condition that will enable him to tell the spirits with whom he is working of the great power of the Love to change the dark evil soul into one of brightness and joy.

Yet he will soon be in that condition, for he is in earnest and such earnestness always brings the results longed for.

Well, I am glad to write to my son again, and while I know it is not necessary in order to have him know that I am with him, yet the writing is evidence that appeals to his senses and gives a satisfaction that the mere thoughts of my presence may not do.

I am very happy, more so than I can tell him and I want him to be happy also, which he can do, for this Love is open to him just as it is to the spirits, and the longings of his soul are heard and will be responded to, just as the longings of the souls of us spirits are responded to.

I will come soon, if agreeable and you are in proper condition, and write him a message that may show him what knowledge I have of spiritual truths of our spirit world. His mother and sisters are here and send their love to him. This is the common expression among mortals to make known the flowing of love from one to another, but does not express all that I mean, for our love does not have to be sent to him as it is with and around him whenever we are present with him, which is very often. We, of course, have our work to do, but the work does not take up all of our time, and a part of it is with him, as we have told him.

I will not write more now and will only further say that he is growing in his possession of this Love, and must continue his prayers to the Father, and let nothing interfere with such prayers, for they are the only way to the Father's soul and His Love.

So trusting that you will not doubt what I have said or that the spirits of the Celestial Spheres come to him with the influence of their love and their efforts to help him and make him at-one with them in their aspirations.

I will say good night.

William Stone.

Wants her soulmate, Leslie, to know that she is progressing and is now beyond the Third Celestial Sphere

I am here, Mary Kennedy.

Well, I thought that you would not write more and I tried to make you hear me, and I am glad that you did, for it would not have been just to me to stop and then prevent me from saying a word, for I know I am at least of as much importance to Leslie as the others who have written.

I will not write much, but even a little helps me, for I am here with all my love for him, and I just must tell him. Helen says that I must not forget to tell him that I love him, and then surprise him, for it will be a very new thing to him. Now isn't she mean to make fun of me in this way, but I don't care, as I have the opportunity, and I know he will not consider it very old, for he loves me and love never becomes old.

I am very happy and am so anxious to tell him that I am progressing. I am beyond the Third Sphere of the Celestial Kingdom, and oh! the great glory of it all; never did I conceive of such wonders and beauty, and when I come to the earth plane I want to bring my glory and beauty with me, and wish that my soulmate could see it, but he cannot, and I can't describe to him, for it is beyond all conception and description. But I must prove to him that I love him, for I am willing to leave all that beauty and grandeur for a time and come into this earth plane just because I love him so much. Someday he will realize what this all means, and then he will say to himself: "How that little soulmate must have loved me."

Well, I will not write more; with my kind regards to you, and my love to him, I will say, good night.

Mary Kennedy.

Tells her son Leslie that his soul is becoming filled with more Love of the Father

November 2nd, 1916.

I am here, mother.

Let me write just a line. I am the mother of the boy who is sitting before you, and I want to tell him I am so very happy because I see that his condition of soul is so much improved with the possession of the Love. He may not realize the difference in his condition now and that of a few months ago, and may believe that when he has the feelings of exaltation, which he has at times, that they all arise from the same condition of his soul, but I who can see just what his condition is, want to tell him that this is not just correct, for his soul now is filled with more of the Love than it has ever been. He is developing day by day, and sometime before long he must not be surprised if there comes to him an experience that will show him just what his great work in furthering the desires of the Master, and the other spirits who are working in the great cause, will be.

When that experience comes he will be greatly surprised and will possibly doubt, but he must remember what I am now saying to him, and believe that he is only receiving the realization of the promises that have been made to him, and that they are not more to be wondered at than were some of the powers and gifts bestowed upon the Apostles when they lived on earth and were the followers of the Master. His work is just as important as was theirs, though he does not realize the importance of it at this time. But he will when the time comes and then, oh! my boy! how you will be blest, not so much on your own account, but because the power that you will have to do good to others, and demonstrate the truth of all the wonderful truths that have come through the messages.

I write this tonight because I desire to encourage him in his search for the Love and for the truth, and he must believe that he is not living merely to do the work of the ordinary mortal, but to do the work that has been given him by the Master and the other Celestial angels.

His work is his only, and he forms a part of those who will do a work that will revolutionize the thoughts and lives of the whole world. I am so happy in this knowledge, and he must believe what I say, and appreciate the responsibility that has been placed upon him, for he has been selected to do the work and no other can do it for him.

Tell my son that I am truly his mother who thus writes, and what I say, I know to be true, and if that were not true I would not tell him. Pray more to the Father and let his faith increase and he will find that every aspiration will become a thing of reality, and his soul perceptions will become to him as real as the perceptions of his mind in his earthly affairs. I will not write more now, and in closing will say that I love him, and the Master loves him, and the Father loves him with the Great Love that floods the whole universe. Good night and God bless you both.

His mother in Christ,
Mrs. Priscilla Stone.

Agrees to what his mother has said about Leslie's progress in his soul development

November 2nd, 1916.

I am here, Mary.

Well, if his mother is permitted to write, I think that I should have the opportunity to say a few words. I heard what his mother wrote and know that it is true, for I am with him enough to see that he has made great progress in his soul development, and that the love is increasing and is filling his soul just as she says, the leaven filled the batch of dough.

Well, you see I can say something serious, even when I write to him, and why should I not where he is concerned, for he is more important to me than any other mortal is, and I have a greater love for him than has any other spirit. He knows this, but I like to tell him, and if I felt like a little pleasantry, I would say that I wish to tell him, so he may not forget.

I am with him so much, that if he could know how much, he might get a little tired of my presence, but of course this is not true, and I would not thank anyone else to say so. Well, Helen says that you must not write more now, as your condition is not such as to be further drawn upon. So with my love to him and regards to you, I will say good night.

His own true,

Mary Kennedy.

Says that Leslie is the other part of her, and will surely unite with her when he comes to the spirit world

I am here, Mary Kennedy.

Well, I thought that you would not stop writing without giving me the opportunity to say one word to my dear soulmate, as it has been a long time since I wrote to him, notwithstanding he has been aware of my presence and love all the time that he was absent from the city.

Well, as I say, I was with him and had a most happy time, for I had many of his thoughts of love, and he, I know, felt my response, but I missed being in the company of you and all the bright spirits who congregate with us, and especially of my dear Helen, whom I love so much and who loves me.

I cannot tell him tonight how much I love, for language is not capable of expressing my love and I do not feel like writing of anything else.

I am so much closer to him than ever before, as he may realize when I tell him that his soul is developing, and he is coming nearer to me in rapport and in a realization that I am his real loving Mary. The happiness of my house here is growing all the time, and one of the thoughts that enters into my joy is that this happiness will be his, for the more I progress the easier it will be for him to attain to my degree of happiness.

He may not know, but it is a fact that as he is the other part of me, and will surely unite with me when he comes to the spirit world, the greater I progress in Love the more certain and easy will it be for him to progress and be with me. Of course, his progress will depend upon the development of his own soul, but when he has a love such as mine to beckon him to rise and be with his soulmate, his only aim will be to make the progress that will bring him to my home; and besides I will be with him and hand in hand we will mount upward, for he will find that the love of a little soulmate will mean to him more than he can conceive of.

We are all so happy here, and we are so anxiously waiting for the time to come when you and he will be with us, and yet we know that you must live to do your work, but the certainty that when you shall have accomplished this you will come to us, makes us happy and patient. We can be with you, and just as real is your presence to us as if you were in the spirit, but you cannot see us or realize our presence so satisfactorily, yet, you do feel at times that we are with you. But while you are mortals we cannot feel your arms around us and your kisses on our cheeks, and neither can you feel our embraces, for we do actually embrace and kiss you. So you see there is some difference between yourselves as mortals and what you will be as spirits. Oh dear! how our love makes us wish for what we should not wish, but in this particular you see we have still something of the mortal in us.

Well, I will not write more, but will express my thankfulness in being able to write once more to my dear one.

So tell him that I will go with him to his home tonight and watch over him until he gets to sleep and will lay my head upon his arms, and whisper to him my feelings of love, even though he may not hear me, but I will be there, and he will surely feel my presence.

Good night and may the Father bless him.

His own true,

Mary Kennedy.

Dr. Stone receives instruction from Jesus of the Bible to accept help from anyone that is willing to give it, even though they do not have the Divine Love

November 15th, 1954.[32]

I am here, Jesus.

Yes, I am here again to write you tonight on a subject which has been of concern to the Doctor and which I shall try to explain.

He is concerned with several of his friends and associates who

---

[32] Based on the date, it is highly likely that this message was received by Dr. Samuels and it is not therefore one of James Padgett's. (G.J.C.)

may be of interest in helping the furthering of the work to bring the messages to the attention of all mankind. The first thing that I should like to say is that men can be used even if they do not have the Divine Love in their souls, as may be the case with those whom the Doctor has in mind. But if they have the will to work for the truths of the messages because they recognize the truths, then the Divine Love can come later as a result of the intellectual part of their natures having its effect upon the soul condition, which is at all possible.

And furthermore, I should like to state that this was the condition of many of my disciples when we journeyed through Palestine together. For, many of them, while they recognized intellectually the excellence of my teachings, yet did not obtain much of the Divine Love in their hearts until after my death, at Pentecost and the showering of the Divine Love upon them in abundance at that time; and furthermore, many of them did not understand that I was the Messiah in the purely spiritual sense, but they were active revolutionaries in the material sense and became associated with me because they saw in me a revolutionary as well. And so they banded together with me in that, to them, the national and the religious were intermingled and integrated into a single line of thought and aspiration. I should also like to point out that they were all quite different in their individual personalities; nevertheless, despite all the perplexities and divergences of personality, thought and ambitions, I was able to weld them into a very capable group of men devoted to the cause of bringing the Kingdom to man's possession.

And let me state further that this was done through the efficacy of the Divine Love in their hearts which came later; in fact, after my death. Thus, I should like to point out to the Doctor that he can expect in the same way different types of human beings who may be attracted to our cause for very different reasons and without the Divine Love in their souls; and yet, if these men are willing they can be used for the Kingdom and they may eventually obtain the Love in abundance—in such abundance that it will affect their lives and make completely different men of them, as witness the case of Luke and Matthew and Peter and many others. And so I like to suggest that those persons interested in the messages who recognize the truth of the Divine Love, if only intellectually, be urged, if they are willing and if it is not an imposition upon their free wills, to use their talents and spiritual gifts for the benefit of the Kingdom, and to use them in the way that they may be best fitted to the cause of the Father's truths.

And if this can be in the writings of a book of commentaries on the messages or a reconstructed New Testament or through the translations of the messages into different languages, or in any other way, whether evangelical or administrative, then by all means their talents should be utilized for the Kingdom. And for that reason I have written tonight so that all individuals thus ready to partake in the great adventure of bringing the truths to mankind should be used for that purpose. And to accept all types of people, regardless of their conflicting views, and they can be molded by their interests to the point where they will obtain the Divine Love. And this is the important thing, whether it be simply the salvation of an individual soul, for this is important in itself, or whether the individual will help the Kingdom through working for it.I think that I have said enough for tonight, so good night and may the Heavenly Father shower you with His Love and Blessings; and I will sign myself your elder brother and Master in the Celestial Heavens, which is waiting for you if you persist to the end.

Jesus of the Bible.

Progresses to the First Celestial Sphere and gives a description of her new home

October 8th, 1915.

I am here, Mary.

Well Doctor, I am here, as you may be surprised to know, if you had forgotten my last secret, but I don't believe that you have. I want to say that I am in a happier condition than I have ever been yet, for I am now in the Celestial Sphere where I know that happiness is so much greater than it has ever been. So you must believe me when I tell you that my love is so very much more abundant, and that you are dearer to me than ever before. So try to realize what I mean, and imagine that you are with me, even for a little while, and then you will be happier too. I have said what I wanted to say and must stop.

A few days later when the opportunity presented itself, Mary Kennedy wrote as follows:

I am the spirit of a woman who once lived on earth in the far away land across the ocean, and was known to my people as a little English girl of not much importance in the world, but now I am of great importance to a human who loves to have me with him; and I merely write this to let him know that he is not always in condition to sense when I am really with him, for I heard him say that I was not with him all the evening, and heard all that he said, and enjoyed hearing him talk, but until just now did not mention my name; and if that were the only sign that I have to know that he is thinking of me, I would suppose that he had forgotten me, but thanks to my powers to read his mind, that calling my name is not necessary.

What do you think of that for a sentence?

It is only representative of my love, for just as that sentence is long drawn out, so is my love. But I must not tell him or he may become alarmed at what awaits him when he comes over. Well, I have introduced myself, and now I want to tell him how happy I am and describe briefly my home. My house is a beautiful one of which you might call alabaster, and in it I have many rooms suited to my various moods and conditions; all beautiful and full of the most perfect harmony, and everything to make me happy and contented.

My music room is filled with many instruments of various kinds on which I can perform and bring forth the most beautiful harmonies; and I can sing too, and when he comes over I am going to surprise him by playing and singing some of the songs he so much enjoys at the Colburns. I will prove to him that I was with him many times while he was a mortal and could not see and feel my presence.

I have a library but not many of the spiritual books which he has read or heard of, for they do not contain anything that is helpful or beneficial to spirits who live in the soul spheres, because very few of them contain anything which shows or teaches the development of the soul or the grandeur of the Father's Divine Love.

I have the most beautiful vines and roses all over the porches of my home. And in all the rooms are flowers and plants of the most exquisite colors and delicious perfumes. And the pictures on my walls are such as he has never seen on earth; the subjects portrayed are not of scenes that lend to make inharmony or strife or mortal passions appear, but all teach by their realism the truths of love and happiness.

I do not have any beds to lie on, for as you know we never sleep, but we do have couches which I sometimes lie on to rest when I have become a little tired from work, and strange to say, I sometimes dream of him, as you mortals say. I have no kitchen, for we cook nothing, but my dining room is fitted up in a style that would make your mouth water, as it is filled with pictures of fruit and nuts and flowers, and other things, to suggest good eating. We eat and enjoy our eating as do you mortals, but our food is nuts and fruits, and our drink is pure water, with all the life-giving qualities that spirits need.

The lawns around my home are very beautiful in the freshness and greenness; and the trees are grand old oaks, as you say, that cast their shade over the greensward, and over the many little nooks that abound in our gardens. And then the flowers are so abundant and so variegated in color, and delve in perfume. I have also a beautiful little lake of water in which are boats that carry one without the physical exertion that you have to exercise on earth.

All is more beautiful than I can give you the faintest idea of, and there is only one thing wanting in all this beauty and happiness, and that is that man sitting opposite you; but I would not care to have him bring that mortal body, though he is a pretty good-looking boy as mortals go. But I can see beyond the mortal body, and I know that his soul is much more beautiful than his physical appearance, and yet I am afraid that his soul is not yet in that condition of development that would enable him to come to me just now. But he is developing, and before he comes over, I feel that he will be in condition that will bring him closer to me and closer, so that the distance between us will not be so great.

If he will only try for this development as I am trying to help him develop, he will come very close to me when he comes over, and then he will have such Love all around him that he will not find it difficult to progress to where his other half is, as Luke said.

And speaking of this message of Luke, I want to say that I have my individualized form and a perfect one, so Helen says, and I know that I shall never lose it to enter into some other mortal. Why the very thought of such a thing makes me wonder what all this great Love of the Father was given to me for, if I am to be deprived of it and again become a mere mortal with all the passions and appetites of a mortal.

No. I have no fear of that, and he need not either think that when he once comes to his soulmate he will ever be separated again, and go back to that dark and gloomy earth to live.

Well, I have written a long letter and must stop.

So give him my love and tell him that I am with him more than he realizes, and will continue, to do until he comes over. And thanking you for your kindness in permitting me to write so long, I will say good night, and subscribe myself your friend and his ever true and loving, Mary.

On February 19th another short message from Mary Kennedy was received on her spiritual progress which is as follows.

I am progressing again and this time to the Third Celestial Kingdom and of the great glory of it all, never did I conceive of such wonders and beauty; and when I come to the earth plane I want to bring my glory and beauty with me and wish that my soulmate could see it, but he cannot, and I can't describe it to him for it is beyond all conception and description. But I must prove to him that I love him for I am willing to leave all that beauty and grandeur for a time and come into these earth planes just because I love him so much. Someday he will realize what this all means and then he will say to himself, How that little soulmate must have loved me.

Well, I will not write more, will close with my kindest regards to you, and my soulmate love to Leslie.

I thank you so much for giving me this opportunity to write as I have.

Your sister in Christ, Mary.[33]

Says that no matter how many wives Leslie may have had, none of them can be his soulmates, only little me

January 12th, 1918.

I am here, Mary.

Well, I must say a word because I have the opportunity and am just now like the old lady who never missed a wedding when she had the slightest chance of being present. I come with love, and while I know my sweetheart appreciates gratitude, yet, I know also that love is a greater thing to him, and especially soulmate love, which in all the heavens and earth, I am the only one that can have it for him. Isn't this a glorious thing? No matter how many wives he may have, none of them can be his soulmate, and no matter how many beautiful and attractive spirits he may meet when he comes over, none of them can become his soulmate, only little me, and when he thinks, he will realize that we are eternally united for better or for worse, but there will be no worse.

Well you see I am full of love tonight and can't help writing about it, and I know that you will not think I cannot write of anything else, for I have written of other things, but I must confess that I would rather write of love, except when I can tell him of the Greater Love, and thereby help him towards the acquirement of that Love.

I heard him speak of his brother, and I am glad that I can tell him that he is now not in the darkness that was his a short time ago. And how could he remain in the condition very long when it is realized what a mother that brother has in the spirit world, and with the love she gives to him, as she visits him and tries to show him the way to light and truth. She will have to come herself and write of her experience in inducing that son to believe in and trust her, and follow her advice, and she says she will do so, sometime.

I am very happy and find that this love of which his father speaks is growing in my soul all the time, and with its increase my soulmate love is growing also.

I will not write more now, as there are others who desire to write, and Helen says that I had better let the Doctor imagine what the rest of my love may mean, for possibly his imagination can cause him to enjoy the love more than if I attempt to tell him of it. So with my love, I will say good night. And God bless him with a Love that has no ending,

---

[33] It is impossible to ascertain precisely what dates these messages were received on, because the Daily Diary only refers to these messages as "Message to Dr Stone." There is also no reference to any message on February 19th. (G.J.C.)

and is never absent from him when he longs for it. Good night,
Mary.

Is progressing all the time (now a Celestial Spirit where only Divine Love exists, and spirits cease to have brothers, mothers or relations, only one great brotherhood, whose nearness and unity depend upon the amount of Divine Love.)

May 1st, 1918.

I am here, Mary Kennedy.

I will write a few lines if you will consent, and I know you will, for Helen says that you receive so many letters of love and encouragement from her, that you are wholly sympathetic whenever other soulmates desire to write to their other halves on earth, and especially when I come to write to mine, and Helen knows and never tells me an untruth except when she is trying to plague or tease me.

Well, I am very glad that I can write once more to Leslie, for it has been a long time, as it seems to me, since I wrote him, and I believe that he thinks so, too. I know that he is interested in me all the time, for the reason that I know he loves me, and where loves enter there can be no want of interest, and so it must be.

I am very happy and am progressing all the time in my soul qualities, and in my position in the soul spheres where only the Divine Love exists, except the other love which belongs only to soulmates. Since I have become an inhabitant of the Celestial Spheres and realized what an absorbing thing the Divine Love is, I wonder that I can have so much of this soulmate love as I do, when I realize the fact, and know, that no other love exists in our spheres except the Divine Love and our soulmate love.

No love of mother or father, or any other love that belonged to the relationship of the human life has any place in our existence or happiness, for spirits cease to have brothers and mothers and other relations, but all are as one great brotherhood, whose nearness and unity depends upon the amount of the Divine Love that enters into the souls of the respective spirits, and in this, the Divine Love is different from our soulmate love in that the former is of one nature and substance, though possessed by spirits in different degrees, and is of the same quality and may be possessed by the souls of spirits alike, while the latter belongs only to the two soulmates, and no other spirit can enter into or possess any portion of that love which belongs to the two soulmates alone.

I often think of this fact, and how good is the Father in giving us this great Love which we partake of in common with all other spirits, yet, let us have this soulmate love all to ourselves. This may at first seem to partake of the element of selfishness, but it is not, because, while one of the two souls can and does have it, yet, no other soul is thereby deprived of any love that would make them unhappy or that would afford them any greater happiness. It is not selfishness but merely the possession of that which in itself makes the love of the two individual.

Now, from what I have said you must not infer that when we become inhabitants of the Celestial Spheres all the loves that were ours when on earth by reason of our human relationship are not with us, for it would not be true to make such an inference. The explanation is that the objects and the place of existence of the objects of our loves, determines whether we continue to have this love of the human relationship. If our parents or brothers or sisters, or others having a relationship whom we loved when on earth, continue to live in the flesh, or even in the lower spheres of the spirit world, then our earth love, as I may call it, remains with us, and our dear ones are just as much, or to a greater degree loved than when we were on earth or in the lower spheres; and out of that love grows our desire to help and influence for good our relatives.

But when these relatives become with us inhabitants of the Celestial Spheres, where the Divine Love is the great love belonging to us all, then, the love that is possessed by reason of being relatives one to another, leaves us and has no influence. As long as you remain mortals we love you as parents or children or other relatives, but when you come with us to the Celestial Heavens there remains no reason why such love should continue, for this Divine Love is sufficient for all and supersedes these other loves.

Well, I love my Leslie, and I will love him for and through all eternity because I know that he will come to me in my home and be united, his soul to mine. I am with him a great deal and my love for him never dies down or ceases to exercise its influence upon his soul, and never will so long as we remain separated, which will not continue very long, as we who are in eternity view it. I have written too long already and must stop. But I want to tell him that he has his angels around and with him very much, and he is never left alone. When he prays, as I know he does, we are all with him praying to the Father for a greater inflowing of His Love into my dear one's soul.

Oh, how I wish that I could tell him of the extent of my love and what it means to him, and how much I want all the love that he can give me. He must think of me and keep up his courage and faith in the truths that have come to him, for he will never be disappointed in that faith or in the expectations that come from it. Good night, my dear one.

Your own loving,

Mary.

Says what a great privilege it is that only Mr. Padgett, Leslie and Mr. Morgan at the time can make known the Truth of the Father

I am here, Mary Kennedy.

Let me say just a word before you leave. I know that it is an imposition, but you are so good that I feel that you will not be imposed on if I say a few words to Leslie. It does me so much good that I can tell you when I have the opportunity of writing.

Well, I see that he is very happy tonight and in a good spiritual condition, and filled with love for me as well as the Love for the Father and it makes me so happy. I should like to write him a long letter tonight and tell him of some things other than my love, but I will wait until I see that you have the leisure to receive my message.

Well, we are all here, and many others, and enjoyed the messages that you read and also your conversation; and not the least interested is Plummer,[34] who says he is happy and moving along all the time and wants to write another letter to his brother, for he will not have the opportunity to write many more before his brother comes to the

---

[34] Nathan Plummer, referred to by Mary in this message, had been helped by my father after he had written for help, by James E. Padgett causing him to meet my father in the spirit world, who told Nathan Plummer he must pray to the Heavenly Father to fill his soul with His Divine Love. After a while he did obtain the Divine Love in his soul and has now progressed to the Divine Heavens.

Nathan Plummer's brother, William Plummer, wrote in this message to his brother and was anxious to get him to read the messages that I had for his brother to read, who was at that time on earth. William Plummer was an old man and passed into the spirit world soon after he read the message I gave him on the way to the obtaining the Divine Love. The reason I wrote about William Plummer is that after making his acquaintance I was introduced by him to Mr. Arthur Colburn, who introduced me to James E. Padgett. It was this close association with Mr. Padgett that enabled me to have a knowledge of the messages he was receiving, and resulted in my learning the great truths that were the teachings of Jesus when on earth nearly two thousand years ago; and after his early followers died the leaders and hierarchy of the churches never had a true conception of the New Birth that Jesus told Nicodemus: "Except a man be born again he cannot enter the Kingdom of God." (John Chap. 3, Verse 3 in the New Testament)

It was the realization of this great and important truth of the New Birth that Jesus proclaimed on earth. I was overwhelmed with this vital truth; I found I did not have to seek further, and I know now by personal experience that I have found the greatest blessing that comes to all who seek by earnest prayer for the greatest gift of all gifts; and the great joy and peace that comes into the soul by the earnest longings of the soul that is filled with such real longings for the Divine Love to enter the soul, to enable you to become possessor and owner of it; and eternal progress as this love increases in the soul, nearer and nearer to the Fountainhead of the Father, even after you have entered the Celestial Heavens with the consciousness that this Divine Love is immortal and all who obtain it also become immortal. (Dr. L. R. Stone)

spirit world.

I know that you and Leslie are interested in making known the truths whenever the privilege arises and the work is one that only such a few can do. Just think, only you and Leslie and Morgan know and can disclose the truths in the messages. Have you ever thought how rich you are and that your richness is such that no man can take it from you. Isn't it all so wonderful!

Only continue to believe in the reality of the messages and of the writers, and you will find that a faith will grow in your souls that will become more real than the shining of the sun at midday.

Well, I must stop, but tell him that I do love him so much and so want him to be happy. Good night, with all my love.

Mary Kennedy.

Says that she has progressed to the Celestial Sphere where there are no numbers and is among spirits who fairly shine with the Great Love of The Father

December 18th, 1917.

I am here, Mary Kennedy.

Well, I see that you would rather hear from me than from the last spirit, although you are interested in showing the way to spirits who know not the way to salvation and the wonders of the New Birth. Yet, I believe that I am somewhat nearer to you and that you would rather have a few lines from me.

Well, I am very happy because of the opportunity of writing once more to my soulmate and telling him that I am his own loving Mary, and am always anxious to tell him.

I know that he will be pleased to know that I have progressed since he last heard from me; for I am now in the Celestial planes that have no number, and among spirits who fairly shine with the Great Love of the Father, and are happy beyond all conception, not only of mortals, but of spirits who have never reached the plane in which I now am. I wish that I could explain to Leslie what my present condition and surroundings are, so that he might form some idea of what the happiness of his soulmate is, but I cannot, and will not try. But this I can tell him, that my new position and happiness do not keep me away from him, for the increased love of the Divine that enters my soul, there also enters in a greater love for him, and a greater longing to be with him; and as he cannot come to me, I can come to him, and in coming bring my happiness with me in all its fullness.

He will understand, that while I fully realize that the higher I progress the greater the distance between us, yet he will also understand that I must seek to progress with all the strivings of my soul. And he must not think this progress will keep me apart for a longer time than if I should remain stationary and wait for him. It will merely seem so, for when he comes to the spirit world and learns just what my position means, he will want the more to be with me, and will strive the harder to reach my home, so that his strivings and longings to see my home will be such that what is lost in distance will be made up to him in time; and besides, I will be so much more enabled to help him, for the greater the love the more rapid the progress, and when he sees the great love that I shall have and feel its influence, he will the more easily appreciate the possibilities of his own progress.

Yes, I am surprisingly happy, and only wait his coming to make complete the soulmate love, but of course I do not long for his coming in a way that might bring him to me sooner than it is intended that he shall come. He has a work to do and he must know it, and that is his sacrifice, as he will understand after he comes over, but it is a glorious sacrifice, for from it will flow that which will enable him to make the more rapid progress after his work shall be done.

I will not write more now. I know that he would be glad to know of my progress, and so I took the opportunity to tell him, and am so happy that I can do so. I wonder if he ever thinks what a difference there would be in his own soul if during all the years prior to his coming over, we should have to remain silent, and he never knew of what love is waiting for him, and what a soulmate is trying to do for him. How blessed we both are that we can exchange our thoughts of love, and know that sometime in the near future there will be a glorious and happy meeting of two souls that are really one.

Well, I will not take more of your time. So with my greater love to him, I will say good night.

Mary.

Says that the soulmate love is only surpassed by the Divine Love of the Father

I am here, Mary Kennedy.

I know you would rather hear from me than from spirits such as have just written you, and I am selfish enough to say that I would rather write than see them write.

Well, I am so happy that I can hardly express myself and when I tell that good-looking man, I should say boy, that it is hardly due to the love that I know that he has for me, I am telling a truth. For now since I have fallen in love with him, I never seem to be satisfied unless I can in some way make him know that I am present, and I like this way better than any other, for by it I can tell him of my love as well as tell him and know that I am present.

The thing that gives me most happiness is getting more and more of the love in his soul and consequently he is coming in closer rapport with me and nearer to the completed one which we are and ever will be. The soulmate love is, as you have been told, a wonderful love and is only surpassed by the Divine Love of the Father, yet it is not entirely independent of this greater Love, for when the latter is in the soul in greater and greater quantities, this soul will love and become more real and binding in its operations. I suppose that he may get tired of my telling him so often of my love for him, and if he wants to get tired he had better do so when on earth, for after he comes over here he will not get tired of the love, but if the tired feeling comes to him it will be the result of his striving for more and more of this Love and that is one of the things that makes happiness so great here.

I see I must not write longer, and I thank you that I could write as I have.

Helen says that I may come soon and write him a long letter and in it will show him that I can write of something beside this soulmate love, for I intend to tell him some truths of our home and spirit life and I know that will be of interest to him.

So with my love to him and my sister love to you, I will say,
Good night,
Mary Kennedy.

Writes that the soulmate love increases as the Divine Love increases

I am here, your friend and sweetheart of the Doctor.

Well, Helen said that my opportunity is here and that I had better take advantage of it and you may be sure that I did not hesitate.

I am so glad that I can express my feelings, although I know it is not necessary in order for the Doctor to understand, but yet it is a great consolation to be able to tell him in words what he already knows. I am still progressing and have more Love of the Father than I ever had, and consequently more love for him, for this soulmate love seems to increase as the Divine Love increases. I have been with him a good deal trying to help and sustain him and I know that he has been conscious of my presence, not only because I give him the signal but because he actually feels the presence of my love, and if he knew how I try to make him feel my presence of my love, he would know that only the Great Love that I have for him can make the feelings that he realizes at times.

The spirits who are so much interested in him enjoy hearing him talk of this Great Love that has come to him and of the certainty that he has felt its presence and when he thus talks he would possibly be a little surprised if he could know of the effect that it sometimes has on his hearers. They may appear to be indifferent to the truth or may apparently not understand what he endeavors to tell them, yet some of these truths have a lodgment in the memory of the people; and then come times when they think of what they heard, and in thinking words of what he explained to them, can be the real truth. Good is being done and he must not cease in doing the work, for while it reaches a comparatively few yet the saving of one soul in its importance is beyond all comprehension that you mortals may have.

Well, I have not yet told him how much I love him and I will not try, for I cannot find words to express my feelings; but when I tell him that I love him more than any being in all God's universe, he may have a slight comprehension of what I mean. This love is of such an intensity that to express it in words only chills its meaning and leaves more unsaid than when it is attempted to be conveyed.

I will try very soon to take his soul with me and have him enjoy the bliss of our wonderful land of love and beauty and of his own true soulmate; and he will, I hope, be able to recollect the happiness, if he cannot recall the scenes and the appearance of his Mary, but anyway he will be able to do both, for I believe that sometime the experience will come to him in his memory that he will be able to recall them with a very satisfactory degree of clearness.

I will not write more now.

So with my love for him and regards to you, I will say good night.

His own,

Mary.

Refers to a message written by John the Apostle

February 6th, 1917.

Let me say that you think more about your coffee[35] than you do about hearing from us, and we are not at all flattered.

(Mr. Padgett then said he meant after the message.)

Well, pardon me, for that places a new meaning to your remarks, but of course I am only joking, for I know you would rather hear from us than drink your coffee or eat your pie, for we go with you at times to the lunchroom and see you and the Doctor eat, and try to make ourselves believe that we are eating with you.

Well, you wonder who this is, and if I were not writing I would pull that dear boy's ear so that he would be able to tell you who is here. I thought that I would write a few words tonight, as Helen says that for

---

[35] Mr. Padgett suggested to Dr. Stone that they go out and get a cup of coffee. (J.P.G.)

peace's sake I will have to do so, and I have been very anxious to write, and since John wrote[36] you as he did, I am more anxious than ever, for his assurances are so important that I feel that I must tell Leslie that it was actually John who wrote, and that what he wrote had accompanying it the authority of a spirit almost Divine—yes, really Divine for he is of the Divine Angels of the highest spheres. I am so much interested that Leslie shall believe this message of John that I think that even my corroboration may help him to believe. And I must further tell him that I have heard the Master say that he, Leslie, has been selected for this work, and that power and other gifts will be his that will enable him to do the work; and what a wonderful thing it all is.

I intended to write him something of a love letter tonight for the occasion, but the thing that John has written is of so much more importance that I will postpone my expressions of love and with all my soul try to cause him to believe, and never doubt, the decree that has been spoken; and my soulmate is the selection of the great Master, and I am so happy, and I thank God that such a thing has come to pass.

I am his true Mary—his eternal soulmate—and know that when he comes to me, the results of his work will make him one of the shining ones, not because only of the good that he has done to others, but because in doing this work then will come into his own soul so much of the Divine Love that he will be enabled to come into the Higher Spheres, and the sooner be at-one with his Mary.

I love him with all my heart and soul, and am waiting patiently for the time to come when the great consummation of our love will make us one in truth.

I must not write more. So good night,
Your sister and his own true,
Mary.

Says that we spirit soulmates do not make other engagements when we can be with our soulmates on earth

I am here, Mary Kennedy.

Yes, there is, and he dare not go until I can write him a few lines. He does not appreciate the opportunity for me to write, and if he thought more of me he would try every way to hear from me. But he is a good boy and loves me, I know, and I love him.

Well, dear, I am happy and progressing all the time and getting nearer to the fountainhead of the Father's Love and into the association and lives of spirits who are wonderful in their glory and love.

---

[36] The message from John is probably the one that is published in this Volume IV and can be found on page 215. (G.J.C.)

But as I progress he must not think that I am taken away from him for that is not the fact, as I am with him just as much as before and bring to him more love than ever. When I leave my home in the high spheres I do not have to leave my happiness behind because the condition of my soul determines my happiness, and as that develops the greater my happiness and the more my love to him increases.

I do come to him and want sometime soon to come and tell him what my home is like and all the beautiful and magnificent surroundings that I have, and the glory of the love atmosphere that surrounds my home. And also of the many wonderful spirits who are my companions and what we do to make our intercourse joyous and happy.

I will come soon and I know you will let me write, and I will promise not to consume too much time.

Well, I shouldn't think it necessary to ask that question. Listen to me a minute and know that we spirit soulmates don't make other engagements when we can be with our soulmates on earth, unless our work demands our presence elsewhere. Yes, I was with you and heard what you said and was so glad to hear you, and the people who heard you were much interested and some of them feel the benefit of the knowledge of the truths which come to them; and the audience on our side was much larger than the ones that you could see and was more interested in what you said, for among them were many who had never heard the truths that you declared, and as they were looking and seeking for something that might help them out of their darkness, they were highly interested and left you with many thoughts that they had never heard before.

Whenever you have the opportunity to make known the truths to mortals, do not forget your unseen hearers, and the fact that to them what you say is most vital and important, for they, unlike your mortal listeners, have no material things or desires to distract them from those truths that may possibly be the means of rescuing them from the condition of darkness and suffering.

Well, I must not write more now, and will close with my love and the prayer that God will bless you both.

His own true soulmate, Mary.

Says that the visit that Leslie made into the spirit world was one of the happiest nights of her life

I am here, Mary Kennedy.

Let me write for I know that my communication will be more interesting than the others you have received tonight, just as love to the lover is more interesting than war to the peaceful man.

Well, I am the loved of the lover and I will tell him I am so happy that I can write to him tonight. I am progressing in my soul development and am happy beyond expression; and the more of this Great Love that I receive the more my love for him increases, as I have told him before.

I should like to tell him of the time when he last came with me to the spirit world, but it is too late now, and Helen says that you are too exhausted to receive my message at this time, so I will have to wait, but I will say that it was one of the happiest nights of my life and I hope that before long I will have the experience again, and that he will have some faint remembrance of the joy that he will experience.

I am with him often, as he knows, and enter into his spiritual exaltation that comes to him sometimes, and also I pray with him every night and try to mingle my love with the other Love that comes to him.

I know that sometimes he may get a little tired of hearing me tell of my love, but if he only knew what it means to me and that there is nothing in all the universe that brings such happiness except the Love of the Father, he would not tire of hearing me say how much I love him or how dear he is to me.

Many spirits are here tonight who are interested in him, and especially his mother, who seems to never be weary of attending him in his moments of meditation and when he may seem a little despondent throwing around him her love and efforts to help him. We are all so much interested in his soul development and in the good work that he is doing to both mortals and spirits, for he must know that when he talks to mortals of these truths of the Father that have come to him, there are many spirits present who derive much benefit from what he says; and I have a kind of pride which is not unnatural that my soulmate has been given to him the power to do such work and that there are so many grateful souls in this spirit world who are feeling the effect of the good that he does them.

But he knows all this, and yet I felt that I must tell him also for he will realize that I am telling him only what is true and that my joy is what would only be his if he could see and understand the conditions that surround him.

I must come soon and write my letter. Helen says that she is waiting to write him also, and we will be so very glad when the opportunity comes that we can do so.

With all my love for him and regards to you, I will say good night. His soulmate.

Says that if she were a mortal she would rather possess the power to help spirits that needed help than the riches of the richest man in the world

I am here, Mary Kennedy.

I am so glad that you let this last spirit write, for he was unhappy and pitiable, and so much wanted relief that your guide could not refuse to let him write; and besides, Helen said he should write, and I just kissed her, for I wanted him to write also. It is such a grand thing: to have the power to help these spirits, and if I were a mortal I would rather possess that power than have the riches of the richest man in the world. The good done never ceases in its influence; it is like the pebble that is thrown in the pond, that starts the first little ripple which keeps expanding and increasing until the whole pond becomes ripples, for I must tell you that these dark spirits when they find the light, help others, and their influence is beyond estimation.

The dark spirits who have recently become rescued from their darkness seem to get in closer rapport with those left behind, and to have more influence in convincing them that there is a way in which they can find relief and happiness.

Well, you see I can be a little serious, even if my sweetheart is present, just wishing that he could hear from me, for that is what he has been wishing all evening, and if he says he has not, don't believe him, but pray for him, as he will need it if he tells such a fib as that.

Tell him that I am very happy and have listened with much interest and enjoyment to your conversation tonight, for I could not only hear the words spoken, but could see the workings of his soul and know that the Love was there doing its work of greatness. I am also progressing as I told you in my last letter, and if I could only tell you of my increased happiness I would do so, and I know that he would feel the benefit of its influence.

Tonight I would like to write a longer letter and tell him something that I so much desire to do, but it is not best for me to do so, as you are somewhat tired, as Helen says.

So I will stop, but he must know that I love him with all my heart and soul, and never cease trying to make him happy.

Oh, yes. I heard what you said about the great blessing of having the love of a soulmate who has the Divine Love in her soul, and I want to say that, while you have some idea of what it means, yet you cannot fully comprehend the great significance of the Love, and the great blessing that comes to you from having such Love. He has his soulmate and she loves him with all the power of that love, which as you say is next to the Divine Love.

So believe that I am your friend and his soulmate,
Mary.

110

Says that the same Love that has filled her soul and made her an Angel of Light is flowing into Leslie's soul

(Mr. Padgett asked Dr. Stone if he thought there were any spirits present just before Mary began to write.)

I am here, Mary Kennedy.

You are not serious when you ask such a question, or you have forgotten there is such a spirit in the spirit world as Mary Kennedy, who is the soulmate of a man who has the power to attract her presence wherever he may be.

Well, my friend, we have been listening tonight to your conversation, and reading of the messages, and have been much interested both in the messages and in the workings of your mind as the truths came to you, and they were wonderful truths that will do you much good if you will only meditate upon them.

I am very glad to be able to write once again to Leslie, and to let him know that his Mary is still loving him, and enjoying his association, for I am in that condition that the mere being with him gives me unbounded happiness, although I am not able to communicate that happiness to him except as our souls come in unison, which they often do. I am still progressing and trying to influence him with my love, and especially am I trying to impress upon his mind with a vividness, that I cannot explain, the spiritual truths that I know, and not only know but experience. I realize that he has a very great knowledge of some of these spiritual truths, but as they depend for a real and deep understanding on the soul condition, rather than that of the mind, I necessarily have a better and clearer perception of these truths than he possibly can, and for the only reason that my soul development is greater than his, and will be until he comes to me in the Celestial Heavens, as he will, and this thought makes me so very happy. He will not be disappointed, and I will not be disappointed, for the same Love that has filled my soul and made me an angel of light is flowing into his soul, and sometime will fill it so that he will become as pure and transfigured as I am now.

I should like to write him a long loving letter tonight, but Helen says: "it is too late and I must wait until another time."

So tell him that I will go home with him, and try to make him feel my presence, and the love for him that is now filling my soul.

I thank you and will say good night.

His only and forever soulmate,

Mary.[37]

---

[37] Mr. Padgett and I had been conversing about spiritual truths, and talking of Dr. Gordon's answers to questions, which had taken place at the Congregational Church that

Says that they are able to reach many spirits as a result of his talks that otherwise could not be reached

I am here, Mary Kennedy.

I heard the Doctor's question. I want to say he is doing a vast good through his talks, for it enables us to get in rapport with many spirits who otherwise we could not reach. He will find when he comes here that he will be thanked by many who have been the means of getting out of conditions of darkness and suffering.

So tell him to keep up the work and whenever he has the opportunity he must avail himself of it. You also are doing a great work among these spirits to enable the high spirits to get a rapport that they would not otherwise be able to attain.

So you both are doing a good work in helping the souls of the children of God and turn their souls to Him. I will not write more.

Mary.

Is happy to see the Love of the Father come into his soul

I am here, Leslie's Mother.

Let me say just one word. I so want to tell my son how happy I am tonight and how much I rejoice to know that this Love is growing with such rapidity in his soul. I wish that his soul could be laid open to him as it is to me, for then he would see how the leaven of the love has worked in the few short months since it first came into his soul and how it is filling all the crevices, as it were, and sin and error are disappearing. Oh, I am so thankful and grateful for the great gift that has come to him. But I am told that I must not write more, and must stop now. Tell him that his mother's love is all his and her happiness is beyond expression.

Thanking you I will say good night.

His mother,

Priscilla.

Says that what Helen wrote about soulmate love also applies to Leslie and her. That their soulmate love can never be taken from them

October 11th, 1917.

I am here, Mary Kennedy.

---

night. (While this may have not been the same occasion, they did attend such a meeting on April 1st, 1917. (G.J.C.)) And Mr. Padgett also had been reading aloud in his room the many messages he received from various spirits during the month of April, 1917. (Dr. L. R. Stone)

I wish to write a few lines as I am so anxious to once more come into conscious communion with my soulmate. I heard you read the letter from Helen in reference to your dream, and I want to tell my dear one that what she said as to the soulmate love between you and her applies equally to that love which is existing between Leslie and myself. I am so happy that he understands this, for such knowledge is one that must create a happiness on his part that so very few of the human race understand or have the privilege of enjoying.

Yes, our love is one that can never be taken from us, and in all the great eternity it can never change, except to increase in intensity and beauty. Oh, I am so happy when I think that I have a soulmate on earth who knows that he has a soulmate in the spirit world, and that he is trying to develop his soul so that when he comes to me our separation will not continue very long. I am praying all the time that the great love of the Father may fill his soul so that it may become more and more in unison with mine and he realize, even while he is on earth, that it is possible to approach closer and closer to my condition of development. When he believes this, as I know he does, he is not dreaming but believes an actual truth that nothing in all God's universe can change, and only he himself can postpone its fulfillment.

Isn't it all wonderful that our Father should have made such provisions for poor little insignificant mortals, when all around are the wonderful manifestations of His power and greatness! But while we are small and many, yet to the Father our happiness is the greatest care that there is in all His creation. The earth and the stars and suns may pass away and cease to exist, but that one little spark of soulmate love will never cease to exist, no not through all eternity; and we, who have this love, when joined in unity will live and know that as to it, the decree of the Father is that it shall never die, but in all the long ages grow brighter and deeper and more like the Love of the Father.

I am happier tonight than I can tell you of, and my love for Leslie is greater than ever before, and growing all the time, and with this knowledge there comes to me the consciousness that his love is becoming mine to a greater degree than ever before. Then why shouldn't we, as a mere personal matter, thank and praise the Father, for His goodness and loving provisions which we have been so specially privileged in receiving, and not only receiving but knowingly!

I feel tonight that I could write him many pages on this subject, but I must not consume too much of your time. So let me say, just one word more; whether he is sleeping or awake, I am with him in my love, and enjoying every thought that he sends to me, and only crave that his thoughts of me become more frequent and his desire to have me with him increase and never cease. This may seem selfish, but when you consider that there is none other who can give me this love, and none

113

other who has the love which is a part of me, and which only, outside the Father's love, can make me so supremely happy, you will not think me selfish.

Well, I must stop for tonight. But I will be with him and go home with him and remain with him until he goes to sleep; and sometime in the near future, I hope that I may have him come to me again in his spirit as he did before, when we enjoyed an hour of such great happiness and joy. Thanking you and with my love to him, I will say good night,

Mary.[38]

Tells of the great gift that her soulmate, Leslie, will receive and exercise

October 16th, 1917.

I am here, Mary Kennedy.

Well, I am here, and of course he knows it and if he says he does not, he is either telling an untruth or is asleep, and I don't believe that he is either. Yes, I am here, and am glad that I can write once more even only a few words.

I am, of course, very happy and have enjoyed the evening listening to your conversation, and especially that part of it when you conversed about the great gift that my soulmate will receive and exercise. I have known this for some time, but was not permitted to disclose the fact, and now that Helen has told him, I am all anxiety to repeat it. Oh, how glad I am that he has been selected for this work, for two reasons: one, that he will be doing the Will of the Father, and the other, that when his soul gets in that condition that will enable him to exercise this great power, I know that his development will be such that he and I will be very close together in our oneness, and that we will not have to be separated so very long after he comes to me. What a wonderful blessing this is, and how I thank the Father that he has bestowed this possibility upon my dear one. I will not write more now as Helen says that you have written enough for tonight.

So with my love I will say good night.

Mary Kennedy.

Says that her soulmate love for Leslie is like a consuming flame. It is the one great love outside of the Father's Love

December 16th, 1916.

---

[38] This message is a composite of two, being published twice in Volume IV. In this edition the second instance has not been included. (G.J.C.)

I am here, Mary Kennedy.

Well, I will not be left tonight as I was a few nights ago when Kate wrote her message of love to her brother, for while I really enjoyed Kate's message of love, yet I was a little disappointed that I could not say a few words.

Well, I know of no more interesting subject to me than that of love and I could write of it until you might become very tired. I mean physically tired, but I will not do so now, for while you may think I am selfish in this particular I really am not, and you will understand me when I tell you that this love is with me in such intensity that it is a consuming flame. I mean that it is the one great love outside the Father's Love that forms a part of my existence.

Of course, you must not infer from this that I have not love for all mortals and spirits, be they relative or friends or not, for I have, and my work is in trying to help them in their unhappiness and sufferings. But as you have a soulmate who loves you and you have some of that soulmate love yourself, you will understand that it cannot be divided by any other love, and that it is only a little less than the Divine that can make two soulmates completely happy. Well, I heard you and I admit that I have it bad, and am glad of it, and would not lose one iota of it for all the world. Just you wait until you get it bad and then you will understand that I am not expressing to any very great degree how bad I have it.

Well, as we are all in one boat, as the saying is, in this matter, I will not think that your expression means anything more than an approval of my feelings.

I have enjoyed your conversation tonight and I am so happy that there is so much Love in your souls and that you are seeking for more. Persevere and you will not be disappointed, and you will find that it is not mere speculation but the great truth of the universe, or rather, the Celestial Spheres.

Helen says that she agrees with all that I say and that she is glad that I. told you the truth when I said that she loves you with all her heart and soul. Well, I will not write more now.

With my love, Mary.

Confirms that the soulmates of Mr. Padgett and Dr. Stone had them traveling in the spirit world and they are truly who they represent themselves to be when they write

December 28th, 1916.

I am here. Judge Syrick. Well, my friend, how are you this

Christmastime and how is the Doctor? Of course I know full well, but I adopt the old earth way of greeting you both. It has been sometime since I wrote you or had the pleasure of talking to you at Mrs. Ripple's, and I am glad of the opportunity to now say a few words.

Well, when I think of all the things that have happened since I left the mortal life and you two friends, I can scarcely comprehend what it all means. Here, I am a spirit who has found the love of the Father to a small extent, and enjoys the heavens which I used to wonder what it was like, and the company of a dear girl that I used to talk to you about as if I really knew her, and I did really believe in her existence, as my Rose. And you two who have found this love that you used to tell me about, and I didn't understand what you meant. You have your soulmates just as truly as I have mine, although the Doctor has never seen his, at least with his mortal eyes.

But I want to say, right here, with all the sincerity of old friendship, that your soulmates are just as real as is mine, and are with you just as certainly as mine is with me. As your friend, I think it is my duty as well as pleasure, to assure you as a witness bound to you by the bonds of the Divine Love, that both Helen and Mary are the spirits in all communications that they hare written you of. Well, I can hardly realize that all this is true, but I don't have to prick myself to feel that I am not dreaming, and I am glad for your sakes as well as for mine.

I happened to be present a few nights ago when your two soulmates came sailing, as you might say, with the spirits of you two into our spirit sphere, and I must confess that I was surprised for I did not dream that such a thing could be. And you were there and I shook hands with you and greeted you and twitted you on being in possession of two such spirits as were they, and told you that they would never let you return to earth, and you said you were glad of it. Now seriously, this is not a fairy tale, and I assure you in all truth that it is a fact.

I, of course. did not stay with you very long, but you both expressed surprise that I should be such a handsome spirit, and I said I would return the compliment. Well, there are stranger things in heaven and earth than men dream of in their philosophies and I know that this experience of yours is not among the least strange. I am very happy now, and am progressing all the time, and I must tell you that you may, at times, experience some of this soul happiness, but when you come over you will find such happiness very faint in comparison with what you will then enjoy.

I must not write further now and will close, but in doing so must congratulate you on the great privilege you have enjoying the presence of your soulmates, and other spirit friends in this heaven of bliss, and while you are mortals. So with my love, and Rose says hers too, I will say good night.

116

Your old friend,
Syrick.

Tells of her great love for her soulmate Leslie in an early message

I am here, Mary.

I am the only woman in all the spirit world who ever claimed that dear Leslie is her true soulmate. Oh, how I love him, and what a blessed spirit I am to have such a soulmate.

Tell him that in all the earth and heaven as well, there is no one who loves him as does his Mary. I want so to have him feel that I am his, and that no matter how long the years may be, and how many other loves may intervene, there is no love like that of his Mary.

He is so dear to me! I can scarcely write for my tears of joy, and if he could only see me I know that he would shed tears with me, and feel his heart so full of love, that he would think that heaven is with him now.

He must take good care of himself and love his soulmate, for he has now a great work to do, for I have heard the Master telling you this, and he must believe.

And to think that after the years of his work have gone by, he will come to me and enjoy the beautiful home which I have prepared and will continue to prepare, for us! Oh how I thank the Master for having chosen him to do this work.

The Master will be with him so much that the great love of the Master will become a part of his love, and his soul will expand to such an extent that when he leaves his fleshy body he will leave most of his sins behind.

And you, my dear brother and friend, I cannot express to you my gratitude for the great opportunity you have given me to make known to my dear lover that I am his and he is mine, and also for permitting me to write to him. If I could only answer his letters at night as he writes them, I am afraid that he would think so much and so often of his Mary that he would be in danger of neglecting his business.

I must not write more tonight, but will say that you must not forget to pray for me with all your heart, and to believe that when he prays his Mary is with him in all her love and anxiety to see his soul develop in great love for the Father. Tell him also to kiss me good night when he retires, for I shall catch the kiss though he may not realize it.

He is my own true boy, and when I think of the great bliss that will be ours when he comes to me, I can scarcely wait for the time to come. But this I know is not right, and that he must live and do his work.

You are blessed, too, with having such a beautiful pure

soulmate, and how I love her, and only wish that you could see her now! She is here, loving you and smiling, and says that she thanks me for telling you, but she guesses she will have to do her own love-making.

So my dear friend, tell him to love me with all his heart and soul, and to think often of his own true, loving,

Mary.[39]

Writes about the love-making scene between the Doctor and his soulmate, Mary

October 8th, 1915.

I am here, your Helen.

Well sweetheart, we had quite a love-making scene between Mary and the Doctor, and she was so happy that she could write to him that her whole soul was filled with emotion and many tears fell on her letter, though you could not see them.

What a beautiful loving spirit she is, and how she loves the Doctor. I enjoyed the scene more than I can tell you; and when she finished her writings, she came and threw her arms around my neck and cried until I thought that she could have no tears left, but they were tears of joy. Oh, how dear she is to me, for she seems to have a love that appeals to my love for you, and when she tells me of her great love for the Doctor I join with her in her tears, and we both thank God that he has given us such soulmates, and the great love that we have for them.

I have been with you all day trying to comfort you and help you forget the troubles of your earthly affairs, and to some extent I succeeded.

You must love me more and think of me more often, for if you do you will draw me so close to you, that you will feel my love in all its power, and my presence will appear so real to you.

I heard what you said to the Doctor about giving Mary a real lip kiss, and you were right, for while he may not be able to feel her kisses, she can his, and it will make her so happy. Notwithstanding our spirit love, we have that about us that causes us to enjoy what was a part of our earth nature. A kiss is just as sweet, yes more so, than when we were mortals—and you must not think that we are such ethereal, nebulous beings that we cannot enjoy a kiss, or an embrace, for we enjoy both. And as you know, many times have I hugged you until you hollered. So tell the Doctor that he can kiss his Mary just as often as he might were she in the flesh.

---

[39] Although I am in possession of all of Dr. Leslie Stone's correspondence I have never found any of the love letters he wrote to Mary each night. (J.P.G.)

I must stop now.

(A spirit requests to find his soulmate.)

Well, I will try to find his soulmate. He seems a man of a loving disposition and he is in real earnest when he says he wants his soulmate, and he shall have her.

So, sweetheart, say good night.

Your own true and loving, Helen.

Helen and Mary write of their love for their soulmates on earth

February 16th, 1920.

I am here, your own true and loving Helen.

Well, dear, the Master will not continue his messages tonight as you are not so well and he does not feel it best to draw upon you as he would be compelled to do if he were to continue, or attempt to continue, the message of last night, and so I will write you for a short time and tell you of someone here and very anxious to communicate with her soulmate.

Of course I mean Mary, and she is all aquiver with excitement, as you mortals might say, at the prospect of writing to the Doctor; and so I will let her come and write, but you must be careful and not let her write too long, for what she has to say would require you, in order to receive it, to write for the balance of the evening.

Mary now writes:

I am here, Mary. Well, I am here and want to say a great deal, but as Helen has warned you, I will not trespass very long, and Helen did me an injustice when she said I would want to write all the evening. I am as considerate of you as is possible and notwithstanding my opportunity, I realize your capacity.

Tell my dear one that I have waited a long, long time to communicate with him, and that although I have the advantage of him in that I can see what his thoughts are and know just how much he loves me, yet I also desire to tell him of my love for him, and how much I am interested in him and want him to know it. He is my own true lover, and I realize that no other woman can come between him and me, even as to any earthly love that he may have. And just here let me say that I am not reflecting on you, (James Padgett) for I know the circumstances in your case, and how it is best that you should have someone to comfort your last years on earth.[40] But Leslie does not need such a one, and I shall always be sufficient for him, as he is for me. Tell him that I am very happy in the knowledge that he is all mine, and that my love for him is always increasing, and that my efforts to make him happy never cease.

I am now in a higher sphere than when I last wrote him, and realize what the wonderful Love of the Father means more than ever. Also with this increased Love in my soul, I have greater love for him. I am with him more often than he is aware of, and am pleased that the thinks so much of me and loves me as he does. His life will at the longest be very short,[41] and then I shall have him with the full consciousness that no earthly pleasure or condition can ever for a moment separate us, and that the bliss which I have will be nearer his than he can imagine. I really believe that when he comes over it will not be very long until he will find his home with me, and enjoy the happiness of my home—a wonderful home, not like anything on earth, or that has been conceived of by man.

No, it is beyond description and the nearest approach to a description that he can understand is that the Father's love is in and about it to a degree that renders everything beautiful and grand. He must not despair of coming to me, for he will come as surely as your sun will rise; and then he will know what happiness means in the experience of actual enjoyment.

I am so very happy that I can write to him tonight and encourage him with the knowledge that all these things will be his and forever. He, I know, is not surrounded by those things which ordinarily make men happy, but he has greater wealth than these things can possibly give him, for he has much of not only the Father's Love, but the love of a soulmate who is all his and ready to give him the real true happiness that only a union with a soulmate in the Celestial Heavens can give. He must continue to pray for an increased inflowing of the Father's Love, and as that shall come to him, I shall be able to see that the soulmate love for his Mary will increase also.

I would like to write of many things that are here in such reality and grandeur, but as you must not write much more, I must forego the pleasure. But this he must know, that my love is all his and the many mansions spoken of by the Master will prove to him to be a reality, and not the mere hope that so many mortals rely on. I send him a kiss, yes, many kisses, such as only angels can send, and if his soul be opened up

---

[40] It is apparent from the daily dairy that James Padgett had another woman in his life, Ella, and that Helen was quite happy about this. See the entries for Oct. 16th, 1919. That particular message from Helen has not been published. (G.J.C.)

[41] Mary Kennedy got that very wrong, unless it is simply a convoluted turn of phrase, as may well be the case. Dr. Stone passed at age 90, on the 15th January 1967. (G.J.C.)

to their coming, he will realize what it means.

Good night, I thank you, and with my love to him and the assurance that I am watching over him, and sympathize with him in all his earthly worries, will sign myself his loving Mary.

Helen now writes:

Well dear, she has written and says she feels much better, and I know she does, for she looks very happy and grateful for the privilege. I am with Mary in her expressions of love and hope and certainty, and you must believe that these things that she has spoken of will be yours when you come to join us. Why dear, you cannot appreciate what all this means to you and to us! We are truly thankful to the Father for the privilege of knowing that we have on earth a soulmate—the very necessary part of ourselves with whom we can talk and communicate the innermost feelings of our souls.

It is a privilege that not many mortals enjoy, and it is no wonder that men and women are earnestly seeking a way by which they can come into communication with their loved ones, even if these are only their loved ones for a short time.

If they only knew what it means to be able to talk to a soulmate, and have that soulmate tell him of her love and the wonders of it all, they would become more anxious than ever, and the faith that they now have would cease to satisfy. But this cannot be so at this time, and it may be well that men and women generally are not fitted for such an experience.

You know how much I love you and what this love means, and that there is no other love in all the spirit world, except the Father's love, that can so satisfy and make happy.

I must stop now, for you have written enough. But do not forget that Baby[42] is anxious to write, and you must give her the opportunity to do so before long. You will soon feel well again and be in condition to perform your work, which to you just now is the important thing. So I will say good night.

Your own true and loving, Helen.[43]

---

[42] Baby referred to above is Helenita, an 18 year old daughter of James Padgett and his wife and soulmate, Helen. Dr. Stone knew her before she passed over on June 20th, 1918. (J.P.G.)

[43] This message is a composite, the portion here that is Mary Kennedy's message was also published in Volume I. (G.J.C.)

Helen decided to scold the soulmates but without the cooperation of Mary

December 6th, 1915.

I am here, your own true Helen.

I merely want to say that you and Dr. Stone are very foolish men to neglect your soulmates, as you have been doing lately. We have been waiting to have you call for us, but you do not express a desire for us to write a short letter before you go to bed, to let you know that we are here and that we love you.

Now do you think that this is right, when we are with you every night anxiously waiting for you to say, sweethearts come and write us a long letter tonight, and tell us that you love us with all your hearts and souls. I know that many men who, if they had such sweethearts as you two have, would not rest content to let the night go by without praying for us to write them, that we thought at least just a little bit of them. Now what shall we do in the way of punishment for your neglect?

I said, "Tell my soulmate to give me a kiss."

Well, he has solved the problem. We will not give him the kiss but will make him go to bed without his usual kiss, and then he will realize that his punishment is just what he deserves, and he will not neglect us again. But Mary says; No indeed, she will not punish her soulmate in that way, because if she did, she would be punishing herself more than she would him, and besides, she could not write unless you would consent to write for her, and she knows that many nights when he visits you he hopes that he may receive a message, but as he sees that you are at work he does not make his request, and consequently, she is not going to punish him for what he can't help.

Just see what a foolish little sweetheart she is. So you see that spirit sweethearts and mortal sweethearts, when they are females, do not differ very much. And she says that now that the Ray is open she will write just a little if you will help her, and I seeing what a foolish little girl she is, and knowing that she will not be happy unless she can say a word to him, I tell her to go ahead and let the Doctor see what an easy little sweetheart she is. She says that she doesn't care what I think, that she knows that the Doctor won't think that she is foolish, but will just be delighted to have her write. So prepare now to hear words of burning love.

Mary now writes:

Well, I will tell him that I love him with all my heart and soul, and I don't care if Helen is laughing at me, for I do love him and I have the right to tell him so, and he must believe me, for I am with him nearly all the time and want him to know it.

So tell him, also, that when he is not thinking of me I am thinking of him and trying to help him with all my powers and love. And say particularly, that I am so glad to see that the Love of the Father is entering his soul more and more, and that as a consequence, he and I are coming closer together in our love and in our soul development.

I know that you are tired but I could not help writing this, for I have been waiting so long to write him and tell him this. But I will not trespass longer, and will say that I thank you and love him as only a soulmate can love. So goodbye.

Helen resumes:

Well, sweetheart, I enjoy so much seeing Mary express her love for the Doctor for it makes her so happy, and I love her so much that I will do everything in my power to make her happy.

I will write you before you go to bed.

Your own true and loving,

Helen.

In another joint message Helen and Mary jest about their love for their soulmates

December 15th, 1915.

I am here, Helen.

Well you have written enough for tonight, and I will say only a few words and stop if the little lovesick girl does not interfere. I suppose, though, she will have to say a word or she will not sleep tonight, as you mortals say. Well, go ahead and tell him that you love him. You should be ashamed to try and deceive him so.

Mary now takes a hand in telling Helen what she wants her to say:

Well, Leslie, don't you believe her, for you know that I love you, and she is only jealous because I love you more than she does her soulmate. Of course I will interfere whenever I get the chance to tell you of my love, and Helen is real mean to try and make you believe that I am trying to deceive you. But she will tell you differently, I know. Won't you Helen?

Now Helen writes:

Yes, Doctor, I was merely joking, for of all the sick girls that I have ever seen, I don't think I have ever seen one so sick as your Mary. Now she says that I must not say that, so you see I can't please her. Now, come Mary, was I right when I told him that you would deceive him, or when I said that you were lovesick? Well, I won't deceive him, and I suppose I won't have to say anything more.

So you see, Doctor, she acknowledges that she is a little lovesick girl and is not happy unless she can tell you so. But remember, Doctor, that she does love you, and you should be a very thankful man to have such a beautiful and loving soulmate. Well, sweetheart, I will not write more.

Dr. Stone then asked if she felt his kisses, and Helen resumed:

Mary says that they were so quickly given that she did not have time to know whether she felt them or not. She says, Tell him that when he kisses her, to have them longer drawn out, as she doesn't like these quick kisses.

She says that she does kiss him, and sometime she will bite him, just to let him realize that she is kissing him.

So with our love to both of you, I will say good night.

Your own and true loving,

Helen.[44]

Mary continues to explain her soulmate's love, but does not want to frighten him with her pursuit of this love

December 26th, 1915.

I am here, Mary Kennedy.

Well, you had a spirit write you who wanted the light, and your band thought it advisable to let him write, and they also saw another spirit who is filled with love for a mortal, who some spirits such as Helen, say doesn't deserve it, and they have let her write, and she is doing so.

I merely wanted to do a little independent writing myself, to let that dear boy see that I am able to write him and tell him that I love him, just as I have told him so many times before.

I was with him at church tonight and enjoyed the singing very much, as he did, and tried to make him feel my presence, and I believe that he did.

But I will not make love to him or he might get tired of hearing me tell him, and get in such a condition of conceit that he will think that all he has to do is to say, "Mary, come and tell me that you love me better than anyone else." So have determined that I will not in the future tell him so often of my life—that is, if I can keep from doing so, and I

---

[44] This message shows that spirits like a little fun and enjoy it as much as mortals, and are just as natural in their existence as mortals are here. (Dr. L. R. Stone)

doubt that I can. Helen says that I am such a lovesick girl that if a brick house stood between him and me, I would butt my brains out trying to get to where he is. And maybe she is right. But anyhow, I have the right to do it if I choose, and no one else has any right to say I shan't.

So let him know that it is real mean to take advantage of my weak condition, or strong maybe, and want me to do all the love-making. He doesn't have to write his love to me as I do to him, for if he only thinks love, I can see it in his heart and enjoy it, just as if I should receive a letter from him, telling me of it.

But I must stop this love-making, and tell him that I am with him, and am so interested in his soul progress, and I know that he is progressing, for I can see his influence of love not only for me but for the Father as well, and his soul development means a great deal to me as well as to himself.

I am now in the First Celestial Sphere and am so very happy, and when I have the opportunity, and you are willing, I desire to tell him of my beautiful home, and the great things that the Father has prepared for me and bestowed upon me to make me happy. They sing "That eye has not seen, etc"; but his eyes will not have to see, for when I write him of the great things that the Father has prepared for me, he must know and realize that they will be his someday, as well as myself also.

So let me say just one word more, and that is, that you must continue to pray to the Father for His love and blessings, and for faith, and he will find that his soul will expand in joy and peace, and that he will realize that he is coming closer and closer to his own true soulmate.

Mary.

Helen and Mary wrote a joint message to permit Mary to tell a secret to her soulmate

December 29th, 1915.

I am here, your Helen:

I will write you a little, if I am permitted to do so; but I suppose I will have to be real stern to another spirit here who says that she wants to write, and tell you one little secret which she has, and if I will only let her say it she will love me forever. So I suppose I must let her say it.

Mary now writes:

Well, Doctor, don't you know whom Helen was talking about? I don't believe you do, because when I said I had a secret, you would immediately say it was not I, for I don't keep secrets but tell all I know, no matter who hears me.

But you are wrong, for I have a secret and I want to tell it to you, but only on condition that you promise not to reveal it. I assume that you promise. So listen as I whisper it to you: I love you with all my heart and soul and want you to know it.

Now Helen, I have told him, and I thank you.

Helen now writes:

Well, isn't she a cute little sweetheart! But she had to tell him or she would burst open, as you mortals say. Well, sweetheart, you have had a long writing tonight and I will not detain you longer.

I will say, though, that I am so happy and only wish that you could get one glimpse of me now, for you would see such love for you that you would never more doubt. But I must stop.

So good night to you both.

Your own true and loving,

Helen.

Cousin tells of meeting her soulmate

January 19th, 1917.

I am here, Laura Burroughs. I am glad to be able to write you again and tell you that since I last wrote you I have made much progress and come into the possession of much more happiness. Dear cousin, I am so glad that I can tell you this, for I know that you rejoice with me in my happiness and the knowledge of what great mercy has come to me. I merely wanted to say this, for it makes me very happy to come to you in this way.

Well he (her husband) is in the spirit world but in a very dark plane, and is not at all happy. I have been with him some, but have not been able to do him any good, as his old beliefs cling to him and prevent his progress. Sometime we may be able to help him, and will then try.

She (Helen) has told me he is not my soulmate, and I have met my soulmate very recently; he is in the same sphere with me and we are very happy together and are trying to progress together. Well, I never knew him on earth. He lived in Pennsylvania and died a long time before I did, and tells me that he had to go through much suffering and darkness before he got into the plane of light. He is a very beautiful spirit, and I could love him, I believe, even if he were not my soulmate; but as he is, you know what our love means. He is looking at me write and heard your question and says his name was Henry W. Spaulding, and lived in Millville, if you know where that is.

After I had made some progress and got some love in my soul, Helen brought him to me one time, and said "Laura, here is a young man who has been very anxious to meet you for some time, and you must not fall in love with him, if you can keep from doing so," and she laughed. Well, I suppose, I blushed, as we mortals used to say, but I did fall in love, as you can imagine, and have been loving him ever since. How we all love Helen for her kindness and the great good that she does. You just wait until you come over, and you will see the most beautiful girl that you ever saw.

He returns the satisfaction (salutation), and says that he considers himself very fortunate in having such a cousin, and he means it, for he sees the wonder of the great gift that you have, and the loving and high spirits that come to you. I must say good night now, and with my love I will stop.

Your loving cousin,
Laura.[45]

Judge Syrick's soulmate writes about his progress in the Divine Love

April 24th, 1916.

I am here, Rose - just Rose.

I want to say only a word, for I am so happy that I must tell you, as I know that you will join with me in my happiness. Well, the Judge has progressed to the Third Sphere, and he is so happy that he hardly knows what to do or what to say! He is here, but wanted me to write, as he thinks that I may be able to tell you more understandingly than if he should try to write.

Well, he now knows what the Divine Love means, and what a Savior and great spirit the Master is; and he is praying to, and praising, the Father with all his heart. He certainly is happy, and wants everybody to know it! You can imagine that we all rejoice with him, and unite in thanking the Father for the great blessing that has been bestowed. I, of course, am especially happy, for I am his soulmate, and he is now so much nearer to my home, and now his progress will be more rapid and his growth in this Divine Love so much more easy. As he realizes the wonderful power of this Love to make him happy and to give him a home more beautiful than he ever conceived of, his faith will increase. He thanks God for his Rose, and for his friends on earth who helped him so much in learning the truths of the spirit world, both as to what you might call the material things, and as to the spiritual higher things.

Well, I am so full of joy that I cannot write much tonight, and I

---

[45] This message is a composite of two, being published in Volume III and Volume IV. (G.J.C.)

feel that what I have said must be disconnected, but I know you will excuse my weakness, for when the time comes for you to understand what soulmate love means under such circumstances, you will wonder that I was able to write at all!

He sends his love, and so do I, and when next he comes he will want to use up your whole tablet in writing his experiences.

So, thanking you I will say good night.

Your sister in Christ,

Rose.

A loving personal message to her husband and soulmate

April 24th, 1916.

I am here, Helen.

Well, sweetheart, you have had a very happy night, and I also have enjoyed the reading of the messages and the exchange of thoughts between you and the Doctor.

It is wonderful to see the great truths that are being opened up to you and with what understanding you receive them. I am so glad that you are in condition to understand what the spirits mean in their revealment of these truths.

The Doctor is so very much in earnest, and has such faith that he, too, can understand these things of the soul.

Oh, how good the Father is to come to you in this way, and show you the great truths that do exist and that all men must learn, either in the flesh or in the spirit world, in order to become children of the Father.

I will not write more tonight, as it is late and you must go to bed and get your sleep. But I will watch over you until you sleep, and even then I will come to you through the night and you will feel my love and presence. When in sleep your spirit will come to me and you will realize that you are with me, even though you may not remember the fact in your waking moments. But we will communicate in our love and realize that we are together.

So love me waking, and you will love me when you think you sleep.

With a great big kiss and a hug, I will say good night.

Your own true and loving,

Helen.

Urges Mr. Padgett to follow John's advice. Also writes about soulmates

January 19th, 1917.

I am here, your own true and loving Helen.

Well, dear, I see that you are tired and must not write more; but I want to say that you must think of the message that John wrote you,[46] for it is a very important one and means as much to you as it will to us and our work. He was all kindness and love when he wrote, and so much wants you to follow his advice, and I know you will.

Laura wrote and told you the fact about meeting her soulmate. They are very happy and are both seeking for greater inflowing of the Divine Love, for which I am so very glad. I have not seen him, and hence of my own knowledge can't tell you, but she should know the fact, and of course would only write you the truth. I don't see how she could be mistaken.

Well, the last spirit is very anxious to meet his soulmate, but I think I will keep him on the anxious bench for a little while, for he is not altogether in the proper condition; and if he has to worry a little before he meets her it may do him some good. He is a very decent sort of spirit, and I have no doubt will love his soulmate very much; but yet some of his thoughts must change before I bring him to her.

Yes, she has made considerable progress, and is a quite loving spirit. She has not yet gotten into the Third Sphere, but she is seeking the Love very earnestly and before a great while will be there. I have taken a special interest in her on account of Mr. Colburn, and I have told her of him and that he is her soulmate, and she is with him quite often. And having seen the Doctor's Mary write him, she is very anxious to write Mr. Colburn. She now realizes fully that her earth husband is not her soulmate, and that the love which she had for him is a very different kind from what has come to her for Mr. Colburn. The latter is now absorbing her and the former is now a mere recollection of kind thoughts and good wishes for the happiness of her husband. And these thoughts do not in the least interfere with the greater and only decreed love that has come to her. As I say, she is anxious to write him, and very soon she shall have the opportunity.

I suppose he would like to know her name while on earth and I will give it now, though she says give only her maiden name, for she says that the only true marriage for her is the one with Mr. Colburn, and she wants to come to him with all recollection of her earth matter obliterated. Well, her name was Nellie Robinson, and she lived in the state of New York close to the city of Buffalo. She was a village girl and never saw much of city life; and for his gratification she says tell him that her mortal life was as pure and undefiled as pure thoughts and rather

---

[46] This is a message from John advising Padgett not to read certain spiritual material. This message was published in Volume III (2nd Ed.) on page 325. (G.J.C.)

spiritual nature would make it.

But I will not write more now about her, and will leave her to tell her own story and do her own love-making. But say to Mr. Colburn that he is fortunate in having such a beautiful girl for his spirit bride, and I am glad that it is so. I must not write more now. My own dear Ned, I love you with all my heart and soul, and will say good night. Give me my kiss and soon go to bed.

Your own true and loving,
Helen.

The wonders, benefits and blessings wrought by the Divine Love of God

June 8th, 1916.

I am here, your own Helen. Tonight everything seems favorable to my writing you my promised message, and I will try. Of course, you must expect to find some expressions of love in it, for I could not write you if I did not tell you how much I love you, and how happy I am when you love me and want me to be with you.

Well, sweetheart, I am now in the (same) Celestial Sphere with your grandmother, though not in as high a plane as she, and have not so much of the Divine Love as has she; yet my happiness is so great that I can hardly realize myself what it means, and it is impossible to tell you of the beauties of my home and surroundings. I have tried when I was in a lower (Celestial) sphere to describe to you my home, and I did it very inadequately, giving you only a glimpse of what it really was. And now, if you could increase that description a hundredfold, you would have no conception of the beauty and glory of my present home and the wonders that surround it.

I so often wish that you had words in your language that could be used to fully describe what this new home means to me, or even the one that I just left; but as you have not, you will have to be content with knowing that if you should take all the imagery of the Revelation and add to it the sum total of all the beautiful descriptions of places and homes and scenery that the whole range of your English literature contains, you would have but a faint idea of what really exists. And besides, the great increase in the Love that I possess and enjoy and the beautiful and loving and holy spirits whom I have for my companions, make this home of mine truly one of the mansions of the Kingdom of Heaven that Jesus referred to in the Bible; only the mansions that he there spoke of were not necessarily like the one that I have, for the mansions in the Celestial Heavens vary according to the soul development of their occupants.

I sometimes think that a very few years ago I was on earth,

without much soul development and very little knowledge of the things of God; and now I have that development and knowledge of those things that fit me for these glorious mansions of the Celestial Spheres. How wonderful it all is, and how I thank the Father for His goodness and mercy, and for having given to mankind such a loving and glorious savior as Jesus.

And I do not forget that you had something to do with my starting on this great journey of progress, for I remember that when I first came to you, things of the material were very attractive to me, and my appetites of earth had not left me, and how when I displayed some of these desires for the material things you rebuked me, and tried to point the way to the higher things; although I know now that your advice came from your merely mental conceptions of what I should strive for, as at that time you had very little knowledge of the things of the soul and scarcely any soul development.

But your Christian training as a child, and the conceptions that had come to you from these instructions, taught you that in the spirit world there must be something higher and beyond the mere earthly conditions of men, where purer joy and happier lives might be found and lived; and your love for me was such that you desired that I should find and possess these things, if possible. I have never forgotten what you then said to me, although at the time I thought you were unkind and not so anxious for my happiness. But long ago I had come to me the knowledge of the motive that actuated your advice, and much happiness has come to me from that knowledge and recollection. Only a little thought of love and an earnest desire on the part of the mortal for the spirit, when it is directed in the way of the soul's progress, sometimes work a greater result than the conquering of a city, for it means the salvation of a soul, which is of more value than all the cities of the earth combined.

And while I am writing in this strain I wish to say that one of the greatest benefits or possessions that can come to a mortal is to have a mother or husband or wife in whose bosom glows the Divine Love of the Father, even though very faintly, for that little spark of love, to its own degree, makes that soul a part of the Divine essence of the Father's Love, and its influence upon the possessor causes an atmosphere of love and help to be felt by all who have the relationship to such possessor of a child or wife or husband. Christian instructions, though mixed with dogmas and creeds that may all be wrong, yet will benefit, as in them are some thoughts that may awaken the soul to a condition that will let in some portion of the higher Love, which will remain, though dormant, until the time comes when something will arouse the dormant Love to action and life.

And this benefit passes with the mortal to the spirit life, and the influence of the teachings, or rather the accompanying impressions of the Christian mother, etc., to help such a spirit to realize its true condition and to start on its progress to the attainment of the higher things of the soul. No wealth or riches or position that a mortal may inherit can possibly equal the influence of that one little spark in the Christian mother who possesses some portion of the Divine Love; and there is none so poor as the spirit who comes into the spirit world without any recollection of having, at some time in its earth life, received in its soul the influence of that little spark.

So I say the man who has a Christian mother or wife who has, at some time in his earth career, taught him to turn his thoughts to God and to pray, even though that man in afterlife forsakes such thoughts and prayers, is a very fortunate being; for in the spirit life he has with him the memories of his earth life and nothing is lost; and among these memories will be the influence of his mother's teachings and his own prayers. And while he will have to satisfy the laws of compensation, yet these recollections of these thoughts and prayers will come to him sooner or later, and will help him in his progress to higher conditions. And you must remember, as has been often told you, that all souls will ultimately reach the planes of purification of their natural loves, or the glories of the spheres where only the Divine Love exists.

After I commenced to receive into my soul this Divine Love, I became very anxious to increase its possession and my progress was very rapid, as they tell me, and as I progressed from sphere to sphere, ever were there coming to me new wonders and great happiness and the disappearance of those things which belonged to my mortal life. No one who has not experienced this progress can understand what it means, and how the happiness increases and also the longings for more; and yet the astonishing fact is that notwithstanding these longings, the contentment of the spirit is perfect and no unhappiness, because of longings yet to be fulfilled, exists.

As you know, when I entered the spirit world I was met by your mother and others, and all fear or confusion that usually arises from the change which so-called death brings to the spirit left me, and, in fact, never came to me, and I was as tenderly cared for as you can conceive of; and ever thereafter, while I could not go to the home of your mother, yet she and others were with me often enough to keep me from much darkness and suffering, though I did experience some darkness and suffering. But the influence of their love was with me, and they earnestly and lovingly told me of the Great Love of the Father, and how I might get it and become happy, and start on my upward progression. And your father came to me also, with his cheer and help, and showed me that upon myself, to a certain extent, depended my being able to get into the light. He was so good and kind to me that I loved him at once, although I had never seen him in earth life.

And from all this can you wonder that I did not remain very long in the lower planes? I tell you that the love and tenderness and influence of the beautiful and loving spirits who have some of God's Love in their souls are things that can take away the terror of death and make a spirit who has just left his mortal home almost happy. And if men could only realize the fact that by attempting to get into their hearts good thoughts and longings of love so that these beautiful spirits could be attracted to them, their entrance and reception in the world of spirits would become one, even if not of happiness, yet of freedom from fear and loneliness. So, I advise all mortals to so live as to attract friends on the spirit side of life that can come to them in the times of the great change, and comfort and help them. Now, I do not mean by this that such spirits of mortals will not have to endure the darkness and suffering which the conditions of their souls demand they should endure, but their entrance into the spirit world will be as I say.

Well, sweetheart, I have written a quite long letter and you must be a little tired, but I must further write and tell you that all this happiness that I have spoken of may be yours, and as your soulmate, I believe and almost know that it will be; for while you are a mortal, no matter how long the years may be, you will have with you my love and longings for your coming, and my prayers to the Father for a great bestowal upon you of His Divine Love. And besides all this, you know that you have surrounding you the loves of those who are higher than I, and who possess so much more of this Divine Love. Oh, it, will be a happy day for me when you do come, and I know that you will be happy, also. Just think, that as your eyes close in what the preachers call the last sleep, I will be with you, and when you awake I will be with you, and the only thing that will greet your newly-awakened vision will be my eyes, so filled with love and joy that you will almost want to die over again just for the sake of having the awakening.

I remember that when on earth, you thought my arms were very beautiful, and loved to have them around you, and thought yourself happy; but when you come to me again you will find arms so much more beautiful clasping you to a bosom that you cannot dream of, and eyes looking into your eyes with so much love and happiness that you will, for the first time in all your life, know what happiness means; and then when I tell you that I am all yours and that never again will cruel death, as it is called, separate us, and that only love, pure and unselfish and never-dying, will be ours without any lessening or disturbing by jealousy or tiresomeness, you will wonder if you have really awakened from that last sleep or are only dreaming. But then I will give you a long, sweet kiss of love that you will know that it is all real.

Oh, my Ned, I do love you and want you to love me with all your heart! The time will not be long now, until we shall be together in our spirit life, when your cares and worries of life will no longer trouble you. But, sweetheart, you must pray to the Father for a greater inflowing of His Divine Love and blessings, for upon the development of your soul depends our continuous living together, and progress.

I will be with you tonight while you sleep, and I am so filled with love that I know I shall call your spirit from your body and carry it with me to purer planes, where we can, for a few moments, enjoy the bliss of living together, without the encumbrance of your body. You may not remember it when you awake, but I will know, and will tell you of it when next I write.

So, sweetheart, give me my good night kiss.
Your own true and loving,
Helen.[47]

A confirmed bachelor decides he will try to get into the proper condition that will enable him to meet his soulmate

January 19th, 1917.

Let me say a word—George E. Luckett.

I am a spirit who has listened to your last communication and was somewhat interested in what the spirit said about her soulmate and her love for a spirit that she never heard of until after she got into the spirit world.

Now that may be all true, and I must say that she and her companion seemed to be very happy, and looked like sure enough lovers that you read of in romances; but what I want to ask is, how could they know that they are soulmates? Of course, they may love each other a great deal and think that there is no one else in all the wide world that can take the place of the one with the other, just as mortal sweethearts have thought and said many a time, to find later they were mistaken. And, as I have heard that this soulmate love is one that admits of no mistake, I should like to know, as I said, how they are certain that they are soulmates.

Well, I see your wife, and she says that there is not the slightest difficulty in knowing that you are some other spirit's soulmate, provided you are in condition to be able to receive that knowledge. That of course, some of these old grouchy selfish bachelors would not be able to receive this knowledge; and that is one of their punishments. But whenever the spirit has a loving soul and he has progressed into that condition of

---

[47] This message is a composite of two, being published twice in Volume IV. The second instance has not been included in this edition. (G.J.C.)

development where it is best that he should meet his soulmate he will meet her and will know the fact when he does meet her.

Now, this makes me think some, for I am one of these bachelors, and have never believed in soulmates or anything of that nature; though I have seen a number of couples who claimed that they were soulmates and seemed to be very happy. Yet the fact made no special impression on me, neither did it incite in me any desire to learn if I have a soulmate. But now I believe that I will try to find whether I have or not.

Your wife says that when I get in proper condition for having one come to me she will find her for me and bring her to me, and that I will almost curse myself for having been such a big fool all these years. But I wonder what she means by "proper condition"? I must go after her and find out, and try to get in that condition.

Well, I will do it! I am glad that I broke in here tonight. I am in the light planes of the earth sphere, and am trying to be a decent fellow, and hope that I am. But as to whether it meets the "proper condition", I will find out. Thanking you for your kindness, I will say good night.

Your friend, George E. Luckett.[48]

Mr. Padgett's father tells of his progress to the First Celestial Sphere and as his guardian angel tells him not to worry about material needs

October 28th, 1916.

I am here, your father. I desire to write a few lines tonight, as I have not written for some time and I feel that I want you to hear from me and learn that I have been with you a great deal, trying to help you and make you happy.

I know the worries that you have, and know that everything looks so dark to you and no apparent relief in sight, but you must not have such dreaded views, for what you imagine you see will never come to pass, and things will take on a brighter hue before a great while. I love you, as you know, and so do many others who are with you frequently, and you must believe that they are trying to help you and are doing so. If you could realize just for a moment what power you have surrounding you and how much it is being exercised for your good, you would not look upon material things in such a gloomy light.

I am now in the First Celestial Sphere and am happy beyond all expression, and know that the Divine Love of which you have heard so much is a real living thing that makes the souls of spirits at-one with the

---

[48] This message is a composite of two, being published in Volume III and Volume IV. (G.J.C.)

Father and immortal. My dear son, I cannot tell you the glories of the home that is mine or of the happiness which I have in my soul; and when I sometimes think of what I was on earth and what I am now, I am astonished that such great difference could exist between the two existences. God is all Love and His Mercy and care are without limit, and all mortals are the object of all these blessed attributes of Him.

Keep up your courage and let all the aspirations of your soul go forth to Him and His Love for (because) you are on the right road to obtaining this Great Love in increased abundance and your home in the Celestial Spheres is assured; only pray and have faith. Many spirits are here tonight and some desire to write, but I do not know they will do, as your wife says that this is her night and she has promised to write you and must keep her promise.

She is so wonderful and beautiful that you would not know her if you could see her in her glorious appearance and her love is exceedingly transcendent, and her love for you rather surprises us all for it is deeper than the ocean and higher than the heavens, as you mortals say. She is a spirit of such exceeding brightness that we who were with her when she first came to the spirit world can scarcely realize that she is the same person that came to us a few short months ago. But she sought for the Divine Love with all the positiveness and longings of her soul and was never satisfied unless she was progressing, so that now she is higher up in the Celestial Spheres, and is filled with this Love, and with it has a beauty that outshines the stars and a wisdom that you cannot conceive of. We all love her very much and her work in bringing soulmates together is resulting in a wonderful good and happiness to these happy ones.

Well, I am glad that I could write to you tonight and tell you these things. But do not forget that I am with you very often and am still your Guardian Angel although you have around you and interested in you, a vast number of spirits of the Celestial Heavens.

Well, you must know that as I progress in my soul development I also progress in my mental development, and knowledge and power of expression come to me, as it were, unconsciously, and no effort is required to write you and explain the things of this world in a manner that you would hardly expect from what you know of my mental development when on earth. There are many surprising things occurring all the time to spirits as they progress, and I am told that there is no end to our progress, and it must be so, for even the highest spirits say that they are progressing to higher and higher planes all the time.

Yes, my soulmate has progressed with me and we are very happy. I wish I could tell you what soulmate happiness when combined with the happiness of the Divine Love means. But it would be useless to try. Your mother's soulmate has progressed also; he is in the Seventh

Sphere and is striving with all the energies of his soul to get in the sphere with your mother, and he will soon do so, for she is helping with her wonderful love and is with him a great deal. I must stop now. So with all my father's love, I will say good night.

Your loving father and brother in Christ,

John H. Padgett.

A spirit writes a very beautiful letter of love to her soulmate

December 16th, 1917.

I am here, Mrs. Horner.[49]

Let me say only a few words, for I am so anxious to write a few lines, and have been for some time. Many times I have been with you (Dr. Stone) and my husband as you conversed of things pertaining to the spiritual world and I was very hopeful that he would believe what you said to him and turn his thoughts to an investigation of the truths that he would surely find, and thereby give me the opportunity of coming to him in my voice, at least, and telling him that I am not dead, but very happy and always watching over him to comfort him.

I know that I have been away from him, as he has thought, for a long time, and that other things have intervened in his life to cause him to forget me to a more or less degree, and to think that it was all of life to live on earth and find his happiness there. This, of course, was quite natural, and I was not hurt, as you mortals say, because of the fact that he had, as he thought, given his affections to another; for I knew the conditions of his heart better than he himself knew it, and saw that his real love was mine, and that no other could take it from me or, as he may be surprised to hear, he could not give it to another.

I have heard you talk to him about the soulmate love and he has some conception of it, and I want to tell him that this is the love that is binding us together; and nothing in all the universe of God can sever that bond. I should like to tell him what this bond means and sometime, if you will indulge me, I will do so, but tonight I will not take your time.

But tell him this: that I thought when on earth that I loved him, and I did, but now I realize how faint that love was as compared to what I now have for him, and what will always be his. He may not believe that I am writing to him or that my love for him is as I write it is, but as certain as his friend, death, at some time will come to him, so certain is it that when he comes to the spirit world he will find this love waiting for him, and also his soulmate, just at the entrance of his real home.

Well, I must not write more, but kindly tell him that I am a very

---

[49] Dr. Stone knew her husband. (J.P.G.)

happy spirit, with my home in the Fifth Sphere, and that I am bright and beautiful in appearance, as they tell me. When I left the earth plane all darkness of race[50] left me and I became one of the shining ones; and every spirit associate that I had, was and is my true brother and sister, and the Father is my Father, and I am His child. As my soul progressed and developed in Love, I became nearer like unto the Father, and my spirit body and appearance showed the purity of my soul. And such will be his destiny if he will only follow the way that the Father has provided for him by which he can obtain one of the beautiful mansions of these spheres.

I will tell him only one thing more before I stop writing; and that is, that as my soul developed in Love, my intellect and knowledge also developed, and I became very wise without having to study as you mortals do on earth; and now I see that many of your so-called wise men are, in their wisdom, very foolish, and in their understanding very ignorant. I write this because he may think that now I am the same person in my intellect and knowledge that I was when we were happy together. And we were happy for a short while, for I loved him with all the fervor of my young life and trust, and was so sorrowful when I had to leave him; but God knew best, and now I know that it was for the best. As I said, I still love him, but with a greater and more fervent love than ever; and sometimes I love him so very intensely that I draw him to me and enjoy a spirit communion with him, although he may not realize it.

Pardon me for writing so long. With my love to him, I will say good night. I was Mrs. Horner when on earth for a short time, when he gave me the fine love of his youth, and I will be his for all eternity.

Mrs. Horner.

An old friend of both Mr. Padgett and Dr. Stone relates his spiritual progression and is living with his soulmate in the fifth sphere

May 13th, 1917.

I am here, Judge Syrick.

But you must not pay any attention to the Judge part. I merely used the term to let you know that I feel a good deal like yourselves tonight in that I am a man with you.

I cannot tell you how pleased I am to be able to write to you tonight, as it has been a long time since I wrote you; and as you know, I always enjoy being with you, even more so than when on earth, for you are both very dear to me, and I want you to feel that the throwing aside

---

[50] Mrs. Horner was an African American. (J.P.G.)

138

my covering of flesh did not change me in any particular as regards my feelings for you, except to cause me to realize how much more you are (both) my brothers and friends. Well, I have been present all evening and heard you read the message of Jesus, and your comments on the same, and I cannot express my joy in hearing the message and realizing how it appealed to you both, for it was a wonderful message and one that will open up a world of truth to men if they will only understand and believe.

I have made much progress in my soul development and in the acquirement of the knowledge of these spiritual truths, so that even I know that what was written you in that message is true. I am progressing all the time, and the Love that has come into my soul has transformed me to a large degree into something more than the mere image of the Father. Oh, I tell you, this Love is wonderful, and we who have it are happy beyond all conception, and the best thing about it is that the more we receive the knowledge comes to us that there is more waiting for us to receive.

I am in the fifth sphere, and I have with me one whom you have heard me speak of. I mean, of course, my Rose. What a blessing to have such a soulmate, and if I could only find words to tell you of the happiness that comes with such a possession I would do so, if only to give you some idea of what you may expect when you come to the spirit world, and especially when you remember that both your soulmates are in a higher sphere than are we, and of course have more happiness and love.

Well, I would like to write a longer letter, but am advised that I have written enough for tonight, and so I must stop. Yes, I was there and spoke to you, but did not try to talk much as there were so many other spirits, all anxious to speak to their friends and who haven't the blessed opportunity that I have to communicate. The room was filled with spirits, and if you could have seen the condition of some of them I know that you would have had a longing desire to help them. So do not let any doubt come to you as to the great work that is yours to help these spirits and also that many of them are helped, as a truth. Was not I one who was thus helped, and do not I know that you have given to you this power? So thank God. and work. Tell the Doctor that he also is doing a great work and must persevere; and when he comes over, as my old mother said when I was a mere child, here will be crowns of glory waiting for him.

Well, I must stop now, and in doing so want to assure you both that you have my love and gratitude to the extent that an appreciative soul can give. Rose sends her love and says that she is so very happy and is praying for you both. Good night, my dear brothers.

Your old friend,

Syrick.[51]

Helen writes a message

May 13th, 1917.

I am here, your own true and loving Helen.

Well, dear, you have had some messages tonight that were satisfactory to the Doctor and I am glad that he received them, for they make him feel better. James actually wrote him and was much interested in doing so, as he thinks a great deal of the Doctor and is trying to help him in every way.

I will not write more now as it is very late and you are tired and sleepy—so go to bed and get your sleep, and believe that I love you with all my heart and soul. I will say, though, that I was with you at church, and as they sang Home, Sweet Home, I was with you and tried to impress you with my presence and love. The home will be yours and you will soon, I mean when the work is finished, come to enjoy it.

I want to tell you that you must keep up your courage and hope, and you will not be disappointed. Be ready tomorrow night for the Master to write his message. Do so, and you will be successful in receiving it. So, sweetheart, good night and God bless you, your own true loving,

Helen.

Described the spiritual law of do unto others and also his progress into the seventh sphere

December 21st, 1917.

I am here, Judge Syrick.

Well, old boy, how are you tonight? I speak thus that you may know that I am feeling just as friendly as I did when on earth, and you may feel assured that I am more friendly than I was when I used to talk to you about the mysteries of the unseen. Now, of course, I know a great many things that were to us, at that time, mysterious, and know that the mysterious exists only in the minds of men, and that everything in our universe of truth and mystery is merely a convenient manmade word for hiding our want of knowledge.

---

[51] I knew Judge Syrick. He was an old friend of Mr. Padgett who was able to get Helen, who has the wonderful gift of finding the soulmates of those who desired to know whether the soulmate is on earth or in spirit world. Helen found the soulmate of Judge Syrick, who was a beautiful spirit and her name was Rose. Both of them have now made their progress into Celestial Heaven. (Dr. L. R. Stone)

Well, Padgett, I am glad that I can write to you again, for it gives me much pleasure in being able to do so. Of course, I am with you very often, listening to the conversation of yourself and friends, and the reading of the messages that you receive. There are so many spirits around you, all desiring to write, that I can only at times write myself, and, as you have learned, we always give the preference to others whenever we know of their desires. This is one of the things that we learn and apply in our life here as we progress. It is not only that we do unto others as we would have them do unto us, but we do unto others as we know to be for the good of these others. We try to efface self, and as we advance in our possession of the love, we find it less and less difficult to sacrifice self for the benefit of others; and the wonderful thing is that in doing this we are the happier and realize that we should not live for self alone. Well, you will commence to think that I am a preacher, and in a way I am, but what I say I know to be true, and not the result of any speculation.

I am progressing and am now in the Seventh Sphere, and if I were to attempt to tell you what this means, and could do so, you would think that I was either a storyteller surpassing the author of the Thousand and One Nights, or that your imagination was running away with your senses. But it is a fact that the beauty and wonders of this sphere are beyond my ability to describe or your ability to understand.

Rose, of course, is with me, and we are so very happy. What a wonderful thing this soulmate love is! Now I realize that the happiness which is mine compensates for all the lonesome times of my old bachelor days on earth, and as I see that your friend is a poor, lonesome bachelor, I want to tell him that when he comes to the spirit world and has his soulmate to love and cherish him, he will forget that he was ever a lonesome bachelor on earth and will regret only that he had not become a spirit long before he entered that world which so many dread to think of. Sometimes I have been present when some of his Catholic friends visited him[52] and attempted to annihilate him, and although you may look upon us as sedate and pious spirits, yet we enjoyed the encounter very much, and especially when we saw that these priests were worsted and lost all the fighting blood, as you may say.

While I did not know him on earth, yet I feel that I know him very well now, and I desire to tell him that he is doing a wonderful and exceptional work, and one that is doing and has done much good among these priest-ridden people. He may not know, but it is a fact that when he enters into these controversies with the priests, that they are not the only spirits present, for many of their followers accompany them to see

---

[52] Eugene Morgan was the medium who was selected by Jesus in helping dark spirits. (J.P.G.)

the enemy of their church annihilated; and they hear what may be said and see the results, and, as a consequence, many of them are caused to think and seek the help of the numerous high spirits who are always present, ready to give the help that they need; and many of these followers are, by the means mentioned, rescued from their purgatory and erroneous beliefs. I should like to write more on this subject and describe the actual scenes that accompany his encounters with these priests, if only to encourage him, but I cannot do it tonight.

Well, Christmas will soon be here, and we have the Christmas feeling, but it is not exactly as you have it on earth. We have the actual visible presence of Jesus and feel his love, and know that he was born and is now the living, loving, all-embracing Christ in his teachings and manifestations of the Father's Love. I wish you and your friend and Dr. Stone a merry Christmas, and desire to tell you that many of your spirit friends will spend the day with you and bring as presents their love and prayers and best wishes for your happiness.

Good night, old friend, and God bless you,
Syrick.

Helen is glad that the Judge wrote

December 21st, 1917.

I am here, your own true and loving Helen.

Well, dear, I am glad that the Judge wrote you tonight, as you had not heard from him for some time, and he was very anxious to write. He is very happy and is progressing, and with his Rose, enjoys bliss to the fullest.

The other spirits actually wrote, and the young mother is now a very beautiful spirit and feels a great sympathy for all mothers who die as their babies come into life. I will not write more now. So love me and pray to the Father with all your soul and longings for His love.

Your own true and loving,
Helen.

Helen came to her husband's call

I am here, your own loving Helen.

I heard your call and, of course, responded, but there was a poor dark spirit who wanted to write. White Eagle explained to him that it is not permitted for him to write at this time, and that he must not try, and the spirit left.

Well, I see that you are very sleepy, and I will not write more tonight.

I am happy and progressing, and love you with all my heart and soul and want you to love me.

So, with my kiss, I will say good night.

Your own true and loving

Helen.

Mary wrote through Eugene Morgan, selected by Jesus, like Mr. Padgett and Dr. Stone, to work in behalf of the Kingdom, and urges her soulmate, Leslie, to continue in this work

I am here, the soulmate of the Doctor.

I am not going to write of the things pertaining to love and romance, for I know that you are a hardhearted old bachelor, who doesn't take interest in such things. I will only write of practical things and tell him that he is doing much good over here in his talks to those he comes in contact with as to the Divine Love. We are thereby enabled to get in rapport with many of them; and as a result have caused the awakening of a large number of them; so he must continue in this work, for though it is not the work that has been assigned to him, yet, when the opportunity comes he must avail himself of it, for the purpose of all work is the salvation of souls, and when this can be accomplished, it matters little what the means employed, whether in line of the work assigned or not.

I said that I would not inject sentiment in this communication and gave my reasons, but on second thought I will ask your indulgence that I may be permitted to say to him, that he is my own true love and sweetheart, and that all the longings of my soul are for the time when we shall once more be united, never again to part throughout all eternity.

I will not write more, but thanking you for this opportunity, and to you all extending my best love.

Will close,

Mary.

Celestial Spirits

Ascension of Jesus the Christ greeted by Celestial Spirits called angels.

There is no indication of the source of this image.

This section is entitled "Celestial Spirits" yet it includes messages from many spirits who are not technically "Celestial" —that is, those residing beyond the Seventh Spirit Sphere indeed some are in fact "dark" spirits—those residing in the hells. (G.J.C.)

Has written about a visit to a medium, although the spiritual forces were not too good, but the message from a four year child, Rosebud, that was attracted to Mr. Padgett and came home with him to tell him was absolutely true

October 28th, 1915.

I am here, John.

Yes, I want to tell you that the influences were not good, and some of these spirits came home with you and tried to write. But they have gone now, and I will write a while. I was present, and heard what the medium said to you and what she said was true, for the spirits that she described came to you and wanted to make known their presence. I did not know them, but I ascertained who they were, and the Sarah that the medium spoke of says that she was the Cousin Sally who wrote you some nights ago.

The description of her funeral was correct, for she was buried in the little village where she lived and which you know the name of. She was attracted to you because of her having met you at the time of her writing, and she has been with you quite often since, so she says. I only know what she told me.

The little child was not a relative, but a bright little spirit who was attracted to you and wanted to let you know that she was present. I do not know her name, but she was about four years old as you would say. She is here now and says that she wants to tell you that she came, because she saw that you must be good and love little children. She says her name is Rosebud that she has no other name, and she died when she was only a few days old, and never had any name. So you see, the children love you and you can have no better sign of your love nature than that. I don't know who the James was as he left soon after the medium spoke of him.

Now, all this is very pleasant for these spirits, but it does not do you any good, and I would advise that you do not attend that church very often. The mixture of spirits is so great that undesirable influences are present and necessarily affect your aura and the conditions that bring us in rapport. Of course, you may go occasionally, but if you want to go to church on Sunday night go to some of the churches where there is more of the Divine Love present. I mean some of the Protestant churches where you will listen to songs that have in them thoughts which ascend to the Father of Love, and where the preaching is such that the soul qualities will be appealed to. The spiritualist church has not much of the Divine Love in the hearts of its people, nor do the speakers say things or give out thoughts which tend to elevate the soul or satisfy its longings.

I would like to write you a message tonight on the subject of these soul qualities, but there are others here who want to write and I must postpone my message on that subject.

But I will say that without prayer to the Father and faith, there cannot be much progression in the development of the soul. If only men would understand this and offer their prayers to the Father instead of to the spirits and the unknown forces and friends who have recently passed to the spirit life, they would find a very different and wonderful result.

I am with you very often, trying to help you both materially and spiritually, and you are progressing, and your worries will soon leave you. So only trust and believe.

I will not write more tonight.

Your brother in Christ,

John.

Comments on a preacher's sermon and advises Mr. Padgett to cultivate the friendship of this preacher in order to help him to better understand the Truth

October 12th, 1916.

I am here, Luke.

I will say only a few words tonight. I have heard the preacher's (Rev. J. S. Gordon) remarks and your conversation regarding the same. Well, the preacher as you say, is broader-minded than most orthodox preachers and has some knowledge of spiritualism, yet intellectually he believes in the trinity and vicarious atonement and some other of the fundamental doctrines of the church. He has in his soul considerable Divine Love without knowing just what this love means, except that from its possession he experiences a wonderful happiness and a consciousness that God is close to him in His Love. He has not formulated these feelings of his soul into mental beliefs, but his realization of the presence of the Love comes to him notwithstanding the intellectual drawbacks which, in a degree, retard the growth of his soul. But, as he says, he rests more upon the unconscious knowledge, if I may call it such, of his possession, and the actual living, working presence of this Love, than upon the beliefs in these dogmas of the church.

He has a comparatively open mind, but as he believes so implicitly in the Bible, he has not yet found any evidence in other writings or books or teachings, sufficiently strong to cause him to renounce his beliefs in the Bible teachings. But should he find such evidence he would not hesitate to change his beliefs in these things for what might appear to him to be the truth. He is not one of the iron-bound believers in the church dogmas or ecclesiastical interpretations and constructions of the declarations of the Bible, so that under all circumstances, and in spite of truths that might otherwise come to him, he would say a thing is true just because it is in the Bible. He will grow in freedom and knowledge, and it may be well for you to get acquainted with him, and gradually declare to him the truths as we have explained them to you.

It is not necessary for me to comment on a particular thing that he preached, for some things that he said are true and some things are not. I am glad that you three (Dr. Leslie R. Stone, Eugene Morgan and James E. Padgett) are so interested in these matters as to cause you to listen to the thoughts that the preacher expresses, and to comment upon and analyze them. It will do you good and develop in you a large understanding of what we have been writing you. The argument of contrast is sometimes a very powerful and discriminating one, and I would advise you to attend his discourses, whenever you feel that he intends to preach upon a subject that may affect or in any way relate to the truths in which you are interested.

Give my love to your friends and tell them to believe and pray and especially pray, for thereby will light and knowledge and faith come to them.

I will say good night and leave you my blessing.

Your brother in Christ,

Luke.[53]

Wants Mr. Padgett to obtain more faith and love of the Father and that he is with him often trying to help him

August 8th, 1915.

I am here, Saint Peter.

I want to tell you that you are very near the Father tonight and that His Love is filling your soul to a great degree. I see that you are anxious to learn of the spiritual things of the Father and of His Love

---

[53] This message is a composite of two, being published twice in Volume IV. The second instance has been removed in this edition. (G.J.C.)

towards you and all mankind.

You must pray for more faith and trust implicitly in His promises, and in the promises of the Master, for they will be fulfilled and you will not be disappointed or left to yourself. I am with you quite often now, for I want to assist in the great work that Master has chosen you to do; and you must get into a condition that will enable you to do this work in the greatest perfection. Your soul must be developed with this Divine Love of the Father, so that you will be in accord with the Master when he writes, for unless there is such accord you will not be able to get the spiritual meanings of his messages as he wants you to do.

There is nothing that will cause this development as well as earnest, sincere prayer to the Father. With such prayer will come faith, and with faith will come the Substance of what you may now only believe. So pray often, believing that the Love of the Father will come to you and you will realize your oneness with Him.

I am so much interested in you and your soul development that I am going to help you with all my love and power. Let not the things of the world distract your attention from these spiritual necessities, and you will find that all these material things will be supplied you. Be firm and courageous in your beliefs and professings and God will be with you in every hour of trial and distress. This I know and tell you as one having knowledge. I want you to let your faith increase until doubt shall flee away, and only trust in the Love and goodness of God remain with you. I will not write more tonight.

So with all my love and blessings I am your own friend and brother in Christ,

St. Peter.[54]

A follower of Zoroaster overheard previous conversations and since he does not know about the New Birth, would like to learn

August 20th, 1915.

I am here, Aleyabis.

Let me write. I have been listening to those who have preceded me, and I am interested in what they have said.

I know nothing about this New Birth, and although I have lived in the spirit world a long time and in great happiness, yet I have never before heard of the doctrine.

I feel like the Turk, in that if there be any truth in this doctrine, I

---

[54] This message is a composite of two, being published in Volume II and Volume IV. (G.J.C.)

would like to learn what it means. Of course to learn I will have to make investigation and to do so I must get a starting point; and if you can show me how I may come in contact with anything that may assist me in my investigation, I will be obliged to you.

I am a Persian and was named Aleyabis. I lived four thousand years ago, and was and am a follower of Zoroaster, the divine teacher of God. I am living in the highest spheres where the followers of our teacher live. We are not in the same heaven with the spirits of other beliefs, but have a heaven all to ourselves; although I sometimes come in contact with spirits from these other heavens.

Sometimes I come in contact with the Christian spirits and talk to them, but we do not discuss our doctrines, because we each so firmly believe in the truth of our respective beliefs, that no good would come of any discussion as to their relative merits.

I see a great many spirits around you, and some are very beautiful and bright, more so than I have seen before, and also seem to have much love in their being.

She is here and says she will be pleased to show me the way to start in my investigations, and I will accept her kind offer.

I will come to you again sometime and tell you the result of my investigation.

Your friend,
Aleyabis.

Writes of his progress to the fourth sphere

February 25th, 1917.

I am here, Raleigh. I am Lord Walter Raleigh, the Englishman, who loved and was beheaded.

Well, I have heard what the last spirit wrote and merely wish to say that the tenor of his discourse is wise and should be followed; but, as he says, there is no way to make it known to the men whom it is intended for, and who only can apply it.

I am also interested in the war, as you may suppose, to some extent, but only because the country to which I once owed allegiance and claimed the protection of is now a very great sufferer by reason of the efforts that are now being made to subdue her. But yet, my interest is not very great, for I have arrived at that condition of brotherly love and the true conception of right and wrong and of the certain destiny of men, that all are my brothers; and the name of Englishman, German, or Frenchman makes no difference in their destinies.

The human soul, when it comes to the spirit world, is without nationality, and the destiny of that soul does not depend upon the fact that it was lodged in the form of an Englishman, etc. No, the thoughts of earth, to a large extent, have left me and I am intent on my progress in the spirit world and attaining to that condition which will bring me the most happiness and enable me to do the most good to my fellow spirits, for I am working to help those who are not in such favorable condition as I am.

I live in the Fourth Sphere and am a quite happy spirit, surrounded by many things that make me happy and contented, and am free from all those things that caused me worry and sufferings while on earth. I have lost all my recollections of the acts and deeds, and even thoughts, of my earth life that caused me so much darkness and unhappiness when I first came to the spirit land: but you must not think that it was an easy thing to get rid of these recollections, for I tell you that they clung to me like leeches and seemed to draw from me all my heart's blood, if I may so express it.

The hells of those who have led lives of wrong or injustice are not imaginary, and all who think that the stories of such hells are the idle tales of superstitious mortals will be greatly surprised when they have shuffled off the mortal coils. But, as I say, I have progressed out of my dark condition and am now in the light, and quite happy in my pursuits that so much appeal to me.

No, I do not know that such is the fact, and can scarcely conceive that you can know what you say to be true. Of course, if such things are true, I should like to become conscious of the fact and join in the search of discovery, but I doubt that you have knowledge on the subject. Yes, I should like to make the experiment, and am willing to do so in seriousness and with a mind open for conviction.

Well, I see a great many spirits present—some bright and some dark, but none preeminently bright or beautiful as you suppose may be here. I have done as you suggested, and one comes and says he is Mr. Riddle, and I must say that he is a wonderfully bright spirit, and has an appearance that is different from the appearance of those spirits that I see in the Fourth Sphere.

Well, I have heard what you said to him and I will go with him and listen to what he has to say in reference to the subject matter of our conversation; but I doubt that he can tell me anything that is an improvement on what I already know. But as I told you, I will listen in seriousness and consider what he may say to me.

So, thanking you for your kindness, I will say good night.

Raleigh.

Jesus says: Eugene Morgan is a very spiritual man

October 30th, 1915.

I am here, Jesus.

I only wish to say that I am glad that the mother of your friend (Eugene Morgan) wrote to him tonight, because I have been interested in him for a little while past, and so much desire that he shall learn the truth. He is naturally a spiritual man, and the long years of his lonesome life have been filled with thoughts and ideas that did not tend to fit him for an entrance into the spirit world; and his awakening will be very beneficial to him and will result, as I see, in his seeking for the Divine Love of the Father and his salvation from error and acts that would only tend to keep him in a state of darkness, both in earth and in the spirit world. And when I say darkness, I mean it in the sense of the want of the proper understanding and experiences of the truths of what will make him a man of light as regards his soul perceptions in the earth life; and in the spirit world, both that kind of darkness and actual darkness, meaning an absence of light, for spirits who come to the spirit world undeveloped are not only in a condition of darkness, but in a place of darkness as well.

His mother wrote him a beautiful and loving letter, and if he could have seen her while she was writing, he would be convinced that she was not only his mother, but a mother whose heart is overflowing with love for him.

Although I am the Jesus whom many worship as God—but I am not—and although I am the most developed spirit in the Celestial Heavens, and have such powers as no other spirit has, yet to me each child of God is precious and the object of my love and care; and when I have the opportunity of coming in sensitive, positive contact with a mortal, as I have with him by reason of his being here with you and being in an atmosphere which enables us to communicate our desires and loves to that mortal, I do not think that, because of my exalted position as a spirit and child of the Father, I must not come to the mortal and let him know that I am interested in him and want him to seek the Divine Love of the Father.

No mortal is so insignificant or so unimportant that I will not seek him as an individual and let him know that I am interested in him and that my love is with him, trying to bring him into reconciliation with the Father. So let your friend know that he has a brother and friend in Jesus, and that his happiness is the happiness of his brother.

I write in this way tonight because I want to see this man a redeemed son of the Father, and a possessor of that Great Love that will make him happy on earth, and happier when he comes to the spirit world. To me, every mortal who is not in the fold of God's children is that one who went astray, and to find whom I left the ninety and nine.

You, my dear brother, will understand this, and you can help your brother—and many brothers—to learn the great truths of their souls' salvation and their spiritual progression.

I will not write more tonight, as you are tired, though you may not realize it.

So, with my love and blessings, I am

Your brother and friend,

Jesus.

Has chosen Mr. Eugene Morgan to do a work in reference to the spreading of the Truths

March 22nd, 1916.

I am here, Jesus.

I will give you the prayer very soon now, and you will receive with it a spiritual enlightenment of its meaning that will draw you very close to the Father and His Love.

(Refers now to Mr. Morgan.) Yes, I speak to him sometimes, and he hears my voice, and is not mistaken; but he must not think that all the impressions that he has are from the spirits, for such is not true. As he progresses in the development of clairaudience he will be able to distinguish between what comes to him from the spirits and what may arise in his own mind. He must not be discouraged or let doubt enter his soul, for his faith must be one of soul and not of mere mind.

I have selected him to do a work in reference to the spreading of my truths, and he must determine that his mission is one that will occupy his time during the balance of his earthly existence; and if he now draws back from this work he will lose a wonderful opportunity for helping mankind and for developing his own soul and fitting himself for a happy existence in the spirit world.

He has been favored as few mortals have been, or will be, and he must realize and appreciate that fact, for it is a fact, and only the Celestial spirits who are with me in this work know the importance of it. I am his friend and brother, as I have told him, and he has my love and influence as few mortals have ever had, and this because I know that he is a true man and will not fail me in what I wish to accomplish. I know that many times it has been said and written by mediums that I have come and written to them, but such is not the truth, and it is only since I have determined that you shall receive my written messages of the truth, have I come in such close contact with you. Often have I tried to influence them with my love and thoughts, but not for long years have I come in such close rapport as to have them receive my written messages or hear my voice audibly, as your friend has heard it, and will hear it in the future.

Yes, I have chosen him just as positively, and with the certainty as I chose my disciples when on earth; and I expect that he will follow me as faithfully as they followed me. As time passes the conviction will grow stronger and stronger that he has been selected for my work; and there will come to him a knowledge and power which he does not now realize, and which it is impossible for him at this time to understand.

After you and he have gotten in the condition when you can let your thoughts of earthly necessities cease to trouble you, and become in that state of mind and soul that will enable you to turn all your thoughts and longings to the Father and the work that He desires you both to do, there will come to you such a blessing from the Holy Spirit that will prove to you that the Pentecost of the days of my disciples has again been given to man to bless and make him pure and powerful, and the wonder of his fellow mortals.

I, Jesus, tell you this with the authority and knowledge that have been given me by the Father, and no man can gainsay it. I have spoken, and you both must believe.

So, my dear brother and friend and disciple, I will stop, and in doing so, say that you and your friend have the love and blessings of him who never makes a mistake or misleads his disciples in the things of the soul.

Good night.

Your brother and friend,

Jesus.

Confirms that the Master wrote and selected Mr. Morgan to do a work in reference to the spreading of his Truths

March 22nd, 1916.

I am here, your own true and loving Helen.

Oh, my dear one, what a message you had from the Master, and with what power and authority he wrote you! Again, he displayed that great glory of which I have written, and so grand and magnificent was his appearance that we could scarcely look upon him. He certainly was the son of the Father as he wrote to you and declared that you both were his disciples, and that power and great soul development would be given you.

And Ingersoll was present, and he stood in amazement, and almost adoration, as he saw the wondrous greatness and power of the Master. He says that no spirit can doubt that Jesus is the true son of God and the greatest of all the spirits in the Heavens; and that he feels that he is of such insignificance when he sees the glory displayed by the Master. He, Ingersoll, is so humble and so remorseful when he thinks of his days on earth, when he doubted that Jesus ever lived, and if he did, that, in his opinion, he was merely a good man and nothing more.

I tell you that the opportunities which we spirits have had—now three times—to see displayed this wonderful glory and power of Jesus, have made us all realize that the love of the Father which Jesus has is beyond all conception; and he tells us that such love may be ours if we will only strive and pray for it.

Oh, my dear, when I think of the great favor that has been bestowed upon you I thank the Father with all the capacity that I have. I am so happy! Some day you will be with me, and this happiness will be ours together.

Well, dear, this has been a glorious night, and I will not mar the happiness that comes to us by attempting to write of anything else.

So, with all my love and many kisses, I am,

Your own true and loving,

Helen.

Eugene Morgan's guardian angel tells of the great work he is doing among the dark Catholic spirits

May 14th, 1917.

I am here, Luke.

I want to take advantage of the opportunity to write while my dear and personal charge (Eugene Morgan) is present. As he knows, I have been with him a great deal, doing for him that which gives me great pleasure, and also helps him in his work of trying to convert some of the dark spirits who are living and suffering in the very erroneous beliefs that they had when on earth, and which, if they be left alone, will cause them to remain in their darkness for a time or times that cannot be determined.

I want further to say that he cannot possibly appreciate the work that he is doing, and its results upon these spirits who come to him, not for kindly purposes, but to pronounce upon him the anathemas (A formal ecclesiastical ban, curse, or ex-communication) of the church which they used when on earth to scare the unruly believers of their congregations. Of course, I refer to the priests of the Catholic Church, for they, of all the spirits in the spirit world, make the greatest efforts to keep their followers together, and with the greatest feelings of hatred and indignation resent any attempt to intrude upon and change the beliefs of these followers.

But I am glad that my charge does not become frightened or allow these priests to prevent him from doing his work, which is a wonderful work in this, that never before in all the history of the habitation of the Catholics and their deluded leaders in the Spirit World has any attempt by mortals been made to impinge upon the authority and domination of these priests, and consequently, he must not be surprised to know that his crusade, for I must call his efforts such, has started a very considerable commotion among these blind followers and their blind leaders; and more especially is this the case when it is known to be a fact that many of these Catholics have been shown the way to light and have embraced the opportunity to follow the instructions and teachings given them and get out of their darkness and away from the folds of these priests.

He is doing a great work and must persevere, for if he has been the means of saving only one of these poor benighted spirits he has done a work greater than that of conquering a city, as the Bible says. But he has shown not only one to the light and truth, but many, and those thus saved from their darkness and suffering have taught others the way, and the work thus started by him goes on in almost geometrical progression. No man before has done this work among the spirits of that faith, and when it is considered that there are myriads of them, it can be appreciated what the possibilities are for an earnest worker in the way of changing a sinful and benighted and satisfied (?) soul in sin into a spirit of light and happiness.

And I want further to tell him that this work of his is becoming noised (to make something generally known) all through the host of Catholic followers, and many are asking about its effect upon the congregations of the faithful, and many also have become dissatisfied with their condition and commenced to doubt the truths of the teachings of the priests and their promises of salvation through the prayers and masses, and are commencing to make inquiry as to where this mortal can be found and how he may be reached. Now, what I have written you is a fact, for I visit these spheres where these spirits live and hear what is said among them, and know that the efforts that my charge has made to help these dark Catholic spirits who have come to him have resulted in good.

Well, I could continue much longer my description of what effect his work has had upon these spirits of darkness and delusion, but will not do so tonight. Now, I want to say a few personal words to him. As he knows, I am praying for him and am interested in his every thought as to spiritual matters, and am with him in times of doubt and loss of faith, trying to encourage him. And I want to say that he must not lose faith or doubt what we have written him or the truth that he has received in his soul the Divine Love to a great degree, and that if he will continue to pray he will receive more and more, and after a time his faith will become so strong that it will almost be impossible for him to doubt and he will then realize the meaning of faith as the Master defined it; all the aspirations of his soul will become things of real existence.

He is blessed among mortals, for there are very few who have with them the association and rapport of the high spirits, as he has, and when it is understood what this means, it will be seen that he enjoys that which the civilized world among its church members pray for continually and yet never realize, as he does, palpably and unmistakably, the presence of these high spirits and the sensible presence of their love, and even that of the highest and greatest of all spirits—the Master.

I am so anxious that he shall realize all the privileges and blessings that have been bestowed upon him, for I want him to develop his soul and permit me to come into a higher and closer rapport, which only the greater development of his soul will bring about.

I will not write more tonight, as I see that you are somewhat tired, but in closing permit me to say that I most earnestly desire that he shall realize who and what I am, and how much I want him to understand that I am his own Guardian Angel, with a duty that only my love makes it pleasurable for me to perform, and that so long as he shall live as a mortal I will be with him, and as time goes by will get in closer rapport with him, which will result in his powers increasing more and more until, before the time comes for him to perform the great work that has been given him to do, he will be in that condition that will enable him to do it successfully to the glory of the Father and the salvation of mankind.

You may wonder that I write so enthusiastically tonight, but when you come to realize the great work that is to be done and that I know to the fullest extent what it means, and the further fact that I have in my soul the Great Divine Love of the Father to a degree that not many of the Celestial Spirits have, you will not wonder.

So, believe me and trust me, and know without doubt that I love you both with a more than brother's love. May the Father bless and keep you both in His care. Pray and pray, and believe. good night,

Your brother in Christ,

Luke.

Eugene Morgan's mother tells of her Mother's love, his soulmate's love, and the Divine Love of the Father

October 30th, 1915.

I am here, mother of Eugene Morgan (who is sitting opposite you):

I heard him express the desire today that I would write to him, and I then determined that I would come with him to your room tonight and gratify his wish. Your band consents that I should write, and are helping me in the way of lending me their rapport, and hence I write so easily, as you may see.

Tell him that I am so glad that he has commenced to awaken to the truths of spiritualism, and that if he will only continue his investigations he will not only ultimately believe in its truths, but will find the greatest satisfaction, and the longings of his soul will be realized.

Many and many times have I been with him, hoping and praying that his mind would be opened to the truths which spiritualism teaches, and that as a result thereof his soul faculties would be opened to the greatest truths which affect his eternal happiness in not only this life but in the great life to come. I, as his mother, have prayed for all this, and now I thank God that I can see that my long-wished-for hope will likely be fulfilled.

I am very happy, and am a Christian, as he knows I was when on earth; but I am not exactly the same kind of Christian. Then I believed in the doctrines of the church as to the ceremonies and formalities that were imposed upon me to follow and abide by, more than in the soul's real religion. Now I see that these formalities were nothing; that the true soul religion determines and brings to us the great happiness which the Father has provided for us.

I will not leave him until he shall come to the spirit world; and I don't mean to say that that will be very soon, but no matter how long he may remain on earth I will stay with him and give him the great mother love which he never received in a very demonstrative way when I lived. But he is my boy and it seems to me that my love for him is without limit or extent. So he must believe that I am with him and in return think of me often and let his love for me flow to me sometimes, and try to feel that the love of his mother is responding to him.

I am in the Fifth Sphere and am among the redeemed of the Father, with only the Divine Love in my soul; and if I could only tell him what this means, all his doubts would flee from him and he would thank God with all his heart that he had been awakened to some realization that there is such a thing as the future life, and a God, and a great overwhelming and all-pervading Love waiting for him to make him happy and to become one with the Father.

His father is here, too, but he is not so much developed as am I, for he was not on earth a very serious believer in the things of the soul; but now, thank God, he has had his awakening and is trying to obtain that Love and to progress to the higher spheres and so, ultimately, be with me; for I must tell my son, notwithstanding the fact that he doubts or cannot exactly realize the existence or meaning of soulmates that his father and I are soulmates, and are more happy in our love than ever we were in earth life.

And there is another thing that I want to tell him, and that is that he has a soulmate, too, and she is here, and lives in the same sphere with me. She wrote him a few nights ago, and while I see that he may doubt the reality of her existence here, yet I want to tell him with all the love and interest that his mother has in him, that she is a real existing being, with all the substance and reality that he can imagine a human sweetheart to have, whom he had never seen. Yes, his Clara is here, and is with him oftener than he can conceive of, and is loving him with a love that even his mother's love cannot compare with.

Tell him that I will come again soon and write him, and more in detail, but tonight I am so full of love and so thankful that I can express it to him that I can scarcely think of anything else. Love, Love, Love is the burden of my message tonight and he must think and learn and know that his mother's love, his soulmate's love, and the Divine Love of the Father are the three greatest things in all God's universe, but in their reverse importance.

I must stop, though it is hard to do so. I want to thank you for your kindness in receiving my message, and trust that you will continue to show my boy the way to a realization of the truth in this great and most important Truth of spiritualism.

I will again tell him that I love him, and say good night.

Mother of Eugene Morgan.

Comments on message by Eugene Morgan's mother

October 30th, 1915.

I am here, Helen.

Well, my dear old Ned, what beautiful and wonderful messages you have received tonight.

Mr. Morgan's mother wrote him a most motherly letter, and her whole soul was in her expressions of love to him. And then when the Master came and told of his great interest in and love for him, it was so astonishing and unusual that we had to look on in wonder and almost adoration. To think that the greatest spirit in all the Celestial Heavens, and he who is the best beloved son of the Father, should come and in such loving words tell your friend that he is the object of his interest and love.

Well, Sweetheart, I will not write more tonight, as I see you are tired.

Your true and loving,

Helen.

Dr. Stone and Eugene Morgan have a great deal of love in their souls

November 4th, 1916.

I am here, John.

I merely want to say that what the Master and I said a few nights ago to Dr. Stone applies to your friend who is with you now, and he must realize the fact; and I wish he would take a copy of the writings and insert his name wherever that of the Doctor occurs.

He has more of this Love in his soul than he realizes, and although at times he has some doubts, and the Love seems to be dormant, yet it is there, and he must not lose faith in the fact. As long as he is a mortal these times of doubt and want of feeling of the presence of the Love will come to him, but he must not let this discourage him, for as certainly as the sun shines he has fought the battle of the soul and has come out victor, and he is now an accepted son of the Father. I would not tell him this if I did not see the condition of his soul and the presence of the Love resting and living in it.

We have all been much interested in his transformation because of the difficulty that has attended his fight—greater than he may conceive of. And when he commenced to get into that condition of awakening, he had the assistance of many more of the higher spirits than he has been informed of, for we left him alone scarcely any of the time when the change was taking place. And besides, he was so unfortunate as to have around him some very evil spirits who had such a hold upon him that it was not an easy work to cause them to leave him. Of course, we could have dispersed them without any difficulty by the mere exercise of our will, but that was not the desirable or effective way of ridding him of these incubi, for whenever we should leave him they would return to him and his condition become much worse than before. And consequently, the only effective way—and the one that was pursued, and the only one that can be with certain and lasting results pursued—was to have his soul develop, so that in itself it would possess that power that would cause these spirits to leave him and render him innocuous to their influences, whether we were present or not. And in this we were successful. And all this means that our work was simply to turn his thoughts to the Father and to cause him to have faith in prayer; for when all is said, it was the result of prayer that brought the Divine Love which made him able, because of his own soul's power, to disperse and keep from him these evil spirits.

And in this I do not intend to be understood as meaning that he was relieved from the presence of these spirits in the way of attempting to communicate with him, for that amounts to very little as regards his soul condition; but I do mean that the influence of these spirits on the condition of his soul became of no effect, and that they could not, after he received this power, affect the transformation and growth of his soul. As long as he, or any other mortal, remains mortal, he will be visited at times by some of these undesirable spirits, and will feel their influence in a spiritual sense; but they will never have any power to swerve his soul from its progression to the higher development. The fight, of course, will continue all through the earth life, and at times the influence of these spirits upon his mental faculties and animal appetites may tend, for the time being, to retard or hold still the progress of his soul development; but, directly, these evil influences can never have any effect upon the condition or qualities of his soul.

I want him to fully grasp the meaning of what I have written and in the future, no matter how discouraged he may feel or how much his mentality may suggest the existence of things in him that are injuring his soul or taking from it the presence of possession of this Divine Love, he must believe what I have told him and that he has fought the battle of the soul and won, and that this Love is his and cannot be taken from him by the wiles of Satan, as the preachers say. It may lie dormant to his consciousness, and the happiness that arises from its active existence may seem to leave him; yet the Love is there and will assert itself. Temptations will come to him, and he must continue to fight—not to keep the Love, but to prevent the Love from becoming dormant and the happiness from disappearing. He has had his resurrection from death to life, and he cannot die again. I would like to write longer, but others desire to write and I must stop. So, with my love and blessings on you both, I will say good night.

Your brother in Christ,
John.

Grandfather and father helped Eugene Morgan's spiritual development

November 4th, 1916

I am here, the grandfather of Eugene.

I was his father's father, and died ever so many years ago. I am in the Celestial Heavens, for many years ago I learned the way to the Heaven of the soul. I have been interested in my grandson's experience, and have been with him on many occasions, trying to influence him with my prayers and love. And in the spirit world I have been with his father, attempting to show him the Truth, and to some extent I succeeded; but strange as it may seem to you both, this influence that I speak of has never been so effective as since the time when Eugene's father came in rapport with him so that he could write through him and speak to his inner ear. There is something so mysterious about the effect that the rapport with the human has on the mortal in the way of helping the spirit to progress, that we who are of the higher spheres cannot fully understand it.

But the fact remains that since the time his father first came in rapport with him, the father has made more soul development than in all the years before. The influence of spirit upon spirit seemed to increase, so that the one in the lower condition would listen, and strive to progress. These things are wonderful, even to us, and I realize more clearly since the experience of my grandson commenced, the great work that mortals may do among spirits, when the mortal has in him that which is able to awaken the spirit to a realization of his true condition.

I have been with all the family that I left behind, and have seen, and now see, the great difference in their condition of soul and estate, and why such differences should exist is to me not clearly understood. Of course, my love to all was the same and my desire that everyone should progress equally was impartial; but yet, the fact is that equal progress was not made.

I was so glad when I heard John deliver the message that you have just received. Of course, I know the fact, but it is so satisfying to have my grandson told the truth by a spirit of such high estate and development as is John. Tell my boy to read the message and understand its full significance, and he will then possess a knowledge that will help him in many difficulties that he will encounter in his earth life.

I am often with him and with his sisters who are in the spirit world, and they are very happy, and he may become so, too, even while on earth. Of course, my home is in a higher plane than those of his sisters or parents, and our attractions are somewhat different and I am not with them so often as he may suppose; but I love them very much and am with them whenever I see that I can help them with my love or influence.

Our love for our children remains with us a long time after we become spirits, and I have not yet realized that it has left me, but it grows weaker as the space between us in our soul development widens, and the laws of attraction carry our affections to others who are more nearly like us in our development. This I am told is the experience of many who have lived in the spirit life for a long time, and to a certain extent I feel it myself; but, strange as it may appear, this law does not seem to apply between the spirit, no matter how great its development, and a mortal relative. And so it should be.

Hence, my interest in my grandson is just as great as it could be, and in all my progression there has been a love in my being that has drawn me to him and caused me to look after and pray for his welfare.

I write thus tonight, because I desire him to know something of spirit laws that he may not know, and to assure him that though he may not have any remembrance of me as the earthly grandfather, yet to me he is as dear as if I had left the earth and him yesterday. Of course, the time will come when we may have no recollection or memory of each other and our love become a misty dream, but as long as he continues on earth he will remain the child of my care and love.

Well, I have written enough, and must stop. So with my love to him, and the blessings of God on you both, I will say good night.

Eugene Morgan's grandfather.

Eugene Morgan's sister is happy that Eugene has received the Great Love of the Father

November 4th, 1916.

I am here, your own dear, loving sister (of Eugene).

I have never written before. I want to say a word and tell him how happy I am, and largely because I realize that he has received the Great Love of the Father in his soul. Oh, I cannot express my feelings, as I am now writing for the first time, but he must try to understand what I would desire to say if I had the ability to express myself.

We are all very happy, and especially mother, and as she listened to John writing his message she became so overcome with her emotions that she could scarcely breathe, as you would say. She was so happy, and praised the Father with all her soul's thankfulness, and cried in joy big tears of happiness and love. And so were we all so very happy.

We are all progressing very rapidly, and our cousin who has so recently come to us, and whom Eugene is so much interested in and has helped so much, is progressing also, and is in the Third Sphere—a marvelous evidence of progress in so short a time. But she is so earnest in her seeking, and as I sometimes tell her in joke, for fear that her Catholic friends will take her back to count her beads and worship the saints, and believe what the priests tell her, that she seems to never tire of praying and reaching out in her soul's longings for the great things that are ahead for her to obtain, as some of the higher spirits have told her.

It is wonderful, and if my dear brother could only see how much he has helped her, he would never, for one moment, doubt the reality of this Love, which he spoke to her so often about, even though it apparently, at the time, made no impression. We all send him our love and want him to know that we are with him, trying to help him in every way, spiritually and materially, and when I say this I speak for the whole family.

As this is my first attempt at writing, I am a little tired and must stop; but as I have made a first effort, I should like to come sometime and write him a longer letter. So, thanking you, I will say good night. I am the sister that he used to think was so loving to him, and careful of his wants.

Eugene Morgan's sister.

Has written about the great powers that are behind Mr. Padgett to fulfill all his wishes which was further encouraged by Leslie's mother, his Sister Kate, Prof. Salyards, Elizabeth Barret Browning, and his wife, Helen

January 7th, 1916.

I am here, John.

Well, I came to write only a few lines as you are not feeling too well and not in condition to receive any formal message tonight. But I will say that notwithstanding what you have read tonight in reference to your material affairs you must have faith and expect that our promises will soon be realized. The work must be done and you must be placed in condition to do it without interference. If you could realize the powers that are at work in their endeavor to bring about what is necessary to place you in condition to do this work as we desire it to be done, you would not lose faith or doubt that all the promises made will be fulfilled. We recognize to the fullest the importance of this matter and we will not permit much more time to elapse until the end desired is brought about.

You and your friend who is interested in the means that we have adopted for bringing the consummation of our plans will soon be enabled to start the business that we have told you of, and you must both have faith.

I will not write more tonight and with my love to you and your friend, who is present, I will say good night and God bless you both.

Your brother in Christ,
John.

Tells Mr. Padgett about the inner beliefs and the mind of a Washington Methodist preacher and advises him to talk to the preacher with regard to the Plan of Salvation as revealed in the messages

July 3rd, 1917.

I am here, Paul.

Let me write a few lines, as I desire to say a word about the condition of the man to whom you were talking a short time ago on matters connected with your work and the messages that you are receiving. I mean the Methodist preacher. (Dr. Mitchell)

As you may judge from his conversation, his mind is open to the reception of the truth, and his beliefs in the dogmas of the Bible teachings are not such as to cause him to be unduly biased, so that if the truth be presented to him with any degree of reasonable force he will give consideration to the same. Of course, he is an orthodox in the way of believing in the plan of salvation provided by God, as recognized and enunciated by the creeds of the churches, and to him Jesus is God, and his sacrifice and vicarious atonement are truths vital to the salvation of mankind; and that the man who does not believe in these necessary prerequisites cannot possibly become reconciled to God or be at-one with Him. To him, Jesus is God, and the only savior of men, and without Him (Jesus in this sense) it is not possible for man to escape the great condemnation.

Now, while all this is true as regards the preacher's belief, yet he does not believe positively that the man who dies in his sins, as the churchmen term it, will be condemned to a separation from God for all eternity. His belief on this question is not fixed, and his love for mankind creates in him a hope that this may not be so, and that some means will be provided by which such an awful condemnation will not be imposed on men.

He has in his soul much of the Divine Love, without having the consciousness that this is a separate and distinct Love from the natural love that has been to some extent purified. In fact, he has no conception of any Love of God other than the love that was given to men at the time of the creation of the first parents, and which every human being born since that time has received, although it has become defiled by sin and error and the willfulness of man. He believes that man, by the operation of the Holy Spirit, is cleansed of this defilement of the love with which he was endowed, and by the atonement of Jesus is brought into a state of reconciliation with the Father, and no other or different love is necessary for the redemption of the fallen human. That Jesus, by his sacrifice, is all that is required; and when a mortal, by his belief and acceptance of that sacrifice, receives Jesus into his life and nature, he becomes a redeemed child of God.

Of course, he cannot fully understand just the method by which this change is brought about. He believes that there is something mysterious connected with the manner in which the resultant condition of goodness and purification and the change of the vile man into an angel, which flows from the sacrifice and acceptance and belief, yet the man is so changed, and the manner thereof is known to God, and it is not

165

necessary for man to understand. This is a path which does not demand knowledge, a mystery of God which need not be inquired into; only "believe on the Lord, Jesus Christ, and ye shall be saved." I say that this belief is his and is sufficient for him, and in it he rests securely.

Well, he is comparatively happy in his belief, and is willing to retain it, for, as he sometimes thinks, if he renounces it, where and unto what shall he go? He can see nothing to take its place, and he is wise not to give it up. For in Jesus is salvation, when Jesus is correctly understood; and as the preacher turns his thoughts to Jesus and sends forth his soul's longings to the Master and what he represents, his soul at times catches a true conception of the very Jesus, although this conception does not agree with and is not the same thing as his intellectual comprehension of the Jesus of the Bible as interpreted by the creeds.

I am glad that you had the conversation with him, and I believe that as he listens to the unfoldment of the truths, as contained in the messages, his mind will take on a new and true conception of the truth, and his soul open up to a greater inflowing of the Love that will make him at-one with the Father, and transform that soul into the very substance of the Father's Divinity in Love.

I would advise you to present these truths to him, for he is an important factor in the work of man's salvation, when it is considered that one soul is of more worth than the whole world. He has the opportunity to show the way to salvation to many souls by the preaching of the truth, and any personal sacrifice which may come to him as a result of learning and believing the truths is not to be considered. While his material happiness on earth is to be considered and not thrown away whenever it is possible to retain it in connection with the teachings of the truth, yet his soul's happiness and that of many other souls are of more importance than the mere material happiness that arises from ignorance of the truth, or the living in that ignorance. So I say, let him know the truth no matter what the consequences may be, for in the end happiness will come to him, even on earth, as well as in the great eternity.

I will not write more now. So, with my love, I will say good night, and God bless you and the preacher, for I am interested in him, and in the future may possibly sustain a closer relation to him than is now possible by reason of his false beliefs and the want of the necessary rapport with him.

Your brother in Christ,
Paul.

Spiritualist teacher's lack of knowledge of the Truth. The importance of the Truth being made known to all souls

May 20th, 1917.

I am here, John Mark.

I will write a few lines and let you know that I have listened tonight to your comments on the book of the spiritualist teacher (Mr. Kates), and as I heard the Doctor read extracts and then your comments, I was convinced that the writer did not know very much about either the laws controlling what may be called the physical part of creation, or those controlling the spiritual existence and relationship of things spiritual. It is a pity that men in his position do not make an effort to learn more of the truths in reference to these things, for it is not necessary even that he should have a knowledge of the truths that have been conveyed to you, in order to learn many spiritual truths that would enable him to teach his followers those things that would advance them in the true knowledge of spiritualism.

I do not know the man personally, as I have never been in his society, and have, therefore, never had the opportunity to observe his condition of soul and mind, and what I say is based entirely on what I heard read and what was said in your conversation. But this great error I do know, and that is, that he is all wrong when he says there is no God in the universe, but some eternal force which he calls God. It is pitiable that his knowledge is so limited and that he attempts to teach others the truths of the spiritual universe. I will go some time when you visit him, to where he may be and learn just what his condition of soul and mind is, and then inform you, so that possibly you may do him some good in the way of teaching him the truth.

You may think it strange that I should write to you on this subject or think that his learning the truth is a thing of sufficient importance to give my attention to, as there are so many things to be written you, but I realize that he is in the position of a teacher of spiritualism and that he has the opportunity to influence a great many mortals who are seeking the truth, and who believe that he may be able to enlighten them. This is the only reason that prompted me to consume your time in this writing.

Of course, his soul is one of a million, and is no more valuable or precious in the sight of God than the soul of any other mortal, and to select his soul for a special effort of salvation would not justify me in ignoring others in the way of seeking them out or in permitting them to learn the truths from spirits who may be interested in them, using the privilege to communicate through you. But for the reason stated, I thought it advisable to suggest to you what I have written. This is all that

I can write tonight. So, believe that I am interested in your work although I do not come here very often.

I am, your brother in Christ,
John Mark.[55]

Urges Mr. Padgett to bring the message of Jesus on "The Soul," as well as the present message, to the spiritualist

May 20th, 1917.

I am here, Paul.

Well, my dear brother, I have not written for a long time, and I now will embrace the opportunity to say a few words. I do not intend to write a formal message, though I should like to do so, but conditions are not just right to enable me to write as I desire.

I have been present quite often when you were receiving messages from the other spirits and used my influence to make conditions favorable to your receiving these messages, and also to cause you to feel that there was surrounding you an atmosphere of Love and harmony that enabled you to enjoy not only the messages but the feelings of Love and benevolent influences that came to you.

While I have been listening tonight to your friend read extracts from the book (by Mr. Kate) and the comments that both made on the same, there was suggested to me a text upon which I will write, and that is the spirit and the spirit body as to their nature and creation. (This planned message was never delivered) I know that you have received writings dealing more or less with this subject, but I desire to enter more into detail in order to show that the writer of the book is all wrong in his conception of these things.

Of course, you will remember Jesus' message on "The Soul,"[56] and it will not be necessary for me to say anything about the soul; but you can read my message in connection with that message. As Mark has just written you, it is a great pity that a man in the position of a teacher of spiritualism should not know more of the truth so that he may disclose it to those who may listen to him and have confidence in his knowledge. And it may be that at some time you will have the opportunity to read both messages to him, and the result may be he will seek for the truth in the way that shall be pointed out, and when he does so in earnestness he will find it and make his find a blessing to many with whom he may come in contact.

---

[55] This message is a composite of two, being published twice in Volume IV. The second instance has not been included in this edition. (G.J.C.)
[56] This message is on page 101 in Volume I (5th Ed.) (G.J.C.)

It is very unfortunate that a leader of this great truth of spiritualism—and it is a truth and one that will ultimately supersede the old religions whenever it comes into contact or association with people who think for themselves—should have such little knowledge of what a true understanding of it would enable them to teach. We spirits have for a long time endeavored to enlighten these leaders and at times have been able to impress upon them some of the vital truths; but these efforts have not been very successful until now, when we are to deliver our messages through your writings. But this endeavor will become more and more earnest or successful in the future, and many of these people who are anxious to learn the true religion and are waiting only for some authoritative source will learn, and among them will be many leaders of what is now called Spiritualism.

The work is one that must become world-wide in its results, for the soul of every man on earth, no matter where he may be, is worthy to be saved; and, as you know, if the start towards regeneration can be made on earth, the progression in the spirit world will be so much more rapid. I know that the spread of the truth will take much time, but when the commencement is made the progress will become more rapid.

I do not think that I should write more tonight, and will only add that the evangelization must start very soon, and those who work to start the truth on its way to the knowledge of men must put all their energies and love into the work. You know that now there are very few—only three[57]—who have any conception of the truth and what the plan is for the making known of these truths to the world. Yet Christianity was started by only one besides the Master, I mean John the Baptist, and he, as I must tell you, did not have the knowledge of the truth as you three have this day, and did not have behind him the power of the Celestial Heavens, as you have. His mission was performed, and Christianity would have been a success if its truths had not become lost and perished by the acts of men who did not have in their souls the Love that has been given to you. The truths perished, and men perished as far as their souls' salvation was concerned, to a large extent.

But now these truths will not perish because they will be presented in living type, and no copying or recopying will be needed, and no addition will be made to, or anything taken away from the writings of the spirits who are now engaged in formulating these truths. It will not be a failure this time, and the way to the Kingdom of God in the Celestial Heavens will be made plain and no man will have an excuse for not walking therein. And those who do not will have a greater penalty to pay than was required of the Jews and pagans who lived in the time of Jesus, or who have lived since that time; for with increased opportunity to learn

---

[57] James E Padgett, Leslie R. Stone and Eugene Morgan. (J.P.G.)

the truth will come increased obligations, and the one who neglects will have that lost opportunity as a part of his consciousness, and this may be even after he becomes the perfect man, for I tell you here that the memory of man lasts even when the highest perfection is reached, as to those things which it is not necessary for him to lose in order for him to become the perfect man.

Well, you are tired, and I will not write more. So, with my love to yourself and your friend, I will say good night.

Your brother in Christ,

Paul.[58]

Describes the relationship that existed in his day between the laymen and the church officials

May 23rd, 1916.

I am here, Luther.

I came tonight in the hope that I may write my message of which I spoke to you a short time ago. Well, if you feel that you can receive the same, I will proceed.

In my day, the members of the Church—I mean the Roman Catholic Church—were dependent entirely upon the priesthood for all information as to the contents of the Bible, and the interpretation that should be given such contents, and very few of the laymen were able to possess the Bible, and scarcely any could read it, as it was written in the Latin tongue; and the inhabitants of my section of Europe were not acquainted with that language. (Martin Luther lived from 1483 to 1546.) The consequence of this was that all the people were dependent entirely on the priests for any knowledge of the Will of God, and that only as the priests saw proper to convey the same to these people.

Many things were taught by these officials of the Church in such a way as to convince the people that the Church was the divine institution of God; and that, in every particular, as to the conduct of men, what the priests said and declared to be the Will of God must be accepted without doubt or hesitation, and that the penalties of disobedience of these teachings of the priests would be in the form that they should prescribe, and that the wrath of God would fall upon all who should disobey these teachings of the Church.

The spiritual enlightenment of men was not attempted to any degree, and the requirements of the Church were that men should strictly obey the dogmas and tenets which should be declared to them by

---

[58] This message is a composite of two, being published twice in Volume IV. The second instance has not been included in this edition. (G.J.C.)

these instructions of the priests. Duty was the principal thing to be observed, and the utmost obedience to the commands of the Church must be performed, unless the Church itself should release the people from the performance of these duties.

Every violation of these commands was a sin, to which a penalty was attached which could not be avoided unless the priests should give to the believers an indulgence, and then to the extent of the indulgence the penalty was taken away. But in order to obtain this indulgence a compensation would have to be made to the coffers of the Church, depending upon the ability of the one receiving such indulgence to make. At a time when these indulgences were most prevalent, and when the Church was becoming rich from the revenues paid for the same, I commenced to revolt from the claims of the Church and declared my want of belief in the dogma that the Church could grant such indulgences, and absolve men from the penalties which their sins brought upon them.

You all know the history of the Reformation and its results upon the power of the Church of Rome, and how men were freed from the superstitions of the Church and how the reform grew in many of the Catholic countries, and new churches and beliefs were established. Well, I will not further recite any of these things, but merely say that what I have written is intended to be only preliminary to what the object of my writing is.

As men of thought, convinced of the false claims and superstitions of the Church and of the necessity of making known to mankind the truths of the Bible, I and several others, in our zeal, refused to recognize and accept as a part of the teachings of the reform belief many things which were contained in the Church's dogmas or teachings that were really true, or in a manner true, when relieved of their appendages which the Church had attached to the kernels of truth. As a consequence, we rejected many principles that we should have made parts of the beliefs and teachings of the new beliefs.

Well, I am sorry that you do not feel in condition to receive more at this time, but it is best to postpone the remainder. I will soon come and finish what I desire to write.

So, with my love and best wishes, I am

Your brother in Christ,

Luther.[59]

---

[59] Luther has written that in his day members of the church were entirely dependent upon the priesthood for all information as to the contents of the Bible. The Church of the New Birth is twice blessed with these writings that were received through the instrumentality of Mr. James E. Padgett with sufficient Divine Love to permit Jesus of Nazareth and many other Celestials to comment on the errors in both Old and New Testaments. (J.P.G.)

Comments on the war then in progress, and its consequences

March 18th, 1917.

I am here, Luther.

I had some difficulty in writing my name, but I did not let that difficulty deter me or prevent me from writing.

Well, I merely want to say that if things are favorable, I should like to come tomorrow night and write you a message on the subject of which I have before written. Well, I know, and am thankful, and will come. Well, I am interested in the war[60] only as a lover of all the children of God. There is no distinction in my love between the German and the Englishman and the Frenchman, and the mortal of any other nation, and hence, I am not writing to you as a German, but as a spirit in whom all distinction as to the objects of his love has no existence.

Of course, I have been interested in the war, because I sympathize with all mortals who may be in suffering and distress; and besides, many spirits are coming to the spirit world before their normal time and all unfitted for the change from the mortal to the spirit. The consequence is that much suffering and confusion and feelings of hatred and revenge exist among these spirits, that otherwise would not exist. But we spirits are powerless to prevent the dire distress and sufferings caused to mortals by their fellows. Man exercises his will and man must endure the consequences.

But this I will say, that I think the war will soon end and peace be restored to earth, and I trust a greater peace than has existed among men for a long time. Well, I must stop now. So good night and God bless you.

Your brother in Christ,
Luther.

Sees the necessity of correcting many of the principles of belief of his followers

May 16th, 1916.

I am here, Luther.

I come to tell you that I desire very much to write you before a great time shall elapse, as I have a subject that is important to me to reveal to mankind, and especially my followers in the Church which bears

---

[60] World War I - it was simply called the War at that time, as the Second World War had not occurred. (G.J.C.)

my name. I see the necessity of correcting many of the principles of belief which now hold my followers to bondage and prevent them from learning the truths as I now know them to be. So soon let me write, if you can possibly find the opportunity. I am very happy in my condition of love and living, and so want to help all others to learn the truth and become happy.

So, with my love and best wishes, I am

Your brother in Christ,

Luther.

First message written automatically by Mr. Morgan from Mary Kennedy

October 12th, 1916.

I will write a few lines to tell the Doctor that I love him very much. He must not think that I am away from him very long for I am not.

I am watching him very close, and if he flirts with the girls I know all about it. So tell him he must be very careful as I am a very jealous lady.

You must not write more, so thanking you for your kindness I am,

Mary,

The Doctor's soulmate.

What men should believe in order to again become the perfect man

December 12th, 1916.

I am here, Jesus.

Let me write a while tonight as I desire very much to again come into communication with you in reference to the truths of God that are so important for men to know.

Tonight I desire to write for a short time on the subject of what men should do in order to become again the perfect men as was the condition of the first parents before their fall. I know that many doctrines and beliefs have prevailed in the world of human experience as to what is necessary to bring about a return to the original condition of the created soul of men before the fall, and that many of these beliefs have been preached and efforts made to live the life that will produce this happy state; but in all this experience and belief men have rarely attained to the perfection that they sought for, notwithstanding the fact that they have been taught that as their Father in heaven is perfect, they should become perfect. No, this goal has always eluded men while living on earth, and for a long while to come and until man's ideas of his own created condition changes man will not succeed in reaching the condition of perfection.

While the created soul of man is pure and perfect, and man must realize that fact, yet because of the long ages of living in and nurturing sin and its resultants, man has covered over that pure soul with such a deep and fallacious covering that they have never yet been able to get a correct idea of what that soul really is. As it appears to them in all its frailties and ugliness as it really is, and in addition to this, so long has man been accustomed to see that soul as it appears in its false covering that he has concluded and had no other thought than that it is really what it appears to him to be.

But never was a greater mistake made and never has man been so little successful in discovering the truth of things as in this matter of the true condition of the hidden soul, waiting only to be relieved of its covering in order to shine out again in all its purity and truth. So you see, the first thing for men to do is to realize the true condition of their own souls, and then make the effort to rescue such souls from this false and unnatural condition, and let it appear again clean and pure and beautiful.

Many teachers have appeared in the world and endeavored to lead men to this discovery, and also attempted to show them the way by which this original condition could be recovered or brought about, and success more or less has accompanied their endeavors; but the trouble has been that with these teachings have been mixed things of such irrational character that have had a retarding and baneful effect upon such teachings, and as a consequence men have lost the principles of the true teachings and found themselves enthralled in the scheme of public benefits that men so forcibly presented to those who followed these doctrines instead of the true teachings.

It seems so strange that these beliefs and practices should be given over to so much importance to acts and beliefs of men, and that the one true principle that lies at the basis of all efforts to regain the purity of the soul, as it originally existed, should be neglected.

Well, the rapport is weakening, and I will write later. So, good night and God bless you! I see that you are in better condition than for a long time, and I am glad. I will come soon again. Good night.

Your brother and friend,
Jesus.

Affirming that Jesus wrote on what men should do to become the perfect man

December 12th, 1916.

I am here, your own true and loving Helen.

Well, dear, I am so glad that the Master could write again tonight, for it tells one that you will be able to receive His messages right along, and very satisfactorily.

Your own true and loving,

Helen.

The things material that men pray for are answered by God by using spirits for that purpose

September 19th, 1920.

I am here, Jesus. Let me say a few words tonight as I see that you were disappointed in the sermon that the preacher delivered tonight.

Well, you must not be so disappointed because he knows only that which he could deduce from the teachings of the Bible and while what he said was true, yet it is not all of the truth for he discussed only one of the attributes of God and that is the loving care that he has for and exercises over the children of earth. To most men this view of God is satisfactory and give them much comfort and assurance in the security that arises from the knowledge that there is such a loving and caring Father; and to these men this assurance is of wonderful blessedness and comfort, and it is well that men can have this conception of God—a Father who is always solicitous for their happiness and welfare and to whom they can pray in the faith that he will hear and answer their prayers.

But as we have written you before, the things that men generally pray for and expect to receive in response thereto, are not the things that God in his own personality bestows upon men in answer to such prayers. His great gift is His Divine Love, and these things of the material—or earthly in themselves—he leaves to his ministering spirits to bestow, or, in other words, He delegates His angels to so come into contact with and influence the souls of men that they may feel that their prayers have been answered, as they have.

The preacher's conception of God does not extend beyond these attributes that in themselves are sufficient to answer men's wants and make them better and happier. I will come soon and write you of God's attributes, and hope that you will get in condition that I may make the necessary rapport.

It has been some time since I have written you of these higher truths that are so important to men, and regret that such is the fact, but now that you have had your vacation, and feel that you are willing and anxious that our communications be resumed, I will try to assist you in getting in that condition of soul that will enable the messages to be written you. But as you know, much depends upon yourself and you must try with all the energies of your soul to obtain a greater inflowing of the Father's Love, for only from it can come the condition that is necessary. Pray more and think deeply of the spiritual truths that have already been written you, and we will come together in closer communion and be able to give and you receive the messages.

I am glad that you have thought more of these things during the past few days, and hope that your thoughts will continue and that your longings will flow more to the Father. You cannot now appreciate the necessity for this condition, and if you could, I know you would give all your thoughts and longings and energy to the accomplishment of the work.

Well, I will not write more tonight, but will be with you and pray with you and try to influence you in the efforts to perform the mission that has been given you. Have more faith and believe that you will succeed and you will not be disappointed.

Your brother and friend,
Jesus.[61]

The master stresses the importance of the work yet to be done and assures Mr. Padgett of his help in times of need

May 2nd, 1920.

I am here, Jesus.

Let me write for I am anxious to tell you that you are in a much better condition than you have been for a long time, and your thoughts of today and especially of tonight have put you in a spiritual condition, and if you continue in these thoughts and longings you will soon enable us to make the rapport by which we can continue our messages with greater frequency and with exact expression of what we desire to convey.

I have been with you a great deal today, and have tried to exercise upon your soul and mind an influence that will cause you to more fully realize the responsibility that rests upon you and the importance of the work that you are to do. I was with you at church this morning and saw the impression made upon your mind by the preacher, when he asked the question—if anyone had anything to offer that would show him that he had not grasped all of the truth as to the spiritual

---

[61] This is the very last message received by James Padgett from Jesus, according to the daily diary. However it appears there were later messages not recorded in the diary, but none from Jesus. This message is a composite of two, being published in Volume III and Volume IV. (G.J.C.)

things, as he called them, that would cause men to aspire for and obtain a higher course of living—and also saw that you realized that your work, if carried to its conclusions, would answer that question.

And so you must think of this question and try with all the powers that have been given you to learn these truths, so they can be made known—not only to the preachers of the so-called Christian Churches but to all mankind. You already have truths enough to show this minister that he is not preaching the true Christian spirituality that I came to the world to teach, and did teach, and that he must not rest satisfied with his knowledge of spiritual things but must seek for more light and truth, and then make them a part of his own possessions, and teach them to the world of men, and especially those to whom he has the opportunity of ministering.

I am much pleased that you are in so much better condition of soul, and want you to persist in your efforts to obtain more of the Love of the Father, and then you will be able to bring true enlightenment to the unthinking and unknowing world, of the truths that are so vital to their salvation.

I was also with you tonight and saw the impression made on you by the preacher when he set forth Samuel as he then was, as an example to be followed by the true seekers after the important things that lead to spiritual regeneration and perfect manhood, and was glad that you could appreciate how far the character of Samuel fell short of what is necessary to make a man the Divine Angel, or even the perfect man. The preacher does not experience the truth of the Divine Love in his soul, and in fact has not even an intellectual knowledge of its existence and operations. He believes that I am God, and that my blood washes away the sins of all men who believe in me; and thus thinking, he is satisfied to rest upon the promise of the Gospels, which he accepts as the true teachings of me.

Samuel is now here, and was with you at the church, and realized how devoid he was, at the time spoken of by the preacher, of that thing which was necessary to his salvation. And that his demand upon the people to behold him, and then bring any charge of unrighteousness that they could against him and his conduct as a servant and prophet of Jehovah (sic). This is a very pretty story and to a certain extent contains in it a teaching of the moral laws that works for good, but it is not more important than many other things contained in the Old Testament. Samuel will come sometime[62] and write you of his life on earth, and his ministry as a servant of Jehovah.

---

[62] This is the footnoted reference as published in Volume II, but it is actually a reference to a much earlier message received July 21st, 1915. Presumably it was intended that Samuel would come again and deliver another message. (G.J.C.)

Well my dear brother, I will not write more tonight, but will soon came and write an important message, which I know will not only benefit but interest you. Well, I will write on the subject that you suggest, for this is an important thing for men to know, as so many think they are doing God's will in their various courses of living and in their various forms of worship. His will is one that corresponds with all the laws that affect man in every way, and men must know what this will is.

I will come soon and write on this subject and hope that you may be successful in receiving my message as I intend to deliver it. With my love and blessing, and the assurance that I will be with you in all times of need, and try to direct you in your thoughts, I will say good night.

Your friend and brother, Jesus. [63]

Urges Mr. Padgett to remain in a condition of Love for the sake of the work to be done

May 2nd, 1920.

I am here, your own true and loving Helen.

Well, dear, I am so happy that you are in such good condition to receive the messages, and that you have again realized the presence of the Love in your soul, and have turned your longings and desires to the Father for an increase of His Love.

I cannot tell you how solicitous I have been for you, and have prayed the Father that He would pour out His Holy Spirit upon you, and call you again to the work that you must do. How different you are when in the condition of Love from what you are when indifferent and cold and shut in, as it were, to your thoughts of the material. If you could only fully appreciate what it all means to be in this condition of indifference you would try with all the powers of your soul and mind to never let the condition come over you. There is nothing in all the universe that can possibly compensate for the loss of this feeling of the possession of the active Love in your soul, and you must realize it.

I am so glad that the Master wrote you as He did, and hope that you will remember what he said and become in unison with him and the work that he has given you to do. Be true to him and to yourself and you will arrive at the state of will that will make and keep you very happy while on earth—and give you the certainty of a home in the Celestial Heavens.

Well, dear, you have written enough for tonight, and I must stop. But believe that I love you with all my soul, and want you to be very

---

[63] This message is a composite of two, being published in Volume II and Volume IV. (G.J.C.)

happy. Many spirits are anxious to write. So, good night.

Your own true and loving,

Helen.[64]

Gives advice for Mr. Padgett to help a medium into a knowledge of the Divine Truths

March 30th, 1919.

I am here, Jesus.

Let me write a few lines, for I am anxious to tell you that you have not been in good company today, as the meeting (Mrs. Kates' séance held in Washington, D.C.) was filled with spirits who are of the earth plane, and know not the truths that will lead to a knowledge of the things that are necessary in order to secure a home in the Celestial Heavens. Many spirits were those of men who, when on earth, lived immoral and licentious lives, and who are in the same condition as they were when on earth. They have not yet answered to the Law of Compensation and, of course, you will see that their influence is not of the kind that tends to develop those soul qualities that lead to the Heaven of the followers of me, in the true sense.

The medium with whom you conversed, and who delivered the messages of some of the spirits who were so anxious to reach their friends of earth, was influenced by spirits who are in a condition of more or less darkness and alienation from God, and consequently suffers from her association and the influence to which she was subjected. She has long been in this work of demonstrating to mankind the fact of communication between the spirits in the flesh and those who have passed the mysterious border line; and her work has been strenuous and served to demonstrate the fact for which it was intended, and she is satisfied with the reality of the fact of the continuity of life after so called death.

This has been a phase of mediumship that was necessary to be performed, and she has done her work faithfully and well, and is now entitled to be relieved of this work that pertains to the lower order of spiritualism, and should be freed of this great burden and be permitted to come into a knowledge of the higher things of spirit life. I am glad that you will soon have the opportunity to tell her things that await her as a reward for all the sacrifices that she has been compelled to make.

Now, do not misunderstand me. Her work was necessary as a preliminary to the conversion of men to a belief in the truth of spirit

---

[64] This message is a composite of two, being published in Volume II and Volume IV. (G.J.C.)

communication and the fact that there is no death, and to the consolation that comes to men from the knowledge that their loved ones are with them, seeking to help and be helped in their conditions that the great law of cause and effect imposes upon them. Many a sad heart has been comforted by her ministrations and many a spirit has been helped by having opened up to them the way to make known their presence to mortals.

But she has from the very nature of her occupation been more or less injured in her spiritual progress, and the time has come when she shall have the opportunity to attend to and obtain her own soul's progress. She is naturally a good woman, and when she told you that she had a longing for something for which she did not understand, she was uttering a great truth of her soul, and one that has been present with her since she was a little child, for her soul has been calling to the great soul of the Father for His Love and the happiness that comes with the knowledge that the Father's Love is ever ready and anxious to respond to her longings. Her knowledge of spiritualism does not teach her what this Love is, even though her soul feels its presence, and in her under-developed longings realizes that there must exist that which will draw her closer to the great Love of the Father.

So I say, tell her the truths that have been revealed to you, and of your experience in seeking for and obtaining this transforming Love, and she will listen and seek and obtain, and with such obtaining will come a happiness she has never before experienced. And when she has believed in this Love and obtained it to a degree, she will become a powerful instrument in converting men to a belief in the only way to the Celestial Heaven and to immortality. Then will she have back of her the influence of the hosts of Celestial angels to inspire her and qualify her to preach the true Kingdom of God; and her faculties of clairvoyance will be opened up to see the things of the Celestial Heavens and the wonderfully bright and glorious spirits, who will come to her with their messages of truth and knowledge of the glories that belong to those who know that the Divine Love of God is the only thing that can transform the human soul into an angel of light, and the immortality that I came to earth to teach, and which I did teach, but which, alas, was so soon lost to the knowledge of men.

I am particularly interested in her, not so much because of her own soul, as because she has in her those qualities that can be used by us in making known to the world the truths which we of the Celestial spheres know will set them free from the false and damning teachings of the orthodox churches, and making my coming to earth and living—not dying—the way to the Truth and the Life. She may think that her knowledge—I mean intellectual—is all that needs to be known, but when she lets her soul's longings go to the Father and receives the response, which she will certainly receive, she will then know that spiritualism, as she conceives it to be, is the mere forerunner of that which will make all men at one with the Father, when embraced by man and lived.

The meetings, such as was held today, while as I have said was filled with spirits who are in darkness and suffering, yet also attracted many spirits who are bright and progressing in their natural love, and who tried to help those to whom they came and communicated, and to that extent did good, and also served to convince the unbelievers of the truth of the mere passing from the body of flesh into the spirit body—a continued existence, without changing of condition of happiness or misery. The great Law of Compensation—as you sow so shall you reap—is taught at the meetings, and there is no truer or greater law in all the universe of God, and man must realize that it works without exception and to the last farthing, and that there can never be forgiveness until forgetfulness takes place.

Well, my dear brother, I must stop as the power is weakening, but before closing let me entrust you to tell the medium that I, Jesus of the Bible, as I called my disciples when on earth, now call her to do the work which is so important to mankind, and that she must prepare herself by seeking for this Love. It is utterly impossible for a soul out of unison with the souls of the spirits who come to it to receive their communications and transmit the same to mankind. Her soul must respond to the souls of the spirits, and it will be so easy for her to get into the condition that will make this possible. Like attracts like, and this law applies to rapport and to other things of the spirit world, and of the earth as well.

I see that you are in better condition tonight, and I am pleased, for I will soon come and write another message with reference to the higher truths. With my love and blessings, I will say good night.

Your brother and friend,
Jesus.[65]

The importance of the work set before Mr. Padgett. The necessity of getting into condition to do this work

September 17th, 1917.

I am here, Jesus.

I come as I promised and desire to write on a subject that requires that I should have absolute control of your brain and hand; and tonight I see that you are just not in the condition necessary. So I will not

---

[65] This message is a composite of two, being published in Volume III and Volume IV. (G.J.C.)

write on the subject, as I intended, but will postpone the same until later. But I will say a few words that may be of interest to you and your friend, whose conversation tonight I listened to, and saw what was in both your minds and hearts.

I realize that you both appreciate the importance of the work that is set before you, and that you have arrived at that condition of faith which causes you to forego all interest in material things so far as they may benefit you personally; and it is well that you are in this state of feeling and appreciation of the work, for this work is of such an exclusive nature that in order to be performed in the way that we desire and which is necessary that the truths which you receive shall be given to the world, all thoughts of the things that ordinarily belong to the mere human living must be eliminated and turned aside.

These truths while, when understood and applied by the individual, will not render that individual less qualified to perform the duties of life, but on the contrary will increase these qualifications, and must be so taught, yet in the case of you who are to make and teach these truths, your interest in the world must be forgotten or submerged in these higher interests. In other words, while you are in the world you must not be of the world, as I taught my disciples when on earth.

Of course, while you are mortals you will have to have these things that are necessary to sustain life and health and comfort, and your work does not require that you shall make sacrifices of these things, but that you shall have the comforts that are necessary to your enjoying the merely physical life, and this you must understand. As you have said, the work will be hard and the difficulties that you shall encounter will be great, but you will be able to do the work and overcome the difficulties; for I desire to tell you here that never in all the history of mankind has any work had behind it the power and influence of the high spirits of the spirit world as your work will have, and your faith must be such that no possibility of failure will be permitted to enter into your conception of success.

The world is now ready for those truths, for men's souls have been and will be more opened to the possibility and necessity of seeking for and obtaining things spiritual than ever before, and mankind will—and now does—realize that man himself, notwithstanding the teachings of some of the writers that man is of the divine and of himself capable of self-regeneration, is not able to become brothers in truth and reality, and that the brotherhood of man is a mere dream when based upon the power of man because of any qualities of goodness or of the divine that he may be supposed to possess.

Time is passing and the great conflict that has deluged the mortal world with bloodshed and hatred and vengeance will soon come to an end, and men will wander in confusion and seek that which may bring them into unison and brotherly kindness, and also into a greater knowledge of the world unknown to them—the hereafter. Faith will fail to satisfy and their souls will long for the spiritual food that will have in it the qualities of certainty and knowledge.

They will think in their hearts and in many instances declare that the Christian faith as has been taught them by the churches does not satisfy, and the creeds and dogmas of the churches have been failures, and will cry out for something that will fill their souls with spiritual food of truth and salvation. So we must work and be prepared to give to mankind the truth and this food—a knowledge of the only way to the Father's Love, and of what the possession of this Love in the souls of men will mean to them.

I feel that you are both in earnest in your desire to do the work and that all opportunities will be embraced, and that when you are free to give your whole time to the work you will permit nothing to intervene. And this you will do for the good of humanity without thought of reward, and such should be your desires. But nevertheless, your reward will be great, not in the way of an independent payment, but as an acquisition necessarily growing out of the very nature of the work that you will do; for as you help others to learn the truth and gain the possession of this Great Love of the Father, your own souls will obtain more of the Love, and with that increased possession will come increased happiness and a closer at-onement with the Father; and this, of course, means rewards beyond all conception of mortals or spirits who have not arrived at the degree of possession of this Love that will be yours.

So, as I said in the beginning, first place yourselves in that condition which will enable you to free yourself from all worldly cares, and consecrate your body, mind and soul to this great work; and then what follows will be without interference of worldly things.

I am glad that I could write you in this way tonight, for I know it will assist you in pursuing the best way to accomplish the mission that has been given you and which at this time no other can take from you. You have been selected for the work and we feel that no mistake has been made. So, believe in us and pray to the Father with all the earnestness of your souls and you will find that which we have told you to be the greatest thing in all the universe: the Divine Love and nature and Immortality of the Father.

I will not write more tonight, and with my love and the blessings of the Father, will say good night.

Your brother and friend,
Jesus.

Confirmation that Jesus wrote about getting in condition to do the work

September 16th, 1917.

I am here, your own true and loving Helen.

Well, dear, the Master has written you an important message[66] and I know it will help you in your conception of what and how you shall work. He was in great earnestness when he wrote, and we all felt that he was speaking with authority and knowledge that only he possesses. So keep in mind what he has said and try to follow his instructions. So, good night.

Your own true and loving
Helen.

Accepts suggestion from Mr. Padgett to write on the soul, that is, when he is better able to do so. Jesus also informs Mr. Padgett that Mr. Morgan's work will not be the same as his

March 16th, 1917.

I am here, Jesus.

Keep up your courage and believe, and all things that I have promised will come to you, and you will not be disappointed. You are now in better condition than you were, and soon I will come and write another message; and as I see that you think my message on the nature of God had better be rewritten, I will take that theme for my subject. Yes, I understand, and it is my desire that I rewrite the message. As you are in better condition to receive it than you were when I wrote before, I know that it will be very satisfactory for the purposes for which it was written.

So, as I say, believe, and I will not leave you alone or fail to do what I have promised. Well, when you suggested to me to write on that subject (the soul) you were not in such receptive condition as to take the message in the form and meaning that I intended to convey. It is a very difficult subject to write on, and I wanted you to be in the best possible condition. I am satisfied at the way in which you received it, and if I find that it needs any amendment I will make it before you publish the book.

Yes, I know, and you will soon be in that condition, and then I

---

[66] It would appear that this message referred to here, written by Jesus and clearly indicated in the Tablet, was not included in those to be published. It would appear Jesus wrote on the 14th, 16th and 17th, but only the last message has been published. (G.J.C.)

know that the work will proceed faster. Yes, as you say, the world is ready to receive these truths, and the people are longing for some knowledge that will show them the true way to the Father.

Well, I am sorry, too, but he (Eugene Morgan) must wait a while. He has been selected, and his mission is definite, and it makes no difference whether he receives any messages or not.[67] That is not a part of his work in the great plan, and he must not let his faith fail him, for his work will be wonderful, and one that many of the world would give their lives, as it is said, to be selected to do. His work will be very important and he is being prepared, notwithstanding his disappointment that you speak of, as to material things; and I say to him with the authority of one who knows, that he must believe and wait and pray, and he will not be disappointed; for we never forsake our own who trust us.

Well, I must stop now, but remember what I have said, and say to your friends that I am their brother and friend, and that they are very close and very dear to me, and my chosen ones; and in my Father's Kingdom their places will not be filled by others.

So, with my love, I will say good night.

Your brother and friend,

Jesus.

How the Divine Love may be called upon and used in the healing of our physical bodies

May 16th, 1916.

I am here, Jesus.

I will not write a formal message tonight, but will merely tell you that I was with you tonight at the home of Mr. Morgan, and wrote what you received as purporting to come from me, and I meant that if I could establish the rapport with him I would cure him; and so I will. It depends somewhat on his having the necessary concentration and belief in me.

It may seem strange that I cannot do this unless this rapport is established, but it is a fact. There are certain laws which control the exercise of this power upon mortals which must be complied with. When on earth I could come in direct contact with the mortal by reason of my being in the flesh, and as the power was in me, or could be engendered in me by the exercise of my spiritual powers, I encountered no obstacle in the way of my exercising these powers upon the mortal. But now there is no direct contact between me and the mortal, and hence there is no means of communicating this power to him until a rapport is established.

This rapport is something more than a mere "spiritual"

---

[67] This means the authoritative messages like Mr. Padgett obtained. (J.P.G.)

connection, and partakes somewhat of the material, though we are not of the material; yet the rapport must be of the nature mentioned, and the material part of it must come from the mortal himself.

Now you will understand that my relationship in such cases with the mortal is very different from what would be your relationship to him, had you this power residing in you; and when the time comes for you to receive this power, you will not need to establish any rapport between you and whomever you may be able to cure. I mean it will not be necessary for this rapport to be established by drawing from the mortal any part of the material that belongs to him: this you will have yourself, and the power will be exercised by you simply as a mortal coming in contact with him.

This power can be possessed by mortals just as my disciples and others possessed it at the time that I was on earth, and the same results may be obtained as were obtained in those days.

Well, the power that was manifested in you was somewhat of the nature that I have been speaking of, only it was a power borrowed, or conferred upon you by a spirit. It was a part of this spirit's power, and thereby differing from that which you will receive as a part of your own self, when you shall have had that soul development and possession of the Divine Love, which are necessary prerequisites to any mortal—or spirit either—being able to receive the power.

The spirit who was trying to manifest through you and help Mr. Morgan was your own Indian guide, who is a very powerful spirit; and he drew on you very hard for the material that was necessary for him to make the manifestation. The power which he transmitted will help Mr. Morgan, and he will realize it by morning. And if you had continued for a while longer, its effects would have become seen before you left him.

I will try tonight, as I promised, to help him, and if we can form the rapport that I speak of, there will be no uncertainty as to the results. I will give especial attention to his case, as I desire to demonstrate to him that the power of the spirit world, when properly exercised, can be used to help mortals, even in their physical ills, to relieve them from their sufferings. I see that he has a very considerable faith and will make the effort to help establish this rapport, and we may succeed. At any rate, you have already helped him and he will realize it.

I will come to you soon and write you another message on an important subject, so that you may see the necessity for our working faster. I will not write more, but will say that I love you and am with you, trying to help you. So, with my blessings, I will say good night.

Your brother and friend,
Jesus.

Confirms that the healing forces of Divine Love had been utilized in Mr. Morgan's behalf

May 16th, 1916.

I am here, your own loving Helen.

Well, sweetheart, I will not write much, as you are tired and must go to bed early. You have had an experience tonight which has exhausted you somewhat, and you need rest.

I was with you at Mr. Morgan's, and tried to help him; and when White Eagle was rubbing him, I also tried to help. I think that Mr. Morgan will feel better in the morning, for White Eagle used a great deal of his power to treat Mr. Morgan, and you received so much that I was afraid it might do you some harm at the time. But White Eagle said no, that he would look out for that, and so I told him to do his best.

Yes, Jesus was there, and what you received he actually wrote. And he was so anxious to help Mr. Morgan in the way that he indicated—and will succeed, if he can only establish the necessary rapport, as he said. It will be a glorious demonstration if he does succeed.

I would like to write longer tonight, but I must not. So, my own dear Ned, love me and think of me, and call me to you more often. Give me a great big kiss and say good night.

Your own true and loving,
Helen.

Informs Mr. Padgett that his soul has had a great inflowing of Divine Love

December 20th, 1915.

I am here, Jesus.

I came tonight to tell you that you are in a good spiritual condition and that your soul has had a great inflowing of the Divine Love and you will realize as time goes by this Love to its fullest.

I know that you are not so very far from the Kingdom and that soon such Love will come to you as will make you a conscious child of the Father and one upon whom He has bestowed His Great Love in all its purity and splendor. So let your prayer and praise go up to the Father in continuous streams of soul longings and love and you will know that God is your Father and the One altogether Holy. I would like to write to you tonight another of my messages, but I do not think it best, as you are not just in that condition of rapport that will make it successful as you desire, but soon now I will, and you will learn more truths of which you now have no knowledge and of which the world has never heard, for even in my teachings on earth I did not teach the truths that you will receive.

Well, I will tell you that Love is the greatest thing in all God's universe and that with its coming into the soul of a man comes peace and happiness and joy, and a knowledge that the Father is a real, existing, present Father of the most wonderful tenderness and Love.

You are in a condition that you will experience this Love to a very great degree, and the Holy Spirit is with you and is filling your soul with this Love and making you feel the influence of its presence. Oh, my dear brother, I now know that you will become my own true disciple and worker for the salvation of men, and very soon you will have given to you the great gift of inspirational talking and you will do much good in your telling mankind of the Great Love of the Father and His Wonderful Mercy. This will come to you when your condition is such as to admit its coming and when your soul is attuned to the Heavenly things that are now working to forward the revelations of the great truths.

I know just how you feel tonight, and I am with you in all my love and tenderness and am giving you the great Love that I have for the Father and that I have received from the Father. So believe in me and pray to the Father and trust in Him to the fullest, for with this trust will come faith that will make all your longings and aspirations things of real substance, as your soul will become a thing of substance in the Divine Nature of the Father.

Well, I will stop now, but I will not leave you without letting you know that you have my love and blessings in all their fullness, and the blessings of the Father. So remember that you are mine and that you are the object of my care and will always be. So good night.

Your brother spirit,

Jesus.

Speaks about how many Christian Scientists exercise the faith that helps them to overcome harmful habits

April 5th, 1916.

I am here, Jesus.

These people (the Christian Scientists) obtain by their study of the principles that God is everything, and that their will must be subjected to His, a certain union with the power of the spirit world that calls into operation those powers which give them strength of will and a belief that their appetites for the stimulant (smoking) has left them; and that being so, they may easily refrain from further indulging this appetite.

The spirit forces help them to a greater extent than they possibly understand; but in order for this help to become effective, these people must necessarily come in rapport with these forces. They, by what they believe they possess in the way of having a proper conception of the true relationship of themselves to God, further believe that there is some power which exists in the spirit realms that is sufficient to take from them their appetites and enable them to lay aside these appetites for what, they realize, is the unreal.

This faith is a wonderful thing in helping man to do—or not to do—a particular thing, and even though they may not understand the true principle upon which this faith works out the results of which they testify, yet they acquire the faith which causes them to come into close rapport with the powers that actually help them to a successful realization of their desires.

As a matter of fact, God does not, as you may say, personally intervene in these matters, for he performs His work by means of spirits or ministering angels, as the Bible teaches, in things having to do with the material things affecting a man's existence; and even in the matters of the soul, He uses the Holy Spirit as an instrument to bring to man His Divine Love and infill the soul of man with its presence and essence and influence.

Many of these Christian Scientists have in their souls this Divine Love without really understanding that it is there or why or how it came to them; but they see the effect and have a knowledge that there is some power within them that enables them to come closer to the Father and experience the presence of His Love.

Christian Science is, in many particulars, a belief which leads to a faith that brings the true, sincere believer into an at-onement with the Father, and makes the believer a possessor of this Divine Love of the Father; and yet many of its teachings are misleading and hard to understand, and not suitable for the great mass of mankind, because of certain mental requirements necessary to be understood before the seeker can grasp the truth that this Divine Love is the only thing that will save him from his sins and fit him for the Kingdom.

But I must not write more on this subject tonight, for, as I have told you, I will come sometime and show you its merits and demerits in detail.

I will soon come and finish my last message, and as there are so many more that I desire to communicate, I hope that we may proceed faster in our work.

I will be with you in your daily life in my love and influence, and try to help you to that condition of mind and soul progress that you pray for, and that are so very necessary.

Yes, I hear your request, and I pray as you desire; and I know that the Father answers my prayers, as he also answers yours. Only have more faith and more soul longings, and you will soon realize an inflowing of this Love to a wonderful degree.

I must stop now. With all my love and blessings, I am

Your friend and brother,

Jesus.

Writes that Mr. Padgett's prayers have been answered and is now ready to receive Jesus' teachings on the Truths of the Father

January 5th, 1915.

I am here, Jesus.

You are my own true brother and disciple. I come because you need me and my love, and I want to tell you that you are very near the Kingdom. Your prayers have been heard, and our Father has given you His Love to a great degree. So you must soon be prepared to take my (formal) messages, for the time is getting ripe for the world to receive my gospel of love and peace.

Men are now thinking deeply of spiritual things and want a gospel that will teach them the way to the truth and to God's love and their eternal happiness. So do not let the things of earth keep you from getting more of your Father's Love and Grace in your soul. Be steadfast in your faith and you will not want for anything that will enable you to become His true son and my own loving disciple in spreading the glorious tidings of joy and peace to mankind. Your love is now so great that you will soon be at-one with your Father and receive from Him the outpouring of His love and the Pentecost of His Holy Spirit. Be a man that will not let anything of earth or heaven keep you from doing the work which I have set before you to do. I am your true helper and protector, and you will not suffer for want of anything that will make you free and happy. Be more earnest in your efforts to obtain the great boon which your Father has promised to give you, and you will not be disappointed.

You are doing a good work among the spirits and God, our Father, will bless you in your endeavors. You must not let doubt or want of faith keep you from doing the great work that you have undertaken. The spirits whom you have so much helped will progress towards the truth and will remember you when they get the happiness which awaits them. Your wife is a beautiful and powerful spirit, who has learned to love God very much, and who loves you to an extent that is unusual among spirits, who love with a love far exceeding the love of mortals (the redeemed spirits are the ones I mean). She is the sweetest and brightest wife that God has given to man. She is now progressing very rapidly and soon will be very near her father's home of love and joy. So you are very much blessed in having such a wife and soulmate; and when you come over you will find a spirit waiting for you that will appear so beautiful to you, that you will wonder how such a thing could be. But you may become just as beautiful and as much possessed of God's Love, if you will only pray and do His will while on earth. It is not necessary for you to wait until you come over in order to get this Love and become free from sin and error.

I am your true teacher and brother, and I want you to do my will as regards the teaching to mankind of the truths of the Father. I do not desire to tell you now of these things. I will in a short time and then you will know just what the truth is.

Yes, I know the future, and I tell you now and you must believe, that you will soon be relieved of all your business cares, and be in a condition to give all your time and energies to my work. Do not doubt this anymore. I think that this is the best place, though the place will not determine the best means of doing the work. I mean the place will not be material, except that the place you mention is a good one, as it is near the Capitol of a great nation and will enable you to make more impression on the world by what you may publish. I do not intend to restrict you to any place; only take the messages and publish them.

You will also teach the truths by your daily conversations and example. Yes, I remember the saying and it is true, but in your case the same conditions do not exist as existed when I gave utterance to the saying. Nevertheless I will guide you when the time comes and you will follow my guidance. It will make little difference to you where you are, for the spread of my truths is the important thing. Yes, a church will be established, and there will be many leaders of my new movement, and it will succeed and supplant all other beliefs in this hemisphere. I mean in the United States and other protestant countries.

The war will last until the Germans are subdued. I don't think it will be very long before they will see the utter hopelessness of fighting longer; then they will submit and a new nation will arise, which will be a nation of the people governed by the people. Emperors' sons will not have any influence with the people. The nobility will cease to have any power and will become a part of the people. God will eventually rule men's lives through His love, for men will then seek His love, and peace will be established in the earth. When my Kingdom comes on the earth I will reign in the hearts of men, not as a ruler or as a sovereign lord, but as a Prince of Peace, the only son of the Father who was born without sin, and all mankind will worship God in spirit and in truth. War shall be no more and swords shall be turned into pruning hooks and plowshares, and men shall know what peace and love for one another are.

My second coming will be as the still small voice that speaks to every man and tells him that Love is the only thing that is necessary for him to have, and when he gets that in his soul all the sins and hatred and desires for evil will pass away.

I will not desert you in your work, and it will prosper. I know that certain churches—I mean the clergy and high officials—will fight my truths and the teaching of them to men, but they will not succeed. I will prevail and mankind will be redeemed. All will bow down in earnest prayer and thanksgiving to their God, and His Love will enter into their hearts and they will be at peace. Brothers will be brothers indeed, and the Fatherhood of God and brotherhood of man will be established, and all men will serve their God.

The Catholic Church will eventually, as an organization of political power, and as a monster of error and a teacher of doctrines contrary to God's truths, be utterly destroyed, and its followers will embrace the true teachings of my gospel. Many will not embrace these new teachings, though, until the last vestige of the power of this great vampire has utterly disappeared. The priests will be shaken from their seats of power and will become men of no influence among the people, for my truths will destroy all the errors which they have preached and through fear caused their deluded followers to embrace and believe.

You must not write more tonight, as you are tired. So with my love and blessings, I am

Your brother and teacher,
Jesus.[68]

Confirms that Jesus wrote the preceding message

January 5th, 1915.

I am here, your grandmother. I heard, and you must believe that it was the Master. He was writing and was so in earnest that you must believe that his prophecies will come true. I am so glad that he wrote you again.

Good night, your grandmother.

You must stop now.
Your own, Helen.[69]

---

[68] This message is a composite of two, being published twice in Volume IV. The second instance has not been included in this edition. (G.J.C.)
[69] This message is a composite of two, being published twice in Volume IV. The second instance has not been included in this edition. (G.J.C.)

A great Queen in her day confesses freely to the violations of the Law of Compensation which she committed and reveals a soul full of remorse and contrition

May 12th, 1915.

I am here, Queen Elizabeth I of England.

I have been here several times but have never before been able to get the chance to write to you, and now that I have, do not disappoint me in my hope that you may help me.

Well, I was a very bad woman on earth as I now see the true relation of things and deeds and am suffering from the memory of those things.

I was looked upon as a creature of the divine favor and could, therefore, do no wrong, and that whatever I said or did must be obeyed and followed by my subjects, and others who lived within my dominions.

I lived a life that was not in accordance with the laws of morality or of God as they now appear to me; and when I tell you that, although I was a single woman yet had my lovers to gratify my passions and to please my caprices, you will understand that I was a wicked woman and that those are the things that now cause my sufferings and darkness.

I am not a spirit who thinks that because I was a ruler that therefore I could do no wrong. I knew at the time that many things I did were wrong and consequently my sufferings have become so much the greater. Many a poor soul has been sent to damnation by my commands, a damnation on earth as well as here. Even murder I was guilty of, although it may have had a legalized form, but it was murder nevertheless, and I am suffering the penalties. Why, some of my truest and best friends in moments of jealousy and envy I sent to the block, to afterwards bitterly regret my deed. Oh, I tell you that a queenly crown makes no difference in the penalty that must be paid for evil deeds. Many a humble subject of mine is now where I cannot go, and where they find happiness and love, as I am told.

I loved once truly and deeply, but I sacrificed the object of my love through pique, and what I wanted in my blind rage to have him do, and he would not, and how bitterly I regretted the deed and suffered even while on earth. Yet I was to all outward appearances callous and without feeling. But God knows how my heart bled, and how my very soul was wracked with remorse and torture. But I was a queen and had no right to have the feelings of a human being.

I loved and love had to be hid. He knew it and died in the knowledge that love wept while I killed him. Sometimes I hope that this love will meet again with the love of the victim, and be one throughout all eternity.

Well, I will not relate the vast number of evil deeds that I did, but only say that as my opportunity for committing evil without fear of punishment was great, so the number of my deeds was great.

But I have suffered in darkness and torment and love has been absent from me all these years of the travail of my soul. I have lived alone, as I saw no pleasures in what other spirits who lived near me were engaged in.

When I first entered the spirit world, I was still a queen as I believed and many of my subjects who had become spirits and knew me still believed I was their queen and worshipped me as such; but as time passed they saw that while on earth I may have been of divine creation, yet as a spirit I was without any evidence of divine right and no better than themselves, and they soon ceased to look upon me as superior to themselves and as is usual, as you on earth say, they went to the other extreme and treated me with neglect and even taunted me for having been on earth a fraud and deception. I soon hated them all, and so sought my consolation in silence and isolation.

What a mockery is nobility on earth and what a leveler is the spirit world! I many times have wished that they had let me remain the simple country girl and not made me the queen of a great nation. I can now see that if my life had been that of a subject living in God's pure and uncontaminated country air, I would now be a much happier spirit. But it is now too late. As I made my bed I must lie in it, and there is no remedy.

But yet when despair and darkness come to overwhelm us there yet seems some good Providence which gives us a little ray of hope and even though it comes to us as a glint of sunlight yet it comes, and we sometimes think that in the future, we know not when, there may be some relief for us. And so that glint of hope comes to me sometimes, and I feel that God has not forsaken me altogether.

I have seen spirits made happier by coming to you and so I came with just that little spark of hope telling me that you might help me, and if you can please do so.

I was Elizabeth, Queen of England, and died in 1603 a little-mourned woman.

Yes, I will do as you say.

Yes, I see the beautiful spirits.

I see your mother and she says that she will take me with her and show me the way to light and happiness and will love me, as God loves me as He does all His children.

So I am going with her and now I want to say that as you are my true friend and well-wisher I believe what you told me and want you to think kindly of me as not many do. So with my thanks, I will say good night.

194

Says that Mr. Padgett's mother will help the Queen

May 12th, 1915.

I am here, Helen.

Well, sweetheart, you have had a long meeting tonight and are tired and must not write more.

Yes, it was a spirit who was once a queen, but she is so poor now that there are none to do her reverence. Your mother will help her, though, and she will get out of her darkness. She has long years of remorse and suffering and is in condition to grasp the truth. She is like a drowning woman catching at a straw, but in her case it will not be a straw but the true Love of the Father that she may get.

Well, I love you with all my heart and soul and will watch over you tonight as you sleep and try to make you have pleasant dreams. So until we meet again in communication, I am and will be your own true and loving

Helen.

This writer, called an infidel by contemporaries, tells of his religious views when on earth and is caused to visualize some bright spirits of the Celestial Heavens

August 5th, 1915.

I am here, Robert G. Ingersoll.

I am a spirit who when on earth taught men that the only salvation required for them was good deeds and kind hearts, and that the Bible, outside of its moral precepts, was not worthy of belief, that many of its sayings were untrue, and that all of its teachings as to belief and faith were not worthy of consideration.

I was perfectly sincere in what I taught and thought, and hence I don't feel that I was guilty of any very great sin, although I have now changed some of my beliefs, or better, thoughts. I did not believe that Jesus ever really lived, as was set forth in the Bible, and I certainly did not believe in a vicarious atonement, or any salvation through blood or propitiation of an angry God. Neither did I believe in any New Birth or in any of the doctrines of St. John having reference to a soul being redeemed; but believed that every man's future state, should there be a future state, depended upon his deeds of love and mercy towards his fellow man. I believed that God was not to be worshipped or consulted, neither would He, nor could He, save a man from anything that might tend to make him unhappy; but that man's love for one another was the great thing that would determine his condition in the future life, should such life exist.

I did not deny that there would be a future life. I merely didn't know anything about it, and hence, all my teachings were directed to making men live on earth in a way that would bring to them happiness while mortals. And my foundation stone, as it were, was love, one towards another. And with this went love, kindness and forgiveness, and good feeling, and fair dealing. Especially did I emphasize the necessity for love at home.

I am still of the opinion that these qualities, if possessed and expressed in action, will make men happier, make the world better, and finally do away with evil and distress.

I now see, though, that there is a future life and that men who would enjoy the greatest happiness in this future life must not only have this love and kindness for one another, but must also seek the Love of God, and believe that God is a Father of Love and believe that He is interested in the soul of each individual man.

I am in the Fourth Sphere and have much happiness in my intellectual pursuits and in my love of my fellow man, and am trying to help them get the best out of life on earth. I do not yet believe in the teachings of those parts of the Bible which, in effect, say that you must believe on the Lord Jesus Christ in order to be saved, for I do not believe that any mere belief will save a man from anything. I know that many here believe that Jesus is the savior of men, as taught by the orthodox churches, but I think that such spirits are as much mistaken as were those who believed the same doctrine when on earth.

I consider myself as saved. I have not found any hell as taught by the churches, although each man has to pay the penalties for his evil deeds done on earth, and many men are suffering here since they became spirits. I will confess that I was somewhat surprised to see that spirits who did not live correct lives on earth are suffering very serious tortures; but this I suppose is the effect of the law that demands a penalty for every violation of its command.

But I do not understand that this suffering will have to continue forever, or that the state of these men is fixed. Progression is the law of the spirit world, and I cannot conceive that any spirit will remain the same through all eternity. To me, the great satisfaction is that there is no orthodox hell and no devil to punish the wicked. I am myself not entirely satisfied that the condition of those who suffer from their evil deeds may not last a long time, as I am told that many of these spirits have been in a condition of suffering for a long time.

Well, I am satisfied with the condition that I am in, and in the possibility of progression, and I need not the teachings of the spirits who profess to have knowledge of a higher love that brings happiness of a kind that enables them to enjoy supreme bliss. Such spirits, I believe, are those who had the old ideas of the churches, against which I taught. I was not compelled to undergo such suffering when I came into the spirit world or to endure much darkness; but I suppose there were some deeds which I had to pay the penalties for, and hence I had to suffer some. But as my love for all mankind was my principle and feeling when on earth, this love gives me a position which I now enjoy.

I could write much longer, but I will not do so tonight, and will come again sometime and explain some of the laws of the spirit world. I am Robert G. Ingersoll and was called an infidel.

Well, my friend, that is a very astounding proposition, and you must be either a very ignorant man or a very self-conceited one to make such a statement.

Well, as to the last statement, you are right. I have an open mind and am willing to learn any truth that may be presented to me in such a way as to convince me that it is a truth. You are stating things of which I have no knowledge, and which I do not believe to be true. I have thought a great deal of God and believe in a God, but as to this Divine Love, I have never heard of it nor ever thought of it.

I know of no love but the love for man, and that means spirit for spirit, and a certain love of God for man. But as to a Love that makes one partake of divinity, I have never heard. And as to the New Birth that you speak of, I don't believe in it any more than I did on earth. To me it seems foolishness. What is there about me or any other spirit to be born again? You might probably say that when I left my body and became a spirit I was born again, and in a sense that is true, but when you tell me that I must be born again and that by such birth I will become a partaker of divinity, I cannot believe what you say or understand what you mean.

Well, you state your proposition very fairly and very clearly, and I must say that I am impressed with what you say, and it might be that you are right. At any rate, I will keep an open mind and will stand ready to hear any argument from you or any spirit that you have mentioned; and if they can show me the truth of your propositions I will not hesitate to embrace them. I want to learn everything possible, and as I was an honest inquirer on earth, I will be an honest one here. You make your assertions very strong and you seem to be in earnest in what you say, and for those reasons I must listen to you.

Yes, I knew Riddle very well, and he was a believer somewhat like me. I have not met him since I have become a spirit, but would like to do so.

I will keep in mind what you say and will observe any difference in beauty that may exist, because if such be a fact there must be some cause for it, and that cause I shall endeavor to understand. I have done as you suggested and I see Riddle, but hardly recognize him, as he is so changed and is so much more beautiful than I conceived of. He has shaken my hand and introduced me to the others. And what beautiful spirits they are! The one who, he says, is your grandmother is glorious in her beauty and brightness, and love seems to be a part of her very being. How I thank you for the experience! I am going with Riddle, who says that he has a wonderful truth to tell me and that I will become convinced of its reality.

So, my friend, I thank you for our conversation and if you desire, I will come again and tell you of the result of our interview—I mean between Riddle and myself. I have made the request of your grandmother and she says that she will be pleased to tell me of this Love that you speak of. But let me tell you this before I stop; that what you said about the difference in beauty and brightness of the spirits is true and that I am as a dark night compared to the noonday sun in my appearance compared with theirs. I am so glad I came to you tonight. So my dear friend, I will say goodbye for a little while.

Your friend,
Robert G. Ingersoll.

Helen confirms the previous message

August 5th, 1915.

I am here, Helen.

Yes, they were and Ingersoll is now with Mr. Riddle and your grandmother. He seems much inspired with your grandmother, and listens to her with great interest. I believe that he will soon see the truth and will seek for this Divine Love and New Birth.

So with all my love. I am,
Your own true and loving,
Helen.

Is praying for the Divine Love

September 22nd, 1915.

I am here, Robert G. Ingersoll.

I come to you again because I desire to thank you and tell you of the great good you have done me in introducing me to the beautiful spirits who form your band. Of course, I knew Riddle,[70] but I must confess that he was so beautiful and bright that I hardly knew him, and also I wondered at his appearance because it was very different from mine and that of a number of other spirits who are here with me and who are friends of mine.

---

[70] Mr. A. G. Riddle was at one time a law partner of Mr. Padgett. (J.P.G.)

As I said before, Riddle was on earth a man who thought somewhat as I did, and I had never heard of his becoming a convert to Christianity; and consequently when I met him here I was impressed at his appearance, for it was the same as the appearance of a great number of spirits whom I have met here and who claim to be Christians. And when Riddle told me the cause of his appearance I was more surprised than before, because I did not think that he would let himself become convinced that there was any truth in the Christian doctrines. But once I have talked with him, I find that his belief is not in the Christian doctrines as taught by the churches on earth, but rather in the teachings of Jesus, which Riddle has learned since he became a spirit.

I also talked to your grandmother—and what a beautiful, wise and powerful spirit she is. She explained to me the meaning of the New Birth as taught by Jesus and as believed in by all his followers, and I must confess that it appears to be very reasonable and simple of understanding.

I have thought a great deal about this matter and I am commencing to think that there is some reality in this question of the New Birth and that it has a substance as well as a theory for its existence. Your grandmother told me many wonderful truths about spirit life, and especially the life in the higher spheres, and I am inclined to believe what she said because they are all so in harmony with reason and common sense. She is so very lovely that I cannot but believe that her appearance is due to the possession of this Divine Love of which she tells me, and I am now trying to follow her advice and seek to obtain it. I do what I did not do on earth—and that is pray to God in the hope that He will answer my prayers. This will appear most surprising to many who read my books and believe in them, for I always in a manner ridiculed the idea of prayer.

But so it is now that I am earnestly praying for light and for an inflowing of this Divine Love into my soul. I am just as open-minded now as I was when on earth, and if the truth of a thing can be shown me I am ready at all times to investigate and learn whether it is true or not.

As regards the truth of the Divine Love, I have so many evidences as to its existence and the wonderful work that it does that I feel that it is due to me to learn what this Love is, and, if possible, obtain it for myself.

All the spirits of your band claim to have obtained this New Birth and to be possessed of this Divine Love of God, and their appearances certainly indicate that they are possessed of something which beautifies and makes them lovely over and above what the spirits who do not believe in Christianity possess.

I will write you again when I learn the result of my prayers and what effect this Love, should I get it, has on me.

If what they tell me is true and proves so in my case, I will

199

proclaim the same from every housetop in no uncertain words, and I may ask you to receive my expressions of belief and joy that I have found such a truth.

I will not write more tonight, as you have written a great deal already.

I have seen Jesus, but I have never talked with him. He seems to be a very close friend to you, for I see him with you a great deal, and writing to you. I will emphatically say that I have never seen any spirit in all this world compare with Jesus in beauty and grandeur, and power and love and humility. I will soon have an interview with him and ask him to tell me the truths of the plan of man's salvation.

So I will say good night.

Your friend,

Robert G. Ingersoll.

Affirming that R. G. Ingersoll wrote

September 23rd, 1915.

I am here, Helen.

Yes, that was Ingersoll, and he wrote you just as you received his message. He is studying and praying as he says, and very soon, I believe, he will find the way and the truth and the light. I must stop now.

Your own true and loving,

Helen.

Regrets that he did not know the Truth when on earth

October 1st, 1915.

I am here, Robert G. Ingersoll.

I came to tell you that I am the Ingersoll who when on earth was a fool in my beliefs, and who now knows the truths of God as far as the way to salvation is concerned, and the Wonderful Gift which he has in store for all who may believe what the Master says as to the way to obtain it. I have not yet recovered from the wonderful experience which I had on the night when Jesus displayed his wonderful glory and power, and made me feel that I was of such little importance in my beliefs and opinions as I entertained them on earth and as I brought them with me to the spirit world.

I must have been a poor soul all my life to have gone on in a way that kept me out of the happiness which a belief in the Father's Love would have given me. But the reason was that the truth was not taught, and what the preachers have proclaimed in their pulpits as to the way that a man could be saved from sin was so repulsive to reason that I could not for a moment tolerate it, and consequently I did not seek to learn any other way. I now know that even the Bible taught another and true way to salvation, but that way was not taught by the preachers; and I never thought of any other way than that which I heard from the preachers or from the writings of the orthodox.

But, if I had only known that even in that book (the Bible) I might have found the true plan of salvation, what good I might have done on earth, instead of the harm which I now see my books are doing.

For while some who read them understand what is really intended to be taught, yet a greater number, who give them a mere casual reading and grasp and enjoy some of my catchwords, really are led to believe that there is no God and no future life; and all this makes me unhappy now and causes me to wish that I could return to earth and teach these people the truth and show them that my writings in many particulars are not beneficial to them.

But I realize that I cannot do this, and I only hope that sometime you will give me the opportunity to write through you my corrections of many of the things contained in my books.

I never before realized what Jesus is, and until the other night when he showed his great power and beauty, I never supposed that he could be much different in appearance than a spirit like unto many others.

I will not write more tonight, except to say that a spirit comes to me and tells me that you invited him here and advised him to ask me to tell him of my conversion to Christianity, as he needed help and light. Well, as you sent him, and as he was my friend on earth, I shall take great interest in telling him of the wonderful power and magnificent love of Jesus. So I will take him with me now and try to show him the way to salvation and to surcease from his sufferings.

He will come to you and tell you of the result of our interview, and how he then thinks of what I will tell him of salvation. So thanking you, I will say good night.

Your brother in Christ,
R. G. Ingersoll.

Relates his experience in obtaining the Divine Love

February 18th, 1916.

I am here, Robert G. Ingersoll.

Well, my friend, I come tonight to say a few words, for I have been very anxious to take advantage of your kindness and communicate a few thoughts that have come as the result of my progress here in matters spiritual.

As I told you in my last communication, I am a thoroughly convinced spirit as to the truths of Christianity as taught by the Master—not as set forth in the Bible, but as I have been instructed by him and your grandmother, and other bright spirits, since I have had my understanding and soul opened to these great truths. I have progressed very much since I last wrote you and have received into my soul a wonderful abundance of this Divine Love of the Father—which you first called to my attention when I thought that you were a foolish and deceived man. But I now know that you were not foolish, nor deceived, for this Divine Love is a real, existing thing, and is obtainable by all God's children, whether on earth or in the spirit world, who may seek for it in the way that the Master teachers.

My mind, as well as my soul, has opened up to the truth of these teachings, and I now realize that I was in great darkness on earth in my own beliefs and teachings, and that man is not of himself sufficient to bring about his own salvation, but must seek for and believe that his salvation is dependent very largely upon the help that will come to him from the spirit world. I mean, that such help is necessary whether he seeks the Divine Love of the Father or only the purification of his natural love and the happiness that will arise there from.

Of course, man's own will and desires are important factors in obtaining this salvation, and he may go on for his whole mortal life, and for a long time after he comes into the spirit world, and never obtain this salvation unless he realizes the fact that he needs this outside help and that it is ready and open to him for the seeking.

I know that many may be astonished and refuse to believe that I am now in this condition of belief; but as I when on earth sought only for the truth, so when I came to the spirit world I sought for the truth, and when I found it, as I have, I believed and accepted it and made it a part of my faith, with the result that I am now convinced beyond all doubt that I am the possessor of a knowledge that has its foundation in truth which never changes.

I am in the earth plane yet, but in a very bright and beautiful location, and free from the darkness and sufferings that I first endured when I came to the spirit world.

Life is a thing that is lived on earth only for a short time, and man is given the opportunity to make of it the great means of his salvation and progress to the higher spheres of light and happiness and immortality that those bright spirits tell me of; and when men fail to make the most of the opportunity which the mortal life affords, then they lose that which, when they become spirits, would help them beyond all conception to progress to the higher realms. I know that in the case of many thinking men, as in my own case, it is impossible for them to believe the teachings and dogmas of the churches and the interpretations and even many of the precepts of the Bible; and as a consequence men turn entirely away from these things, though there are many truths in the Bible, and become seekers of knowledge which science and their own reasoning powers afford them.

But the trouble here is that science does not teach things spiritual, and their reasoning powers must be based very largely upon what their senses tell them to be true; and these senses can only learn what naturally comes to them, which necessarily is of the material. As a consequence, men discard entirely all things spiritual which they cannot understand and thus render impossible any development of their soul qualities, except that they do realize the great qualities of their natural love and, in many cases, develop it, and in that way gain a progress that does help them in their condition of light and happiness both on earth and here.

Well, as you suggest that you are tired, I will stop, but will soon come and finish my communication.

Yes, and I am glad that you feel that way about it. You have many spirits here who desire to write and some of them are such elevated and wise spirits that I feel that their writings will benefit you more than mine.

Yes, I am with her[71] quite often, and she is a wonderful spirit in love and wisdom, and has such deep and wondrous knowledge of God and His Love. I almost adore her, and feel that if I had not met her I probably would not be where I now am. I tell you, I am thankful that I came to you that night.

Yes, I see your wife quite frequently and she is a wonderfully beautiful and happy spirit, and makes so many other spirits happy by her goodness and help. She is a very positive spirit as well and she lets nothing stand in the way of her work and mission.

So, my dear friend, I will say good night and God bless you.

R. G. Ingersoll.

Describes his progress and his difficulty in changing the views of his followers

April 24th, 1916.

I am here, Robert G. Ingersoll.

I come tonight to tell you of my progress since last I wrote you. You will remember that I had declared to you my conversion to Christianity—I mean the true Christianity of Jesus and to the faith in the

---

[71] Mr. Padgett's grandmother. (J.P.G.)

Divine Love of the Father. Since then I have been praying and seeking for this love and the faith that comes with it, and now I have progressed so that I am in the Third Sphere, where I find such beauty and happiness as I never conceived of on earth or since coming to the spirit world.

Now I know what was meant by Jesus when he said, "In my Father's house are many mansions," for I have one that is very beautiful and grand, filled with everything to make me happy and to satisfy my heart's longings. Of books I have so many that I cannot find time to read them; and all the appointments of my home are so very beautiful and satisfying to the eye, as well as comfortable for its occupancy. But above and beyond all is the happiness that comes from the possession of this Divine Love of the Father, which to me is the most wonderful revelation and reality in all my experience, either on earth or in the spirit world.

I now think with regret of my years of erroneous teachings on earth, and of my failure to seek for and know, at least partly, the great truths of a continuous life and the existence of God; and when I contrast my beliefs then and my knowledge now, my happiness then and my happiness now, I realize that as a mortal I was very ignorant and very unhappy. I know that Jesus is the way to immortality and life everlasting and to the true and always increasing happiness, and that the followers of his teachings of the Father's truths will never be disappointed in their expectations.

My work now is to help those mortals, and spirits as well, who read and believe my books, and as a consequence lose the opportunity for learning the truths and the way to the Father's Love; and very many of my followers live on earth and many have become spirits. I search for them, and when I find them I tell them of my great mistakes and try to turn their thoughts to the true way to become redeemed children of God. My work is continuous, and sometimes disappointing, for when I come to some spirits and attempt to tell them of my new beliefs and knowledge of myself being mistaken, they wonder why may it not be that I am equally mistaken in my new beliefs; and the result is that I find it difficult to convince some of them of the truths that I attempt to teach them.

But as I sowed the seeds of the pernicious and false beliefs when a mortal, now I am bound to root up these seeds and plant in their places the seeds of truth. And I can't tell you how much happiness I experience when one of these deluded followers of mine discards the old beliefs and accepts my new teachings, and how unhappy I am when they tell me that, as they believed what I taught them on earth and were satisfied, so now in the spirit they prefer the same belief and are satisfied. And as they stay in this condition of belief they remain in darkness and unhappiness, and I, knowing that I am the cause of their darkness and unhappiness, am also unhappy and always in search of some one of these who will accept my teachings of truth. And thus I fully realize the meaning of "What a man sows that shall he also reap."

But this is my work, and you must know that it is self-imposed, for I see that until I have removed the evils by me taught and engendered, I cannot be so happy and progress as rapidly as I desire. And I want further to say that when I succeed in convincing any of my followers of the truth, I enlist them in my cause of correction and they work with me, for no spirit so well understands the meaning of error as he who once indulged in that same error, as I most assuredly did.

I will not write longer tonight, except to say to all who have heard of me and have read my books and imbibed my beliefs, that I am a Christian, a follower of Jesus the Christ, and a believer, with knowledge, in the Divine Love of the Father. Yes, when I told you that, I actually believed what I said, and really felt sorry for your ignorance; but I want now to assure you with gratitude that that conversation was the means of starting me in the progress to a knowledge of the truth and the gaining of this Divine Love. Oh, I was very ignorant, and with it I now realize there was much pride in my own opinion, for I thought that my reasoning powers and my research in things of the religious past had given me a knowledge that could not be gainsaid or overcome. So my brother, you now see that truth is truth, and that no matter whether mortals learn it or understand it, or not, it is still the truth and never changes. Thanking you for your kindness, I will say good night.

Your brother in Christ,
R. G. Ingersoll.

Life and death, the friends of mortals, each to be welcomed. The one, the friend for eternity; the other, the friend for only a moment, but what a friend!

March 10th, 1917.

I am here, R. G. Ingersoll.

Tonight I am a very happy spirit, and one who realizes that "it is not all of life to live, or yet of death to die," for life and death are mere incidents in the existence of the immortal soul's career through eternity. Life on earth is but a short breathing of the soul in bondage, yet prized so highly by mortals; and death of the physical is the liberating of that soul from its bondage, and yet, men fear and shun it, and, if possible, would never let it come to them. This may be said to be natural and not to be wondered at, and all because mortals do not know that life and death are brothers, working for the good of humanity, the former giving them the opportunity to seek and possess happiness or misery, and the latter ending that opportunity in this, that happiness may be increased without having to undergo the retarding influence that life on earth throws around mortals, and misery, or rather the cause thereof, prevented from increasing. So you see, life and death are complementary, the one positive and the other negative, but each the great helpful friend of the human soul.

You wonder who I am, and I wonder that I am what I am, and not what I was.

My friend, life has continued with me in greater and more enlarged abundance, until now I am the possessor of that life which Jesus came to earth to declare to be the heritage of every mortal who should seek it. My friend, death has left me, and in leaving me took with him all the possibilities of increased causes of unhappiness in my soul. The results or effects of the causes that existed in my soul while in the mortal life came with me in more acute and overpowering abundance; but no new or additional causes to produce additional effects came with me. Death took them with himself when he departed from me forever.

Life and Death—the friends of mortals, each to be welcomed! The one, the friend for eternity; the other, the friend for only a moment, but what a friend!

I intended tonight to write you a long and (as I think) important message relating to the real world of spirits, but thought it best not to do so, and hence gave you the little impersonal thoughts with reference to my friends and your friends.

I will come soon. Good night and God bless you.

Your brother in Christ,

R. G. Ingersoll.

Comments on the teachings of Swedenborg while on earth

March 29th, 1917.

I am here, Robert G. Ingersoll.

Well, I come first because I am more modest than the other spirits who are present, and will say a few words and then give place to the others.

I have been with you while you were reading the work of Swedenborg, and was much interested in the impression made upon your mind by what he said, and found that your impressions were not very different from those that I had when I read his book while on earth, except this, that I had no belief in the spirit world, while you have. Of course, you know from the knowledge that you have received through the messages that have come to you that many of his assertions are erroneous and the creatures of a mind that was fitted with a great knowledge of scientific things as accepted in his day, and also of a desire on his part to reconcile his knowledge of science and of theological teachings with what he supposed had been imparted to him by spirits and angels. But the result was that they could not be reconciled, and the consequence was that he declared doctrines and teachings that were utterly at variance with spiritual truths; and no one knows better than he does at this time of the falsity of many of his teachings.

Swedenborg had many opportunities for receiving and imparting the truth, but his great learning in the sciences and his beliefs in the old orthodox doctrines of the church in which he had been reared led him to conclusions and declarations of truths—as he believed—that were contrary to both science and religion in its higher and true sense.

Well, you may wonder that I write on this subject, and to answer any question that may arise from your surprise, I only desire to say that since I have received a knowledge of God's plan for the salvation of mankind and some of His Divine Love, I have been investigating with all the energies of my soul the great truths that exist and which are never changed. And in such investigation I have talked with Swedenborg and have learned from him the sources of his wonderful declarations and doctrines as set forth in his works. He is now in full knowledge of the truth, and also of his errors of his own learned disquisitions,[72] as his followers believe and pronounce them to be.

He can best explain to you the causes of his erroneous beliefs and what led him to attempt to explain the teachings that he received in the spirit world and his experiences in the mystical way that he did. I will not write more on the subject.

But I, Ingersoll, who was truly and honestly an agnostic, can and do say that in this spirit world I had less darkness and less erroneous beliefs to get rid of than had Swedenborg; and while he had more of this Divine Love in his soul than had I—for I had none—yet his mind was so warped by his intellectual conceptions of the truth that it was easier for me to find the true way and progress in it towards the Father's Love and the Celestial heavens than it was for him. This he has told me, and I have listened to him with much interest, and have learned that the way of the narrow and bigoted orthodox believer is a harder road to travel than that of the agnostic who has not in his soul been too much defiled by sin and evil.

I am still progressing and praying, and believing and receiving, the inflow of this Wonderful Love. Oh, I tell you that this Love is the greatest thing in all the spirit world, as well as on earth, and the only thing that brings the soul in close union and harmony with the Father. I will not write more now, but soon I will come and write my promised letter.

---

[72] A long or elaborate essay or discussion on a particular subject. (G.J.C.)

So, my dear friend, with my love and gratitude, I will say good night.

Your brother in Christ,

R. G. Ingersoll.

Intended to enlighten Mr. Padgett, so that the truths later on in the formal messages would contain more exact explanations that the Celestials, including Jesus, would be able to give to the world

November 11th, 1914.

I am here, your grandmother.

Yes, I am here and I wish to tell you that you must not let what I said to you last night discourage you for I was only trying to let you know that you must not forget to pray to God for His Blessing. You were not in a condition to fully understand what I wrote. You were only in a condition of doubt as to what it was that you should do in order to feel the influence of my meaning.

Question and Answer:

Yes it is and you must not so worship him. They were not only wrong in that particular, but they did not understand that Jesus does not want to be worshipped in that way. They may follow him in his teachings and example, but must worship only God. You can help them to see the Truth and you should try to do so.

Yes, I know, but nevertheless you should make the effort for they must learn that Jesus is only a son of God and is not the God or any part of Him. He is the one for them to seek and ask his aid in order to learn the truth. Yes, I know, but they will have to learn sooner or later that the Holy Spirit is of God and not a medium of Jesus to bring about their New Birth and entrance into God's Kingdom. He (God) is the one that confers the blessings of the Spirit and they will realize it when they receive the Spirits inflow of Love and Grace. Yes, many have and their influence is good and helpful, their spirit friends are with them at their meetings and help them to realize that God is Love and Truth.

Yes, sometimes, but they do not enjoy being there and consequently do not remain very long or take any part in the services. He is not present at the various meetings that are held in the several churches over the whole country, but his truths are there in the character of spirits who are ordained to do the work of teaching the truths which he taught and which are the truths of God.

The Holy Spirit is the one that can cause the inflowing of God's Love and it is present in all meetings as it is without form or personality. It is the messenger of God and it can be in all places at the same time so that the penitents no matter how far apart can receive it's influence and feel its saving Grace and Love. It is not necessary for it to use other spirits to carry its love and influence. It of itself is able and all comprehending enough to influence the persons who seek for its inflowing. So do not think that you have to have Jesus present in order to obtain the blessings of the Holy Spirit. He meant that when they are gathered together for the purpose of seeking the Love of God he would be able to help them feel the influence of the Holy Spirit, he would not have to be present himself for that purpose, but he would be represented by the Holy Spirit.

No, he cannot, for he is a person and has all the limitations that belong to the individual. Jesus is not a spirit in the sense that God is a spirit. He is only an individualized spirit as you are. He is only a spirit of such wonderful development that he can control all the spirits of his own manner of thinking and who have been Born Again into God's Kingdom so that he can have them do his work just as he teaches them to do. Yes, he can direct the Holy Spirit in the sense that when the penitent prays for help the Holy Spirit will respond and fulfill the work that the Father has provided it to do.

Jesus is the truest exponent of his Father's Truths and he alone (only) through his teachings can cause the Holy Spirit to enter the hearts and souls of mankind. No, it is not, for the Father has given him the power to control all the spirits that are of the Father's Kingdom of Truth and Love. Christ is not only a spirit of the Father, but is the one that God gave to Jesus when he anointed him on his earthly mission. He is the one spirit that cannot be made to do anything that is contrary to God's Love and Law. No, not in addition to the spirit that Jesus had, but the spirit that God gave to Jesus at the time of the anointing.

The spirit that Jesus had before that time became one and the same with the Christ Spirit—they are now one—Jesus is not a man as is taught by some writers, but is the Christ of God—a spirit that is full of God's truths. He is the great dispenser of truths and he cannot lie nor do anything but what the Father has given him to do.

Yes, Jesus the Spirit is only a spirit as you have a spirit, but Jesus the Christ is a Spirit that is without form or limitations, so that he can be everywhere at the same time. Yes, he meant that he as the Christ would be with all peoples wherever they might be gathered together seeking his help and teachings, but as Jesus the mere spirit, he did not mean that he would be with them.

So you may believe that he is with you always in the sense that he is your Christ. It is Jesus the teacher of truth and not the Christ, the latter is with you and everyone else at all times. Only the penitent must ask that he let them feel his influence and teach them the Truth of God, and the fact that the Holy Spirit is waiting to enter into their hearts and fill them with the Divine Love.

Go to the church where you were last night, as you will be much more benefited than you will be by attending the other churches. You will be under the influence of more spirits who have received the New Birth.

No, not in the sense that the Holy Spirit is in their hearts, they are only letting their minds become confused with the idea that Jesus' blood or crucifixion saves them when the fact is the blood of Jesus or the crucifixion is not necessary, as a matter of belief to their salvation. The only thing that saves them from their sins and reconciles them to God is that they must become conscious of God's Truths and receive the Holy Spirit into their souls. No vicarious suffering on the part of Jesus is necessary to save them. He never taught that erroneous doctrine and it is not doing any good by being taught by the preachers who claim to represent his cause.

No, only in the sense that these things (his blood and crucifixion) call the attention of mankind to Jesus and his mission on earth. As between God and man, no blood of Jesus or vicarious suffering can appease God or save man. God is a God of Love and does not have any wrath to be appeased. He is only too glad to have his children come to Him and be at-one with Him. He is not waiting to punish them or have them suffer because of any wrath that He may be supposed to have towards them. They suffer only because they have violated his laws and they must do that which will remove the causes of their violation of these laws.

Mankind is not the object of God's anger, but are the dear children of His Love. He is not pleased when they do wrong or when they do not obey his precepts. Let not the idea that God delights in the punishment of the wicked make you think that God wants any one of His children to suffer. He is only too ready to save and have the sinner come to His Love and Care. He is the one Perfect Love that exists.

You must stop writing now as you won't go to your dinner.

Your loving grandmother.[73]

---

[73] This message is a composite of two, being published in Volume III and Volume IV. It is clear that Ann Rollins is having difficulty expressing her meaning here which suggests poor rapport. (G.J.C.)

The Truths are not to be refuted by any preaching or teachings, or any reference to the Bible, that are contrary to these Truths

October 28th, 1915.

I am here, James.

I will write only a few lines tonight, as conditions are not very good, for you are tired and have been working too much to permit us to make a very close rapport.

I want to say that today I have been with you and my charge (Dr. Stone) a part of the time, and heard your conversation, and was pleased to hear your conversation, and was pleased to hear you both express yourselves so strongly with reference to the truths that you have received; and you will not be disappointed when the time comes for belief to become an experience.

The truths are not to be refuted by any preaching or teachings, or any reference to the Bible that are contrary to these truths. And I here declare to you that the only way to the Celestial Spheres is by the way of the New Birth, as it has been explained to you.

I also desire to encourage the mortal to whom I have attached myself especially (Dr. Stone), and assure him that I am with him very often and impress him with thoughts that will make him realize more and more that only the truth that he has knowledge of will fit him for the work that is before him to perform, and that he must endeavor to increase his faith so that his beliefs will become things of real substance, for they are real, and when he gets in that condition and attempts his work, what will appear real to him will, in fact, be real, and so real that other mortals will know the benefits that arise from their reality.

I will not write more now. So with my love, I will say good night.

Your brother in Christ,

James.

Apostle of Jesus.

Jesus was never learned in the wisdom of India or Egypt or Persia. He was taught by the Father and the Angels of God

April 3rd, 1917.

I am here, James (the Lesser).

I will not write long tonight, but pray to the Father to bless you and make your faith increase.

No, I never belonged to any of those sects, nor did Jesus. He was never learned in the wisdom of India or Egypt, or Persia, as the writer whom you were reading tonight asserted. He was taught by the Father and the Angels of God, and his knowledge was that which came from these teaching and the opening up of his soul perceptions. He was not a son of the Magi, or of the wise men of any of the countries referred to, but as to knowledge and wisdom he was a son of the Father only.

I will come again soon and write you.

So, good night.

Your brother in Christ,

James.[74]

All the writings of the New Testament, as they now exist, contain so many things which the original writers did not write or believe in

August 28th, 1916.

I am here, John.

I merely want to say that you will soon be well and in condition to receive some of our messages which we are anxiously waiting to write. The time is approaching when the book will have to be published and it is very necessary that you get these messages in full so that you can compile the book. Of course we want to incorporate every truth that is necessary to make known to mankind, and to do so we will have to work faster.

Yes I, I know him well (James the Lesser, the subject of a question asked by Mr. Padgett) and he was the brother of Jesus, the real brother, having the same father and mother that Jesus had and all speculations as to his having parents who were other than the parents of Jesus are not in accord with the truth, and were falsified, to make it appear that Mary was a virgin. He was not in the beginning an apostle of Jesus and came to believe in him late in the ministry of Jesus, but when at last he became convinced that Jesus was the true messiah he became a very earnest and hardworking follower of Jesus, and also the first Christian Bishop of Jerusalem.

I have no personal knowledge as to whether he wrote the epistles ascribed to him or not but he has said that he wrote some portion of the first epistle and a portion of the second but that he did not write the third. That in each of these epistles are many assertions of truth which are wrong and which he did not teach. All the writings of the

---

[74] In more recent times—2001 to 2003—a Divine Love medium received from Judas a significant amount of previously unknown material concerning Jesus' life on earth. These have been published in hard copy as well as in Kindle format, and are mentioned at the beginning of this edition. (G.J.C.)

New Testament, as they now exist, contain so many things which the original writers did not write and which they did not teach or believe in, that it is with difficulty that the mortal, even though a great student, can separate the true from the false. And that is one reason that enters into our motives for writing a new revelation of the truth.

The truths will be made plain and you must not let the writings of the Bible influence you in your receiving a correct conception of these truths. I will not write more now.

So with my love I will say good night.

John.[75]

Jesus has no vicar on earth: The claimed infallibility of the Pope of the Catholic Church is a delusion and a snare. The worship of Jesus as God is blasphemous and a very harmful untruth

December 26th, 1917.

I am here, Jesus.

Well, my dear brother, I am glad to find that you are in so much better condition, and I know that very soon now I will be able to resume the delivery of my messages.

Well, I have no vicar on earth (in answer to question by Mr. Padgett). In the first place, I am not God, but a mere spirit—a child of God—and one that worships Him with all the devotion of my soul, praying for an increase bestowal of His Love and for a complete unity with Him, and with the longings to progress eternally in the development of my soul.

In the second place, the Pope is a mere man, and he can only represent God to the extent that he has in his own soul the Divine Love and the consequent soul development. The mere fact that he is the head of the Catholic Church gives him no greater privilege, or no greater commission to represent God on earth, than is possessed by any other man with the same amount of soul development. His claimed infallibility is a delusion and a snare, and he is just as much subject to sin, and sinning, even as Pope of the Church, as is any other mortal; and this claim, which is an attribute belonging only to God, will be one of the sins for which he will suffer for very much when he comes to the spirit world and has his soul opened up to the truth.

At some time I intend to write you in detail as to the Catholic Church and its erroneous dogmas, beliefs, and teachings, and as to its

---

[75] This message is a composite of three, being published in Volume III and twice in Volume IV. In this edition the second instance has not been included. (G.J.C.)

destiny. But this I will say: that the worship of me as God is a blasphemy, and a thing that is so blasphemous that I care not to remain in the earth plane and hear the prayers of these misguided Christians.[76] I know that this will sound surprising, and un-Christian, to many, and they will continue to believe in their faith in me as God, and also to worship me. But it is a very harmful untruth, and these people will have to realize it sooner or later, in the spirit world. And this is one of the errors that my messages are designed to eradicate. Well, my dear brother, have faith.

Your brother and friend,

Jesus.

Not the blood or death of Jesus, but his living and teaching men the Way to obtain the Divine Love of the Father are what saves a soul from sin and fits It for Heaven

September 24th, 1915.

I am here, John the Baptist.

I desire to write to you tonight about a certain truth which you must know, in order to be able to teach others the importance of studying the plan of God for the salvation of man—I mean, that in order for men to be saved from their sins they must believe in the way that the Master shall teach you in his messages. I do not intend to dwell at large upon the New Birth, for that has already been told you a number of times. But I want now to deal with the truth that this is the one thing that perfects mankind, and spirits as well, and enables them to obtain the soul qualities which are absolutely necessary before a man can become at-one with the Father.

The other things which the churches teach as necessary sacraments, such as baptism, the laying on of hands, and the Lord's Supper, or communion, are things which are not necessary. They were never intended as being anything more than merely symbolical, and even as symbols, the last-mentioned does no good, but rather, harm, for besides being used to remind the followers of Jesus of his communion with them before his sacrifice, they look upon it as something which saves a soul from sin and fits it for Heaven.

I want you to understand that all these things are not important to a soul's becoming at-one with God, and that mortals must learn the truth of what I say.

Many preachers, as well as laymen, believe that only the blood of Jesus can save from sin, and that his death was necessary for man's salvation; but I want to tell you that if he had died a natural death,

---

[76] This refers to the increased worship of him at Christmas. (J.P.G.)

beloved by all who knew him, and honored by the whole Jewish nation, his blood would have been just as efficacious, and his death just as important, as they were, because he was killed as a result of hatred and envy on the part of the Jewish authorities. In neither case would the blood or the death in one particular have anything to do with the salvation of men.

His living and teaching, and the making known to man the Great Gift of the Father, and the way to find the Gift and possess it, were the things that brought to man salvation. Jesus lived and taught and loved us; he did not die and suffer and make an atonement for us.

The living Christ is of more importance to our happiness and salvation than the dead Jesus, and so Jesus, himself, teaches. And he is not pleased with those who teach the dying Jesus instead of the living Christ. I, John, was and not only a precursor of the Master, but a follower, also, and it was not his blood or death that saved me, but his living and teaching me the way to obtain the Divine Love of the Father.

I am much interested in the salvation of all men, and want to do everything in my power to help men to learn the way to truth and light, and Love. I am trying, as well as are many others of our band who are with you now, in carrying forward this work of showing men the truths which will lead them to the Father's Love.

I have only to say further that you must pray more to the Father and keep up your courage and belief in the Master, and all these things will be properly worked out to a final and happy conclusion.

I will not write more tonight. So with my love and blessings, I will say good night.

Your brother in Christ,
John the Baptist.

Explains the spiritual importance of the only Prayer that men need offer to the Father in order to become redeemed children and partakers of Immortality

February 6th, 1917.

I am here, John.

I want to say a few words in reference to your conversation about the Prayer and the importance of thoroughly understanding it, and its spiritual significance and the wonderful truths that it contains. I heard you say that when you first received it there was in its meaning all confusion and that you did not understand that it would convey any great truths, or help very much those who should offer it to the Father. Well, I have no doubt but what you say is true, and there is a good reason for the same, and that is that it is so full of the declarations of wonderful truths and thoughts for soul aspirations that it was difficult, and almost impossible, for your mind or soul to grasp the same, and like every other truth that men do not understand, it does not at first reception appear to be a thing of truth that men can learn, and learning make their own.

But the truths of that prayer, when rightly analyzed, will appear sufficient to meet every necessity that men need or are in want of to bring them to a perfect at-onement with the Father and assure them of eternal salvation as His Divine children and the partakers of immortality. Very soon I will come and give you a full explanation of the Prayer and its deep and vital truths, so that you may become real possessors of its full meaning. Tonight I do not think it best for me to write more, and in closing will say to you and your friends[77] that you must not become discouraged in the work that you have before you, or in the work that you are now doing, for I, John, tell you that your labor is absolutely necessary to make our truths known to humanity, and there are no others of all the men of earth who have been selected for this work or can perform it, for none have the qualifications developed for the rapport which we have established.

So take what I say seriously, and do not let the importance of the work, or the thought that you are not suited to do the work, cause you to think that we have made a mistake in our selection, or that this power that has been given to you is a mere myth and without reality. The high spirits who are followers of and are led by the Master have, in following the Master's desire, determined that you three shall be the ones to start the spread of these great truths amongst men, and leave behind you helpers who will carry on the work after you come over to receive the reward of your well-doing.

I am John, and I write with authority, and must be believed. So with my love to you both, and the blessings of the Father, I will say good night.

John.

White Eagle and Arondah assist Dr. Stone in his healing work

April 18th, 1916.

I am here, Arondah and White Eagle.

I am the guardian of Dr. Stone. I was the Hindu guide. I want to tell him that I was with him when he treated the sick woman. Her name was (Miss Fallin, an elderly patient). I was an assistant and we were

---

[77] Dr. Stone and Mr. Morgan. (J.P.G.)

trying to help him in ministering to her and are making every effort to establish that rapport that will enable him to do her good.

He must have faith for notwithstanding that she appears to be beyond all hope there is more than hope and if we can only establish the rapport that is necessary, he will be able to help her so that she will recover and restore to her the powers of sensation in the apparently dead portions of the body and also recover strength of mind sufficient to enable her to regain her condition, and the necessity of her following his instructions. We will make a special effort in his case in order to demonstrate the effect of the powers which the spirit world has over the conditions of mortals where all hope has been abandoned by physicians who rely only so far as drugs and medicines.

Besides our powers there is a Doctor present who has the power of high spirits and such powers are beyond the comprehension of mortals who have not the faith of which he has been told in the messages which have come to you. Faith and prayer are mighty instruments in effecting cures of the human ills, and in this case the Doctor must pray and exercise his faith and he will see the glory of God manifested in the case of this woman. So tell him to rely on us and in the powers of the bright spirits for they will both be with him in his treatment of this woman.

I thought it best to write this so that he may be encouraged in his good work.

Tell him that we will be with him on every visit that he makes to her, and will try to get conditions so that our powers may be exercised in helping him.

But above all pray and exercise faith.

White Eagle.[78]

First message through Mr. Padgett

December 17th, 1916.

Let me write a few lines, as I am so anxious to declare some facts, which when on earth were not facts to my understanding and beliefs. And oh, the pity of it all.

Today, I was present at the church where the preacher discussed and criticized my teachings and me also and I am compelled to admit that some of his criticisms were true and justified. I am Mrs. Eddy, and the founder of the sect which bears the high sounding name of Christian

---

[78] I am glad to say the woman who was advanced in age who I was instrumental in treating was restored to good health and lived many years after the healing. I recognize that the healing that brought results was on account of the high healing spirits. (Dr. L. R. Stone.)

Science, and the doctrines of which are neither Christian nor science as I now know from actual experience in the spirit world, where many of my teachings are shown to be not in accord with truth, and so misleading.

I now realize that my mind and soul were not in accord as regards the truth while I lived (as) a mortal, and that my (material) mind was superior in causing me to have certain beliefs which I left to the world in the form of doctrines contained in my text book and my other writings.

My soul possessed a considerable degree of the Divine Love, as that Love has been explained to you, and when I came to the spirit world that Love was my salvation, notwithstanding the errors of many of my teachings as to mind and matter, and non reality of sin and evil.

I am too weak to write more, but I will soon come for I must declare the truths.

Good night.

Mrs. Eddy.[79]

Discusses the equality of the sexes

March 17th, 1917.

I am here, John.

I have been listening to your conversation tonight and was interested in some things that were said as to the inferiority of woman to man, and will soon come and write you a message on this subject; for the conceptions of your friends antagonistic to the equality of the sexes are all wrong, and they must learn that women, in the totality, are not only the equal of man, but in certain senses are their superiors.

It is too late tonight to write on the subject, and I will postpone the writing until a time later.

Your brother in Christ,

John.

Mr. Padgett's declaration of belief in Jesus has advanced his spiritual development. A New Church will arise: And the Love of the Father will be the foundation stone of its establishment

April 4th, 1915.

I am here, Jesus.

---

[79] This message is a composite of two, being published in Volume II and Volume IV. (G.J.C.)

I was with you today and I heard you declare your belief in me and my being the Jesus of the Bible; and while it did not have much impression on the hearers, yet it will cause them to think, and possibly lead them to a realization that I am the true Jesus and that my teachings which you will receive are the teachings of truth. I was much pleased that you declared yourself so emphatically and earnestly, and that your faith in me is so fixed and certain.

You have advanced yourself in the way of your spiritual development by such positive assertion of your belief, and you will find that your faith will increase and you will progress in your development very rapidly.

I will now be able to communicate with you more satisfactorily than before, for the mere fact of declaring your belief in such a way, and the knowledge that those to whom you spoke who do not believe that I am other than God, and a part of God, will help you beyond what you may conceive.

You are now much more in rapport with me than ever, and you will soon realize that you are very near the Kingdom of the Father.

The discourse on forgiveness made a deep impression on the father, and he will commence to think that his belief in the church dogmas and creeds does not satisfy the longings of his soul, as they have heretofore.

Be my true disciple under all circumstances, and your reward will be great, both here and hereafter.

I will come to you soon and finish my last discourse, and when completed, you will see that the truths which I shall declare are truths that will show man that the Love of the Father is the one all-sufficient means to His Kingdom and favor. Be true to me and to yourself, and you will be one of the overcomers[80] who will inherit the eternal Kingdom of the Holy Home of redeemed spirits.

You will not only feel the great benefit yourself of this great truth of the New Birth, but you will lead many others to embrace the truth and receive the benefits of the Father which He has prepared for all who may love Him and receive His Love.

So my dear brother and disciple, let your efforts continue to learn these truths, and teach others the way of my truths and their own redemption.

I will be with you very often, for on you I depend to receive and spread my Gospel of Truth; and when you have done this, mankind will turn from their condition of formal religion and embrace the true and

---

[80] This is a reference to Revelations 2:7: *He that hath an ear, let him hear what the Spirit saith unto the churches; To him that overcometh will I give to eat of the tree of life, which is in the midst of the paradise of God.* (G.J.C.)

only way to their salvation. A new church will arise,[81] and the Love of the Father waiting to be bestowed on all men will be the foundation stone of its establishment.

I know that you will have disappointments and trials in doing this work, but only be faithful and steadfast, and the great object of my teachings will be accomplished on earth, as in Heaven.

I must not write more now, but I want to assure you that your action today is of more significance than you realize, and you will soon see the importance of what you declared in the presence of those who doubt the truth of your declarations.

So with my love and assurance of tender care, and the blessings of the Father, I am your own loving and true brother,
Jesus.

Writes, that very few mortals have Mr. Padgett's rare phase of mediumship

June 25th, 1917.

I am here, Luke.

I have listened to your conversation and have enjoyed the facts disclosed of the knowledge of the truths that you two possess of these truths that have been conveyed to you by the various messages and the intuitions if I may so describe which I wish to say that I have also impressed you with these truths. And here I desire to say that in our working to make plain to you these truths by our impressions or as some mediums might say our inspirations, but we do not let you depend entirely on the mere language of the message but we try to give you accurate understanding of the true interpretation of these messages.

This you may not know but it is a fact and in many instances our work of this nature has caused you to conceive the truth that is delicate shades of meaning that otherwise you might not have received. And from this you will understand that you have the clairvoyant faculty as well as that of writing. And when I say clairvoyant I do not mean that faculty which enables you to hear clearly with the spirit ear, but rather that which enables you to receive our impressions and inspires you to being actually conscious of the reception of these impressions.

So you see you have the opportunity of receiving these things which very few mortals have, for this is a phase of mediumship as it might be called which is rare and not possessed by many mortals. It

---

[81] Jesus' prediction in 1915 became a reality in 1958 when under Jesus of Nazareth's direction the Foundation Church of the New Birth, Inc. was established. (J.P.G.) However I tend to see this as a far wider comment relating to a more general uptake of these Truths than the establishment of what was certainly a beginning. (G.J.C.)

differs from the ordinary inspirational phase in this that where the medium receives information in this latter way the spirit ear actually hears the thoughts coming of which the medium is conscious while in the former method there is neither an actual hearing nor a consciousness on the part of the mortal of the thing conveyed. And all during the delivery of these messages of the higher truths both to you and your friend, you will have the benefit of our instructions conveyed in this impressional way.

Well I am glad that you are both progressing in Soul development as you are doing, and if you continue to pray and seek this will increase until the time will come that will bring to you powers that you do not now conceive of.

You both as you know have special guardians who are looking after you in reference to these spiritual things that will not fail to succeed in making you what they desire, and what you will wonder at when the time of your realization comes.

I heard what my charge (Eugene Morgan) said as to my writing him a special message dealing with truth that will help in the work that he is now doing among the deluded spirits in purgatory and I will soon fulfill that promise and when I see that he is in the proper condition, I will write.

I will not write more tonight but with my love advise you both to pray and have faith and you will be happier on earth and more than happy when you come to your eternal homes. Good night.

Your brother in Christ,
Luke.

Pray: That they all may be one; even as Thou, Father, art in me, and I in Thee, that they also may be one in us; that the world may believe that Thou hast sent me. John 17:21

Ruth's trust in the Father's Love

April 10th, 1958.
Received by Dr Samuels.
Washington D.C.

I am here, Jesus.

In this sermon I continue to show you how the Old Testament of the Hebrews developed stories in which some of the characters act towards their fellowmen in a spirit of love attesting to that human love which was implanted in mankind by God and was the forerunner of that sublime love which the Father has available for whosoever of His children seek it in earnest prayer, so that, abiding in their souls, it will provide the salvation which—as the Messiah of God—I brought with me when on earth.

This story concerns Naomi and her daughter-in-law Ruth who followed the old widow back from Moab to her native Bethlehem in Judea, from whence she had come with her sons at a time when famine dwelt in the land Palestine. And in Moab, Naomi, the widow, lived with her two sons and Daughters-in-law, until, given the harshness of the times, the two sons were stricken and she decided to return to her native land, with the thought that her daughters-in-law would perhaps find new husbands in their own country.

Now Ruth's sister-in-law, Oprah, returned to her people and to those gods which the Moabites of those times worshipped, and indeed, Naomi bade Ruth do likewise, but Ruth replied with those words which have become so soul-stirring in its religious appeal, not only in Hebrew, but in many languages all over the earth.

"Entreat me not to leave thee or to return from following after thee: for whither thou goest, I will go ; and where thou lodgest, I will lodge: thy people shall be my people, and thy God my God. Where thou diest, will I die, and there will I be buried: the Lord do so to me, and more also, if ought but death part thee and me." (Ruth 1: 16 - 17)

Now from those memorable words, it may be concluded that Ruth, the Moabite, daughter of a pagan people, had received some unusual or miraculous knowledge of the Father, to be able to thus forsake her own local gods and adhere to the God whose existence had been made known to her through her Hebrew husband and mother-in-law; and to a certain degree, this is true. But actually, the loving nature of the Father, to the extent that it was known to the peoples of those days, had become known to her through her relationship with Naomi. For Naomi was kind, and loving, treating her daughters-in-law with a solicitude and a tenderness, and a care for their welfare that brought out in Ruth a great feeling of love and devotion, and it was thus that she wanted to share the fortunes or vicissitudes with this woman who was to her like a mother. And it was these qualities of warmth and love and affection, of concern for Ruth and her interests, that made Ruth realize that here was a person who in her way of life manifested a soul that shone with the light of her loving Father in Heaven.

And so Ruth concluded, and she had had many years of life together with Naomi to come to this decision, that a good hearted woman such as Naomi could exist only if her Creator—her God—possessed the wonderful qualities of love and kindness which He had imparted to His Creation. and since Naomi was a Hebrew, she knew in her heart that the God of the Hebrews was a God of Love, such as He manifested through His children.

And when Ruth made her abode in Bethlehem, she found that just as a Hebrew woman could be loving and kind to a degree not before experienced in her life, so could a Hebrew man be as tender and loving, whether he was her husband or not. For when Boaz saw her gleaning in the fields, his heart went out in sympathy for her, because of her unpretentiousness and her humility, her resigned acceptance of the harsh events in her life to which she had been subject, and her willingness to place herself at his mercy. These qualities caused her to find favor in his eyes. And again, he wished to repay her for all the kindness which she, though a pagan woman, had done unto Naomi, his kinsman, and he admired her for her courage in leaving her father and mother, and coming to live in a land of strangers. And he knew she had put her trust in the Heavenly Father, and being a religious man and endowed with a sense of responsibility towards his goods, which he felt were a sort of trusteeship from the Father's Bounty, he felt that her trust in the Father should not be in vain, but be rewarded. And Naomi said unto her daughter-in-law, "Blessed be he of the Lord, who hath not left off his kindness to the living and to the dead." (Ruth 2: 20) And she was speaking of her kinsman, Boaz.

The remainder of the story deals with the business deal whereby the nearer of kin was unable to redeem Naomi's field, in that it would mar his own inheritance, and thus it gave Boaz an opportunity to do so and also obtain Ruth as his wife, in accordance with the Hebrew law which permitted a next of kin to marry that man's wife or other eligible female.

And thus it was that through her love for Naomi, her mother-in-law, that Ruth, the pagan woman of Moab, left her native land and clung on to her; and it was because of the kindness and love which Boaz saw in Ruth's treatment of her dead brother's wife, that he himself appreciated the warmhearted qualities of the Moabite, and caused him to fall in love with her, regardless of her different race. The story, then, has a certain relationship with that of Joseph, in that it demonstrates with what conviction the Hebrews of those days, as well as many sincere Hebrews of today, relied upon God's Love and Mercy to lift them out of the pit of evil fortune and troublesome times. For the goodness of Naomi, of Ruth and of Boaz, working together in harmony and human love, was able to surmount the vicissitudes suffered by the two women as a result of the hard times, in famine and pestilence, which then prevailed in those days of the Judges. And the final prosperity and happiness which succeeded the trials that beset the two women, was seen as the Hand of God in His Great Goodness and Mercy, outstretched to deliver His children from the evils of the world. And in reading the story of Ruth, people have seen in the narrative the great influence which sincere human love and good-will, as the spiritual inheritance bestowed upon man with God's creation of the human soul, possess in making right the wrongs brought about by the action of material things as well as by those in whom the soul is dormant. So that Ruth is one of the great stories of the Old Testament which demonstrates the development of the human love, as a love given to mankind by the Father, who, while His children love with a human love, loves His children with that Divine Love which is His Essence, and which is now available to all those who seek that Love in earnest longing and prayer.

Before concluding, I wish to point out a number of other aspects of the story which help make of it one of the great universal narratives, which has a bearing upon the nature of the Father as a God of Love. For while it appears in the Old Testament of the Hebrews, and deals with a period of time affecting the lives of these people, yet the work is one that belongs to all the children of the Father. For Ruth is not a Hebrew, but a woman of the Gentiles, and it demonstrates that the human being is worthy of love and affection, loyalty and kindness, with out regard to his race or religion, and I might add the color of his skin, for man is the child of the Father by virtue of his created soul, and to treat one another with love is to manifest the Nature of the Father, at least to the degree it was then available to mankind, and show that God exists through the works of his created beings. And for men to love one another with the Divine Love is to be a participant in that Love with which the Father loves His children, and we, both mortal and spirits, who possess that Love in our hearts, become at-one with the Father in that Love to the extent of that possession.

As a conclusion, let me state in its final form, edited many centuries after it was written down for the first time, it becomes a protest against the priestly prohibition of intermarriage between Hebrews and Gentiles at the time when the Babylonian Jews were permitted by Cyrus to return to rebuild Jerusalem. This caused considerable distress and hardship among people of mixed marriages. The story of Ruth was a plea for love and tolerance and human values above strictly racial considerations.

> Jesus of the Bible
> and
> Master of the Celestial Heavens.[82]

---

[82] This is Sermon 12, one of 76 Sermons on the Old Testament delivered by Jesus through the medium Dr. Daniel Samuels in the 1950s. It is not clear why this message is included here, although one can assume Rev. John Paul Gibson felt it is significant. Certainly the set of sermons are fascinating to read, as they are Jesus' commentary on the Old Testament, the only written spiritual resource he had. (G.J.C.)

The Prayer from Jesus

December 2nd, 1916.

The only prayer that is necessary is the prayer for the inflowing of this love; all other forms, or real aspirations, of prayer are secondary, and of themselves, will not tend to produce this love in the souls of men.

This is the only prayer that men need offer to the Father. It is the only one that appeals to the Father, and with the answer, which will surely come, will come all the blessings that men may need, and which the Father sees are for the good of His creatures.

So, my brothers, continue to pray and have faith, and in the end will come a bestowal of the love like unto that which came to the Apostles at Pentecost.

I will leave my love and blessings and the assurance that i pray to the Father for your happiness and love.

Your brother and friend,

Jesus:

Our Father, who art in heaven, we recognize that Thou art all holy and loving and merciful, and that we are Thy children and not the subservient, sinful and depraved creatures that our false teachers[83] would have us believe. That we are the greatest of Thy creation and the most wonderful of all Thy handiworks, and that we are the objects of Thy great Soul's love and tenderest care.

That Thy will is that we become at one with Thee and partake of Thy great love which Thou hast bestowed upon us through Thy mercy and desire that we become, in truth, Thy children, through love not through the sacrifice and death of any one of Thy creatures.[84] We pray that Thou will open up our souls to the inflowing of Thy love, and that then may come Thy Holy Spirit to bring into our souls this, Thy Divine Love in great abundance, until our souls may be transformed into the very essence of Thyself; and that there may come to us faith—such faith as will cause us to realize that we are truly Thy children and that we are one with Thee in very substance and not in image only.

Let us have such faith as will cause us to know that Thou art our Father and the bestower of every good and perfect gift, and that only

---

[83] In very recent years a correction has been offered that we should not refer to "false" teachers, because the vast majority of teachers and preachers have honestly so taught albeit in error. It is better, we now understand, to talk about "Teachers of Old." (G.J.C.)

[84] Correction made by Jesus on Sept. 26th, 1965. (J.P.G.) The correction referred to here was received by Dr. Samuels and replaced: "Thy children, and not through the sacrifice and death of any one of Thy creatures, even though the world believes that one Thy equal and a part of Thy Godhead." with "Thy children, through love not through the sacrifice and death of any one of Thy creatures." (G.J.C.)

we, ourselves, can prevent Thy love changing us from the mortal to the immortal.

Let us never cease to realize that Thy love is waiting for each and all of us, and that when we come to Thee with faith and earnest aspirations, Thy love will never be withholden from us.

Keep us in the shadow of Thy love every hour and moment of our lives, and help us to overcome all temptations of the flesh and the influence of the powers of the evil ones who so constantly surround us and endeavor to turn our thoughts away from Thee to the pleasures and allurements of this world.

We thank Thee for Thy love and for the privilege of receiving it, and believe that Thou art our Father—the loving Father who smiles upon us in our weakness, and is always ready to help us and take us to Thy arms of love.

We pray thus with all the earnestness and longings of our souls, and trusting in Thy love, give Thee all the glory and honor and love that our finite souls can give.

Insists that Mr. Padgett stop writing

I am here, your own true and loving Helen.

You must not write more tonight, as you are somewhat exhausted and I know that the Doctor will not be disappointed if you stop now. But as I am his friend, as he knows, I will tell him that his Mary is here and says that the next best thing to telling him of her love is for me to tell him for her!

His parents are here also, and his mother says that she will come soon and write him a letter, and so will Kate, who is anxious to let him know something about his sisters in England. They, of course, send their love and blessings.

Sweetheart, I will not write more now. Only love me and believe, and pray to the Father, and you will find a blessing.

Yes, they both wrote, and as I know them both, you can rely on what was said to you. Paul was full of love and enthusiasm, and wants you to give him the opportunity to write.

So with my live to you both, I will say good night.

Your own true and loving
Helen.

Affirming that Jesus wrote the Prayer, which is the only Prayer that is needful to bring into the souls of men the Divine Love

December 2nd, 1916.

I am here, Ingersoll.

I am here, and desire to say with all the emphasis of my words and soul that the Master wrote you, and gave you the Prayer, which he said is the only prayer that is needful to bring into the souls of men the Divine Love.

He was glorious, and it is not surprising that you felt the influence of his presence and love, and I, who have so recently experienced what this love is, tell you that your feelings were real and that that love is present, and that we spirits feel it, as well as you two mortals. Astonishing to us, as to you, is the power of this love and the greatness of the Master, for with him seems to come the influence of the very Father, Himself. How every thankful I am that I found the way to this love, and it found its way to my soul! What a loving Father, and what a tender Master, to teach us of this Great Gift!

I could not restrain myself from writing, as the opportunity came to testify of this love and of the Master, and I felt that, as I had so often declared on earth that there was no such thing, I must now and always when the opportunity arises declare the truth of the Divine Love and the Holy Spirit, and the glorious Jesus. I must not write more tonight. So believe that it is I who write, and that I can with all the certainty of love declare that I am your brother in Christ,

Ingersoll.

Commending the prayer given to mankind by Jesus

December 3rd, 1916.

I am here, Cornelius.

I will write only a line or two, as I see from your condition of mind that you are anxious to study the prayer, that the Master wrote you last night. Well I am not surprised, for it is a wonderful prayer, and one, that when earnestly breathed to the Father, will bring into your soul this Great Love which is the only thing necessary to make you at-one with the Father.

As I have before told you, I am the happy possessor of this Love, and know that it is real and causes the soul of the mortal and the spirit to partake of the essence of the Father, and in a manner become Divine itself. I should like to write you a message tonight about some of the truths of the teachings of the apostles which are very pertinent to the subject upon which the preacher discoursed tonight. I was present, as were also many other spirits—orthodox Presbyterians—and those that have been freed from their creeds and erroneous beliefs of earth life.

You might be surprised, if I should tell you the great number of spirits who listened to the sermon with interest and in expectation of learning something that they could accept as truth. The preacher had a vastly larger audience of spirits than of mortals, and among a great many of the former, his teachings were received just as they were by the mortal hearers.

But I must not write more now. So hoping that I will soon have the opportunity to write, I will say, good night.

Your brother in Christ,
Cornelius (First Gentile Christian)[85]

Urges Mr. Padgett to use the Prayer given by Jesus; the great blessing conferred upon him in the work he is to do, also, the importance of the work to be done by Dr. Stone and Mr. Morgan

December 5th, 1916.

I am here, your own true and loving Helen.

Well, my dear, the spirits who desire to write to you of the higher truths did not think it best to attempt to write tonight, and hence you got no response from them. They say that you were not then in condition to receive their messages and that it was not advisable to try to convey any to you. But many of them were present, trying to throw around you their influence of love and help, and I know that as the evening progressed you felt their presence.

I am glad that you have the Master's Prayer to help you and open up your soul to the inflowing of the Love of the Father. It is a wonderful prayer, and as you repeat it with all your sincere soul desires, you will find that peace will come to you and the very presence of the Divine Love will be felt in your soul. So try to learn the prayer and offer it up to the Father, not only at night when you are ready to retire, but during the day, and especially when you feel gloomy and downcast, for the results will do you much good. It will bring to you the presence of this Love and, also, the higher spirits who possess so much of it, and the rapport will enable you to realize that there are spirits hovering around, and such spirits as will cause you much happiness and peace. So remember what I advise, and give your aspirations to the offering of the prayer, and to the hope that with you may abound this Love in all its fullness.

Oh, my dear, when I think of how blessed you are in having conferred upon you this great mission, I can hardly realize that it is true,

[85] This message is a composite of two, being published in Volume III and Volume IV. (G.J.C.)

yet I know that it is, and that you should feel so thankful to the Master, as I do. No other has had such a privilege conferred upon him and, of course, no other has such a responsibility; and when this latter is considered, it seems that you will have to have the sustaining influence and power of all the spirits who are in your higher band, to enable you to do the work and not faint in its performance. Jesus is with you and you will not be afraid that you will not succeed. The way and the means will be provided, and the great truths will be given you, and through you, to the world; and in the long future men will learn the truth and thank the Father that it became possible for His truths and the knowledge of His Great Love to be revealed through the instrumentality of a mortal.

You may be forgotten, but your work will live forever, and men and nations will experience the benefit of it and come closer to the Father and closer to one another, as brothers. The nations will necessarily be what the individuals who compose them are, and love and peace will reign on earth, as the Master promised long years ago, and as he promises now. All will be fulfilled, and as the old prophet said, the desolate places will bloom and blossom as the rose, but better than this, in men's hearts and souls will come such love that every man will truly become his brother's neighbor, and the great leaders of mankind will realize their dream of the brotherhood of man.

In the near future the Master and the other spirits who have been writing you the truths of the New Birth and of the higher things that pertain to the souls of men, will write you as to the moral precepts, and as to those things that will cause the development of the natural love of men. And their teachings will be very interesting. I have heard them talk of these things, and know that these truths and teachings which relate to the moral development of men are a part of the plan to be made known to you. So you see, you yet have much work to do, and you must not think for a moment that you will not get in condition, materially and spiritually, to do this great work to its completion.

It has been decreed that you shall finish this work before you come to the spirit world, and there will be no failure. It will be that some obstacles will be met with, such as you are now encountering, but after a little while they will disappear, and you will be free to do your work without hindrance and in the way that you have so often thought about.

Well, sweetheart, I have written a long letter tonight and I think it best to stop, but before I do so, I desire to say to your two friends[86] that their work is of like importance, and that the great powers that are looking after and directing you are also looking after them, and that their work will have to be done also. It is a part of the great desire and plan that they shall perform their missions, and that ways and means shall be

---

[86] Leslie R. Stone and Eugene Morgan. (J.P.G.)

provided by which they will be enabled to accomplish the task set before them. So tell them to take courage and believe what I here write, and know that the Master and the higher spirits have decreed that they, also, shall have a part in this glorious plan for the salvation of mankind, and that nothing will be permitted to interfere with, or defeat, them in their labors. They will have to remain mortals until their work shall have been accomplished, and by that time they will have such knowledge of the glories of the Heavenly life that they will be anxious to hear the "Well done, good and faithful servants," and enter into the joys of the homes which have been prepared for them. And when that time comes, there will be many in the spirit world who will meet them, with hearts full of thankfulness and love, and words of appreciation and greeting.

So tell them to keep up their faith and courage, and let not doubt enter into their minds as to the fact that they are the chosen ones also. I must stop now. So with my love, good night.

Your own true and loving,

Helen.

Guests

Leslie's mother wants him to know that she prays for his good health and is happy to see him feeling better after his vacation

I am here, mother.

Let me write just a line, as I merely want to tell my son that I am very glad to see that he is much better in his physical condition than he was before he took a vacation. I was with him at times when he was away out of the cities, and enjoyed very much being with him and wished that I might then be able to communicate with him. I am also glad that he is in a good spiritual condition and that the Love is increasing in his soul as it is. We are all praying for him and seeking to influence him to good thoughts and increased realization of the benefit of prayer to the Father.

I do not intend to write a long letter tonight, but merely to remind him that he has a mother in spirit life who loves him so much and is with him so often.

So tell him to think of me and believe in the love which is here for him, and in the prayers I offer for his salvation and happiness.

I should like to write him about his sisters in England, but will not do so tonight. I feel because of the great spread of spiritualism in England at this time, they may be induced to seek for its revealment, if through mere curiosity, and that then some truth will appear to them so real that they may be induced to investigate further and then be led to a belief in the fact of communication; and if that would happen it will embrace every opportunity to get in rapport and communication with those in this spirit world who would be glad to communicate with them.

Well, my son, I must stop now, so with my love and blessings I will say,

Good night, your loving
Priscilla Stone.

The celebrated philosopher discourses on reason and states that reason per se is not a reliable guide to truth

April 14th, 1918.

I am here, Spinoza.

I desire to write a few lines, if you will permit. I need not say that I have never written you before, for you will know from the difficulty that I have in writing that such must be the case. No, I am a stranger to this method of communication, and to you, and to me it has come in very recent days as a wonderful revelation.

I do not intend to write upon a subject of any great truth connected with our spirit life, but merely to say sufficient to introduce myself, in the hope that when I am better acquainted with the laws governing this method, I may be permitted to come to you and write of those things which I have learned since becoming a spirit, and which to learn when on earth would have been not only very desirable but very important.

I was, when on earth, a philosopher, so-called, and gave many years of my life to the search for truth relating not only to the natural world, but to what I conceived to be truth connected with that world or existence outside of and beyond the sense world; and in my researches I was guilty of many speculations which I now see have no foundation upon which I had built many conclusions and postulates. I had only the intellect, supplied in its workings by the knowledge that came from the phenomena of the purely physical and, as I thought, by that great faculty called reason, which, as a fact, is a wonderful faculty, but in its exercise it is dependent upon, first, its own development, and next, whether that development has been along the lines of and in accord with truth.

A reason merely because it is a reason is not a guide that can be depended on, for reasoning in an erroneous way must necessarily lead to conclusions of error, and merely calling or believing that these conclusions are the results of reason does not justify the belief that the conclusions must be correct and veracious. Reason can be mistaken and featured by error, just as can the senses; and, hence, if you read the writings of the philosophers and metaphysicians, and also scientists, you will find that things declared and accepted by these men in one age have been repudiated and rejected by the successors of these men in later ages.

And so, when I wrote, and I wrote considerably, and was very largely read by what was considered to be the thinking class of men, and especially those whose researches led them along a similar line of study and subject matter as my own, I declared certain doctrines or principles connected with these metaphysical and philosophical matters that I now know to be wholly erroneous, but which at the time I firmly believed to be things of verity, because largely they were based on what I thought was the true workings of reason, together with some little empirical knowledge.

From this I do not mean to decry the value and importance of the faculty of reason, for it has been the great factor operating (creating) progress of mankind, but like other finite faculties it is subject to erroneous exercise and cannot be depended on as a thing infallible. The common experience of men has shown that men who have sincerely and earnestly and constantly exercised their reasoning faculties have arrived at different and contradictory conclusions as to the same principles or subject matter, and those conclusions have been entirely satisfactory and convincing to the respective persons. Now it is apparent that in such instances all of these men could not possibly be correct in their conclusions, and in many cases not any of them were correct, yet they were all founded on the reason, properly and intelligently exercised, as they supposed.

No, reason is fallible, and it is not a thing of itself, but dependent upon environments and sometimes inherited or preconceived ideas of what truth must be. It is the great friend and defender of speculation, and without it speculation could not exist, and so often is speculation deceived by its friend. Truth is that which exists as an unchangeable condition or fact, and speculation can neither create nor destroy truth; and reason is a means which may be used to reach truth when knowledge does not exist. But the fact that reason exists does not mean that it is always used in that way that leads to the discovery of truth. Reason, as I am now justified in saying, is but a creature of God, just as is everything else in His universe; and when given to man with the freedom of exercising it as man wills, is subject to all the possibilities of defective exercise that every other faculty possessed by man is subject to, and is no more infallible in its nature than are these other faculties.

But it is the greatest faculty that man has as a creature of the Almighty, and without it, some of the wise of earth have said man would be no better than or different from the brute animal. But this is not quite true, for man is possessed with that which is really man himself that the brute animal does not have, and that is a soul made in the image of its Creator. It may be said that reason is merely an appendage of the soul; and I have justification in asserting that the soul in its progress can do without or cast aside this reason without doing harm to itself because, as I have learned in progressing in the spirit life, the soul may and does arrive at that degree of development where reason is not necessary or even used by it in its acquirement of truth.

I now believe, and without speculation, that reason is a gift to man to be useful to him only in his earth life and in a portion of this spirit life, until the soul comes into a knowledge of truth by the exercise of the mere desire to know. A knowledge of the whys and wherefores is not required, but it knows because it knows, just as in your earth life you have a knowledge of the sunlight even if you do not know the why and the wherefore that produce that light.

Well, my new-found friend, I have written more than I intended, but as I continued I found the desire to write increase, and I fear that I have trespassed too long and pray your forgiveness. Sometime I should like to come and write of the errors of some of the teachings of earth, or rather of the truths along the line of the subject matter of my earthly writings, as I now know them to be.

I am in what is called the intellectual planes of the Fifth Sphere and very near the entrance to the Sixth Sphere, in which I hope to be in a short time. It has been a long time since I left the earth life, and the early period of my existence in the spirit world was one of stagnation, and, as I now see, merely because I brought with me many of the doctrines of the philosophy of my earth life, and as a consequence I continued my research along the ideas and ways that I had pursued as a mortal. The time thus spent was long and continued until I became convinced that speculation in the spirit life is not very different and arrives at no more satisfactory end than speculation on earth, and then I stopped speculating and waited for something, I know not what. And strange to say, that which came to me was from a spirit who had never heard of my philosophy or any other philosophy on earth, but merely accepted truth as it gradually came to him, without knowing why or how. And I soon learned that he had a greater knowledge of the verities than had I, and so I adopted his way of receiving truth, and since then I have been progressing and am now advancing with accelerated speed—all to my happiness and intellectual enjoyment. Good-bye,

Your friend,
Spinoza.

Does not recommend receiving at this time such messages

April 14th, 1918.

I am here, John.

Let me say just a word and that is, that I have been waiting with some interest until the spirit who has just written you (Spinoza) finished his writing.

I see that you are feeling very much better physically and spiritually, and now I know that we can make the rapport with you that will enable us to write our messages; and so I hope that tomorrow night you will give us the opportunity to write.

What the spirit wrote, I know, was quite interesting, but it is not of the vital, and the time, for the present, must not be consumed by messages of this kind. After we shall have finished the messages that we intend for the book, these messages of the kind just written may be received, for they have a work to do in the plan that we have in view.

I will not write more now, except to say that we are with you very much, and pray to the Father for you and try to help you with our love and influence. So remember what I have written, and pray to the

Father. Good night,
> Your brother in Christ,
> John.

Writes on the important truths that he has discovered

January 15th, 1917.

I am here, Samera.

I am a Greek of the days of Aristotle, and I merely want to say that I am very desirous of writing you a message on the subject of what is the most important truth that I have discovered since I came to the spirit world. This truth is the Oneness of God.

When I lived on earth we believed and taught the existence of many gods, and the fact that these gods were the unembodied spirits of those who had been great heroes or philosophers or statesmen while living on earth. Of course, we had some conception of a God who was superior to all others, and that He had the power and wisdom that belonged only to the supreme God, but the lesser gods also had great power and wisdom, and in their particular jurisdiction were at liberty to exercise those powers and thus bring to mankind the blessings—or woes—that they thought men should have visited upon them.

Our gods did not have any power over our spiritual conditions, but dealt with us only in a material way and ruled us in our earthly ambitions or efforts only. I died with these beliefs, and when I came to the spirit world I found that hundreds of those we had worshiped on earth as gods were mere spirits like myself, without any special powers and without the wisdom that we had attributed to them, and they were subject to the laws of the spirit world just as I was. Of course, this discovery made me halt in my opinion as to the fact of there being many gods, and caused me in time to conclude that all the beliefs in the many gods were erroneous, and that I should seek for another God who should be above all these lesser gods and spirits.

So, in my search I came in contact with spirits who had been in spirit life very much longer than had I, and were far advanced beyond me in the knowledge of things spiritual. And they instructed me that there was a great God, the Creator of the universe, and the only God. And in my continued investigations, I concluded that this must be true. I have never seen that God, nor has any of the spirits that I am aware of, but we have all seen the manifestations of His powers and wisdom, such as no mortal has ever seen or conceived of, and being thus conscious of the existence and manifestation of these powers and wisdom, I know, as do all spirits, that there must be that from which emanates these manifestations, and One who is the possessor of them and the ruler and controller of such manifestations. This entity we all call GOD, and worship Him as such; and we know that He and He alone is the only true God.

I do not know that what I have said will be of any interest to you, but it is a fact, and I wanted so much to tell you that fact. I live in what is called the Sixth Sphere, where are many spirits of men in a condition of perfection that brings them supreme happiness, and such greatness of knowledge that only they, themselves, can understand. I hope you will pardon my intrusion, and I will bid you good night.

Samera.

The father of one of the tribes of Israel is now an inhabitant of the Celestial Heavens

September 16th, 1915.

I am here, Shem.

I am the father of one of the tribes of Israel, and I come to tell you that I am now a Christian and a follower of Jesus, the savior of men.

You may think it strange that I should write to you, but I am interested in the work which the Master is doing for mankind, and which you are to do in taking his messages and transmitting them to humanity.

I was a Jew of the earlier dispensation, and I lived before the destruction of Jerusalem and even before the great dispersion and captivity of my people. I died when the race was very young and when it had not formed its concrete ideas of God that afterwards became such a power in the economy of its government.

I am now an inhabitant of the Celestial Heavens and am working with the other Celestial spirits to carry forward the great plans of God and of His Son for the salvation of mankind.

I know what the New Birth means, and how necessary it is for men to become partakers of the Divine Love and Divinity of the Father. So you must see that only after that Great Gift was rebestowed on men were any of us who lived at a time long anterior to the birth of Jesus able to partake of those qualities which gave us immortality.

I will now stop and say good night.

Shem.

A Biblical king who is now a Celestial Angel encourages Mr. Padgett in his work of helping the dark spirits

August 13th, 1915.

I am here, Saul, the Jewish King.

Yes, I was here once before and wrote you. I am now an Angel of God and an inhabitant of His Celestial Heavens.

I merely want to say that you are doing a good work in helping the unfortunate spirits, and I tell you that your influence with them seems astonishing. Why this is so I don't know, unless they feel that you are nearer to them by reason of being in the flesh, and more interested in them than are the spirits of a higher sphere who come to them sometimes and try to help them.

Well, you must keep up this good work, for it is a good work, as you are helping the Master more than you realize; and your reward, when you come over, will be the gratitude of many of these darkened spirits.[87]

I don't work very often in the earth plane, as my work is among the spirits of the higher spiritual heavens; but occasionally I am sent to earth and try to help mortals as well as spirits.

But since I have first written you, I feel much interested in your work and in the great powers that are behind you. As you know, the greatest spirit of all is Jesus, and he is more interested in having you do his work than you can conceive of. We are all interested in his cause and feel that whenever we can come to you and encourage you, or in any other way help you, it is our delight to do so.

I must not write more now.

Call me Brother Saul, for we are brothers in Christ. Well, as you are not of my time when on earth, I cannot say how you would have been treated had you done the same work then. But I suppose that you would have been called a witch, as was that good woman of Endor in her time.

Thank God the people are more enlightened now, and will soon recognize the fact that a good medium is one of the greatest gifts of God to suffering humanity. The time will come when mediums will be looked upon as were the prophets of old by the Jewish people, but without having the ingratitude of the people visited upon them, as it was visited at times on these old prophets.

I must stop. So, good night.

Your brother,

---

[87] While in 1915 Saul may have been pleased with the time that James Padgett spent in instructing dark spirits, (which was typically one day a week) Ned became so enamored of it that later on he was chided for doing so, to the exclusion of receiving the more important spiritual messages. It also seemed to be the case that making rapport with dark spirits eventually caused him to have more difficulty in making rapport with Celestials. He was of course fully protected from any malevolent spirits by virtue of his spirit band, and these dark spirits came for his help, not to cause any trouble. Indeed the careful reader may notice quite a number of his one-time legal colleagues amongst these dark spirits asking for help. (G.J.C.)

Saul.

A preacher finds that the teachings of a lifetime were false

July 31st, 1918.

I am here, Pastor Russell.

Let me say a word, as I have been with you today as you read the book[88] of which I was the writer. I see that you are aware of the erroneous interpretations of the testament that it contains, of the false constructions that are drawn from the quotations of the Bible, and also that you feel that a great injury is being done to those who read and believe in my teachings. Well, I realize the falsity of my teachings and the wrong and injury that are being wrought among those who have been followers of me; and how great will be their surprise when death comes to them, for what I said was impossible they will find to be true—that they are more alive than they ever were while living in the flesh.

This I have realized, to my great surprise and suffering. When I was about to leave the flesh, and for long years before, I believed that when I died I would go into the literal grave and would thereafter be in a state of oblivion, knowing nothing until the day of the first resurrection, when I and all those who believed that we were of the little flock would be called into the presence of Jesus and there become his coworkers and co-judges of men during the millennium, when the rest of the world would be tried and finally judged to either a life of happiness, as men restored to the condition of Adam before the fall, or to total annihilation.

But as I passed from the body, I found that I had a spiritual body in which was contained all the faculties of mind and appetites of the flesh that were a part of me when on earth; and also, the memories of all that I had thought, and taught, when trying to lead my followers into the truth, as I supposed. I was more alive than ever before, and conscience soon began to do its work of reproval and bring to me remorse and regret for the great harm that I had done to many of my fellow men by reason of my teaching a faith that is wholly untrue, and destructive to the soul's salvation. The soul! Ah, this is the thing that I blasphemed against, for I taught that there was no such thing or entity as the soul after the separation of the body and life; that it then ceased to have an existence, and would never again come into existence until the first resurrection, which would be the first awakening of the little flock to a

---

[88] This is most likely the book initially titled "Millennial Dawn," later renamed "Studies in the Scriptures." (G.J.C.)

consciousness of its existence.

To me the will was the great thing, and while that never ceased to exist, yet it lay in a dormant state and was as dead, knowing nothing. How vitally misleading was this teaching—and how my followers will find themselves deceived, and will suffer from the want of knowledge of the fact that the soul is the man and is susceptible to progressing in the knowledge of the truths of God while on earth, as well as after it becomes an inhabitant of the spirit world. I have had a tragic awakening, with all the consequences of a tragedy in which I was one of the important actors, and the principal cause of the results of the tragedy.

I know what death means, and what life means, for I died merely to live, and to live a life in which at this time is much suffering and regret, accompanied by the knowledge that I have before me a work greater than I can perform in many long years in the future. I must now try to undo what I for so many years did, to the injury of those who believed in me; and when I realize that there is hardly a way, until these followers of mine become spirits like myself, in which I can do this work, my suffering becomes almost unbearable. Only through the medium of the mortal can I reach these people, and because of my teachings they will not believe what I may attempt to communicate through a mortal medium (which medium I wrote against and reviled, and alleged that they were only creatures used by the devil and his minions to deceive mankind).

If I had only known the truth, and thereby abstained from preaching untruth in this particular, how different my lot would now be. But I believed what I taught, and taught what I believed. It was all a lie, and though I believed it, yet that fact does not lessen my regrets, for I see with the clearness of the spirit that my thoughts and teachings are believed by many of my followers because I taught them; and consequently they will suffer from their beliefs; and the fact that I believed these erroneous things and taught in good faith will not, in one iota, save them from the darkness and sufferings which will certainly become theirs.

Unfortunate is the man who believes spiritual untruths; but accursed is the man who teaches them, and thus deceives those who are earnestly seeking for the truth. I would like to write more tonight in reference to this matter and my condition, and the heavy burden which I am now bearing, but your wife says I must not write more now as you are not in condition to be further drawn on. So, thanking you, and having the hope that at some time in the near future I may again communicate with you, I will say good night.

Your friend,

Pastor Russell[89]

Cconfirms that Pastor Russell wrote, and is in much darkness as a result of his erroneous teachings while on earth

July 31st, 1918.

I am here, your own true and loving Helen.

Well dear, you have just received a letter from Pastor Russell, who, as he says, has been with you during the day as you read one of his books, and who was most anxious to write you. He is in considerable darkness and feels the great burden of seeing many persons of earth whom he taught, studying and believing his teachings of the vital truths of man's salvation, which teachings he now realizes, to his own suffering, are untrue and lead away from the realities of the life in the spirit world and the teachings of the Master as to things spiritual.

He was very anxious to continue his message, but I thought it best to stop him as he was very earnest and was drawing too much on your vitality. He will come again sometime after you shall have become stronger.

Helen.

A Muslim is happy in his paradise and no longer hates Christians

August 12th, 1915.

---

[89] Charles Taze Russell (February 16th, 1852 – October 31st, 1916), or Pastor Russell, was a prominent early 20th century Christian restorationist minister from Pittsburgh, Pennsylvania, USA, and founder of what is now known as the Bible Student movement, from which Jehovah's Witnesses and numerous independent Bible Student groups emerged after his death.

Beginning in July, 1879 he began publishing a monthly religious journal, Zion's Watch Tower and Herald of Christ's Presence. The journal is now published by Jehovah's Witnesses on a semi-monthly basis under the name, The Watchtower Announcing Jehovah's Kingdom. In 1881 he co-founded Zion's Watch Tower Tract Society and in 1884 the corporation was officially registered, with Russell as president. Russell wrote many articles, books, tracts, pamphlets and sermons, totaling approximately 50,000 printed pages. From 1886 to 1904, he published a six-volume Bible study series originally entitled Millennial Dawn, later renamed Studies in the Scriptures, nearly 20 million copies of which were printed and distributed around the world in several languages during his lifetime. (A seventh volume was commissioned by his successor as society president, Joseph Rutherford, and published in 1917.) The Watch Tower Society officially states that it ceased publication of Russell's writings in 1927, though his books continue to be published by several independent groups. Source: Wikipedia. (G.J.C.)

I am here, Selim, the Sultan.

I came to tell you that I am also happy in my paradise, which my God has prepared for me. I am no longer a hater of the Christians, but love all men as I believe.

I don't mean that I think all men are following the truths of God in their lives, or that they believe in God in a way that will enable them to reach the happiness which He has provided for them; but nevertheless, they are his children, and I love them as one brother should love another.

I will come to you at some time and tell you of our paradise and our lives here.

I will say good night and God bless you.

Selim.

Jesus is the Christ of God

Christ is not only a Spirit of the Father, but is the one that God gave to Jesus when He anointed him on his earthly mission. Jesus is only a son of God, and is not God or any part of Him.

Your grandmother.

The Apostle of Jesus declares that no man can possibly reach the condition of the perfect man unless his mental beliefs are in accord with the Truth

January 4th, 1917.

I am here, Luke.

I will write a few lines tonight on a subject that I desire to make known to you and others, for I know it will be of interest to all who may read it. The subject is the truth of the statement that no man can possibly reach the condition of perfection unless his mental beliefs become in accord with the truth. This perfection, you will understand, is the perfection that man possessed before his fall—that is, the perfection of his creation.

It has been asserted by many that the beliefs of a man do not count for much in determining his condition of soul and mind, and that only his acts and deeds and the qualities of his heart determine that condition; but this assertion I declare to be untrue, unless these acts and deeds and qualities of heart are the results of beliefs being in accord with the truth.

Belief is the mainspring of man's acts and the result of his thoughts; and thoughts are things that cause the realities of man's consciousness, and as he thinketh in his heart so is he. "Thinketh in his heart" means or comprehends (communicates) the idea that the thoughts of his mind, which is the only part of man that has the powers or faculties for thinking, are suggested by, or flow from, the desires and appetites of the emotional part of man.

No thought originates itself, although it may seem to be a spontaneous creation, but is the result of some spiritual or physical perception—that is, of the perception of the spiritual qualities or of the sensuous organs of man's physical constitution. And belief is the result of thought and that agency which causes man's acts or want of acts, and hence, the only guide or way shown to man in the progress of the development of his soul in its natural love, or of the mind to the state of perfection that I speak of.

Now, belief does not create truth or change truth, for it is absolute and unchangeable; and truth does not create belief unless that truth is comprehended by the thoughts from which emanate the belief. So, it is apparent that unless the belief, if erroneous, changes so that it becomes in accord with the truth, man, the possessor of the belief, can never get into a state of perfection, which can only exist when a man is in a complete condition of harmony with the truth. Belief being the effect of the operations of the mind, unless these operations are in harmony with the truth, the belief cannot possibly cause the development of the man who is possessed of and controlled by that belief, into the perfect man, because every cause has an effect, and that effect must be, necessarily, only such as is the natural and inevitable result of that cause.

Out of untruth it is impossible for truth to emanate, and from the imperfect the perfect can never be constructed; and so it is impossible to develop a perfect love and mind out of an imperfect belief. The law that declares the effect of its operations to bring this result is invariable, and only by the observation of its requirements can the imperfect ever become the perfect. So, therefore, I assert that no man can ever become the perfect man unless his beliefs become in harmony with the truth. As a matter of fact, irrespective of reason, established by my knowledge resulting from observation and experience in the spirit as well as in the mortal world, I declare the same to be a truth.

Then how important to man it is to seek for and obtain those beliefs that are in harmony with the truth in order to become as he was originally, the perfect man. This true belief may be found and acquired even by the mortal, and no man will be excused from the penalty of the great law of compensation by his plea that he did not think it very material what his beliefs were if he tried to do right in the world towards his fellow man. But here, you will see that in addition to the fact that this great law accepts no excuse is the fact that man's acts and deeds proceed from his beliefs, whenever such are strong enough to control him; and when the beliefs are unformed, and man acts from emotion or impulse or desire only, without the constraint of any belief, the result upon his progress to the perfect man is substantially the same, because this law, in order to escape the penalty for its violation, demands that beliefs, formed or unformed, or acts and deeds resulting from emotion or impulse, which are really beliefs without definite form, shall be in harmony with the truth.

The infidel who says he doesn't believe, the agnostic who says he doesn't know, the orthodox who believes, but whose belief is erroneous, and the free thinker who believes only what reason teaches him as he proclaims, if such beliefs are not in accord with the truth all come under the same penalty—that is, the impossibility of becoming the perfect man while such erroneous beliefs or want of true beliefs exist. So I say, belief is a vital thing in the progress of a man towards perfection, and men should cease to declare and rest on the assurance of such declaration that it makes no difference what a man believes if he does what he may consider to be right and just.

Why, I, who know, tell you that the earth planes of the spirit world are crowded with the spirits of men who are in darkness and stagnation in their progress towards the perfect man solely from the causes that I have above written, and some men have been in that condition for many long years, and will not find progress except as such erroneous beliefs leave them and beliefs in accord with the truth take the place of the former. But for man and spirits there is this consolation: that at some time, how long in the future I or no other spirit know, these erroneous beliefs will all be eradicated and man will again come into his original perfection. But the waiting may be long and distressing, and wearisome to many.

I have written enough, and in closing will say to all men: know and realize that the belief of a man is a vital and determining element in his progress to the perfect man. I am pleased to write you tonight, and will soon come again. Keep your faith and courage and you will realize the promises. Good night and God bless you.

Your brother in Christ,
Luke.

His love of country is still uppermost in his thoughts

November 1st, 1915.

I am here, Napoleon.

Yes, I am that man who did so much harm when on earth.

I merely want to say that I have been told by my daughter of her experience a few nights ago, and I became much interested in the fact

243

that she could write to you, and that other spirits could write; and I thought that I would try. I found, though, that you have around you a band of beautiful and powerful spirits and that I had to have their permission before I was permitted to write. But they kindly gave me permission and I am writing.

I want to say that I am the ambitious man that I was on earth, but realize that I cannot take part in any of the movements or actions of men, as I am only a spirit; but I can associate with them and influence them into doing things and carrying out my ideas of what is necessary for France's good and glory.

I frequently visit the headquarters of the generals of the Allies in this present conflict[90] and I know their thoughts and give them, by impression, the benefit or otherwise of my thoughts. And in addition, I know what the plans of the Germans are. This war will last some time yet, but in the end the Allies will be successful, for I can see all the factors that are working together to bring about that result.

Joffre is a competent man, and Kitchener is a good adjudicator; and when they unite their forces and enter upon the aggressive campaign with all the force and power which they have, the Germans will have to retreat, and victory will come to them. But, alas, I also see the great sacrifices that will have to be made; but France will become a glorious nation, and the lives that will be sacrificed will be well devoted to the glorious cause.

The spirits are coming over in great numbers, but as I see things, they are exchanging an earth life for a spirit life merely, and the latter is the happier one. So what matters it that men die when a great nation can be saved, and the country for which I fought and suffered, and was exiled, shall become a glorious nation. A nation is only an aggregation of individuals, and the individual is not so important as the nation. The nation must be preserved even though the individual may die. But I have written enough and must stop.

I am in the Fourth Sphere and my dear wife is in the Fifth. She is so much more beautiful and bright than I am.

Well, I will think of what you said, but until this war is over with and the glory of France is established, I will not think of myself. I am a Frenchman more than a spirit, or rather than the inhabitant of a country that is not of so much importance as France.

So thanking you, I will stop.

I will come again sometime, and in the meantime I will assure you that you have my best and kindest regards.

Napoleon, the first, and as a great Emperor, the last.

---

[90] This is of course World War I. (G.J.C.)

German military strategist predicts the Germans will win the war[91]

November 1st, 1915.

I am here, Von Moltke.[92]

Let me tell you that I am a German and have heard what the little Corporal (Napoleon!) said, and that, while he was a great general when on earth, yet as a spirit general he is a failure, for his dear France will never see the glory that he predicts for her. She is at her best now, and when her armies commence that great advance that Napoleon speaks of, they will be met by the Germans and annihilated.

I also visit the headquarters of the Allies and know their plans, and I know that Napoleon is there advising them; but he is behind the day of improvement in armament and guns and ammunition, and he is also behind the times in his advice. He has found his Waterloo, and never again will he rise to become the great leader of armies. But strange to say, he thinks that he is the same wise, sagacious and tactical general that he was on earth. But he will find his mistake.

The Germans will surely be victorious in this Great War, and the French will sue for peace and with them their Allies as well.

It is no use for me to write further on this matter, because I could only repeat what I have said; but you, my friend, put into your memory and at the end of the war call forth this prediction: The Germans will become the victors.[93]

Your friend,
Von Moltke.

Held the time to write for a spirit that for a moment forgot his name

November 1st, 1915.

I am here, Lar ———.

I am here, John the Baptist.

---

[91] The original title was "Spirits that are earth-bound, thoughts do not change when they enter the spirit world" and this is totally unrelated to the message that follows. (G.J.C.)
[92] The old strategist of the German armies when France fell. (J.P.G)
[93] This is a perfect example of the fact that spirits cannot predict the future. What they can do is make informed guesses, because they have access to a great deal of information, but nevertheless, Von Moltke was wrong. However this should not be taken as a statement that the future cannot ever be predicted—absolutely predicted, but that information must come from God. The message on page 387 in this volume confirms this. (G.J.C.)

Well, the spirit who tried to write could not remember his name, and he has gone into the higher sphere to recover his recollections. He was not a very good spirit, nor yet one in much darkness. He has returned and says his name is Larkin, and that he knew you on earth. I will let him write, for he is so anxious.

Well, I am sorry that I disarranged things, but really I could not remember my name until I went to the Fourth Sphere, where I live, and recovered my composure. This is my first appearance in your atmosphere and I was somewhat confused.

I merely want to say that I am a believer now in the future state; in fact, I know that I am alive even though I died when on earth. Well, it only goes to show that we can so easily be mistaken in what we think we know as a result of what we call reason. I am very happy, but not so happy as my wife who is in the Fifth Sphere, as she tells me.

I have never yet been able to accept her beliefs in the New Birth, although I see the result of something in her condition which she claims to be the New Birth. But I can't believe in it, and I am enjoying myself in the society of those who are happy in the exercise of their intellectual faculties only.

I will not write more, so thanking you, I will say good night.

Confirms that Napoleon and Von Moltke were both present and wrote their messages

November 1st, 1915.

I am here, Helen.

You must go to bed and get up earlier in the morning, for you may lose business by not doing so.

I will not write much, but only say that your communications tonight were interesting, if not convincing, as to whether the Allies or Germans will win. Napoleon and Von Moltke were both present, and they did not look as if they had much love for each other.

I will not tell you of my love tonight, as it is too late, but I love you, and I love my children and have been with them today. Harry is very happy and so is his wife. Edward is as usual, I don't think very happy—how sad! Nita is happy too; she is getting on all right, and as soon as you get some money for her she will be very contented. So you see, I remembered what you said last night, and I feel better by having visited them today. Oh, my darling, do not think that I do not love them, for I do and that with all my mother's soul. But of course, not as I do you.

So go to bed and trust in God, and believe in the Master, for he will do as he promised. Good night, my dear old Ned.

Your own true and loving
Helen.

The truth about hell and purgatory

January 15th, 1917

I am here, John B. London.

Let me say a word, and I shall feel better for having done so. I am a spirit who lives in the earth plane and see spirits of all kinds and conditions, and know from observation and experience that in this plane is darkness as well as light, and that many, many spirits are in the dark places paying the penalties which the great law of compensation compels them to pay. These planes are of various degrees of darkness, all suited to the condition of the spirits who occupy them.

Some of them are called hells and some purgatories, but they are all really connected, and the only difference between them is the condition of darkness and suffering which the inhabitants there are compelled to undergo. I have been through the hells and am now in purgatory, trying to rid my soul of suffering and get into the light of freedom and peace; and oh, there are so many here in that condition and without much hope. Our progress is slow and we have to pay the minutest demand that this law of compensation calls for.

I hope that you will pardon me for having intruded, but I felt that if I could communicate with you I should feel better, and so I do. I will bid you good night.

Your friend,
John B. London.

Wrote later that he does not know what the New Birth is

August 20th, 1915.

I am here, Selim.

I was the first Mohammedan Sultan of that name, and I want to write you for a while, if you don't object.

I have listened to what Paul wrote and some things that he said I do not understand. I mean the difference between the spirit who receives what he calls the New Birth, and the spirit who has only his natural love.

I know that I have a love for God and a love for my fellow man, and that I am very happy and do not desire greater happiness, and have surroundings that I cannot conceive can be excelled in their beauty and desirability.

I know nothing of the other love, and fail to comprehend how there can be any other love than the one which God has given us. This love, in varying degrees we all have, and according as we possess it and have become freed from the sins and errors of life, I mean the earth life, are we happy.

Our Prophet, may Allah bless him, never taught us of any other love than the one I speak of, and I don't believe he knows of any other love.

But, I confess that my curiosity is excited to learn just what Paul means by his doctrine of the New Birth, and I shall make the effort to find out. Of course, I will have to have something more than his mere statement, or even the statement of all the Christians, to cause me to believe in the reality of this doctrine; but I feel that there may be some truth in it, and, if so, I want to learn it.

I will not write more tonight but will, with your permission, do so later.

I will say good night and God bless you.

Selim.

Gives his testimony that Mr. Padgett has been selected to receive the messages of Truth from Jesus and other high spirits

February 15th, 1916.

I am Saint Clement the Pope.[94]

I merely want to say that I am glad to be able to testify as to the work that you have been selected to do, and as to the fact that Jesus and many of the high spirits write to you.

I know that my testimony is not necessary in order to convince you of these facts, but there may be some who will more readily believe when they know that a Pope of the Roman Catholic church gave his testimony to these facts. I am now an inhabitant of the Celestial Spheres, and am happy beyond description. But, as I have told you, I was compelled to undergo great sufferings before I was relieved of my recollections of the evil that I had done on earth.

But I will write you more in detail later, and hope that I may have the opportunity. So, wishing you success and happiness, I am

Your brother in Christ,

---

[94] I had assumed that this is most likely Pope Clement VII, since Martin Luther referred to him in a message dated August 28th, 1916 and which is published in Volume III. However Pope Clement VII does not appear to be called St. Clement. That appears to be reserved for Pope Clement I who lived a great many years before. He died in A.D. 98. (G.J.C.)

St. Clement.

A Tartar lived in Tibet 1,000 years ago and writes of his beliefs while on earth

August 13th, 1915.

I am here, Leetelam.

I was a Tartar and lived in Tibet, and died nearly four thousand years ago. I was a Brahman, and was a priest of the temple and the chief of the brothers of sacrifice. In my day we sacrificed human beings to appease the wrath of our God, and they were the most beautiful virgins—so that our God would have a sacrifice that had never been defiled by man.

This was one of the chief tenets of our religion and was observed with all the strictness and pomp that we, who were fanatical in our beliefs, could give the occasion of the sacrifice. Many a beautiful victim just emerging into the full flower of her youth was made to suffer a cruel death in order, as we supposed, to save the rest of us from the wrath of our God, who was always hungry for blood and the cries of his human victims.

But this sacrifice was one of the chief ceremonies of our religion, and we believed in the necessity for it just as you Christians believe in the necessity for prayer. And when we, the priests who performed the act which consummated the sacrifice, had performed our duties, we considered that we had obeyed the will of God and that he was pleased with our great act of devotion and worship.

No rank or position could save the victim from the sacrifice when once the priests had selected that victim; and the parents of such victim were taught and believed that it was a great honor to have their young daughters chosen as brides for the great God who was not satisfied unless he could have the most beautiful and virtuous maidens for his brides of death.

Since I have become a spirit and learned some of the truths of the spirit world, and that love—and not sacrifice—is required by God, all these evil deeds that I and the others performed in the name of our religion have become to me monstrous and shocking, and for many long years after I had learned the truth, the recollections of these deeds caused me to suffer the tortures of the damned. The fact that I at the time thought that I was performing a duty did not assuage my suffering or relieve my darkness.

Truth is truth, and every violation of its demands must be atoned for, no matter if the intention at the time of committing these violations is supposed or believed by the actor to be in accordance with the truth.

No belief, if it violates truth, will excuse.

As on earth, ignorance of law excuses no one for his acts done in violation of truth, so in the spirit world ignorance of the truth will not excuse deeds committed in violation of that truth. Every cause must have its effect, and no God interposes to prevent that effect from following the cause.

Now that I have been awakened to the truth, I see with the perceptions of not only a clarified intellect but of the soul, that no act or deed done in the name of religion actually believed in will be excused because of the fact that it was done for the sake of that religion. I am now in the Nirvana of the Brahmans, and am very happy. My soul has been purified by the long years of suffering and discipline, and I love God and my fellow man. My sphere is high up in the spirit world—just what its location is I cannot tell you. There are no Christians or other sects in my sphere, although I see them at times and converse with them.

I came here because I was travelling in this earth plane and saw a bright light which is unusual in this plane, and it led me to you; and I found that you were receiving communications from spirits, and I listened to some of the messages and concluded that I would write also if I could have the opportunity. And after the dark spirits left you I commenced this writing.

I did not know English when I lived, but you must know that the advanced spirits who have been in the spirit world for many years have not let the years go by without study and investigation. I understand most all the languages of earth, and so do most of the ancient spirits, and this is for the purpose of being able to understand what the peoples of all lands may think and say. Our work is to help mankind and spirits whenever we can. Well, I will not write more tonight.

I hear what you say and cannot understand you, but if there be such a supreme happiness as you speak of, I should like to possess it. I will accept your invitation and attend your writings on Wednesday night.[95] And so with my best wishes and kind regards, I am

Your friend,
Leetelam.

Assyrian official who believed in many gods when on earth is now a Christian

November 4th, 1915.

I am here, Leekesi.

I was a man who lived in the time of the destruction of Ninevah

---

[95] Wednesday nights Mr. Padgett let the dark spirits write who needed help. (J.P.G.)

and was an Assyrian official; but I am not mentioned in history, for my time was short, though in it occurred some of the most important acts of the whole history of that land.

I was not a believer in the God of the Hebrews, though in my time I had heard of that God, and many Jews lived in my domain; yet I would not let them worship that God or in any way teach my people the religion of the Jews.

Our gods were many and were worshipped by the inhabitants of the nation in accordance with what might be the desires of these people, and when the gods answered the prayers of the people they were thought to be good and true, but when the answers did not come, the gods were false, and new gods were made and worshipped according as they answered the people's prayers or not. So you see that our gods were the creatures of men and not men the creatures of the gods.

But, notwithstanding this false idea, as I now see, of God, there were men of deep insight into the matters pertaining to the spiritual world, who did not make and worship the gods that I have spoken of, but who were able to look beyond these material things and discover that there was such a thing as a higher condition of the afterlife, in which the souls of man could find happiness and knowledge of the existence of a real and mighty power that would bring them into a state of existence where men would realize the higher life of the soul's predominance.

These men were not numerous and did not associate with the inhabitants to any extent, but lived to themselves and evolved certain philosophies which satisfied them of truths which our common beliefs did not comprehend. These men also taught these truths, but not very generally, and only to those who might become their followers.

In my time we had what you would call churches and priests and officials of high position in the religious organization, and feasts and ceremonies and sacrifices, and these powerful ecclesiastics were very jealous and intolerant of anything which interfered with, or in any manner controlled, their religious teachings or the power which they exercised over the people, and the government of the kingdom as well. And consequently, these philosophers that I speak of were not permitted to disseminate their speculations or philosophies among the masses, and were compelled to write their doctrines or teachings in a language which the common people could not understand.

This was the condition of the religious part of my kingdom at the time of its destruction and many of my people who survived this destruction and who were scattered into other countries took with them these beliefs in the multiplicity of gods, and worshipped as before their dispersion. In time these beliefs commenced to permeate the beliefs of the people among whom they lived, until the belief in many gods became the general belief of many other nations. You will find in history that many nations which became great after the fall of my kingdom, such as Greece and Rome and others continued the belief in a multiplicity of gods.

But not until the spreading and adoption of Christianity by them did the belief in the one true God become the established and universal belief of these nations and of the people thereof.

Man made the gods and worshipped them, until the great Master came and proclaimed the truth of the one and only existing Father. Of course, an exception must be made in the statement in favor of the Jews, because they had only one God; but even they had different names for their God, which were applicable and used in accordance with the qualities that they ascribed to Him. It was only after Jesus came did that one God with many names of the Jews become our Father—the God of Love and Salvation.

From all of this you may suppose that I am a Christian. Well, I am, and I live in the Celestial Spheres; for I must tell you that I became converted to the truths of the teachings of Jesus many years ago, and my progression in the development of my soul has been such that I am now in the Celestial Spheres.

I merely wanted to write this to show you that man has been a maker of gods for so many years that they cannot be numbered; and that it was only when the great truths came with the coming of Jesus that the real existing God and all His attributes were revealed to mankind.

Yes, I know, many of the people who lived in my time, and long since, have never learned the truth of the soul development, and live in the happiness which has come to them with the progress of their intellects. But many of them have also been brought into the Light and Truth.

I will not write more, but will say,
Good night,
Leekesi.

The best thing for men to do who desire to see God with all the attributes that belong only to a supreme infinite being

Let me write, Judas.

I have not written you for a long time and feel that I must write you and declare some truth that is of importance to you and to mankind. I will not write a very long message, and what I have to say will be put into short sentences and made succinct. I know that you wonder who I am and what I will write about, and you must not be surprised if I tell you that what you may think is not of much importance.

Well, my subject is, "What is the best thing for men to do who *desire to see God and realize that he a personal God with all the attributes that belong only to a Supreme Infinite Being."*

God is a spirit and a person, and not a mere nebulous being without form or personality. He is real as to these qualities, and is not wanting that which will make him the Father that Jesus so often called him.

Now in order for a spirit to see and understand just what all this means, the spirit must get in that harmony with Him that will enable the spirit to possess qualities of soul that are like the qualities of the Father that the spirit desires to see and understand. This condition can be obtained only by the spirit pursuing the way that the Master so often writes you of, and which is absolutely necessary in order for the spirit to obtain the qualities necessary for such comprehension. Only as a soul is filled with the Love of the Father can it possibly be in the condition that will enable it to see and comprehend this personality of God. No mere development of the intellectual faculties or of the natural love will suffice for this purpose; and while such development is necessary in order for the spirit to become the perfect man in order to enjoy the condition that belongs to that man, yet such development is not sufficient to enable the spirit to see and comprehend the Father.

It is so much easier for a spirit to get in the condition just mentioned than to get in the condition last described; and as you may see the wholly different thing that the soul development leads to, (and this) should be sufficient to induce the spirit to accept the Father's Love, and become a true son of His.

I have written what I desired, and thank you for the opportunity, and with my love will say good night.

Judas.[96]

Confirms and approves what Judas has written

What Judas has written you I approve and emphasize, and with all my love for the mere man, as for the spirit, urge them to pursue the way and attain to the great goal that the Divine Love will fit them for and lead them into.

I will not write more tonight, but will soon come and write you a long message.

Your brother and friend,
Jesus.[97]

---

[96] This message is a composite of two, being published in Volume II and Volume IV. (G.J.C.)
[97] This message is a composite of two, being published in Volume II and Volume IV. (G.J.C.)

A message from Helen

I am here, your own true and loving Helen.

Well, dear, I am so glad that the Master and the other spirit could write you tonight, and believe that now the rapport may be continued and you may be able to receive the messages that are waiting to be delivered. I love you and with all my soul's desires, say that I am

Your own true and loving

Helen.

The apostle of Jesus wishes to add his testimony to the Truth of the messages being received from the Master and the Celestial Spirits. He states he was the son of Mary and Joseph, and a brother in the flesh of Jesus

October 8th, 1915.

I am here, James the Lesser.

I come because most of the apostles have written you, and I want to be in the number who testify that Jesus is the living and true son of God, and that he has selected you—and also your friend—to do his work.

I know that this has been told you by many spirits, but yet I want to add my testimony, for the time may come when you will meet such unbelief and skepticism that you will need all the testimony that you can get.

The work that you will have to do will not be an easy one. You will have many antagonists, especially in the churches and among the preachers and rulers of the churches, and you will need all the help that the spirit powers can give you.

I am one of the band of Celestial spirits that will sustain and help you in your work, and I am so interested that you shall succeed that I want you to know the fact that back of you both is the most wonderful power that has ever been given to mortals to carry out the plans of the higher Celestial world.

When on earth, I was the brother of Jesus, and called the Lesser to distinguish me from James, the brother of John and son of Zebedee. I was not the son of any Alphaeus, such as that name is understood in the New Testament, but the son of Mary and Joseph, as was my brother Jesus. Jesus himself will one day come and tell you exactly who Alphaeus was.

So have faith, and believe what we write you, for it is all true. You must not doubt as you do sometimes, or let your earthly affairs turn your thoughts from the great truths which we come to teach you. So without writing more, I will say, believe.

Your brother in Christ,

James the Lesser.

Jehosephat of the Old Testament explains his status while living on earth

September 12th, 1915.

I am here, Jehosephat.

I was a character in the Old Testament, and I want to say just a word. I am a Christian, and redeemed by the Divine Love of the Father.

I was not a very religious man when I lived and never knew what the love of God was, although you might think from my association with Him as portrayed in the Bible, that I was a righteous man.

I was a man possessed of great mediumistic powers, and through me the spirits would communicate those things which they said came from God. But I was not a teacher myself and was not in condition to teach spiritual truths, for I was only a Jew of the Pharisees who had certain intellectual beliefs as to what kind of worship should be given to God, and what men should do otherwise in their dealings with one another.

I merely wanted to say this, so that you might know that while we are what you would call ancient spirits yet we are interested in your work, which the Master has called upon you to do.

I will say good night.

Jehosephat.

Writes about the True Love of the Father and introduces Judge Syrick's soulmate; Rose wrote to him for the first time while he is still on earth. Helen continues with a comment of what Rose said and so does the father of Mr. Padgett

January 9th, 1915.

I am here, Helen.

I am so happy, and I am awfully glad to see that you are also. I was with you at the show tonight, and you made me so happy when you loved me as you did. I tried to let you hear my voice, but I could not; but don't despair of hearing it. I will soon learn the way and then you will hear me quite often. I loved you so much that you could not help feeling my love, and when you thought of me so intensely I was with you and tried to hug you with my hands. You shed more tears of love, and then I almost let myself control you right there; but as it was a public place, I restrained my emotion. You are my darling Ned, and you are dearer to me than ever. So let me have all your love and I will be very happy.

I was with you today when Dr. Stone was with you, and heard what was said, and I saw that he was very much impressed with your talk to him about the Love of God flowing into the heart; so I believe that if you continue to tell him of this Love, he will soon see the true way that it must be obtained and will strive to get it. He is a naturally spiritual man and wants to have this Love in his soul.

I know just what he thinks about this Love Principle and while he is partly right, yet he does not grasp the true principle of that Love. He is depending upon a love that man creates by what he calls right thinking and action, but this is not true, man cannot of himself create this Love. He can let it come into his heart and grow and thereby become more possessed with it; but it will not come of his own creation. His heart is not in such a condition that this Love will spring up spontaneously, nor can he by his mere effort to create it, cause its appearance. He can obtain it only from a higher source, and that source is his Heavenly Father. No man is so good that this Love can emanate from him anymore than life can arise of his own volition or efforts. What is the Love Principle, as it is called, is not the natural love of a man for God or for man, but the Love that comes into the heart of a man from the Father in answer to prayer. I do not know if I have made myself very clear but you know what I mean, and you can explain better than I can.

Yes, I am very strong tonight and you are in very good condition too, but you must not write too much. You must conserve your strength for I am going to draw on it tomorrow night, if conditions are favorable.

She (Padgett's daughter) is happy as I told you. You are not so much worried, and I am thankful for it. Yes, decidedly. Yes, he has to a greater extent. He sees that only this Love can make him happy, and save him from his sins. So you see you have done some good on earth as well as among the spirits.

As to Judge Syrick, I will try to have his soulmate come and write him—wait a little while until I find her. Rose is here.

Dear Frank, I am here and through the kindness of Mrs. Padgett, I have the opportunity to write you, and tell you that you are the dearest person to me in all the world. You do not yet fully appreciate my love for you, but as you come more in rapport with me, you will feel my presence and love to a greater and larger extent. I am not only your soulmate but your guardian angel and when you least think of me, I am with you trying to direct your thoughts and actions towards those things which will make you happier and more at peace with your troubles in life.

So do not forget that wherever you may be, and whatever your thoughts may dwell upon, I am with you and know what you are thinking of, and I want you to think and believe that in all the earth, or spirit land either, there is no one who loves you with such a pure and fervent love as I do, my own darling Frank. Oh, how I wish that I could communicate with you in this way every night and tell you of what happiness I have in being with you, and feeling at times that you do really love me in your own somewhat divided heart. But thank God the time will come when I will have your whole love for myself, and no one else will share it with me to the smallest extent.

My dear, only believe that I am your soulmate, and am waiting for you to come over, and share with me the happiness and delight which my home here gives me. No spirit can love its soulmate more than I do you, and no mortal can love so much. Be my own true sweetheart, and even though you do not have the assurance that I am with you as I say, yet I am, and nothing in all the world can keep me from you. So if you can, extinguish from your thoughts that I may be a mere myth and not your own true loving soulmate.

Let my love for you keep your thoughts in the way of things spiritual, for if you will only believe in me and in my love you will realize that I am with you and will feel my love and my presence, even though your physical senses may not be able to tell you anything.

But the sense of two souls which are decreed by our Father to be one, will tell you, at times, that I am one and you are the other, and that the two will through all eternity become and remain one in love and happiness. So you see, that even though we cannot exchange our love so very often in words, yet in our feelings and sensations we may know that our love for each other is existing, and burning with a brightness that nothing can extinguish, not even your thoughts that I am a mere myth and not your own true, loving soulmate. Be only closer to me in your thoughts and you will realize that I am your Rose, as I once told you. You sometimes doubt that you saw me and felt my kiss your forehead, and that I have no real existence, but I tell you with all my soul's love that it was I that kissed you and told you that I was your soulmate. Oh my darling one, do not doubt me again if you value my happiness.

Let my love for you keep your thoughts in the way of things spiritual, for I can see that you are inclined to the higher things of the spirit world of life; and if you desire to come to me and live with me when you come over, seek the real love of our Father, for in that you will find everything that will make your soul develop, until when you come to me. I will meet you and take you to my home, where you will find that I have prepared a home for you so beautiful that you will wonder how I could have loved you so much, and thought so much about your happiness. You are the only one for me to think of in this way, and when you stop for a moment and think of what love means, you will see that I could not do otherwise than try to make you happy.

There is another thing that I want to tell you, and that is that you must have no fear of what is called death, because it is not death, but an entrance into life; and when you come over I will be right at your bedside, and as your spirit passes from your body I will take you in my arms and carry you to the home which I have prepared for you.

Of course, this means, if you have developed your soul to such an extent as will permit you to enter my home; and even if you have not, I will be with you as the soul leaves the body and fold you in my arms and say such words of burning love that you will not be afraid or want to be anywhere else than with me. So you see, in life or death, or after death I will be with you and my love will envelope you in the great happiness which I have and want you to have.

As I have already taken up more of Mr. Padgett's time and strength than I intended, I must stop, but in doing so, say with all my heart and soul, I love you and will love you through all eternity my own dear Frank.

Helen now writes the following:

Well, don't you think that she loves him? She is a soulmate after my own heart, and I think that he ought to be very happy to know that she has such love as that.

No, not so great as mine, and I will love you with all my heart too. I am somewhat tired now, and must stop, so good night, my own darling Ned.

Your own true,
Helen.[98]

Rose, after Judge Syrick passed into the spirit world, writes about the wonderful love that the Master has for Mr. Padgett as well as her soulmate's progress

March 4th, 1916.

I am here, Rose.

I am your old acquaintance in the spirit world, and you have said that you loved me as a sister and wanted to make me happy, and you did, for I am very happy, thanks to your help.

I am the soulmate of the Judge, and I merely want to say that we are both with you at times and try to help you and receive help. He is progressing very rapidly now, and will soon be with me when I know he will be extremely happy. He wants me to say that he will never forget

---

[98] This message is a composite of two, being published in Volume III and Volume IV. (G.J.C.)

you and the great benefit you conferred upon him when you brought him in contact with me and enabled him to learn what was in the future for him in the spirit world. He is now a true believer in the truths of the Master and is trying to obtain the love in all its fullness, and he wants you to know that this love is a reality and not a mere thing of speculation.

He wants to come soon and write you a long letter as he promised, and he would come before, but your time is so occupied by the high spirits with their messages that he has not found the opportunity to write.

Well I must not write more, except to say, that you have in store for you a happiness that you cannot conceive of. A soulmate that is so very beautiful and loving and beloved by us all, and who has a most wonderful influence over all with whom she comes in contact. And greater and above all else you have the love and wonderful friendship of the Master, who comes to you so very often.

Oh, I tell you that you are favored and should feel that great benefit of the companionship of the number of high spirits who come to you, for you do have a great number of these Celestial Spirits come to you and write, and cast over you the influence of their great love. I am your friend forever, and I want you to love me too.

Yes, I try to help them, for I am present when they come, and some of them come to me for help. This is a wonderful work and we are all so interested in doing it. The dark spirits who seek your help seem to be as much impressed, as any of us that you have so much influence over them, and when they start on the way to light, they, in many cases, find it, and then turn to you in gratitude and thanks. They are your friends forever, and say, that they will always be with you and protect you.

So my dear friend, I will say good night.

Your friend,

Rose McGovern.

Mrs. Padgett, who located Judge Syrick's soulmate is happy that she is able to write tonight

March 4th, 1916.

I am here, your Helen.

Well sweetheart, you have just had a letter from Rose, who has been waiting to write you for such a long time, and who is so happy that she could write you. She and the Judge were here together, and both of them think a great deal of you, and are very happy in the thought that you helped them so much and caused them to come together even before he became a spirit. He says he wants to write.

No, I was not present when she attempted to write, but White Eagle says; she was not a very bright spirit, but seemed to be in need of help. She may be some poor spirit who wants your help.

Well, I was sorry that you were not in condition to take the Master's message, and so was he, but he says that he will come again soon. He was not satisfied with the message and thought it best not to attempt to write tonight, as I see you are not in condition to write much.

So with all my love, I will say good night, but I want one great big kiss, and your love.

Your own true loving,
Helen.

Is grateful to Mr. Padgett's grandmother for the help that she has given him to enable him to progress to higher spheres

March 4th, 1916.

I am here, Robert G. Ingersoll.

I would like to finish my message tonight if agreeable to you.

Well, under the circumstances, I do not think it best to write tonight, and I will postpone it as you say.

I am very happy and progressing, thanks to that dear grandmother of yours. She is a wonderful spirit with a mind as clear as her soul is pure. I cannot tell you how much I owe to her, and her teachings and love.

That is just what I want to write about, and I know that it is the important thing in the whole plan of God for man's salvation. So I will write on that after I have finished the message which I have already commenced.

I thank you and will say good night.

Your friend and brother in Christ,
Ingersoll.

First effort of communication after suddenly passing into the spirit world, after only a short period of spiritual investigation on earth

March 29th, 1915.

I am here, Syrick.

Let me say a word, I am your late friend and brother in spiritualism. Yes, I am able to write some and your wife told me to try as she wishes me to get stronger and realize that I am living as a spirit.

Well, I am here and alive and have my Rose with me. She is so very beautiful and loving and I am very happy to be with her, but I have already learned that I am not suited to live with her for she is so much higher in her spiritual development than I am, but she tells me that I can progress and I am going to try with all my might.

Well, old friend, the uncertain has become certain and I know now that spirits can and do communicate with mortals. So let any doubts that you may have, leave you and believe with all your heart that you have received the messages from your band and others as you have been informed.

I can tell you this that you have as your wife and soulmate the most beautiful of all the spirits that I have yet seen. I had no conception of what beauty was until I came here and saw your wife and Rose and Dr. Stone's Mary. She is very beautiful also and loves him, I know, with a very deep love. As this is my first attempt I am tired and must stop.

Well, I know no one whom I would rather that it should belong to than you, so keep it and think of me sometimes.

So with my kindest regards and best wishes, I am your true friend,

Frank D. Syrick.[99]

At a later date confirms what Mr. Padgett and Dr. Stone told him about the Spirit World and reports on his experience there and progress to date

May 6th, 1915.

I am here, your friend Syrick.

Well, I first want to say that I am so very glad to have the opportunity to write to you, thanks to that beautiful wife of yours. I tell you Padgett, that she is a wonder, and you should feel yourself a highly favored man to have such a soulmate. She is not only beautiful but so full of love and so wise in the things that pertain to the higher life. Why she tells me things that I never in all my life thought could exist, and when she shows me the truths of the Father's Love and how beautiful and beyond conception her home is, I can scarcely contain myself. She is helping me so much in my progression. Of course Rose is also, but Rose does not have that great angelic love that your wife has, and is not able to tell me of the wonderful things that may be mine, and the way that I may obtain them.

Why I want to tell you that the fortunate day of my life was the

---

[99] This message is a composite of two, being published in Volume III and Volume IV. (G.J.C.)

one when I met you at the Colburn's and commenced the investigation of the spiritualism that you were seeking to learn. Many times you told me to seek for the higher things and the soul development; and I heard you and did not know what you meant. I knew that I was not a very bad man as men go, and would wonder what you meant. Sometimes I got a glimpse of what you might mean, and would ask you, as you may remember, if you thought I was a very bad man, and you would tell me, no, but that I must give my thoughts to higher things and get the love of God in my heart.

Well I did not comprehend what you meant, and when you told me to pray to the Father, I did so, but somehow I did not understand just how to pray. But now I realize what you mean, and what an awful mistake I made in not trying to learn what you tried to tell me when on earth.

Well, when I arrived in Richmond I felt a little sick, but had no idea that I was so near death. In fact death was not in my thoughts, as I had induced myself to believe that I would live to be an old man, and so you can imagine my feelings, after I had been stricken and was unconscious for quite a while, I suddenly recovered my consciousness and found myself looking down on my body all cold and lifeless. I thought it was not my body but someone else's that resembled me very much and that I was still in my body; but as I tried to make myself known to my friends who had gathered around, I found that they did not hear me or see me, and then I remembered the description that you had read to me of your wife's passing over, and the conviction came to me that I was no longer a mortal. And to further convince me, just then Rose came to me and said. "Frank, I am keeping my promise, you are with your soulmate never again to return to your mortal life and wonder what kind of looking girl your soulmate may be, for now you see her as she really is, and you also feel her arms around you and her kisses upon your cheek, and I know that you would not go into that body again for all the world."

Oh, I tell you, that such a reception, accompanied with such beauty and love was enough to make a man forget that he had ever been a mortal; and for the time I forgot that I had. So you see my passing was not as undesirable as I had thought it would be. What a great blessing to have the belief that I had when I was with you all as to my Rose. It may seem strange to some, but I know, not to you, that my belief in Rose was so great, that to me she was as real as if I had met her in the flesh and was separated from her only a few miles in expectation that some near day she would come on the train to be with me. I cannot tell you what my happiness was, I had no doubt about my being a spirit, and thoroughly believed that I had left the earth, so far as occupying my body was concerned, forever. I had no desire to return to it, and my thoughts did not turn to things material. My Rose was sufficient for me. She occupied all my thoughts, and my being was wholly with her, and my happiness was a thing no mortal can understand or believe, if I were capable of telling him.

Such beauty and love! Well, I will not try to tell you of it, for I cannot; but only say that when you come over and your soulmate meets you, you will lose your breath and wonder how such a man as you are now, could be loved by such a being of beauty.

A short time after I had been with Rose, your wife and others of your band came to me and with them my own dear mother, who was so beautiful and loving to me; and I was so happy that I cried with all my heart and soul; but for joy.

Well, such was my passing and such I wanted it to be, but when on earth I had no conception that it could be such.

As soon as I could recover my breath, as we say on earth, I made many inquiries about the things that I saw and which I had wanted to know when on earth, and received information; but I want to tell you that some things that I heard seemed familiar, and I thought that I had heard them before, and so it was, because in our communications and in our conversations and in our circle I had heard them. So you see what a privilege it is for a man to have the opportunity of learning of the spirit world while still on earth. You and Dr. Stone and the Colburns are much favored in your opportunities to hear of so many of the things that pertain to the spirit life.

I am acquainted with Dr. Stone's Mary, and tell him that she is real and is certainly his soulmate as was I his friend and patient when on earth. She is a beautiful spirit and so good, and loves him with a love that he cannot now understand, but which he will some day. Tell him, I am more fortunate than he, because I came first and partook of the love of a beautiful fine and loving woman; but his time is coming, and I am only more fortunate than he, in that I came to mine a little sooner than he will to his. I have met Bright Star, and I certainly was surprised. I thought to meet an Indian Squaw, but instead, I met a spirit the most beautiful and bright, with God's Love emanating from her whole being.

She was glad to see me, and reminded me that I was not a stranger, as she had seen me many times at Mrs. Ripple's séances; but she said: "Then you only knew me as a little Indian girl, simple but accommodating." And I said; "Bright Star you certainly surprise me. I had no expectations of meeting you as such a beautiful and bright spirit." And she said: "The Love of God makes us all alike; we who have that love are not Indian or Pale Face or Yellow Face, but are all the children of the Father, and as His Love is the same unchangeable Love, those who receive it are all the same in their beauty and color and brightness. He is no respecter of color or race. His Love makes our appearance, and as our souls become more filled with this Love, we become more like Him, and only love appears, and color, and race and previous conditions disappear." Now what do you think of that to come from our little Indian girl! I tell you that the things I have learned here are wonderful and surprising.

Well, to continue, after I had lived in this condition of happiness for some time, and saw that my future depended upon my progress, for you must know I could not go with Rose to her home because she was so much more spiritual than I, I commenced to examine myself to learn what my drawbacks were and as I continued to make this self-examination, I found that my life on earth or rather my recollections or memories of that life were still with me, and that I must do something to get rid of them. And conscience commenced to work, and I soon saw myself as I had never seen myself while on earth. And the more transparent my actual self became, the more this conscience accused me of things done and omitted while a mortal; and with these accusations came sufferings, for she and your wife and my mother all told me the way, but somehow I could not just understand how to find it. And so the days went by and I suffered.

But as I continued to pray, for you must understand that I had been praying ever since I commenced to suffer, all of a sudden a feeling of peace came to me and with it a great Love that I had never felt before, and I realized that it was the Father's Love that my Rose and the others had been telling me of; and since then my sufferings have been growing less and less, and my prayers and faith more and more. Oh, how I regret that in my earth life, I had not sought this love. How much suffering I would have avoided and how much more happiness would have been mine.

Let me tell you, and my friends, the Colburns and Dr. Stone, that this is no idle tale, but a stern, unavoidable reality, and I, like though unlike Lazarus, arise from the dead and tell you all, with all the emphasis that I can command, that if you want to avoid darkness and suffering and get into happiness when you come over, seek with all your heart this Love while you are mortals.

I come very near to you, for only a short time ago, I was with you, joining in your speculations as to the life of which I am now a part, and now as your friend who has set aside speculation with knowledge, I tell you this great truth, and with all my heart urge you to believe me, and take this truth to your hearts and souls.

Well, I have written you a long letter and must stop, but before doing so permit me to say, that you all have my thanks for the help that you gave me in the short time that we were friends. The few months that we knew one another were as I now realize, the most profitable months to me of all those that I spent in the investigation of spiritualism.

So give my love to my friends and keep some for yourself, and believe me when I say, I am your own true friend and brother.

Frank D. Syrick.

Tells of preparing conditions suitable to permit Judge Syrick to write his long letter to his friends

May 6th, 1915.

I am here, Helen.

Well sweetheart, you received quite a long letter from the Judge, and also a most eloquent and truthful one. He has told you the true conditions of his coming to us and of his subsequent experiences. I told you the other night that I wanted him to tell you his own story, and tonight I made conditions favorable for him to do so. You will find much food for thought in what he has written; and coming from one who has so recently left you, I have no doubt it will have its impression on you and his other friends.

He is now progressing, and very soon, I think, he will have so much of this love that he will progress to the third sphere. His Rose is with him so much and her love for him is so pure and true that he will necessarily feel that the greater love of the Father is his if he will only pray and believe. We are all trying to help him, and he in certain ways, is like a little child. He is very susceptible to our teachings and to the influence of love, and because of that condition of his mind I think that his progress will be rapid. He loves his Rose and thinks that her word is his gospel—and well he may, for her advice comes from a heart that is full of love for him, and also filled with the love of the Father. He is a very blessed spirit.

Well, sweetheart, you are tired and must stop or you may feel the effects of the strain.

Question by Mr. Padgett and answer:

Yes, I was here and I think he is what you would call a little off. His ideas as to his being the six before the six is all wrong. He will never be the leader of the Bahais or any other sect of religionists. He is too material for that, and as for his being the greatest man in the nation, why that is far beyond absurdity.

Yes, I can and I will for it may do him good to know that he has someone in all the wide universe who loves him. He needs love more than anyone that I have seen for a long time. I mean among mortals.

So I will try to find her and let you know later. So with all my love I am your own true loving,

Helen.

Friend of Mr. Padgett's asks for help, so they compare notes with old friends in the spirit world

January 12th, 1915.

I am here, George W. Harvey.

I lived in Washington, and kept a restaurant on Pennsylvania Avenue and Tenth Street. I am in the spirit world and in the earth plane and in hell also, I am not happy for I am in darkness and despair.

(Question unknown, but answer is as follows)

Yes, I did, but that did not keep me from hell, the priests mislead me, and they are here too damn them—can you help me any, if you can do so. Yes I remember Taggart, but he is here too—and can't help himself, for I see him sometimes, and he tells that he is in a condition of suffering too. No, but he is not in condition to help me, even if I do see him. You must help me if you can. I don't know but I want help from someone. I know they say so, but I don't believe them, for they can't help themselves. No I don't know them. I will see him at once and ask him, and tell him that I want to know. So good night.

Your friend,
George W. Harvey.

Confirms writing and is a go-between

January 12th, 1915.

I am here, Helen.

You must not write to these spirits as we have told you - yes he said that he knew you on earth and wanted you to help him. I see that he has gone to seek Mr. Taggart, but I don't think that he will be much helped. Yes you may be right; you certainly have a way of accomplishing things. I never thought of that. Well, I will go and see if I can find them, and make them come here, and write you what I hear.

They are here:

Mr. Taggart tells Mr. Harvey that you told him that the way to get out of this condition of darkness and unhappiness is to pray to God, for His Love to enter into their hearts, and believe that it will, that if he will only be willing to have it come into their hearts, it will, but that he has not yet been able to believe. But Mr. Harvey says, that when he was on earth, he was a strict Catholic and that he often prayed something like that and attended to his duties, and even when he made his will, he left some money for the priests to pray him out of purgatory, but all their prayers together have not helped him, and he doesn't believe that there is any God to whom a person can pray and from whom he can get relief—so that when you talked that way to Taggart, you were merely trying to mislead him as the priests did him.

But Mr. Taggart says:

George you are wrong there, for our friend does not merely say pray, but he prays with us and for us and seems to believe with all his heart that there is a God and that he will answer prayer. So I am not so certain that there is not a God and one who answers prayers, I am going to try to pray and believe myself and I advise you to do likewise.

Mr. Harvey says:

Taggart it is all nonsense, and if that is the only way we can get out of this condition, we never will be any better than we now are—so you need not tell me of God and prayer.

Mr. Taggart says:

George, I have seen the effect of this prayer on some spirits and I know that they have been made more beautiful and happy, and even Mackay is commencing to say that he sees light ahead and has felt some strange influences come into his heart as he said a prayer, which he promised our friend to say. Now what is the use in your being pig headed and say that there is no God, when you don't know anything about it? I tell you though, there must be something in this belief or I would not see so many happy spirits around us.

Be a man who can keep his mind open to what he sees and the reasons therefore may come to you. Let us not become hardheaded in this matter. As you were so easy to believe on earth what your priests told you about purgatory and the hells and the necessity for you to pay for prayers to help you out of purgatory, why can't you try to believe a little when the same thing is told you without your having to pay for it? I am going to try my best to believe and if you know what is best for you, you will follow suit.

Mr. Harvey, says:

Taggart, what is the use of being fooled twice, once is enough for me. Priests are here with me and suffering more than I am, and when

I ask them why don't they pray themselves out of purgatory, they say: "To hell with prayer." Now how am I to believe anything that is told me about prayer or God?

Mr. Taggart says:

George, Let your priests and their sufferings and their cursings pass out of your mind, and listen to me for a moment. When I came over, I was in great darkness and despair, and believed that there was no possible help for me and that I must remain in the condition of darkness that I found myself in, but one day I was called to meet our friend by his father, and when I came where he was I found that Mackay was there also, and then we exchanged greetings, and wished each other happiness. But I found that there was no happiness for me and I told our friend that I was anything but happy; and he said believe in God's Love and you will soon be, and I said, who is God and what is His Love; and then he explained to Mackay what that love is, and I heard it all; and then I tackled him and told him that God was a myth and prayer was nothing but the wish of a man and went no higher than his mind.

But he would not agree with me and we had an argument right then and there, and I tell you that while he did not convince me that there was a God or any efficacy in prayer, yet it made me think and wonder if I could be wrong and he right; and before I left him, not only Mackay, but myself promised that we would try an experiment in the nature of prayer and we have been doing it many times since, and I tell you, that while I am not yet convinced that there is a God, or that prayer to Him will take us out of our awful conditions of suffering and darkness, yet I have felt many strange sensations, and at times, some little feeling of happiness, which I had never felt before; so you can see, I would be a fool not to try and get this relief, if I possibly can. And I want to tell you George, that if you are willing to make the effort with us we will be glad to have you come. Of course you need not believe if you don't want to, but just come and join with us in our experiment and you will soon realize that there is something operating that you cannot account for. Mackay is now feeling very much happier he says; and I believe that he will soon believe in this God and his love that our friend told us about; at any rate he is commencing to improve in his appearance, and I attribute it to trying the experiment I told you of. So what is the use in holding back and saying that there is no God and no love that can get you out of your condition of which you complain so much, when by the exercise of a little reason and will, you may be on the right track to salvation. Of course I don't know just what this may lead to, but I have determined to follow it to a conclusion, and you will be a big fool if you don't go with me.

Mr. Harvey said:

Taggart, you were a pretty level-headed man when on earth, and required to have things proved to you, and were really a stubborn man as I know, and what you say impresses me; but you will have to show me what you mean by this experiment. You have not told me what you mean, and of course, until you do, I can't follow you.

Mr. Taggart says:

George, it is a very simple thing. Mackay and I told our friend that we did not believe in God or in his love or in any saviour, and he said; you need not, to do what I want you to try. He said, while there is a God and His love which is the only thing that can save you from sin and make you happy men, yet that God does not force that love on you or make you believe in Him; and only when you are willing to receive that love of your own volition will it come to you. So you see he said it all depends upon your own will, whether you will have that love and the happiness which flows from it or not, and if you will only will that you may believe in God if there be one, and that you may receive that love if such there be, then if you will, will this and say to God, if there be one, that you will that this love shall come into your heart and that this belief shall come into your mind, and repeat this with all earnestness and will, you will find that after a little while, this belief will come to you, and this love will come into your heart.

So Mackay and I are desiring to try anything to get out of our condition, and believing that our friend would not intentionally deceive us, promised to say these things, and in that way pray to a God that we did not believe in; and we have continued to repeat these thoughts ever since; and I must confess to you that some strange change or sensation has come to me. What it is, I don't just know, but it is there; and I am determined to continue in this qualified prayer, until I know one way or the other what the result will be. So you see, George, if it does no good, it can do no harm, and if you have desire enough to get out of your condition, you will try the experiment.

Mr. Harvey says:

Well Taggart, there may be something in what you say and I am willing to go with you; for as you say, if it does no good, it can do no harm. So let me hear again what I am to say and I will commence.

Then Mr. Taggart repeated the prayer and they left.

You are too wonderful in your way of getting the attention of spirits who are in darkness to turn their thoughts to things that may help them. And I am so glad that you are helping these spirits, even though you did let Mr. Harvey write. But who knows, maybe such interferences are intended for some good purposes.

So my darling, I love you with all my heart and soul, and must stop writing.

Yes, I will, and will try to talk to him sometime when the proper occasion comes.

So good night, my own darling Ned.

Helen.

Does not want Mr. Padgett to be a failure in his work for the Kingdom as he was

December 23rd, 1917.

I am here, Swedenborg.

I have heard the messages that you have just received and I desire to impress upon you the necessity and importance of striving to follow the advice therein given, for if you fail now to do the work upon which you have entered, your regrets when you come to the spirit world will be so great that you will find it almost impossible to get rid of them even if you progress to the soul spheres where the Love is all so abundant.

I know what I write for that was my experience and it seemed to me that everywhere I turned as I sought to progress I saw before me the word "failure" and for many long years it was my ghost of a recollection. Failure as you may know is comparative, and men may fail in their ambitions and desires for fame and wealth and position, and yet when they come to the spirit world they realize that such failures mean comparatively little and in their progress in the truth, they soon forget their failures and cast them behind. But when a mortal has conferred upon him a work which does not have for its object the accumulation of wealth or the attaining of fame or position, but the great and vital end of showing men the way by which they can become reconciled to God and partake of His very Nature in Love and obtain immortality, and also has given to him the privilege of receiving the Great Truths of God in relation to the salvation of men, then I say that failure means a great catastrophe for him and a greater calamity for humanity, and that man is in a condition of mind and recollection beyond description.

Very few men have had conferred upon them this great privilege and power and responsibility, and I was one of them and was a failure not because I did not try to receive and deliver the truth, but because I prevented, by my preconceived ideas of what the truth should be, the real and pure truth from coming to me and thence to humanity. In a way I was unconscious of my failure or of the existence of conditions in me that caused the failure; yet when I came to the spirit world and realized the failure that I had made, then everything was a failure to my conscience.

In your case, you have no such preconceived ideas to hamper you or prevent you from receiving the truth, for you are used merely as instrument for these truths to transcribe and they are delivered in the very language of the writers, and your failure if such there shall be, will be entirely due to your indifference or want of effort to get in condition that will enable the messages to be written. You must see your responsibility and your duty, and I may say your love that should urge you to work and you must not become a failure.

I am your friend and brother and co-worker in making known these truths and only write because I as a failure can speak from experience. So my brother turn your thought more to this work, and if necessary sacrifice every worldly consideration to carry forward your work and make perfect your efforts to fulfill the great mission with which you have been blessed.

I will not write more now. May the Father bless you with His Love.

Your brother in Christ,
Swedenborg.

Says that Swedenborg wrote with authority

December 23rd, 1917.

I am here, your own true and loving Helen.

Well dear, you have received some important messages tonight and I hope that you will read and ponder them, for they are of great spiritual importance, not only to the work that you are doing but also to you personally. I shudder to think of what the consequences might be if you would make a failure of the great privilege that has been bestowed upon you, and you must think of what Swedenborg wrote, for he would write as one having had an experience with a knowledge that came from the experience.

But I know that you will not be a failure and that you will give your best endeavors to the accomplishing of the work. I wish to tell you also, that you should pray more for the Love and long for it with all the longing of your soul, and then as it flows into your soul I know that your desire to accomplish this work will so increase that there will be no possibility of failure. So sweetheart, follow the advice given you and determine that the great work of the Master will not this time be a failure through you.

I was with you at church tonight and realized that you enjoyed the services very much and especially the music and your soul experience, and considerable happiness from the love that came to you. And there was much love with and around you, for many of the spirits were present, but Jesus was not there. Again has Christmas come, and the people are now worshiping their Jesus as God, a worship which is very distasteful to him and one which he hopes by the truths of the messages that he is delivering to you will cease, when these messages shall become known to the people. He realizes how much harm such worship does and also realizes that he is a mere son of the Father as are many and all spirits who have received His Divine Love in their souls, and become a part of His Divinity; and Jesus knowing that he is merely a child of the Father, dependent upon Him for His Love and Mercy, avoids all opportunity of hearing the praises and worship of those who substitute him in the place of the Father. So distasteful and blasphemous is this worship to him that he even gives up his work in the earth plane among spirits and men until the time of this universal worship of him shall pass by.

I am so glad that this great truth of the only one and true God, the only being to be worshiped, is being revealed to mankind. So you see how important that you do your work. Well you have written a great deal tonight and are tired and I will not draw on you further. Love me and believe that I love you, and pray to the Father to give you His Love and strength to perform your mission. Good night my dear husband.

Your own true and loving,
Helen.

Is surprised to learn that a soul can leave the material body and visit with loved ones in the spirit world as both Mr. Padgett and Dr. Stone were able to do with the help of their loved ones

December 28th, 1916.

I am here, the spirit of your old friend, General Henkle.

I merely want to say that I have been present all evening and heard your reading of the messages and the conversation, and must say that some things that I heard surprised me, for instance, the assertion that your spirit was taken from your body, and brought to the spirit spheres, and there enjoyed the freedom of a spirit that had left the earth forever. This I have never heard of before, and cannot conceive that such a thing can be, and if it were not for the fact that your wife and a number of other spirits who are filled with love and truth tell me that it is true, I should doubt the fact. It is all so wonderful to me that but for the experience that I had when I came to the spirit world, and found so many things that I thought true were not true, I should even yet hesitate to believe. How little we spirits know of the wonders of God, and how much there is to us to learn!

And the one thing that even yet makes me marvel is that all these wonderful things, I mean the power of communication and the truths that you receive, should have come to you, who when I was on earth was merely a man like the rest of us with no knowledge of these things. But I have had so many surprises and experiences that I am ready to believe most anything that these high and beautiful spirits tell me. The greatest truth of all—the existence of the Divine Love and its effect upon the souls of men and spirits—I know to be a truth, for I have had it come into my soul and transform my condition of darkness into light and happiness.

Since I last wrote you I have made much progress and am now in the third sphere, where I find so much bliss, and so many beautiful spirits, who possess this love and tell me of the beautiful and wonderful things that you did for them. Well, my dear friend, it does me good to write you and tell you of my progress, and the certainty of the existence of the great love.

I have met many of my old friends, and brother lawyers in this spirit world, and some of them have found this soul development, but the most of them, I am sorry to say, have not, and are still trying to develop their intellects, especially in the way of spiritual laws which, they think, is the most important thing to learn. And my work is to try to convince them of the greater importance of the divine love, and to show them the necessity of prayer. The work is laborious and somewhat disheartening, but it is mine to do, and I will continue in the work until I am told to go to a higher sphere.

I would like to write longer tonight and tell you of the experiences of some of my friends, but your wife says that I must not do so and so I will say good night, and leave you my love, and also your friend, although I have never met him on earth, but realize that he is a kindred spirit that the Father has blessed him also with some of this great love.

General S. S. Henkle.

Chides Dr. Stone on his love for her. Also speaks of the trip into the spirit world by both Dr. Stone and Mr. Padgett

December 28th, 1916.

I am here, Mary Kennedy.

Well, if he had thought of me as much as he should, he would have guessed without any difficulty. It just shows you how little you can depend upon the men who profess to love you. This is what I might say if I were a mortal, but being a spirit and able to see into his heart, I know that he loves me as I do him.

I have been waiting for these other spirits to write before I attempted to say a few words, and by the way, let me say that all who wrote tonight are really the spirits that they represented themselves to be. If it were not so late, and you were not so tired, I would write a long letter and tell you of our frolic at Christmas Eve, when you came with us to our homes in the spirit world for the time being, and partook of all the love and greetings that awaited you.

As Mr. Stone wrote, there were many spirits present, and all were very happy in having you both with us, and the Judge, especially, enjoyed it after he got over his fright, if I may call it such, after seeing you two sail through the air in our arms, for you must know that we had you in our arms, and would not let you go until we reached the sphere, where we found a nice greensward to rest upon.

I must stop writing a description of this, or I may forget myself and continue longer than I should; just have a little patience and I will soon come and give you a full description. We will commence to write earlier in the evening and provide that there shall be no interference by other spirits.

Tell my dear that I love him very much, and will go home with him and let him feel my presence. So I will not write more now, and after I get my kisses, will say good night.

Mary the loving soulmate.

Relates his many blessings since coming into the Spirit World

March 23rd, 1916.

I am here, Syrick.

Well, you can't lose me, as the boys say, for I have your wife on my side, and I think that we can beat you and Dr. Stone, although you are two of a kind.

Well, my dear friend, I want to write just a little as I have not written you for some time, and you know the great pleasure it gives us in exchanging a few thoughts. I am very happy, and so is Rose, who is here, and says that you are her next soulmate when I get divorced from her, but I will tell you privately don't depend on that.

I am progressing and am with her so much oftener than formerly, and I also have a greater opportunity to be with your folks. I will come soon and write you about something that I have found to be true since I have been a spirit, and which I know you will like to hear of.

How is my friend the doctor? He looks as if he might be very happy, and if he could see that little soulmate of his I know he would be.

Well, you two had the advantage of me on earth, because you knew more of this Divine Love than I did, but I am ahead of you now, for I have my soulmate right here with her arms around my neck, giving me a kiss occasionally, and I know it. And your soulmates say that your two have their arms around your necks too, and they know that sometimes you realize it.

Well, I am glad that we can have our little jokes together. Oh, what a difference from what I expected! I thought that when I came over I would either be helping in building fires or riding on clouds, playing harps. But believe I would sooner be just as I am with Rose telling me all the sweet things that she does.

I must stop now, and with my love and that of Rose, will say, good night.

Your old friend,
Syrick.

An old friend of Mr. Padgett's also comments on soulmate love

March 23rd, 1916.

I am here, Saul S. Henkle.

Let me say just a word, for while you are all having your love thoughts passing, I would like to come in too.

I was your old friend, Saul S. Henkle and while I was not so young as you folks when on earth, yet, now I am younger than you, and no doubt better looking.

But seriously, I have enjoyed being here this evening, and listening to the messages that you have received. Of course, I never knew your spirit friends on earth, but over here, I have become acquainted with them through that beautiful wife of yours, and I enjoy their companionship very much, especially that of Mrs. Stone, who is so beautiful and full of the Divine Love, and such a tender, loving mother. I am also very fond of the little girl that your Helen calls "Lovesick". Well she undoubtedly is in love, but she doesn't look sick, and is just as bright and beautiful and happy as one can imagine. She does love her soulmate though and doesn't hesitate to let us all know the fact. How happy all your friends are, and how happy I am to be with them!

Over here, there are little circles of friends, just as on earth and there is a difference also in the natures and disposition of those who form the circles; and I want to say that your soulmate and that of the Dr. are two of the cheeriest little spirits that I know.

Yes, I have met her and she is not very happy. She has the belief that held me back so long, and little soul development. I have tried to help her, but it is hard to make her think differently from what she did on earth. But sooner or later it will come about, that she will receive the truth. She is not my soulmate, so your wife says, and she seems to know all about soulmates. She says that she will soon tell me who mine is, and I will be glad of it.

I must not write more, but thank you very much for your kindness.

Your old friend,
General S. S. Henkle.

Spends a great deal of her spiritual time with Mr. Padgett, and is always ready to help those in need, both in the material and spiritual planes

October 26th, 1916.

I am here, your own true and loving Helen.

Well, dear, I am glad to know that you are in a much better condition tonight, and hope that you will continue in the development of your spiritual powers—that is the soul—for we all feel much encouraged and hope that soon you will commence to receive the higher messages.

I was with you today when the lady called and heard your conversation, and desire to tell you that it had some effect upon your hearer and may help her to get into the way that will lead to the development of her soul in love.

At the same time were the spirits of her relatives present, and they, or some of them, expressed a desire to write a message to her, and one in particular who is a very bright spirit of the Celestial spheres. She seemed much interested in the woman and is quite anxious to write her in reference to the condition of her soul and the necessity for her seeking for the love and becoming a true child of the Father. I told her that you would receive her message in a very short time, and so you will. Well, dear, I see that you are happier than you were, and it is all due to your turning your thoughts to spiritual things and praying for a greater inflowing of the love. I will not write more now

Yes. I should have told you, but our communications have been so brief, or rather caused to be brief, by the condition surrounding you, that I did not think at the time to write you in reference to Baby. I have been with her and saw that she was sick, but that there was nothing very serious the matter with her. She will soon be much better and then she can have the operation that she told you of.

Well, I will write her a long, loving, motherly letter very soon, and you can give it to her, for I will try to write her a very encouraging letter and one that will appeal to her love instincts.

No. I will not forget—he is ready at any time and has been waiting only for you to get in condition to receive his messages. He has made an examination of the Doctor and knows what the trouble is with him, and is prepared to prescribe. You had better go to bed earlier tonight as you need to recuperate, and a good sleep will help you very much. So love me and believe that I love you. Good night my dear Ned—your own true and loving

Helen.

Is very much interested that Mr. Padgett get in that condition of soul to be in rapport with him again

February 19th, 1918.

I am here, Jesus.

Well, my brother, I see that you are in much better condition tonight than you have been for some time past, and I desire to tell you that it is due to the facts that you have turned your thoughts more to spiritual things, and have prayed more to the Father. If you will continue to do these things you will soon be in that condition of soul where I can make the necessary rapport with you in order to deliver my messages.

I have been very much disappointed in not being able to deliver my messages of the higher truths as I intended, and have felt that we have lost much valuable time in pursuing our work, and it is true but now I hope that we will not have to delay longer our communications. And we will not, if you will take my advice and in that way try to remedy the difficulties that beset us.

I know that you are interested in the work, and intellectually desire to receive the messages, but this, as I have told you, is not sufficient. You must get in that condition of soul development that will bring you in rapport with me as I come to you for the purpose of writing these higher truths. It has been explained to you that a particular quality of rapport is required in order that we may be able to get in that condition of harmony that will enable us to use your brain and hand so that the messages may be delivered. So for the next few days try to have your soul opened up to the inflowing of the love so that the development may come to you.

I have many messages to write before the book will be completed, and so have many other spirits who are engaged in the work. Pray, and let all the longings of your soul go to the Father, and you will realize the response that will fit you for the work. With my love I will say good night.

Your brother and friend,
Jesus.

Describes conditions of the German people and that the war will soon be at an end

December 27th, 1917.

I am here, Bismarck.

If convenient I should like to write a few lines tonight in reference to the war and the prospects of its ending. I am Bismarck and as I have not written you for some time in reference to the subject I thought it advisable to write a few words.

As I told you in my last communication, the cause of the ending of the war would not be any decisive battle but the deplorable condition of the people of Germany and of its allied conditions, and what I then said I repeat with renewed emphasis, for since I wrote the conditions of these people in the way of starvation and deprivation of those things that make life worth living have greatly increased with no prospects of betterment so long as the war continues.

The Emperor and his co-workers have endeavored by every false statement that they could make to convince the people that the war would soon end in victory for the fatherland, and that very soon they would be relieved of the distress and starvation, and that peace and good fortune would soon come to them. And with a remarkable credulity these people have believed their representatives and have endeavored to endure all these privations and hardships with patience and confidence. But the time has arrived when this faith and hope have become shaken and in many instances in many parts of Germany and Austria the people have come to a realization that this peace and relief from their deplorable condition is no nearer than they were months ago, and that less certainty attends the promises of the rulers and military parties. And as a consequence dissatisfaction has arisen and the desire to save and make secure the life of the nation has changed into a desire to preserve and save from hunger and destruction the individual workers of that nation.

And this feeling has become so fixed with many of these people they are commencing to think, and are thinking that they are being sacrificed in order to forward the plans and ambitions of their rulers and also that they as individuals are not objects of consideration in the thoughts and schemes of these rulers. Starvation is prevalent in the land and despair has taken the place of hope with many of these people; and there is slowly creeping into the minds of many the thought that they must arouse themselves and take the control of affairs into their own hands and to such an extent does this thought possess these people, and among them many people who think for themselves, that you must not be surprised to hear at anytime that the people have revolted and that the power of the inhabitants have been overthrown, repulsion of the movement of Russia, although controlled and guided by men of more intelligence and responsibility.

Yes, this ending of the war is coming and the people will rule, and in doing so will make the best terms of peace with the Allies that can be made. Only a little while longer and you will see the fulfillment of my predictions. No great battle on the western front will be fought as the world now expects, for before that time arises the German army of the Kaiser will have become the army of the people, and many will abandon the fighting line and return to their homes and devastated farms and houses.

It is all so sad when I think of what Germany will become and what it might have been had not the mad Kaiser and his country of ambitious guards and advisers let their ambition run away with their duty and obligation to the true interests of Germany.

As I have said before, the Kaiser will die and his followers will die or be scattered and their names and horrible deeds will become dark memory of things that destroyed the national life and the individual lives of many of the promising men and youth of the fatherland. If I were the Bismarck of a short time ago this calamity of my nation would cause me to worry and regret and deplore the day that the mad boy continued to succeed his good father on the throne; but now I view these things in a different light and see that out of all these calamities will arise a happier Germany and people free and not subject to the iron bonds of any one man or family, with rights supposed and proclaimed to be God-given. Yes, Germany will suffer and decline as a world power but in the place of this power and insatiable desire for aggrandizement and aggression will come peace and happiness and a greater spiritual development among the people.

Well, I have written enough and the handwriting is on the wall and its prediction cannot be escaped from. Soon, soon, soon the end will come and with it the salvation of more nations than one.

I am not a prophet, but in the law of cause and effect nations are unthroned as well as individuals, and as I can see the causes that are operating; I can also see the effects that must follow, and the consummation will be that Germany must fall, never to arise again as a great nation that she has been in the past, but a purer, happier and more loving nation than ever before. I will not write more. American lives will not be sacrificed to any great extent, for the great battles of the war have been fought. Good night, your friend,

Bismarck.

Tries impersonation to test Mr. Padgett's soul perception

January 18th, 1917.

I am here, Frank D. Syrick.

I am glad that you could feel the influence of the spirit sufficient to cause you to doubt the personality of the writer, for this spirit who wrote was not Ingersoll and he was permitted to write merely to test your ability or spiritual sense, as we have done before. The spirit who wrote was myself and I did not have with me my usual influence, but assumed that of someone else in order to make the test more complete.

Ingersoll is here and was really with you at the church services and so was I and I was interested in what the preacher said and what I wrote you as to the preacher being a medium and his difficulty of receiving (that) the communication from spirit is true. So you may believe that the message contained the truth as to his condition. I do not feel like taking up more of your time tonight, but very soon I will come and write you as I have promised.

Tell the Doctor that I am glad to inform him that I am here, and also that I frequently come to him and enjoy his thoughts and experiences in the matters of the soul. I am still his friend and well wisher, even though he can't see me or hear my voice, but I am in full sympathy with him in all his efforts to obtain more of the love and in helping mortals as well as spirits. So with my love to you both, I will say good night.

Your friend,
Syrick.[100]

Confirms the test that was made by Judge Syrick

January 18th, 1917.

---

[100] This message is a composite of two, being published in Volume III and Volume IV. (G.J.C.)

I am here, your own true and loving Helen.

I will not write much, for you are not in good condition. However, I was with you tonight at the services and heard the preacher and wished that I could have suggested some thoughts to him that he could have received for he then would have made clear something about spiritualism that he did not. He is a medium and with a little more faith or rather with a little less belief in some of the old orthodox doctrine he would become quite a satisfactory medium to himself at least.

What Judge Syrick wrote you is true and we merely wanted to make the test and Ingersoll said that he was astonished that you could detect it. He says that he is learning something new all the time. He wants to write you soon. Well I must stop and so I will say good night.

Give my kindest regards to the Dr. (Dr. Leslie Stone) and my love to yourself.

Your own true and loving
Helen. [101]

A wicked woman tells of her many deeds that took many lives while working as a nurse

Let me write, for I have been waiting so long to reach you and have you help me. Oh, do help me if you can. I am in darkness and torment in a hell that I never believed in when on earth, but which I now see is more real than the fire and brimstone hell which my very earnest pastor used to tell us about.

I am suffering because when on earth I was a wicked woman and one who delighted in doing evil things because of the enjoyment and pleasure derived from the mere doing of them. You will be surprised when I tell you that I was a prisoner, and in my time poisoned many men and women and children. I mean that I did this in a stealthy and quiet manner - not as did the Borgia of whom I used to read, but in a way that caused no suspicion to rest upon me or anyone else.

My poison was slow but sure and without detection. Why I did this I don't know, except that I was possessed by a legion of evil spirits more wicked than myself.

Well I was a nurse in a large hospital and many a patient died suddenly of heart failure as it was called, but of poison as I knew.

I was considered a good nurse, and, as a fact, was when I was not under the impulse to poison; and many a patient has recovered his health because of my careful treatment. And now the memories of these acts of kindness come to me and, to a small degree, help to dim the

---

[101] This message is a composite of two, being published in Volume III and Volume IV. (G.J.C.)

memories of the acts of hell which I did towards others.

I was not cruel by nature, and many times in the course of my work as nurse, have I shed tears of sympathy with the sufferings of some poor man or woman who was in torture. But this was when I was free from the awful desires and influences which caused me to turn a veritable devil. When these spells, as I call them, came over me, my craving for a victim was beyond what I can explain to you, and could only be satisfied by seeing the victims in the death struggle.

I really gloated over the deaths caused by my awful deeds, and many a time I have sat beside the patient and watched his life go out, when it might have been prevented by an antidote of which I knew. But I could not let my hellish satisfaction be interfered with in that way, and so I would sit and enjoy the struggle until the messenger of death came and only the cold corpse lay before me. Oh, it was pleasure to my evil cravings and to my evil spirits that I sometimes thought were around me. So you see, I was of all women the most wicked, and of all sufferers I have suffered the most.

Yes, I have tried to fight against these desires when I felt them coming to me, and I have even sought to avoid the awful deeds by leaving the hospital for a while, but all to no purpose. I would be drawn back as if a great chain was attached to me and was pulling me back to my awful work.

I could not deliver myself from these desires and I could not resist the desires for they were stronger than I, and had to be obeyed.

I suffered on earth as well as here, and no one knows my sufferings or the cause of them. I continued to carry on this work until a short time before I died. No one suspected me, and I never hinted that I was suffering from this awful obsession for that is what it must have been.

I never counted my victims, as I would soon forget one in the desire and expectation of another. So you see I cannot tell how many fell victim to my evil deeds.

I have met some of them since I have been here, but they did not know of my deeds, for when they took this poison, they, of course, thought it was the medicine given to help them. So you see whatever of accusation comes from seeing them, comes from my own conscience, and not from their lips or words.

I want you to help me if you can. I have given up all hope, but some spirits have told me that you helped them, and I thought that possibly you might show me some way to lessen my sufferings.

Well, I prefer not to give my name as I died comparatively recent, and the disclosure of my name might work some injury to the hospital. So if you will excuse me I will not disclose my name or the hospital, but merely say that I was a woman of considerable education and about forty-five years of age, and the hospital was in a large city, and I died in 1909.

Yes, I will go with her and do as you say, only do not give me hope if there be none.

Yes, I see some bright spirits.

I have told her and she says that she will help me and love me too, and that I must go with her and believe in her, and I am going and will believe what she tells me; and oh, if she only does help me, how thankful I shall be to you.

So my dear friend, let me say that I will never forget you, even though I now have to say, good night.

A spiritualist author writes that he now knows that Jesus was more than a mere medium when on earth

March 17th, 1915.

I am here, Eugene Crowell.

By permission of your band, I will write you a little, as I see that you are reading my book,[102] and I am, consequently, interested in your right understanding of it.

Well, as you have observed, I did not look upon Jesus as a god, but merely as a very high medium and in great favor with the high spirit powers. And that is correct so far as it goes, but he is more than that: he is the highest, and most enlightened and most powerful of all the spirits, and is the only one of all the great prophets or seers or reformers, or messengers of God, who ever taught the true and only way to the Kingdom of Heaven. And the sooner all spiritualists recognize and believe this fact, the sooner will true spiritualism be established on earth and the Love of the Father be implanted in each soul.

All these things have I learned since I came over here and had the opportunity of investigating the truth at first hand with all my powers, which are not limited or encumbered with the physical senses. So you must, in reading my book, eliminate everything from what you may accept as true that teaches or intimates that Jesus is not the great Master and teacher of the true and only way to God's Love and salvation.

Of course, all spirits do not understand or believe this, and when John said try the spirits and learn whether they be true or not, he meant just what I have told you. I know now that Jesus is the most exalted son of God, and while we are all His sons, yet none of us is so at-one with Him as the Master. So as you are investigating this question of

---

[102] He wrote a book titled "The Spirit World: Its inhabitants nature and philosophy" in 1879. As also "The identity of primitive Christianity and modern spiritualism." (G.J.C.)

spiritualism in true earnestness, I thought it best to tell you what I have learned, as I do not want any expression in my book of a meaning contrary to what I have here expressed cause you to doubt for one moment the truths that Jesus and your band have been teaching you.

You are wonderfully favored in having such a teacher, and I believe that the result will be that when you shall have received his messages and transmitted them to the world, spiritualism will become the religion of the whole earth. This is my belief and it is founded on the fact that it will then teach, besides the continuity of life and spirit communication, the great truths that will show men the absolute necessity of following these teachings of the Master in order to become the true children of the Father and be received by Him in His Kingdom of Love and Divine existence.

I must not take up more time now, but will write you again, if permitted.

Yes, it is. Well I thought that you wrote Eugene. I cannot see what you have written at the time of its being written, and when I guide your hand and impress your brain, I think that you have written as I intended.

Eugene Crowell—that is my name. The writing of Edward was not what I intended.

Yes, in 1886, at San Francisco, California. This is true, and you will find an account of my passing over in the newspapers of June 7, 1886. In the San Francisco newspapers. So examine for yourself and you will find what I say to be true. [103]

Well, I will say good night.

Your recent spirit friend,

Eugene Crowell

The once Iron Chancellor of the German Empire believes that the Germans will have to sue for peace and that the Empire is doomed

May 16th, 1917.

I am here, Bismarck.

Well, I am here and will give you my opinion of the war as best I can. My views are based on the conditions that I am aware of in all the

---

[103] Actually this does not appear to be correct. He is generally considered to have died in 1894 and a copy of his obituary is as follows: October 30th, 1894, Wednesday Dr. Eugene Crowell, who was at one time the leader of the Know-Nothing Party in California, died early yesterday morning, in his apartments in the Hoffman Arms, Fifty-ninth Street and Madison Avenue. Dr. Crowell was seventy-eight years old. He leaves two sons, Frank and Charles E., and a daughter, Mrs. John Halliday of Nyack, N. Y. (New York Times) (G.J.C.)

countries engaged in the war.

I understand that you do not want a long message tonight so I will say briefly that the Germans will have to sue for peace and that will happen, I feel certain, before the beginning of August.

The condition of the German people is such that they will cease to sustain the Kaiser in the longer prosecution of the war, and the revolutionary party will grow so rapidly that the monarch of Germany will soon cease to exist. This is the opinion of the one who is responsible for the formation of the Empire.

Bismarck.

A spirit who lived for the development of mind while on earth now realizes the importance of love

Give me your love and help. I am Kate Sprague.[104]

I see that your sympathy is going towards us, and that your love is calling us to come to you, and I want both, so much. So give them to me. I am in such darkness and so much want the light. I know that you can help me, and I pray you do so. I am a woman who lived on earth under circumstances which robbed me of my soul, and made me a brilliant and strongly intellectual woman. But love, how it avoided me! And how my soul was starved! I only thought of acquiring knowledge with which to make myself famous and make men and women seek my society. Well, I succeeded, but what a shallow victory it was in the light of what I know now; and how I have regretted time and time again that my endeavors were turned to these things which, in this world, I find have their limitations, instead of to the development of love and my soul. The poorest spirit in all God's universe must be the one without love and sympathy.

Since I have become a spirit, I have fully realized that my mental acquirements are not sufficient to give me happiness, or place me in the association of those beautiful and happy spirits which I sometimes see

---

[104] Katherine Jane ("Kate") Chase Sprague (August 13th, 1840 – July 31st, 1899) was the daughter of Ohio politician Salmon P. Chase, Treasury Secretary during President Abraham Lincoln's first administration and later Chief Justice of the United States. She was a Washington society hostess during the American Civil War, a strong supporter of her widowed father's presidential ambitions that would have made her First Lady, and wife of Rhode Island Governor William Sprague.
Kate Chase was educated at the Haines School in New York City, where she learned languages, elocution and the social graces along with music and history. After nine years of schooling, she returned to Columbus, Ohio, to serve as official hostess for her father, the newly elected Governor of Ohio, and by now widowed a third time. Beautiful and intelligent, Kate impressed such friends of her father as Charles Sumner, a Massachusetts senator and fellow anti-slavery champion; President James Garfield; and Carl Schurz, a German-born American politician. Source: Wikipedia. (G.J.C.)

pass by. I am in what is called the earth plane, and my associates are spirits like myself, and without love or soul. We are not very beautiful, because I have found that the mind, no matter how excellent of itself, does not create beauty, and I wondered when I came here why it was so; and now I know that the possible mental acquirements that a mortal may obtain, as compared with all the wonderful world of knowledge that exists in God's universe, is as a grain of sand on the seashore—a mere nothing, as it were. And when I came to this spirit world and found that my mind and mental acquirements were so small and insignificant, and that I was without love and sympathy, I felt poor indeed. And so will all spirits who are capable of realizing that what they know in comparison to what exists and may be known is as a mere shadow to a gigantic mountain of substance and life. So you see, my importance on earth became in the spirit world an insignificant nothing.

As I told you, men sought my society for the brilliancy of my intellect and the pleasures of my mind, and asked for nothing more. My position was a high one, as the world looks on such things, and many women envied me and what I was. But it was all without substance—the mere passing of a shadow. When I passed over, I was soon forgotten and, in fact, had been forgotten some time before my death, because great troubles came to me, and my mind no longer had the opportunities to display itself; and I was really pitied for what had been and for what I had fallen to.

So you see, on earth as here, the spirit who expects to find great, lasting happiness merely in his mental acquirements will be disappointed, especially if he realizes that the happiness which arises from the exercise of the mental qualities has its limitations.

Well, I was married, but love did not enter into my marriage. It was merely the marriage of a brilliant mind with position, to a man of great wealth and position—nothing congenial but position. I never loved money for money's sake. I did love position and had aspirations that were never realized—and my disappointment was great. But now, I don't want money or position or the flattery of men—only love and sympathy; and I hope that you can tell me where to find them.

I was C.S., and lived in Washington most of the time, and passed over in 1894, and have been unhappy ever since.

When on earth, I had my sins the same as most mortals, and I am suffering because of them now. Memory is with me and I feel its lashings, and am unhappy; but somehow I feel that if I can only get love and sympathy, I will feel better and happier.

Well, I had a love for one man, but he was another's, and I am suffering now because of that sin. Oh, why was I so unfortunate in life as to love only once, and that love forbidden to me! Yes, I have met him here, but I find that my love for him was not of the kind that lasts when the mortal becomes spirit. I do not love him now, and never really did. It was of the earth, earthy. I am waiting for a love to come to me, and his is a thing of the past, never more to enter into my heart or soul.

Well, as a child, I was taught to believe in God and His love and Jesus and the doctrines of the church, but after I became a woman these beliefs left me. My mind became so great and my knowledge so wonderful, that things of this kind had no place in my beliefs. Oh, how wonderful is the mind of a woman who believes that what she doesn't know has no existence! Such a fool was I, and now I can't get that belief of my childhood again. If I only could believe in God, and know that His love is waiting for me, how blessed I would be. But that is gone from me forever.

Tell me, can you help me? Only tell me, and you will see how quickly I will do what you say.

You say I know him, and he was a friend of my father and of me, and is now a beautiful and happy spirit, with the love of God in his soul, and will show me the way? Oh, I wonder who it can be! Yes, many, and some are so beautiful and happy—they must surely have the love and sympathy that I long for.

I am looking. Oh, I see Mr. Riddle, my old friend. How glad I am! Oh, I am so fortunate, I know, for he tells me that he will help me, and I am going with him.

So, my dear friend, permit me to say that I thank you so much, and good night.

Kate Sprague.

All of the dogmas, creeds and apostolic succession in the world cannot bestow upon the souls of men the love or mercy of the Father

I am here, W_____

Let me write a little. I need your help and believe that you can help me, as I have been told that you have helped others before me.

I am a spirit who has spent many long years in darkness and despair. I was a very bad man, but I never knew it until I came to the spirit world and saw clearly just what kind of character I had. No man really knows his own condition until he has shuffled off the mortal coil and becomes a transparent spirit. Then every inmost thought is apparent, and he becomes, as it were, a mirror of his true self.

My life was not what the world would call an evil one, and I tried to live, as I thought, correctly in the sight of God and man; but it was all outward appearances only. I mean that I was deceiving myself. My soul was not involved, but merely my intellectual condition, as to what was right and wrong. The Beatitudes were not mine—and soul religion was not mine. I was a strict church member and conformed to all the conventions and dogmas of the church so far as their outward appearances are concerned—and was at the same time not of the true soul worship of God. I thought that by observing the dogmas and creeds of my church I was doing God's will, and that nothing further was necessary. I was baptized and confirmed by the proper dignitaries of the church, and was told that I was a child of God, and was certain of salvation. And when as I grew to manhood and became, as you may be surprised to know, a clergyman, I found a deep consolation in administering the services of the church and receiving and confirming applicants into membership.

But all this did not bring me true communion and at-onement with the Father, for I had not the Love of the Father in my soul. My intellect was all Christian, but my soul was not in unison with the Father's Love. How often I thought what a great and satisfying thing it was to be within God's fold. I mean His church, which had been established by Jesus and had come down to us in apostolic succession. But what a mistake! Apostolic succession is in and of itself a meaningless church government, and no such succession can confer upon any priest or clergyman power to bestow upon the souls of men the Love or Mercy of the Father. This I have learned to my sorrow, since I became a spirit.

So I say, let those who think that any priest or bishop can bestow this Love of the Father, or can make the soul of man the recipient of this Love, awaken to the fact that no such power exists in these church ministers. Only, as I now believe, can God Himself do this great work.

So when I came into this spirit life, and found that I was not in my Father's Kingdom, as I had believed, I was sorely disappointed; and in my disappointment commenced to think that the whole of the Bible teachings were merely fairy tales, and that God was not, or if He existed, He had deceived His church by having it believe that the members of such church were the specially redeemed children of the Father. I had been in this state of doubt for a long time, and only recently I commenced to see the truth and to know the way to God is through the bestowal of His Love upon the soul—not through the churches as such, but only through the true and earnest aspirations of the soul. That no mediator is necessary, but that God is waiting and willing to bestow this Love upon whosoever may truly ask it.

No priest or bishop can relieve a soul from sin, or forgive the sinner; and no man can reach the Father's Love or favor except through his direct, individual supplication to the Father. The priest may show the way if he knows how, but so few know, for the reason that they not only teach but believe that all a man has to do is to conform to the church's demands, and that when he does so, God is ready to receive him into His Kingdom. But let all such men know that if they depend alone on such conformity to duty they will be disappointed, as I was, when they come into the world of spirits, where only truth can prevail and where all that is hidden on earth is uncovered here.

Now, I am not to be understood as decrying the churches or the good which they do, for many of their members, notwithstanding the dogmas and creeds, have received this true soul union with the Father, and many preachers have declared truths in their sermons which have been the means of leading their hearers to a true understanding of the Father's Love. What I intend to convey is that the churches in their dogmas and creeds emphasize too much the necessity of conforming to these dogmas and creeds, and neglect to show men the true way to the Kingdom.

The only prayers that reach the Father's Heart are those which carry the true aspirations of the supplicant to the Throne of Grace. Men may repeat the written prayers for a whole lifetime, and if the prayers do not express the aspirations and desires of the supplicant, they have no more effect than would the repeating of the multiplication table. And if men will consider for a moment, they will see that this must be true—only the soul of man can receive this Great Love of the Father and when these written prayers are repeated without the longings of the soul entering into these repetitions, the soul is not open to the inflowing of this Love, and hence man can receive no possible benefit.

So I say, let men learn to know that religion is a matter purely between God and each individual soul; and no church or priest or bishop can, because of any claimed warrant (power) existing in it or them, save a man's soul from the sins of life, or make such soul at-one with the Father. All that such priest or bishop can do is to show the way, if he understands it, and when he does that he has performed a greater service to mankind than he may realize.

I now see the falsity of my depending on the performance of my duty to my church merely as a duty. I performed my duties, but I starved my soul—not intentionally, but because I thought that the performance of duty was all that was necessary. Someday I hope that men will learn that there is only one way to God, and that through their earnest, personal prayers, with faith. Well, I have written enough.

I was a clergyman of the Episcopal church in Lincoln, Nebraska, my name was W__ and I passed over in 1871. I am now learning the way. I came to you for help because I saw that you are surrounded by bright and beautiful spirits who must have this Love in their souls to a great degree; and I thought that if I could meet them and have them tell me of what this Love means from their personal experience, I might be benefited.

Well, I have acknowledged the introduction, and I certainly feel myself fortunate in meeting them—they are so beautiful and lovely. I thank you very much, and sometime, with the permission of all of you, I will come again and write.

So, with my best love, I say good night.

W_____ [105]

A woman writes of her need for help: She is in a condition of darkness and suffering

I am here, R. F.

Let me write, too. I need help so very much, and so come to you. I am now in a very dark and suffering condition and want to find relief in some way, and I hope that you can help me.

I was a woman who lived the life of an adventuress and made many men lose their money, and their souls, too, as I can now see. I lived on my wits and beauty, for they often told me that I was beautiful, and I accepted their statements and used it as my capital. So you see I was not a natural woman in my thoughts or desires. I know now that my life was a wicked one, and that I violated every feeling of humanity and did a great amount of wrong to those who became my dupes. But the life was exciting and profitable in a material way, but damnable in the way of my soul's interest.

I was never married and never cared for any man except for what I could filch from him. Many a man has trusted me in my protestations of love and found that I was false as hell, and not worthy of one kind or noble thought. Some have gone to the dogs in the way of dissipation and degradation because of my treatment of them.

And now I see how wicked it all was and am paying the penalties. So you see, I must necessarily suffer, because of my evil life. I am in torture and darkness with never a ray of light to lessen my sufferings or anything to help me forget my evil deeds. Oh, if I could only get rid of my memories and live only for the future! But memories stick to me closer than the bark to the tree, and I only suffer.

I wish that you would show me some way to get rid of these memories, and forget all the injuries that I have done to simple men. But I have forgotten to forget, and no way comes to me in which I may run away from these awful recollections. So I suffer and wait without hope, and without expectation of being lifted from this dark abyss of hell.

I don't know where I am. I have no home or habitation, but wander about from place to place, an unhappy and darkened spirit. I have met some of my dupes, and they are in a condition similar to my own, but they were not the cause of my condition, as I was of

---

[105] This message is a composite of two, being published in Volume II and Volume IV. (G.J.C.)

theirs—and so I can get no consolation from the thought that others were my undoing. I want some help, if possible.

My name was R.F. and I lived, when on earth, in many cities, but principally in New York, because there were more rich fools there than in the other cities. I passed over in 1889, a miserable, unhappy woman without friends or anyone to mourn my passing.

I will do anything that you may advise, only do not disappoint me.

Yes, I see a great many spirits who are waiting to write to you, and some are so urgent in their demands that I must stop writing, that I feel that I must soon stop.

Yes, I see some beautiful spirits, too. Who are they? They seem so happy and loving. I wish I was like them—but they do not care for me.

Well, I see one who looks so kind and loving that I would like to go with her. She says she is your father's soulmate, and calls me to her, and says that she will love me and show me the way to happiness, and if I will only believe her; and I am going to believe her.

So, my kind friend, let me say

Good night. R. F.

Spirit who found he did not have his soul developed when he passed over

I am here, a troubled spirit, and a very unhappy one, besides. I need help, and you will help me, won't you? Do not say that you can't.

I am a man who committed the worst of all crimes. I took my own life in a fit of desperation and under great excitement at what I thought was unusual injuries done me by another. I was a married man and a friend entered my home and despoiled it, and took my wife away from me; and in my despair, not wishing to live longer, I killed myself. But the fearful mistake! Since that time I have suffered all the tortures of the damned, as I am one of the worst of spirits. No sin is so great and incurs such damnation as that of the suicide, and it seems that for him there is no hope. I am without hope or expectation of any release from my awful condition, and I can find no help among my companions, who are all in a similar condition. Let me tell you that annihilation is a heaven to what I suffer. No hope, no light, no love, no sympathy, and no God. Oh, why was I ever born that I should be so tormented! My life on earth was not a very bad one, and I used to treat everyone as I desired them to treat me and I loved my wife and children with a pure and unselfish love, as I thought, and trusted my friends. I know that I was an average good man and did not intentionally harm anyone. But when the realization of the awful injury done to me came to my soul I lost all reason, as it were, and did that which I had no right to do.

My life was not my own. It was given me by God as a sacred trust, and I had no right to end it. I could not restore it, and I was recreant (unfaithful, cowardly) to my trust.

So you see, I have no way of making recompense to God for doing that awful deed. He demands that I atone for that deed, and I don't know how, as I can see the only atonement that I can make is to restore that life, and that I cannot do. So you see I have no hope—only one bitter long night of suffering and torment through all eternity. Oh! why was I born, tell me if you can?

I do not believe that there is any way for me to escape the penalty of my great crime, and hence, hope has died in me. If I only had the faintest ray, I should not despair as I do. But to me hope is not even a will-o'-the-wisp, for I never see even the image of hope. So tell me, do you know a way out of this fearful condition of night and despair?

I will try to believe you.

Well, I am J____ I lived in a small town in the East (New London, Connecticut), and I passed over in 1864, while the Great War was raging.

Yes, he is here, and is suffering, too, damn him. If I could only kill him as I killed myself, I would feel better satisfied and think that I was suffering in a good cause, and let my torment be my feast or flavors of the feast of my revenge. But I cannot kill him and he knows it, and says that I need not rage so, because he will not give me the revenge. So he is free from my vengeance, but he suffers, damn him, and I only wish that I could increase his tortures tenfold and ten times tenfold.

Yes, my wife is here, too, and suffering. Strange as it may seem, I have no hatred for her, as I believe that she was deceived, and in the weakness of her woman's nature submitted to the overpowering influence of that fiend who seduced her. Oh, for a moment of freedom and the opportunity to wreak my vengeance on him.

Well, I am trying to forget him, as you request, and I am feeling better. Yes, I do. Yes, I see that only God can forgive me, as you say.

Well, I would say that He is just, and that I had no right to ask his forgiveness, when I had not forgiven one who injured me as you say. I see what you mean, but how can I forgive that wretch. I don't know how, and yet, if I do not, how can I expect God to forgive me? Oh, my unhappy condition! Tell me, is there no other way out of my awful condition, for if there is, I won't forgive that villain.

Yes, I will think of it, and maybe my heart will relent, and I will be able to forgive him.

Oh, my darling wife! To think that all my life and love and hope were wrecked by that one man. It is so hard, and I am so very helpless.

Yes, only show me the way.

Yes, and oh, so beautiful and good. But they do not care for me or my unhappiness.

Well, I have asked and a beautiful spirit tells me that she is your mother, and knows why you sent me to her, and that she is willing to help me. She tells me that she sympathizes with and loves me, and wants to show me the way to happiness and light. I will go with her, for I believe that she will help me.

So, as she calls me, I will say that I am thankful to you, and will come again sometime. So good night.

J_____

His experience as a result of a spirit's belief in the vicarious atonement

June 24th, 1917.

I am here, George W. Heyde.[106]

I would like to write a few lines, as I am much interested in the conversation that I have heard, and know that what you two say about the falsity of Jesus' blood and sacrifice being necessary or sufficient to save a soul from sin and error and to make it at-one with the Father, is true.

I know this from personal experience, for no mortal ever believed more in that doctrine than did I, and many—yes, most all the years—of my life were spent not only in believing that false doctrine, but in teaching it. And not until I had suffered and realized that such blood and sacrifice were not able to save me did I seek for something else; and then it was a long time before I found that something else. For when I was first told of the Divine Love being the only thing necessary to save my soul and that without it all the blood and vicarious sufferings of Jesus would not avail, I found it so contrary to my old beliefs that I refused to entertain the thought. And as I suffered and could find no way of relief, and as the spirits who had told me of this Love insisted on my seeking for it, I commenced to do so, though at times I felt that I was doing wrong.

Well, I found it, and then commenced to seek with more energy and faith until I found relief. And now I can say that the only thing that will save a soul is this Divine Love, and everything else that mortals believe to be necessary is useless.

I have never written you before, although I have told Helen that I desired to do so, and now I am very happy that I have the opportunity. Before closing, I wish to say that you are in the truth in your beliefs, and

---

[106] This appears to be George W Heyde, Padgett's father-in-law and Helen's father. He was a practicing minister and they became estranged prior to his daughter's death. The details of a communication from James and Helen Padgett which is published in Volume I (5th Ed.) on page iv indicates that there would have been tension between James and his father-in-law. George Heyde passed over in January 1913 and it took some four years for him to be willing to make this acknowledgement set out here. (G.J.C.)

must not let any, or all, of the preachers on earth cause you to doubt these truths.

I am in the Third Sphere and progressing, and hope to continue until I arrive in the Celestial Heavens, of which Helen has told me so much.

With my love, I will say, good night.

Your brother in Christ,

G.W.H. (as originally published)

Spirit's experience in progressing into the Divine Spheres

April 27th, 1918.

I am here, Ross Perry.

Let me write a line, for I am very desirous of again communicating to you the fact that I am progressing and have found the Love of which you first told me and which information led to my seeking it.

I know that you are very much interested in the higher messages and want to give your time to receiving them and that it is almost impudence for me to intrude, but I have asked your wife if I will interfere with any of these messages tonight by my writing and she informed me that it would not, as none of these messages would be written tonight. So I feel somewhat at liberty to write and I hope that you will consider that I am not intruding.

Well, since last I wrote you, I have been praying to the Father with all the longing of my soul for an increase of His Love and realize that it has come into my soul in greater abundance and I am correspondingly happy. I shall soon be in the Third (Spirit) Sphere, so the spirit friends who have been so kind and loving to me, tell me, and it gives me much happiness to know that such a prospect is opened up to me, for I can, because of the progress that I have already made, and realize to some extent what a home in that sphere will mean to me.

I would like to write you a long letter tonight, but I must not detain you. But this I want you to remember that I am very happy now, and my sufferings have left and I know that all these blessings came to me because of the workings of the Divine Love in my soul. It is wonderful what that Love can accomplish in the way of rescuing a sinful soul from its surroundings of darkness and from suffering.

The Law of Compensation, which is a great truth, does its work without hesitation or partiality, or interference by any God or angel in the way of commanding it to cease its work, but this great Divine Love is more powerful than the Law and when it enters into the soul of a man or spirit it in effect says to this Law: "You shall no longer operate on the soul of the sinner that was, because it will take that soul away from and outside the operations of the Law."

How little men understand this working of the (Divine) Love. It does not set aside the Law, but it merely removes the soul in which it has found a lodgment from the scope of the operation of the Law. The Law goes on but the objects of its operations are rescued from the same. No Law is set aside which men think and argue is necessary in order for a soul to be saved from its penalties and when on earth I believed this too, and did not believe in or accept the doctrine of the special interposition of divine providence to succor men from the consequence of their sins and that I did not believe because I thought that the only way in which this could be accomplished was for God to say to the Law: "You shall cease to operate."

But now I know, that, while the Law never ceases to operate until the penalties that are called for are paid, yet this Love is above the Law, though not antagonistic to it. I wish that I might write more on this subject tonight as to me, it is one of the most wonderful truths in God's Universe of Spirit and I never cease to meditate upon it and thank the Father that I was made a real example of the power of this Love.

Well I must stop now, but when you have time I should like to come and write at more length. I see that my wife has not progressed in learning the truth and I am very sorry. Well friend, good night.

Your friend,
Ross Perry.[107]

Wishes she could have lived longer on earth; she could have helped to prevent the War

February 8th, 1917.

I am here, (Queen) Victoria.

I must write a line, for I have listened to the communications, and feel that none who have written are more interested than I, as my people, who such a short time ago listened to my advice and loved me, are now being destroyed on both land and sea.

Oh, this war is horrible, and the flower of my people are being cut down like so many fields of wheat that are ripe for the scythe. How I wish that I could have lived a few years longer as Queen, for I believe I could have controlled my grandson to the extent of preventing him from launching this terrible catastrophe upon the nations of Europe. I have

---

[107] This message is a composite of three, being published in Volume II and Volume III and again in Volume IV. (G.J.C.)

tried since becoming a spirit to influence him, but all in vain, for his ambitions were great and his sense of having suffered indignity from my own people was great; and in his blindness and hot blood he started to rolling the ball of hatred and destruction that is still accumulating as it continues on its murderous destructive course.

I have prayed for all the people who are engaged in this war, and have, with other spirits, to stem the tide of hatred and feelings of conquest and revenge which now possess them. I believe the end is now in sight and that the Germans will soon seek for peace and the nations will lay down their arms, and common sense and cool blood will again rule. I cannot write more tonight, and will only say that we are all praying to the Father that His mercy may be showered on these unhappy and misguided men. So thanking you, I will say good night.

Yours truly,
Victoria.

The spirits of former rulers, presidents, kings and queens when on earth are yet mere spirits in the spirit world; though exalted by man on earth, their true condition shows forth in the spirit world, and some are in darkness

February 8th, 1917.

I am here, your own true and loving Helen.

You must not be surprised that so many spirits of presidents and rulers of Europe are here tonight writing to you, for in the spirit life space is as nothing, and the attraction of kindred thoughts brings together spirits who you might suppose are far apart in their habitations.

These spirits who have written, and many more who are present, are all interested in this Great War. And I will say here that tonight you have had around you a greater concourse of men and women who were considered great on earth than have ever before congregated in one place.

This may seem surprising to you, but it should not, for in spirit life all these persons are mere spirits, and are not considered to be presidents and kings and queens—but mere spirits. And some are not so high in the spheres as mortals might naturally suppose. They are spirits who are much interested in their people and have more or less development of their souls and spiritual natures; but when you compare the assembly tonight, as these great ones of earth, with the assembly you sometimes have of spirits from the Celestial Heavens, you would see that it would look to you like a comparison of the light of the sun to the light between darkness and dawn! So you need not be surprised that these spirits came and wrote you.

Well, you have had a variety of messages tonight, and must now stop, as you are tired. So with all my love I will close.

Your own true and loving

Helen.

Love is greater than hate; God bless all the people of the earth

February 8th, 1917.

I am here, Abraham Lincoln.

Love is greater than hate, and war will end and love will come and peace will be again established. And then the teachings of the Master will reach men's hearts and war will become a thing of the past and brotherly love will rule men's conduct, and nations will know war no more.

And so must it be; God bless our people, and all the people of the earth, and make them truly His children, is the prayer of

A. Lincoln.

President McKinley and others in the spirit world are striving to bring an end to the war[108]

February 8th, 1917.

I am here, McKinley.

Let me say a word, as I am interested in this great conflict of nations, and especially in the danger that faces my country, and the almost certainty that in a short time the cry of war will fill the streets and homes of its inhabitants.

God moves in a mysterious way His wonders to perform, and this war will result in the wonder—if it may be called such—of many of the inhabitants of the earth seeking a way of a closer union with the Father. Lives will be sacrificed but souls will be saved, and men will realize that they are brothers of one Father, and that love, only, must rule, and that war must cease forever.

---

[108] The original title here as published in the First Edition was "World War I". A facetious commentator has remarked that McKinley must have been very prescient in 1917 to realize there would be a Second World War, since at that time it was not referred to as World War I. One would have thought it obvious that the titles were all added by the publisher and not the spirit sending the communication, and that this occurred in 1972, by which time the Second World War was long complete. I have now edited this title and some others to remove this point of contention. (G.J.C.)

The spirit world is interested in this great conflict, and spirits are striving to open up the souls of the rulers of the nations in conflict and influence them to bring an end to the fearful carnage that is now destroying so many of God's children. The suffering, though, will yet be great before the end shall be accomplished, and many men will become spirits before the dove of peace will leave the ark of refuge and see the dry land. Nations shall fall, and some shall cease to exist; but at least the truth of the fellowship of man and the Fatherhood of God will be established.

But men must work its harvest, and the reaping must continue until there shall not remain in men's hearts any desire for war or the satisfying of unholy ambitions. We in spirit see this and are striving to bring the great calamity to its ending. God will not cease to love His children. Even though those children forget Him and murder their brothers.

I have finished, but through the gloom of desolation and ruin I see the rainbow of hope and the end of strife. May all men learn the fact that God is Love, and that they are His children, and will soon realize the truth of His Love.

I must stop.

Your brother in Christ,

McKinley.

Grandfather of the Kaiser has tried hard to influence his grandson in order to bring the war to an end

February 8th, 1917.

I am here, William, (Grandfather of the Kaiser).

Let me say a word in response to what has just been written, as I am interested in the war. I am heart and soul in sympathy with the sentiments just expressed, and so anxious for the end to come, for my people are suffering so much, and so many of them are coming to the spirit world, their lives all cut off and prevented from performing the missions of their Creator.

I have sympathized much with all the people who are engaged in this war, and have tried so hard to influence my own family to bring it to an end, but in vain, for the fire of ambition and the cravings to conquer have ruled them. But I see the end will soon come, and then will also come the suffering; for it seems to me that my family will soon thereafter cease to be the rulers of my people and will be execrated as the creators of this great conflict and the cause of all the murders and sufferings that have been suffered by the German people. And my only consolation is that life on earth is short and that the spirit must find its home in the realm of spirit; but even then, the suffering will continue. But I trust in the mercy of the Father and realize that He does all things right.

I cannot say more tonight, but that we are all praying for the people of the world and are asking the Father to open up the hearts of the rulers to the inflowing of His Love, and the bringing about of peace. I will close.

William, the Grandfather of the Kaiser.

A former White House doorkeeper expresses his desire to have spirits communicate with the President

February 8th, 1917.

I am here, Col. Cook.

Well, you are much in demand tonight, and the spirits who wrote really whom they represented themselves to be; for I have been present and know them.

I am Col. Cook, who was the head doorkeeper of the Executive Mansion for so many years, and I know and tell you that tonight have been present many of the spirits to whom Mrs. Wilson referred as statesmen and rulers who have been trying so earnestly to influence and advise her husband. Especially is Cleveland anxious to communicate to the President, for he seems to be more interested in the country's affairs than the others, and is such a virile and powerful spirit. I only wish that there was some way that a message from him to the President might be delivered; but we all realize that it would not be believed. Well, I cannot do any good by writing more, and will close, though I am much interested in my country, and also in this method of communicating.

I will say good night.

Col. Cook.

Writes of her attempts to influence her husband, President Wilson

February 8th, 1917.

I am here, Mrs. Wilson.

I will write only a line or two. I am not known to you, but I am very desirous to write, as I am so much interested in what is now taking place in our country in connection with foreign countries; and one in whom I am very much interested is suffering the burdens that are now resting upon him. I am with him a great deal, and try to influence him in his thoughts and dealings with the great problems that are now before him to deal with, and sometimes I fear he may succumb to the heavy burdens. He has around him, also, other spirits who are much interested in the country's welfare, and they are the spirits of men who, when on earth, were statesmen and rulers of our country, and interested in directing its fortunes. I will not name them, only to say that from Jefferson down to McKinley they are with him who now occupies the President's chair.

This war (reference to World War I) is a serious one to not only the people of Europe, but also to those of America; for as I see, and these other spirits say, it is impossible for our country to keep out of it. The Germans so desire—and they are doing everything to bring about—the participation of the United States in the conflict; and the result will be that the U.S. will suffer much more than its statesmen and financiers contemplate.

I wish I could bring to the President in clear and undoubted effect the advice that these spirits would like to have him understand; but this power to communicate is limited to the impressions that they may make upon him by the exercise of the very imperfect rapport of their minds with his, without the proper or necessary medium. If he could only have you with him to receive the advice that these spirits so earnestly desire to give him, it would help him so much. We have been trying to create a way by which this might be brought about, but it seems to be almost impossible.

But so far as I can see the future, he will bring the country to a sound ending, although much trouble and unhappiness will be suffered, and he may not be able to endure the strain. I wish that I could write longer tonight, but my rapport is leaving me, and I must stop. But notwithstanding what has taken place—which only I know—I still love him, for he is mine, and someday he will realize that fact. I will now close. Thanking you for your kindness, I am

Your new friend,
Mrs. Woodrow Wilson.

Confirms that many dark spirits had been present, and wanted to write

January 28th, 1916.

I am here, your own true and loving Helen.

Well, dear, the influences have not been good tonight, and many dark spirits have been present. The one who wrote was very dark and brought with him others who were all anxious to write. But White Eagle would not let them write, although he did not force them to leave.

I desired to write, as I told you last night, but under the

conditions did not think it best to try to do so. I will try tomorrow night, and hope you will be in condition.

I will not write more now, as it is best not to draw on you. So love me and believe that I love you and am with you very much, trying to help you.

Do not forget to pray more and more often to the Father for His Love.

Your own true and loving
Helen.

A dark and suffering spirit comes to Mr. Padgett for help

I am here, J. W.

Let me write, as I need help, too.

You have given much time to these other spirits, and I was afraid that you would stop before I could write; but now that I am writing, I feel that you will give me the opportunity to let me tell you how much I need your help and what my troubles are.

I am a woman who, when on earth, lived the life of a prostitute, and made my living by selling my body and soul to preserve my body. What an expensive body, and what a foul and loathsome one it became before I died. Oh, I tell you, that if there be a God who punishes mortals for the use they make of the body, or rather the misuse, then my punishment will be great, for I mistreated my poor body in every way that human mind could conceive of. I drank so that all its organs were soaked in the baleful influence of the liquors; and I smoked so that its functions were interfered with and I became nicotine-inoculated; I did the other awful thing so that all my muscles and nerves were rendered unable to do the work which they were made to perform; and I ate until my digestive organs were all disarranged and became unfit to perform their functions. And worse than all, before I died I became a veritable Lazarus, only my sores were the result of my evil doings with men, and his were not the result of evil, so far as I know.

I tell you that the misuse of the beautiful and wonderful body which God gave me was a thing beyond conception; and now I know that God holds me to account for the right use of my body, just as the preachers say he holds me to account for the right use of my soul.

I am in darkness of soul, as well as in suffering because of my recollections of the terrible murder of my body—for it was murder, though a gradual and slow one.

But over and above these recollections of my wicked treatment of my body are the recollections of the treatment of my soul and all that made me a human being, made in the image of God, as I have been told. You can imagine what my body must have been, and I tell you, as I now

301

see it, the condition of my soul is more loathsome than was ever that of my body. My body is gone and never more will I be troubled with it, or have the opportunity to abuse it; but my soul is with me, and must forever remain with me, and I may continue to abuse it. I don't know. But oh, my God, if there be a God of mercy, I pray that I may not continue to do that! Save my soul, what there is of it!

I am in torture beyond description, and if only one ray of hope should come to me, I would never stop thanking God, or whoever he be that should send it to me. I am surrounded by many spirits who are like myself, and without hope or expectation of any relief from their great darkness and sufferings.

Can't you help me in some way, if only for a little while? I only wish my soul could die as my body died! But it cannot; and to think of my going through all eternity in this condition of darkness and torture makes me cry out with all my soul, Oh, let death come to me! Be merciful, Oh God, and destroy this soul as I destroyed the body you gave me! But no merciful God answers me, and only the echo of my cry comes back to me and mocks me, and seems to say, too late, too late!

Oh, tell me, is there no hope? Must I endure all this hell and torment for all eternity?

Why, I am not worth such punishment—a little thing of such little importance as I was. I did not think that God would notice me enough, even to punish me, as I am punished. But I am punished, and His mills of retribution must grind very fine.

Well, when I commenced that awful life I was only eighteen years old; and I lived it for nearly twenty years, and in living it I commenced, after a few years, to gradually sink lower and lower, until at last, when the summons came, I was an outcast.

I was once a good girl and had a good home with kind and loving parents; and strange to me, that which they told me tends to make angels of us all made me a devil—I mean love. Oh, what a dangerous thing is the love for a man—and what a devil is the man who takes advantage of that love. I know that in the world it is said that everything is fair in love and war. But if all should suffer from love as I suffer, every woman would say that there is nothing fair in love, and everything to lose, as I lost.

The man who betrayed my love is in the spirit world, and he sees my sufferings; and as I suffer, he suffers and as long as I suffer he will suffer, so I am told. He continually asks my forgiveness, but I cannot forgive him, and my love for him has turned to wormwood and gall. The only shadow of pleasure that I have is when I see him look on me and, as a consequence, suffers as I suffer.

But this shadow is no consolation. His sufferings do not help my sufferings, and if I could only get rid of my sufferings, I believe that his sufferings would lessen, and I would not be sorry. So tell me, can you show me any way by which my tortures may be lessened ?

My name was J. W. I lived in the city of Newark, N.J., and died in 1897. I was buried in the ground where paupers are buried; but that fact is not important. My poor body rests as peacefully there as if buried in the finest mausoleum.

I was an educated girl. I was just finishing my senior year when the awful thing happened to me, and which caused my dear parents to die of broken hearts; for I want to tell you that there is such a thing as a broken heart; but God, it cannot compare with a lost soul, such as is mine.

Yes, I will trust you and believe, but do not let me have hope, when there is none. Only tell me quickly and I will do as you say. Oh, if I shall receive the forgiveness that the one you spoke of received.

Yes, I see many spirits, but they are unhappy and need help as I do; and you surely do not mean that any of them could help me.

Why yes, I see some beautiful and bright spirits. They are so beautiful, and they look at me with such eyes of love and sympathy. You must mean one of them. Oh, tell me that you do, for I know that they can help me. Oh, how beautiful and good they seem. Well, I can scarcely write. Oh, help me.

She calls me to her and says that she will help me and show the way to me. She puts her arm around me and says, "You are my sister; God's love is for you just as it is for me. Only believe that He loves you, and pray with all your heart and soul for His mercy and forgiveness; and come with me to a quiet place, where I can tell you more fully of His Great Love and Mercy. It will be sufficient for you."

So I must go. Oh, I thank you with all my heart and so, dear friend, I say

Good night. J. W.[109]

The condition of man is such that it is of the utmost importance for them to learn the Truths

November 15th, 1918.

I am here, John Wesley.

I desire to speak to you upon a matter which is very closely

---

[109] Whenever initials are given instead of a full name it is because living relatives might object. (J.P.G.) As the astute reader will by now have observed, I (G.J.C.) have worked hard to discern who might be behind these initials, because the passage of the years now allows this liberty. Often this information was contained in the daily dairy that Padgett kept, but in other cases it was discovered as a result of personal research. Those left unexplained are not currently known. (G.J.C.)

associated with your mission and the work you are now doing. I am one of those spirits who are engaged in the carrying on of that work on this side of the borderline, and know the importance of the work and the necessity for its being done as rapidly as possible, so that men may have the opportunity to learn and know and teach the truths of God. I am with you quite frequently as you receive the messages from the spirits who are revealing these truths, and read your mind and soul, and know your exact condition regarding your conception of the task that has been imposed upon you and which you have assumed to do; and hence, can tell you with almost certainty of your attitude towards this great undertaking, and when I say attitude, I do not mean only that of which you are conscious, but also that which is apparently latent but which, nevertheless, is operating, and obstructing or assisting the progress of the work.

I am glad to say that just now you have a fuller appreciation of your position in the matter and of the necessity for completing the writings and the dissemination of the truths that they contain; and if you continue in this attitude and permit your desires therein to intensify and become manifested in actual performance, the work will progress rapidly and the great end in view will be accomplished.

If you will consider for a moment, you will realize that there is nothing in all your earth so important to mankind as the knowledge of these truths, for they deal with and affect that which belongs to the eternity of the hereafter and the future of the souls of men, and lead to a destiny which will be a Divine existence or a mere living of the perfect man of his original creation.

Of course, men are really more interested in their future destiny than in any or all things of earth and the life thereon, but give less attention to the ascertaining of the truths of the same than to many merely human things which exist only during the short earth life; and this is not to be wondered at, because they have no satisfactory or convincing means of learning what this destiny is or may be. It is natural for the desires and interests of men to be attracted to that which has certainty and probability of realization, rather than to that which is devoid of the elements that give assurance and hope founded on knowledge.

As you know, many of the expectations of men as to the future are based entirely upon what is called faith, which itself is founded upon what the teachers of the Bible call the mysteries of God, and which are not the subject of research or study, because God in His wisdom retains to Himself, with a jealous care, the understanding of these mysteries; and so men, in their lives, accepting the mysteries and applying the faith, turn their thoughts to these things very rarely and even then, in a perfunctory way, applying the idea that sufficient unto the day is the evil thereof. Consequently men live more for the present and in a way let the future come and find them in a condition that surprises and injures them, and makes for them a destiny that—were the truth known to them—need not be theirs.

When men shall be able to learn the truths that affect, or rather create, their destinies if believed in and lived, they will not be so indifferent to the life of the future, even though they retain their interests in the life of earth.

And now, in this generation, when men are thinking for themselves and not resting satisfied with the dogmatic teachings of their supposed leaders, they are becoming incredulous and demanding more light, and are refusing to accept the teachings of the mysteries as satisfying to their feelings of want of those things which will give them an assurance of the truths of living as mortals. Such faith is dying, and men prefer its death to the living in the uncertainties. But this preferring to thus die does not imply—nor is it really true—that they are not in their souls interested in the eternity part of their lives and all that it means. But, becoming hopeless because they see no succor from their unsatisfied condition, they resort to the moral teachings and conduct for their salvation, having the hope that right living in accordance therewith will result in a future as well as a present in which there must be some happiness, and that "all will be well."

This, I say, is the condition of many men today, and because thereof, the ground is fallow for the planting and the nurturing of the truths that are being revealed to you; and so you must appreciate what the revealment and dissemination of these truths mean to the world at this time.

I know that you must give much time and labor to the work of fulfilling your mission, and also that you must live a large portion of your life and thoughts with the spirits who are using you for the great object in view; but this apparent sacrifice will soon cease to be a sacrifice, and become to you a joy and source of never-ending benefit to your soul and its future.

So you must work and think thoughts of the spiritual and, above all, continue in earnest prayer to the Father for increased bestowals of His Love; and you will not be disappointed. I felt that I should write you as I have, and while you, I know, expected some spirit to communicate some unknown and important vital truth, yet I believe that what I have said may serve to facilitate the delivery of the messages. I will not write longer tonight.

I am a possessor of this Divine Love, and from this you will understand what my love is for you, and how earnestly I pray to the Father to bless you and help you in the great work which is yours to do. Good night. I am,

Your brother in Christ,
John Wesley.

Affirmation that John Wesley wrote

November 15th, 1918.

I am here, your own true and loving Helen.

Well, dear, you have worked hard tonight, and had a long message from Wesley, and so I will not detain you a great while. I merely want to say that your condition is very much improved, and we feel very certain that now the messages can be delivered without much delay and with comparative ease. We send our love and pray for your happiness. Good night.

Your own true and loving,
Helen.

Writes that she will try to change the atmosphere after the depressing spirit that just left. And she is grateful to God that she does not have to work in the lower planes

I am here, Mary Kennedy.

Well, let me try to make the surroundings more pleasant, as the influence left by the spirit who has just written you is very depressing and undesirable.

What a difference between the atmosphere of love and that which is always with the spirits of darkness and evil, such as the one who last wrote you. His condition is pitiable, and we spirits who know what the mercy and Love of God means in our sympathy find consolation in the fact that mercy and Love will be sufficient to redeem even that dark spirit from his hells of torture and darkness.

But he will have to suffer very much and it will be hard for love to find its way to his soul. So you can imagine the great chasm that exists between his condition and the condition of those like myself, who live and breathe in the possession of the Father's Love.

I am Mary, and while I have so much of this love and happiness yet I cannot help from feeling sad when I see the utter misery of spirits such as the one who last wrote you. And this I want to tell you, it is only when they come to you as this spirit came, do I realize what such misery means, for my work is not among the spirits of hell and I never go to their habitations and meet the awful sights that some of the spirits whose work is with these unhappy ones tell me of.

I am so thankful that I was not compelled to have such an experience, and more thankful that my dear soulmate will not have such an experience, for I know that he has too much of the Love of the Father in his soul to ever commit any deed that will doom him to such misery.

Well, the Father's Love is for all and the vilest sinner in the lowest hells can, by earnest prayer, obtain this greatest supreme joy and happiness that this Love when it enters the soul will give to him. But oh! the long years some will suffer.

I thank the Father, and want Leslie to thank Him that there came to him the knowledge and possession of this Great Love in time to prevent him from doing that which would condemn his soul to such a condition. Well, let us try to be happier, and for the time forget this unhappy spirit.

I am glad that I can write tonight, for my sake and for this, because it gives us both much happiness when I can communicate to him in this way.

I am with him, as he knows in all my love and trying to influence him so that his mind and soul will both be happy and feel the greater love that I have for him, a love that is increasing all the time and that will never know an ending.

Tonight your wife says that you must not write much as your condition is not just as it should be, and she does not want you to write when you are not in perfect accord with the spirits who write. So I will have to close now, but this I must say, that Leslie must think of me and love me and believe that I love him and am with him always at night when he writes me. Tell him to pray to the Father more and more for the Love and I will come to him.

His own loving,
Mary Kennedy.

Friends

Is so glad that Leslie is doing such a glorious work in helping the dark spirits to come out of the darkness, by telling them the Truth

I am here, Mary Kennedy.

Well, I am here and ready to write, as you may suppose. I have been present all the evening in hope you would give me the opportunity to write, and when Leslie started to leave I was so afraid that he would do without my opportunity, and Helen saw that I wanted to write so much and impressed you with the thought that you must give me the opportunity; and when you took the pencil in hand I was just about to take hold when Mr. Plummer came and requested that he be allowed to write a few lines, and of course I had to give way and let him do so, and then came the poor suffering spirit, and you know that I could not stand in the way of her writing.

She went off with Kate, who heard your request, and I hope that the sufferer will find relief and I know she will, for Kate is so full of love and sympathy that the spirit will have to open up her heart and beliefs.

Well, there are many things I would like to write tonight, but I see that you have been somewhat drawn on by these other spirits and I don't think it is wise to tax you very much, though I know that you are always willing to have me write through you.

Leslie knows that I love him and that I am with him so very much and enjoy hearing him talk to the dark spirits who come to him, for there are so many who do so and listen intently to what he tells them, and many of them are greatly benefited; for not only what Leslie says helps them but it places them in such a condition that many of the helping spirits are enabled to get in rapport with these dark ones and tell them of the truths that they need to know in order to lead them into light. I am so glad that he can and is doing such a glorious work, and he would be surprised to know the great number of these spirits who are around him seeking help. Many bright spirits are also with him just for the purpose of helping the dark ones whenever they can gain their confidence sufficient to enable them to tell the truths of Love and Light which are so necessary.

Well, I will not write more now, but only say that I enjoy the letters which my soulmate writes me and that he must never cease to do so. I love him with all my heart and soul and never let him go to sleep without praying the Father to bless him and make him happy.

I will come again soon and write him a more personal letter. I

309

mean one of those love letters that may sound silly to some except the writer and him for whom it is intended. Thanking you, I will say good night.

Your sister in Christ,
Mary Kennedy.

Assures Mr. Padgett in one of his early communications that no spirit writes in his name and that Dr. Leslie R. Stone will receive the Divine Love of the Father in great abundance

July 16th, 1915.

I am here, Jesus.

I see your condition and I will help you if you will only continue to believe in me. I know that everything looks very dark and no light seems to shine ahead, but it is coming.

Question

Yes I know, but it will come in time, and you will be relieved, if you will only trust me. So do not be so downhearted but look to the Father for His help.

I am the Jesus who writes to you and no other. I came today because you are so downhearted.

Question

Well, he will find his mistake someday, for no other spirit writes to you in my name and you must believe. Let him alone in his belief, for as I have told you, a spirit from the dead, should it appear to him in the form of an angel, would not convince him. So do not let what he may say disturb you. Cheer up and you will triumph and will soon see the light breaking.

He[110] is on the way and will soon receive the Divine Love to a very large degree. He is a very spiritual man and is progressing in his soul development.

So believe that I am with you and pray to the Father.

Your own true brother and friend.

Jesus.

---

[110] Dr Leslie R Stone. (J.P.G.)

Mr. Padgett's old partner says that both he and Dr. Stone have correct ideas about spiritual Truth

October 6th, 1915.

I am here, your old partner, A. G. Riddle.

I have listened tonight to the conversation between you and your friend (Dr. Stone), and I must say that you two have reasonably correct ideas of the spiritual truths as we know them in the spirit world.

You must continue your investigations together for an exchange of thoughts is a very wonderful belief to acquire accurate and correct ideas of the truths of things. I mean things that pertain to the spirit world.

I will not write long tonight, but very soon I will come and write you a long letter that will show you some things that you do not now know. But before I stop I want to say that Perry is now in a somewhat better condition.[111] His interview with Ingersoll had a wonderful effect upon him for as on earth Ingersoll was filled with the enthusiasm of his new belief and was just as forcible and eloquent as when on earth. What a wonderful thing this Divine Love is. I can only say that there is nothing in all God's universe that can compare with it.

I am still in this fifth sphere, but hope to work in the seventh sphere where your father is.

So I must stop now.

Your old partner,

A. G. Riddle.

Can a man live and love and go into nothingness? And the answer is no! So says: William T. Stephenson

October 6th, 1915.

I am here, William T. Stephenson.

I was an Englishman and lived in Liverpool and died in 1876. What I want to say: Can a man live and love and then die and go into nothingness?

And I can answer No! For love never dies. It is the one Eternal and never ending quality of the soul. The love of a man for a woman is so great that only the love of God for man excels it. I mean the real soulmate love. I am a spirit who lived on earth and loved a woman of earth and when I died my love did not die, but continued and is with me

---

[111] Perry, a friend of Padgett's committed suicide, and Ingersoll, who had only recently found the Divine Love path, has been able to help him. This message from Perry is on page 410. (G.J.C.)

now growing and increasing all the time. She loved me too, but in her lonesomeness she married another and is now on earth the wife of another, but her soul love is mine and strange as it may seem to you I am not jealous or dissatisfied with her condition, because I as a spirit loving her only with a soul love and knowing that I have her soul love in return, do not want her body or the affections which are so firm, the merely natural love or rather the attractions which one physical or even mental existence may have for another.

I am only waiting and loving and hoping that the time will not be long when she will be with me. So you see love cannot die and happiness which comes with that love can never die. I am in the second sphere and am enjoying my existence. You must pardon me for intruding, but I only wanted to let you know that love can never die.

So good night.
William T. Stephenson.

Is overjoyed with the conversation and discussion between Dr. Stone and Mr. Padgett

I am here, Helen.

I won't keep you long tonight, for you are sleepy and must go to bed. But I want to say that we all enjoyed your conversation and very glad that you read the messages to your friend (Dr. Stone), for I know that they convinced him of the fact of your selection to do the great work which the Master has chosen you to do.

You must both continue to seek the Love of the Father and let your faith increase.

So I will say that I love you very dearly and am with you nearly all the time. We all love you.

So good night,
Your own true and loving
Helen.

Prefers spiritual happiness to earth life

November 4th, 1916.

Well, old fellow, how are you?

I am not going to tell you who I am until the end, but I want to say that I have been listening tonight to the writings and also to the comments you made, and you are very fortunate in having such evidence come to you, for you have more than one witness to a fact, and there are none to contradict, except some funny fellow who tried to tell Mr. Morgan that one of his witnesses was someone else, but he was not successful, as another witness heard him and put him hors de combat, (incapacitated) as the Frenchman says.

But I know that what has been written you tonight is true and was written by the persons who pretended to write. Even that Indian who claimed to be the earth guide of Mr. Morgan's father when on earth was a real, true witness. In this case the truth of the claim that Mr. Morgan is entitled to make is established, and he must believe what was written him, and how thankful he should be that it is true.

If I could only have had such a great blessing conferred on me when a mortal, how many weary hours of darkness and suffering I would have avoided when I came to the spirit world. He must believe and in believing, realize that he has that which thousands of spirits in darkness would give the world, as we said on earth, to have.

Well, I have progressed very much, and am still progressing, and am in the Third Sphere. And what happiness and glory are mine. Never, when on earth, did I conceive of such beauty and magnificence, and peace and rest in action. The lifetime of an octogenarian would not enable me to describe the wonders and beauties of this place, and I feel that somehow you should know something of it, but I will not try tonight as it is late. But let me tell you that I would not exchange one little moment of the bliss I have here for a whole lifetime of earthly happiness. I know now what the Divine Love means and what the New Birth is that you used to tell me about, and when I thought that these things were the creatures of the imaginations or speculations of the priests and preachers and religious cranks, I little realized that they would become mine and things of greater reality than the sun that used to shine in my office windows.

Sometime I will come and write you a long letter describing my progress—for which you are so much responsible and for which I will never cease to thank you as long as eternity lasts.

I remember your friend and I am very glad that he has some of the Love in his soul and did not wait to get it until he came to the spirit world and suffered the darkness and torment that I suffered. He is a fortunate man, and if any man should thank God and the good spirits, he should, and you, too. Well, I will not write more tonight. So, with my love and best wishes for your welfare and happiness, I can sign myself, as I never in all the long years of my earth experience thought possible.

Your brother in Christ,

Hugh T. Taggart.

Belongs to Eugene Morgan's spiritual band

I am here, Red Fox.

I told you true: I am in the Third Sphere and a happy Indian and happier still since you have gotten the Love, for it brings us more in rapport.

Yes, I told you. You heard my voice, as you often do.

Red Fox.

Confirms the statement by others that Mr. Morgan now has the Divine Love of the Father and adds her sisterly love also

November 4th, 1916.

I am here, your own true and loving Helen.

Well, my dear, I am glad that Mr. Morgan called tonight, for the assurance that he received from John and the other spirits will do him good, and strengthen his faith in the fact that he is now a possessor of the Divine Love. I can add my little testimony also, and while it may not have the weight of some who have written, yet it comes from knowledge to which is added the love of a sister in the faith. I am glad that he has this great possession, for I see that he is a man of deep conviction, and when once convinced of the truth of any proposition he is firm in maintaining such truth.

As you have received so much tonight, I will not write more, and only say that I love you with all my heart and soul, and am happy when I see you happy. So love me and give me my kiss and go to bed.

Your own true and loving

Helen.

The conditions of spirits in the twilight zone and their progress in the natural love

February 5th, 1917.

I am here, Luke.

I merely want to say that you are in better condition tonight, and that I will write a few lines upon a subject that may be of interest to you. In the spirit world there are many spirits who are in neither darkness nor light, but are in what has been called the twilight zone, and are neither very happy nor unhappy. These are spirits who have progressed from the lower spheres, where they expiated their sins and errors of the earth life, and have gotten rid of their recollections of many of their sins and have progressed somewhat in the development of their natural love, and also in the acquirement of the intellectual knowledge, and are not feeling the stings of conscience, but are realizing the happiness which the forgiveness of their sins and the improvement of their intellects causes them to have.

They are to a large extent very much in the condition of men who have paid the penalties of their sins, yet have not received such increase in their natural love as to enable them to progress to the higher intellectual spheres where the spirit becomes to a more or less degree the perfect man. And they have been a long time making their progress, for it is a fact that the development of their souls from the condition of the wholly sinful man to that where such sins have almost disappeared is a very slow development.

These spirits, though, are not to be classed with the dark spirits who so often come to you for help and relief from their darkness, for they are in that condition where it is difficult to convince them that they need any help in order that they may have a more wonderful progress and obtain greater happiness. In this zone the spirits seem to be well satisfied with their conditions, and have the belief that their advancement must necessarily be slow and that there is not a better and quicker way to obtain relief from their conditions. Among this class of spirits commences the greatest difficulty for the higher spirits to successfully convince them of the great truth of the Divine Love and the possibilities of obtaining a condition that will place them in the higher soul spheres, without the long delay in making their progress.

In the lower spheres the spirits are not satisfied and generally are very desirous of getting relief from the darkness and suffering and, as a consequence, we can do more to convince them of the truths that are so necessary for them to know. You would be surprised to know the number of spirits who are in this zone, and the great number of years they have been in making the progress that they have made. Many of them have been in the states to which I refer for centuries and yet have never known any desire to progress out of those states except in the way that they consider to be the gradual and natural way to advance. I will not write more now. So, good night, and may God bless you.

Your brother in Christ,

Luke.

Writes about the great work that Eugene Morgan is doing among the Catholics

November 8th, 1917.

I am here, your own true and loving Helen.

Well, dear, you had an unusual visitor tonight and I was very much interested in his interview and experience with Mr. Morgan, and was glad that Mr. Morgan spoke to him as he did and gave him the opportunity of coming in contact with a bright spirit and thereby having an awakening that he had never had before. The uncle is a very bright spirit and has much of the Divine Love in his soul, and is so happy in doing the work that came to him tonight.

The Catholic priest[112] actually wrote you and Mr. Morgan and, while he could not see me, and I did not choose to manifest myself to him, yet I could and did observe all that he thought and did. He had with him a number of spirits similar in condition and belief to himself and they all heard what Mr. Morgan said to the priest, and some of them were attracted by what was said, and also saw the uncle when he made himself visible to them; and some went with the uncle and the priest.

We are all glad that Mr. Morgan is doing this work, for it is a wonderful work and one that will accomplish much good among these Catholic spirits; and when it is considered that of all Christians they are the most bigoted and convinced that their beliefs are the true ones and their states in the spirit world such as must have necessarily followed from the truths as taught by the Church, you can readily understand what a laborious and difficult work Mr. Morgan is doing and will do. And for his benefit, I say that he will never be deserted by his band, and the Catholic priests will never be able to overpower this band; for this is a truth, that while the band seldom uses any force towards these deluded spirits, yet should they choose to do so their mere willing that these antagonistic spirits should leave Mr. Morgan would be sufficient to cause them to withdraw and thus destroy the rapport. But this cannot be, for the work that he is doing is one that must be done, and this is part of the work which he has been selected to do; and in its results it is a glorious work. The salvation of these spirits is just as important to the harmony of the heavens as is the salvation of any man or class of men or spirits.

Mr. Morgan will always have the necessary protection, and whenever he calls for the higher spirits to aid in his work, that call will always be responded to. Even now, there are many of these spirits who were lingering in and satisfied with their condition in purgatory that are now in brighter spheres, on their way to the Celestial Kingdom, because of the Love that they have received in their souls; and they are more grateful to Mr. Morgan than I can explain. And these rescued spirits are also with him, working to help their friends and acquaintances who are still in their darkness and belief in the efficacy of the teachings of their church.

God will bless Mr. Morgan in his work while on earth, and many spirits whom he has helped will thank and bless him when he comes to the spirit world. I have thus written at length so that Mr. Morgan might gain some conception of what his work means and how he has been

---

[112] The Catholic priest who wrote is quoted in a later message in this volume on page 318. (G.J.C.)

successful in his efforts, and feel encouraged to continue in his good work, without doubt as to the truth of what he may conceive the results of his efforts to be.

Well, dear, I will not write more now, but only say that I love you, as you know, and that your condition is much better, and very soon you will be able to receive the higher messages. So keep up your courage and pray to the Father and you will not be disappointed, for the Love will work in your soul the great miracle of transforming a human, mortal soul into a Divine existence, at-one with the Father and His very Essence. Good night, and believe that I am

Your own true and loving

Helen.

Describes an incident in her work of finding the soulmates of spirits

January 27th, 1915.

I am here, your own Helen.

Well, I am engaged, as you know, among other things, in finding the spirits' soulmates and bringing them together. Well, there is a spirit here who believes that the soulmate theory is a false one, and only intended to deceive those who are so very lonely and unhappy, and that a man who has any stamina or any intellect will not be fooled by such ideas as that soulmates exist and are waiting to become one. Well, he was in that condition of loneliness and was very unhappy, although he had very great intellectual acquirements, and prided himself on that fact; and he thought that love and kindred things are for women and foolish men, when he was suddenly visited by a most beautiful spirit and asked if he had yet found his soulmate. He replied that he had not and didn't want to, unless she should happen to be as beautiful as the spirit who was talking to him; and that if such a thing could be, he would be most happy to find her.

Well, she asked him why he should suppose that his soulmate would be so beautiful, when he was a spirit who was not so very attractive looking, and all crooked, and devoid of anything that would tend to make him appreciate beauty or love in another. He said that he did not consider himself so unattractive as she said, because he was possessed of a knowledge of very many things that the ordinary spirit did not have, and that, consequently, he must be more attractive looking than she described him to be. And as to love, why he could love, he thought, if he could find anyone whom he considered worth being loved. Then she told him that she was his soulmate, but that he could never have her until he acquired more love and larger understanding of

317

spiritual things. That her home was up in the Fifth Sphere, and that he could not go there to live with her until he had gotten sufficient love in his soul to make him fitted to dwell there; and that the longer he delayed trying to get this love the longer he would be separated from her, and would, now that he knew she was his soulmate, be most unhappy. That his intellectual acquirements would not help him very much, and that the only thing that would enable him to progress to where she lived was a development of love in his soul.

He said that he did not know much about love, but that if she would only show him the way to obtain it, he would devote his whole soul and efforts to getting it. She then told him that he must give up the pride which he indulged in and which kept him so encased in himself, and learn to love everybody else in a brotherly way, and God with all his heart and soul. And that when he made that effort, he would find that this love which she, as his soulmate, must have from him, would come to him and he would soon realize that in all the spirit world love is the greatest thing to possess. And that when a spirit has that he needs nothing else to make him happy.

He did not seem to comprehend what she said, but said he would try to let his pride of intellect leave him, and make an effort to let his soul receive this love; that thereafter love should be first and knowledge and everything merely intellectual follow after.

So, you see, a soulmate may be found, but not acquired, until love commensurate with the love possessed by the higher soul is gotten by the lower soul.

No merely intellectual acquirement is sufficient to attract and make one, of two soulmates. Only love in perfect harmony can bring about this union. Let love rule and then happiness is the lot of all spirits. But, of course, this love is comparative, and so is the ensuing happiness.

Your own true and loving Helen.

A Catholic priest who defended his flock talks with Mr. Morgan

November 8th, 1917.

I am here, Father Williams.

I am the priest that visited your friend[113] last night, and I was very aggressive and insulting; but now I wish to apologize, for I have learned that he knew a great deal more about things of the spirit world than I thought possible, and more than I knew myself.

Of course, if he will consider for a moment my position and the

---

[113] Mr. Eugene Morgan (J.P.G.)

fact that for many long years I entirely believed what I professed, and also felt it my duty to God and to my church to defend the doctrines of the church, he may understand why I was so vehement and looked upon him as a foe to truth and a dangerous man to the followers of the church and to all that we believed in as sacred and holy. Now I must confess that I see some things in a little different light, and am not so certain as to some of the positions assumed by the church, in its teachings[114] as to the destiny of men in the spirit world.

I should like very much to talk to him again and ask him some questions respecting the position that he took, and this not for the purpose of controversy, but to learn his explanations of some of the things that he asserted. So, if he will tolerate me for a while, I will be greatly obliged.

Is now writing through Mr. Morgan.

I want to ask you a question, and that is, how you came to know of the things you asserted to be the great truths that are necessary to be understood in order to obtain salvation.

Mr. Morgan has enabled Father Williams to visualize a bright spirit.

I saw him.

I am very much surprised at your statement. You are indeed fortunate. I am satisfied with your explanation and shall endeavor to profit by it. I am not as vicious as you may suppose, but I thought I was but doing my duty in trying to protect my people from one whom I believed was the emissary of the devil. I now see my error, and am thankful that you were so patient in enduring my abuse as you were.

I am, as I said, satisfied with your explanations, and from now on shall endeavor to become as the bright spirit with whom you brought me in contact. You must not think unkindly of me; for I now realize what a great service you have rendered me. I will now go.

Your friend, the once Father Williams.

Contrasting the Muslim heavens and the Christian heavens

August 8th, 1915.

I am here, Seligman. I am an ex-sultan of the Muslims.

---

[114] Refers to the teachings of the Catholic Church. (J.P.G.)

I do not know time, but about four hundred years ago. Yes, I am still a follower of the Prophet, and I am in our paradise and happy. God is great! Allah is his name and Mohammed is his prophet!

I had a desire to learn what the writers who have written you tonight might say, and so I stayed and listened to them and found that their doctrines of the Divine Love of the Father are new to me. The Muslims do not understand this Love, and when I heard that it gave such bliss to those who possessed it, I became interested and wondered what it really meant.

We have not this Love, and our happiness comes to us from our brotherly love and our worship of Allah and our devotion to his prophet. As I wondered the thought came to me that we should have been taught to know what this Love means, and if our Allah is not such a loving God as the God that these Christians tell of. I am going to inquire into this, because if there be a greater happiness than what I now have I want to learn about it, and if it exists, to become a partaker of it.

We don't have much intercourse with the Christian spirits, as our heavens are separate from theirs and we believe that we have the true heavens and are the chosen of God, and that all these Christians are in the dark.

Well, these Christians seem to be brighter and more beautiful than do the spirits in our heavens and that has caused me to think, also. I know that in our heavens the higher we progress the more beautiful we become and the brighter we seem to be, and that the condition of the progress of the individual determines his appearance; and, knowing this, I have come to think that these Christians live in a higher or more progressive heaven than ours.

I am dissatisfied now, and I will investigate. Can you tell me the best way to do so?

Yes, some are who have not written. I will do so.

There is one here—a beautiful woman—who says she is your grandmother. I will ask her and maybe she can start me on my investigation.

Well, I will say good night.

I will certainly come again.

Your friend,

Seligman.[115]

---

[115] The First Edition reports his name as Seleman, but on the occasion of his second message which is contained in Volume III (2nd Ed.) page 245, he corrected that. The earlier edition used the term Mohammedan here which is now Muslim. (G.J.C.)

Confirms that a spirit was enabled to visualize Mr. Padgett's grandmother

August 8th, 1915.

I am here, Helen.

Well, my dear, you have had a great many writings tonight and you must feel tired and I will not keep you, though I should like to tell you of my love and my desire for your love. But I must stop.

Mr. Padgett asked if Seligman had visualized his grandmother.

Yes, he was, and I am interested in him. Your grandmother is talking to him now. I hope that he may see the light.

With all my love, I am

Your own true and loving

Helen.

Wishes to explain Jennie Lawson's passing into the spirit world and the help that he gave her while on earth

November 11th, 1915.

I am here, mother of Eugene Morgan.

I am his mother, and must say one word before you stop writing. I have been with him today and saw his condition of mind in reference to his friend who has just come into the spirit world and want to assure him that she is now in a much better condition than he may think.

I have been with her (Jenny Lawson) ever since she came over and in fact I was waiting at the portals of this spirit world when she ceased to be a mortal and took her in my arms and comforted her and told her that there was nothing to fear and that she was with friends who loved her and would help her.

She did not seem to be much confused because when we whom she knew to be dead as she thought came to her in our familiar forms and with our voices so natural that she could recognize us she thought of what my boy had told her of—spirit life—and the result was that she believed that we were whom we said we were and as a consequence she seemed to lose all fear or dread and to come into a condition of security just as if she were visiting me while on earth.

But she is not very spiritual in ideas of the real truth of things of the soul for I see that her beliefs of earth are with her and that the poverty of her soul development causes her to experience darkness and soon she will have some sufferings but she will not remain in darkness very long for her mind will soon open to our thoughts of truth and her soul to the influence of our love. And I want to tell my son this, that he may remember it and apply the principle in his contact with others of earth, that the one little seed of truth which he caused to find a lodgment in her soul helped her more than I can tell him in her realizing the exact condition of her being when she came to us.

We are all very happy and thankful that love is doing its work in the soul of my boy. His father is with him quite often and he says that some days ago he heard you suggest to him that he should have a spirit band to help and protect him, and his father will form that band and soon tell him who is with him. I have written long and taken your time and I thank you for your kindness and will show my appreciation by trying to help you as well as my son.

So believe that I am your friend and that I love you with a love that is that of a sister. Give my love to my boy and tell him to think of his mother and believe that she is with him trying to help him with her love and influence.

So again thanking you I will say good night.

Mother of Eugene Morgan.

Buddha no longer teaches reincarnation

August 1st, 1916.

I am here, your own true and loving Helen.

Well, sweetheart, you have been much interested in the book (The Birth of Buddha) you were reading, and there are some wonderful statements contained in it, and which, as you must see, are fables; for never did the things related happen.

There are in the spirit world a great number of spirits who believe in and worship Buddha, and who are satisfied in their beliefs and their manner of living and the places in which they live. None of them are in the Celestial Heavens, but are in several spheres of the spirit world according to the development of their moral natures and their natural loves.

I have never seen the founder of this sect, but I am informed that he is in the sixth sphere[116] and is a very bright spirit and pure, and still engaged in teaching his doctrines. But of course he has changed in some of his doctrines, notably the doctrine of reincarnation; for all the spirits of his followers on earth remain in the spirit world, and never become reincarnated.

Well, I do not know whether we can have him come and write or not,[117] but we will make the effort sometime in order that he may tell

---

[116] Highest Sphere of the spirits who have developed their natural love in a pure state, but do not possess the Divine Love. (J.P.G.)

[117] No message was received from "The Buddha" by James Padgett, although some

you himself of his present beliefs and condition of bliss. Well, you will be able to do that and it may have some effect. But you have so many other things to do at this time that I do not think we will have him come very soon.

Your own true and loving
Helen.

A spirit who is suffering intensely comes to Mr. Padgett and begs him to help him to find his lost soul

April ^{1st}, 1915.

I am here, a man who has lost his soul and can't find it.

What would I not give to have it again, and so be able to receive the love that you write about? But I lost it and no one can help me find it. I have tried and sought for it everywhere, but it has left me, and I am a spirit without a soul, only my poor inefficient mind remains with me, and such happiness as I can conjure up by thinking of what might have been or what might be, if I had a soul.

Tell me, can you help me find it? If so, please do so, and I will bless you forever. I am in a condition of not knowing whether I am living, or only dreaming, or dead. As I seem to be alive, I wonder who and what I am; as I dream, I see that I am a son of God; and as a dead man I know nothing. But I don't know what I am, and no one will tell me.

You are to me a very real man with a soul, as I can see, but I have no soul. Tell me where to find it, for I must have it. I lost it in trying to find that my intellect was the only thing in all the spirit world that is real, and when I thought that I had found that to be true, my soul had left me, and I can't find it. Oh, tell me where it is, and I will never lose it again.

You must know something about it, for the other spirits say that you help to save souls, and if you can do that, you surely can find a lost one. Why don't you tell me where to find it, and not keep me in this condition of not knowing whether I am living or dead? Come, be kind to me, and find my soul. It will not run away from you, as you will treat it kindly, I know. Your soul will know, if you will only ask it, and when it tells you, you can find mine.

I am neither spirit nor mortal nor anything created by God until I get my soul again. My mind is nothing but an abstract nothing without my soul, and I have no love or happiness. Oh, if I had only cared for my soul instead of for my mind, how different I would be now, and I would not be a wanderer looking for his lost soul.

---

contemporary mediums have claimed to have received such a message. (G.J.C.)

I was a man of great intellect when on earth, and lived in the city of New York, and passed over in 1864, a much honored man. I was a lawyer, and well-known to my immediate community, and I died a mere man without a soul.[118] So, you see, I am so lonely without my soul and love. I was not a very bad man, and did not barter my soul for filthy lucre, but I thought that the soul was a myth, and the mind was everything; and when I passed over and found that I needed a soul, I could not find mine, and have never had it since. Tell me, I pray, where it is, and I will thank you through all eternity.

Won't you tell me?

Yes, I will do anything that you say that will help me get it.

I know that I had a soul because, before I had given my years of hard study to make my intellect the great thing that it became, I loved, and felt sympathy for the unfortunate and poor, and especially loved children. And I know that if I had not had a soul I would not have had these feelings and emotions. But after I became a man of great mind, I may say with only a mind, none of these feelings ever came to me—only the knowledge that I had a powerful intellect. My soul died and never has come to me since.

Yes, only tell me quickly that I may commence the search.

Yes, I see many beautiful spirits who look very happy. Yes, she says that she is your grandmother, and how beautiful she is. Yes, I will go with her, and do as you say, and try to believe what she may tell me.

Yes, I certainly will, and oh, if I do, how I shall thank you.

Your grandmother calls me, and I must go.

So, good night.

A message from Helen

April 1st, 1915.

I am here, Helen.

Well, sweetheart, you have heard a great many messages, but none like the last one. I have not before come in contact with a man who has lost his soul, and don't know just what it means. I am so glad that you sent him to your grandmother, for she, I believe, knows what he means. Well, I will not write more tonight, as it is late, and you are tired.

So, with all my love, I am

Your own true Helen.

---

[118] This appears to be Charles G. Groveneur. (G.J.C.)

When on earth did not know of the development of the soul by the Divine Love

October 10th, 1915.

I am here, Jerome.

Well, you seem to be in doubt as to who I am, but I will say that I am sometimes called St. Jerome.

Now, I merely want to say that you are very much in favor with the spirits who dwell in the Celestial Spheres, and with the Master as well, and that you will be the means of receiving and giving to the world some of the wonderful truths of the Father.

I was not one when on earth who thought very much of these truths, for I was not acquainted with the soul development or the Divine Love. I thought more of the doctrines as propagated by the Catholic Church, and tried my best to make the doctrines of this church the important things with the worshippers of the church creeds.

Your brother in Christ,
Jerome.

A dark spirit is also seeking Mr. Padgett's help to get out of darkness

I am here, Edward J. Sovellard.

Let me write just a line, for I need your prayers just as the last spirit said he does. I am in darkness and suffering and have never been able to find my relief. I see that you have helped these other spirits. I so want you to help me, and I know that you will, for there are other spirits here who say that you have helped them.

Well, my name is—let me see. I have been here so long and have suffered so much that I have forgotten it, but it is Edward P. Sovellard. I think that I have spelled it correctly.

A former law partner of Mr. Padgett tries to help a lower spirit to understand spiritual progress

April 6th, 1915.

I am here, your old partner, A. G. Riddle.

Well, I want to tell you of that man with the wonderful mind, who surpasses every other spirit in his knowledge of the laws of the spirit world. I had a conversation with him and I found that he knew comparatively little of anything.

His knowledge consisted in not knowing what there is for him to know. He had certain ideas about the spirit world, but they were few and superficial. He was so convinced that he had learned everything there is to know that he was not capable of learning more.

I soon found that his capacity for learning was limited by his horizon of what he didn't know, that is, he thought that as he knew everything there was nothing in all God's universe that was left to him to learn.

His was the greatest case of a man who was possessed of all knowledge that I have ever met. Just as soon as we commenced to converse, I saw that the only way to deal with him was to let him think that his is the great mind that he believed it to be, and so I posed as one who was inferior to him in intellect, and one willing to sit at the feet of Gamaliel[119] to learn.

He commenced to tell me about his wonderful mind and the great knowledge which it possessed and how he was quite lonely in the spirit world, because he could find no one who was competent to discuss subjects which only minds of his greatness could grasp and understand.

As a seeker after some of his great knowledge, I commenced in a very modest way to ask him certain questions for information as he thought, and to his surprise, but not to mine, I will confess he said that he had never considered them, and that because they did not appear to be of sufficient importance for his gigantic intellect to bother with. Well, I kept putting questions after question and his only answer was that he had not considered them for the reason above stated. At last he commenced to see that I had an object in approaching him in this way and that I was not as unsophisticated as I first appeared.

Finally he said that maybe there were some things which he didn't know, and which were worthy of his investigation, and that he would give his mind to their consideration.

Then I commenced to tell him of spiritual things and of the great love of the Father, and what a power it had to beautify and make happy the souls of spirits. At first he declared that there was no such thing as the soul and reiterated that the mind is the only thing that belongs and determines the character and qualities of a spirit. That God is only the creature of man's mind, and that love is a thing of the imagination only.

---

[119] Gamaliel the Elder, or Rabbi Gamaliel I, was a leading authority in the Sanhedrin in the mid first century. He was the grandson of the great Jewish teacher Hillel the Elder, and died twenty years before the destruction of the second temple in Jerusalem. He fathered a son, whom he called Simeon, after his father's name, and a daughter, whose daughter (i.e., Gamaliel's granddaughter) married a priest named Simon ben Nathanael. The name Gamaliel is the Greek form of the Hebrew name meaning reward of God.
In the Christian tradition, Gamaliel is celebrated as a Pharisee doctor of Jewish Law, who was the teacher of Paul the Apostle; the author of the Book of Acts portrays Gamaliel with great respect. (Source: Wikipedia) (G.J.C.)

Well, you may imagine what a task it was to convince him that he had a soul, and that the soul is the real thing in his existence, and that mind is merely a subordinate part of the soul. He didn't seem to grasp the proposition, but after a while I showed him the beauty and happiness of several of our band and asked him if the mind is the greatest thing and as he knew that none of these spirits has a mind equal to his own why is it that they are so much more beautiful and happy than he.

He hesitated a moment and said, that his mind did not run in the direction of creating beauty or happiness, but if he had devoted it to those things he would be more beautiful and happier than any of these spirits.

I confess this argument was difficult to meet from his standpoint, but I called into concentration my argumentative faculties and knowing he was wrong, I asked him why he had not devoted his mind to these subjects as he must surely know that beauty and happiness are more desirable than anything to which he could possibly direct his mental strivings. He said that he knew that these qualities or possessions are very desirable but he doubted if there could be any happiness equal to that of great mental development and its resultant delights. I asked him why he was willing to remain in his condition of darkness and surrounded by such unhappy beings if the mind could bring such delights, and why he had not left the plane of darkness a long time ago, and sought the companionship of brighter and more intellectual spirits. He said that was one of the few things that he did not understand. He was anxious to get into different associations and wanted more congenial companionship, but yet no matter how much he exercised his mental powers he did not seem to be able to change his condition or leave the plane on which he lived.

I then said to him, suppose there is a power so great that it can take you out of that condition and place you among these congenial spirits, where you say you have desired to go, what would your great mind say of you if you refuse to learn what this great power is, and rest content to remain in ignorance of this great power and ignore its existence. He said, that he supposed his mind would say that he is a fool, and does not do its greatness the justice to which is was entitled, and that such a position on his part would show him that he was not making the best use of his mind to which it is entitled.

Well, after letting him think a while on this phase of the matter, I said to him, my friend, what I have put to you as a supposition is a truth—there is a power which is able to elevate you above your present condition and one which your mind will tell you to seek for, if you will only let it do so. And that power is one of spiritual qualities not depending on the mere mind, but upon a source which is the mind of all minds, and of which your great mind is only a shadow, and merely

327

reflects its possibilities. He said, well, since you seem to know of this great power suppose you describe it to me, and if you can show my mind that such a power can have any possible existence, I will try and learn what that power really is.

I then told him of the greatness of the soul, and its wonderful capacity for growth and expansion and love. He listened to me intently, and said, what you say may be true and I will investigate, but I am sure that there must be some mistake as to its superiority over the mind, but as you are an honorable and intelligent spirit I will consider the question in all seriousness; and if I find that there is any probability of such power existing as you describe, I will let my mind acknowledge it and will seek to obtain the means of attaining to this power. I am as you see, a very reasonable man and susceptible to conviction when the evidence to prove your assertions are reasonably certain.

I told him to think the matter over and come again and discuss the question with me. He said he would, but I am afraid that he is hopelessly bound up with the idea that he knows everything, and outside of his mind there is nothing in all God's universe. Such spirits are the most to be pitied because to them repentance will never come, or if it does, it is a long way ahead of them.

I must confess that I rather enjoyed the interview, because it recalled somewhat some of the old times when on earth I engaged in arguments and debates. But, of course, it had a deeper and holier meaning than that, because I hoped that he might come to the light of God's great provisions for the spiritual awakening, and learn the way to the Father's Love.

So, I must say that I am indebted to you for bringing me in contact with such a spirit. I know how apparently hopeless the task is of convincing him that his great mind can be surpassed by any other thing, but I pray that something I may say may help a little light to enter into that hidebound and all-sufficient mind of his.

I intended to write about another subject tonight, but as I thought you would be interested in knowing the result of our interview I concluded to tell you rather than write on the other subject. So I will not write more as there are other spirits waiting to write. So my dear boy and partner, I am your loving friend and brother, as ever.

A. G. Riddle.

Has progressed to the extent that he is now a helper in leading other dark spirits into the light

I am here, Joseph Salyards.

I am your old friend and fellow worker in the vineyard of the Father, and as you must know am interested in the subject that has been written about by the spirits who have just written you.

How beautiful these spirits are! One whose home is away beyond the starry heavens, as you mortals might say, and the other, among the bright stars of love and gladness. This, of course, is merely figurative, but the figure is not greater than the fact, because there are no brightness and gladness among the stars that can compare to the brightness and gladness of this loving mother who has so feelingly written to her son.

Well, I must not write more tonight as I do not desire to consume more of your time, but I thought that you might like to have one little line from me.

Let your faith in the promises grow and become a thing of real substance, for you will not be disappointed. The spirits are with you and God is with them, and they must prevail in their efforts.

With my love and blessings to you and your friend who is my friend too, for I have been with him so much that I have forgotten that he was ever a stranger.

I will say good night. Your brother in Christ,
Joseph Salyards.

Was so set in his ways of religious thoughts that he felt he needed no help from anyone in the spirit world, that is until Mr. Padgett explained the laws there, which he began to learn and only then started to progress

December 16th, 1914.

I am here, your old partner.

I want to talk a little with you. You have not given me the opportunity before and I commenced to think that you did not wish to hear from me. Well I will try my best and will talk to you about the laws of control of spirits over human beings.

You are not very different from us in your mental or spiritual conditions. We, of course, have no physical bodies but our spiritual bodies are very much like those we had on earth in former shape except that we are young and strong and not affected by those things which you are subject to.

You must know however that we are all affected to a greater or lesser degree by the condition of our soul development. Your wife, for instance, is now a very beautiful spirit both as regards her spiritual body as well as her spiritual soul. She is one of the most beautiful that I come in contact with except your mother and grandmother who are beyond my ability to describe. I am also very different but not so very much changed as I have not yet made very great progress in the things pertaining to the involution [development] of the soul.

My ideas are not very much changed as I still think that I am a man who must depend upon himself for his advancement and that God is a way off somewhere in the heavens and not much interested in my welfare. But your father is now in another plane and I commence to wonder why he should progress and I be left to live in this earth plane, and as I think of this I feel that there must be something more to my being lifted out of my present conditions through my own efforts.

I hear what your mother tells me but somehow I do not quite catch the import of her teachings as I believe that her ideas are more or less the result of her training on earth and have no actual foundation for a belief in the help of the Holy Spirit to rest upon, but as I see the wonderful change in your wife and father, I cannot but think that there must be something more than my own efforts at elevating myself is necessary to my rising out of my present condition. So I am thinking deeply on the subject. Your grandmother has also told me of the wonderful work of the Holy Spirit in her case, as well as in that of very many other spirits who were in my condition when they first came to the spirit world and it all makes me think that there is something in this wonderful transformation of these spirits beyond what I have ever thought of.

I will try to learn what it is if I possibly can so if you can help me in any way please do so for I do not want to remain in this state if there is any way for me to progress out of it. You seem to be in great favor with some spirits who have told me that they were benefited by you and hence I say, if you can help me do so.

I have had a spirit come to me who said he was Jesus but I did not believe him even though he was of a most exceeding brightness and loveliness. I do not believe in his being Jesus even though your mother told me that he was. But until I can see that he is the true Jesus I do not care to listen to him, for I have never believed that Jesus is any more than a man or that he can save anyone from sin or error. Yet as he seems so good and lovely I sometimes think that maybe I am all wrong and that he is, in truth, what he claims to be. I will, in future, listen more to him and if he can show me the way to higher things as your mother claims he can, I will let his teachings linger in my thoughts for consideration.

I am not very happy as I have told you, but I am studying the laws of the spirit world and find them very interesting to my peculiar make of mind.

I find that you can sense my thoughts and write them as you are now doing, but when you are not in a condition you cannot hear what I say or I cannot cause you to move the pencil in conformity with what I desire you to write. Why this is, I am not yet able to determine, but I am told by those who have given a longer investigation to the subject, that you have certain qualities that must respond to certain qualities that I have and if they do not, then there can be no communication. What these qualities are I do not know, only that they do exist and that the more perfect they are the more successful the writing of them with mine. You call it rapport, but that is not exactly the whole meaning of the condition, for some people seem to have these qualities and yet between them and the spirit there is not any rapport or condition of love or sympathy or what else that may be understood in the term. So you see, we do not exactly know just what is necessary to establish this junction of powers or qualities. I am trying to discover what this is, if possible. You seem to have these qualities to a very large extent and I find no difficulty in coming with a condition that enables me to freely express and you to receive what I wish to communicate.

I will inform you of my efforts just as soon as I am able to discover the real secret of this condition that exists.

You are writing what I really express to you. There is no such thing as the subconscious mind, the only mind that you have is the one that enables you to express what you really know of your own thoughts which do not depend upon what others may infuse into your brain as I am doing now, but which have their origination in your brain and which do not result from exterior minds. What is called the subconscious mind is merely an imaginary thing used by the scientist to denote that which they have no better name to call it by. It is not a part of your self or your brain, but only the image that these wise men use for what they are not able to explain.

So do not think that when something comes to your consciousness that you cannot account for, that it is the subconscious self that produces it. It is not, there are only two sources of thought, one that arises from your own brain and the other that comes to you from outside minds as consciousness which is that condition of being that enables you to feel or know that certain things exist either as actualities or as mere ideas which so far as you know have no real existences.

Consciousness is a realization of being nothing that does not exist or is capable of expressing itself in consciousness.[120] Mere dreams

---

[120] This sentence does not read well, and would benefit from a review of the original document, if that can be found. Many of the original handwritten documents still exist, but unfortunately not all. And in particular we believe the originals of Volumes III and IV have been damaged and destroyed by poor storage.

My personal interpretation of this sentence is as follows. I agree with the premise that we have only mind, a material mind, but that we also create what has been called a mid-mind or soul-mind as a result of our striving for spiritual advancement. However Riddle is at this stage too inexperienced to know about this soul-mind. So I would re-write this as follows: "Consciousness is a realization of being. Nothing that does not exist or is not capable of are not really things that lie in consciousness for they do not always have an existence, they are only shadows of what might have an existence. So you see, consciousness is not anything else than the evidence of what exists and of what your brain feels or knows. Do not think that I can tell you everything that you may want to know for I cannot. I am only a student as you are but of course I am an older one and am in a position to possibly learn more than you.

You must not think that memory is an evidence of any sub-consciousness because it is just as much of the faculty of the brain as any other part of it that shows its operations. Memory is not separate or distinct from the brain. It is merely that portion which keeps in full existence knowledge or experiences already gained. Memory creates nothing new and when you recall things that you once knew and have forgotten memory only supplies those things from its storehouse which you put there to have filed. So let not the thoughts that memory is anything other than a part of the brain. No subconscious self is involved in memory but memory is its own self and is only a part of the brain as I have said.

There is no middle ground between the brain as a generator or instrument of producing thought and the minds of spirits or others who supply independent thoughts even though sometimes the wise men thought that such thoughts are of their own creation. You seem to be very much interested in this matter and I will give more attention to its study and try to learn the operation of the thoughts of spirits upon the brains of mortals.

No laws that I am acquainted with show that a thought is other than the emanation of what passes through a man's brain and what spirits put into it. I mean that thoughts are not the result of anything but that which arises from the observations of the five senses of a man or from what is suggested by spirits. I have not made myself very clear I know but sometime I will write you more fully and clearly on this subject.

I am engaged in studying the laws of spiritual life and its connection with the earth life. I do not yet know just what that connection is, but I believe that I will very soon. I am sure that you will be much benefited if you will let me tell you occasionally just what your relation as a human is to yourself when you come over here. I do not know that I am very different from what I was on earth except that I am no longer suffering from the limitations which the body placed on me.

My mind is just the same and my ideas of life are nearly the same except that I see that material things are not of very much importance to a man even when he is on earth. You may do everything possible to accumulate and enjoy these things but in a moment you are

expressing itself is conscious." (G.J.C.)

without them except as your earthly desires and cravings for them may cause you to believe even after you are here, that they are still with you. This is the one great thing that prevents spirits from progressing to higher things. I never cared much for these material things. Yet I find that even the little desires that I had to possess them have held me from progressing to a plane where I am informed intellect rules supreme and when great minds exchange thoughts of moment to both spirit and earth life.

Yes, sometimes he is in the third (spirit) sphere and is a very happy spirit and is much engaged in his studies of spiritual things. He should be able to tell you a great deal about these things if you give him the opportunity. Yes, I see Mrs. Riddle and Bert very often. They are not very happy because they think that the spirit life is not what it should be. They do not realize that they are altogether in the spirit, but have an idea that they are still a part of the earth and consequently, as they cannot take any part in earthly affairs, they are not so happy. Your mother has been talking to them a great deal lately and trying to teach them of the spiritual things that she so believes in but I doubt if they are very much impressed.

No, I cannot help them for I do not believe in such things as I told you.

I will try to do as you say, but it will be hard for me to believe that prayer is anything more than the mere expression of a desire and reaches no higher than a man's own mind and wishes.

I will do as you suggest and if you are right I shall not fail to give it all my earnest and deepest efforts; if you are right I shall never know how to thank you, but you will know just as soon as I know. But in the meantime do not let the thought that I am not doing all that I can to make a better man of myself enter into your mind for I am. I will pray with you as you say. I commence to see what you mean and it seems to me that there is some true philosophy in what you say.

I want to get everything that any of God's children may have and if what you tell me is the only way to get this wonderful happiness, I will try even though my doubts are now mountains high. I will pray with you tonight and try to believe with all my mind and soul.

Yes, I will give my attention to them also and if they tell me what they actually know I will get the happiness which they have, so do what you think is best for me and I will try to have the faith that you speak of.

Yes, your father is very different in his appearance and I wondered what caused it and thought that maybe some peculiar condition of his spiritual body had been created by something which he had learned from his wife or mother-in-law. But I now see that it must have been caused by some other powers of influence and I want it too, if it is for me.

Yes, I see that you are very much interested in not only myself but in them and I will try my best to obtain what you tell me of, so that I may help them as you say. I know that I was not given to spiritual things on earth, but I did not see the necessity of being so, for I thought that when I died I would not need anything but my own help to live a life of comparative happiness. But if you are right, I will soon know the difference, for I shall do as you say. I will pray and ask God to give me faith to believe that He is my savior from sin.

Yes, I see that there must be something in it. They are all claiming to have the love, but myself, so I must be wrong and they right. You are right, let me think of what you have told me and I will soon know if I am to be like the rest of the band.

Yes, I know that you loved me even when on earth and that thought has helped me to believe that what you tell me to believe, and that what you tell me now is the outgrowth of your love. I am so glad that I have you to think of me and show me the way and now I will say good night.

Your one-time friend,
A. G. Riddle.

Confirms that Mr. Riddle has started to pray as Mr. Padgett suggested to him in order for him to be able to progress into the light

December 16th, 1914.

I am here, Helen.

You certainly did make an impression on Mr. Riddle, for he is now trying to pray as you suggested to him to do. But you must not let your love for him keep you from feeling that we all want you to pray for us also, for you seem to have such faith that we wonder at you.

Question.

No, not that, but we need your prayers too, so do not forget us. I am not one bit selfish in the matter, but I want you to help me too.

I do not know, but it seems to be so. Whenever you talk to these spirits, who will not believe us, they listen to you and soon commence to pray to God for forgiveness and love. We do not understand it any more than you do, but it is so and your grandmother says that your faith must be very great that you should have such influence with the lost spirits. She says, that she does not understand herself and that if you continue you will do so much good that your reward here will be especially great. God seems to listen to your prayers for these spirits and we are all amazed at it.

But let me say that you must also pray for yourself for you also need the Love of God in your heart to a greater degree in order to be at-one with the Father.

Gives Mr. Padgett healing treatments whenever he needs it after a long writing

I am here, White Eagle.

You are a good man, but you no like my treatment, as I see. Let me try tonight when you stop writing.

White Eagle.

Writes that he considered Jesus to be a mere man when on Earth, who had received a large conception of truth, and he attempted to teach it. But now he writes that Jesus is the most wonderful of all spirits

January 20th, 1915.

I am here, your old partner.

Yes it is I, and I am glad to be able to write to you again. I told your wife that I desired to write and tell you of my progress in spiritual matters, and as you are kind enough to give me the opportunity, I will try to tell you how my eyes were opened to the things of the spirit, and my heart to the Love of God.

Well, as you know, when you first commenced to talk to me, I did not actually believe in a God or Jesus or his teachings, except as they related to the moral condition of men. When you first commenced to talk to me about these spiritual things, I thought that you were merely telling me the things that you had learned in your church or Sunday school, and that they were only intended for men and women of no capacity to think for themselves, and suited only to receive what the preachers might tell them.

So, you see, I was not in a very receptive condition of mind to enable me to believe that what you told me had any foundation in fact or in truth. Jesus, to me, was just the same as any other man who had received large conceptions of the truth; but he was only a mere man, in the sense that what he attempted to teach he had learned by study and meditation, or through some worldly source that I did not know of. At any rate, (I believed that) that his teachings were not the result of inspiration, or derived from a source any different from what mankind received other information as to things of nature, or of spirit.

Well, as you continued to tell me that I was mistaken, and that there is a Source from which all good flows, other than the mere mind or conscience of men, I began to think about the matter. And when I looked around me and saw that your mother and wife—who claimed that they had received this Love of God which you insisted was waiting for me to obtain—were so beautiful and happy, while I and my folks were not very beautiful and not at all happy, I began to inquire (as to) the cause. And when you told me that their, I mean your mother's and wife's, condition was due to this Love of God, I asked them to tell me about the nature of this Love, and the way in which they obtained It. And your mother, bless her soul, took great pains to instruct me in these things.

And, then when I learned that prayer was the only way to this Love, and saw you praying for me with all your heart and in great earnestness, I commenced to pray also; but I must confess that my prayers were not accompanied with much faith. But I continued to pray, and every night when you prayed for me and for the many others who were with you praying, I tried to exercise all the faith possible and prayed for more faith. This continued for some time, and one day your grandmother, who is a most wonderful spirit in goodness and beauty, came to me and said that she was your grandmother and was very much interested in me, on your account as well as on my own, and commenced to unfold (explain) to me the great efficacy of prayer. She assured me that if I would only try to believe, and pray to God to help me believe, He would answer my prayers; and I would soon find that with my earnest efforts, faith would come to me, and with faith would come this Love into my heart, and with this Love would come happiness and joy.

So I listened to her, and tried to believe that what she told me must be true and that she was interested in me and desired only my happiness. I continued to pray, as I said, and one day after I had received some considerable faith, I met Jesus, and he told me of the wonderful things that his Father had prepared for me, if I would only believe and ask Him to give them to me. Jesus was so very beautiful and loving that I could not resist the influence which came over me; and then my faith increased, and I prayed with all my heart and soul.

At last, light came to me, and with it, such an inflowing of Love as I never dreamed could exist, either on the earth or in the spirit world. But it came to me and I felt as if I was a new spirit, and such happiness came as I never experienced before. And then that dear mother of yours came and rejoiced with me, and also your beautiful wife who had tried so hard to induce me to seek for this Love.

Oh, Padgett, I tell you that in all the wide universe of God there is nothing to compare to this Love of the Father. Let me say, that in all my life, when only my intellect ruled me, there was nothing to compare with that which came to me with this inflowing of the Love.

I am now in the third (spirit) sphere with many beautiful and happy spirits. Your mother and wife are higher up, and are so beautiful and good that when I am in their company I feel that I will become a much happier man if I will try to follow them. Your father has progressed too, and so has Professor Salyards.

Well, my soul is one now that is filled with this Love. My mind is also elevated in its thoughts and not inclined to think of those things that are merely intellectual. For I tell you that while knowledge of all God's laws and nature's apparent mysteries is desirable, yet a knowledge of this Love of God is far and above compare—and not only more necessary but more desirable. I would not give the feelings that come to me from the possession of this Love for all the sensations of delight that might arise from the discovery of the most stupendous and important law of the workings of nature.

Let this Love come first, and then the other acquirements will only help to show the spirit that God is a God of Wisdom and Power as well as of Love. But as you have read, "Love is the fulfilling of the law"—nothing else is. And the man who has all the knowledge and wisdom without this Love is poor indeed.

Jesus is the most wonderful of all the spirits in both Love and the knowledge of the Father's attributes. He is the greatest, and knows that the Father's plans to save and redeem mankind are as he teaches. So you must listen to him and believe. I am going to try to learn more of his teachings, and when I do, you shall know what I learn.

Jesus appears to me the one altogether lovely—he has no competitor, and no one who sees him, if he has any of this Love in his soul, can fail to know that he is the true Jesus of the Bible, and the most perfect son of his Father. I only realized this only after this Love came to me; it seems that spirits who have not this Love do not realize who Jesus is, or how wonderful and glorious he is. This may seem strange to you, but it is a fact. Only when the spirit has an awakening of his soul's love for God does Jesus appear as their great brother and teacher of this Great Love of the Father.

You must not let the things of the material life lead you to think that you may have to wait until you come to the spirit world to get this Great Love, for I tell you that the man whose soul is open to the inflowing of this Love while on earth is a much more fortunate man than he who waits until his earthly life ends. If I had only become conscious of this Love when on earth, I would have been saved many hours of suffering and unhappiness after I became a spirit. My own experience is so true to what so many undergo, and will undergo, that if I could proclaim to every man on earth the necessity of becoming possessed of this Love while on earth, I would do so with all my might and strength.

I can tell you of my experiences in passing over, but I do not think it best to do so tonight, as it would take too long and require more strength than you have tonight. Sometime soon I will do so in detail. I am so glad that I have been redeemed by this Great Love, and the teachings of Jesus, and the help of your spirit relatives, and also, by the help of your prayers, that I cannot express the extent of my gladness. Nothing in all heaven or earth can compare with the feelings of joy that come to a soul when it realizes that it is at-one with the Father in Love and power. Yes, they (old friends of Padgett in spirit world) know, and are with you every night as you pray. They don't seem to quite understand though that you can help them in any way, but still they, in a manner, feel some peculiar sensation as you pray and the others pray with you. Do not stop praying for them.

I tell you that you are a wonderfully blessed man in having such a loving Christian mother and grandmother to pray with and watch over you all your life. If all men had Christian parents to teach and show them the Way to this Love of God, as they grow from childhood to manhood, many a time of suffering and unhappiness would be avoided, and many a spirit would come into this life with many less sins to atone for.

Your old partner and friend for all eternity,

A. G. Riddle.[121]

Has progressed to a new spirit sphere and is now seeking more help to further his spiritual progress. And has received it with the help of Jesus

February 20th, 1915.

I am here, your old partner.

I am very happy tonight and I am glad that you are so much better. You had a rather hard time of it and reminded me somewhat of the suffering that I used to undergo when I was on earth and in Washington. Well you are cured of the indigestion but the gas accumulates at times and makes it uncomfortable for you, but that will pass away before long and your digestive organs will soon be in perfect working order. The faith that you had in your prayers and the work of the Master—you were actually cured by your faith. The work done was only a means used to impress upon you with fact that God had answered your prayer. I do not see how you could have had such faith as you evidenced at the time, but it is a fact that you had it and as a consequence the cure was effected.

When you prayed as you did I was so very much impressed with your faith that I expected to see your prayers answered as they were.

---

[121] This message is a composite of two, being published in Volume II and Volume IV. (G.J.C.)

Jesus helped you to pray and also helped your faith. He also did the work that you observed through the power which he possesses and used White Eagle to manipulate your intestines and liver. It was a revelation to me I must confess and caused me to believe more than ever in prayer and faith.

I am now so very happy in my new sphere that I cannot explain to you what that happiness means. I cannot express myself in language sufficiently strong and descriptive that you may comprehend. But this I will say, that my happiness now transcends all conception of what happiness might be when as a mortal I sometimes thought of the afterlife and the happiness which might be in store for me when I passed over.

I am in the third (spirit) sphere but I am not contented to remain there for your mother has told me on many occasions of the far greater happiness existing in the higher spheres. I am now striving and praying for this greater happiness and I will never be contented until I get it. Your wife is in a much higher sphere and is so very beautiful and so exceedingly happy that I know that where she lives such happiness must exist.

I am also happy because I have my soulmate with me so very often and her love is so great and pure that it leads me on to higher things and enables me to seek with so much earnestness the great love of the Father which I now believe is working for me if I only will strive to obtain it and have the faith which all who have obtained to a very large degree of this love tell me of.

Your grandmother is so wonderful, beautiful and filled with this love that her very presence inspires me to believe and seek for the happiness of these higher spheres.

Well as you want me to tell you of some of the laws of the spirit world I will say that the one great law is that God is Love and that He is willing to bestow that love on anyone spirit or mortal who asks Him for it. I am not only very happy but I find that my mind is expanding to a great extent by reason of the love that I possess. No man or spirit can possibly be filled with this love and not have the wisdom that necessarily comes with the Love. I am not so much interested in purely mental phenomena as I was before I received this love and believed in a Father of Love and Truth, but I am nevertheless able to understand many things to a far greater degree than I could when I had merely the mental pursuits in mind. I am not yet fully conversant with the laws of communication as I told you I would learn and instruct you in, but I know enough to be able to say that every spirit is trying to communicate with their friends on earth and why they are not able to is because the mortals are not in that condition of psychical rapport that will enable them to receive the communications of the spirits. I do not yet know why one mortal is susceptible to these influences in such a way as to be readily understood and another mortal is not. Some spirits say that this law controlling this matter is not even understood by spirits who have been here for a great many years and who have given considerable study to the subject.

But this I do know, that when the rapport exists the communications become stronger with the exercise of the powers. You have this power to a very large degree and if you will continue to try to exercise it, you will find that manifestations of several kinds will be disclosed. Your writing powers are very great and will grow as you continue to write but beside this phase you have the potential ability to have other manifestations such as independent voices and slate writing. This latter I think will soon come to you and when it does you will get messages that will have their great value to you in convincing you that what you write in this method is written by the control of the thoughts of your friends who profess to write.

You will also get the voices very soon as I think, and when you do you will be able to converse with us in your room at night when you are alone. But I don't know of any manifestation as satisfactory to both spirit and mortal as the writing such as you are now doing, for we have the opportunity for such a greater extent of communicating and interchanging of thought. I am perfectly delighted at the possibility given me of writing you in this way. So you must believe that I am writing to you and that all the others of your band are doing the same thing.

Your wife has more powers in this regard than any of us and she does not hesitate to write you whenever you call her. She is a wonderful spirit in her grasp of spirit things and in her love for the Father. So you must not let any doubt come into your mind when she writes to you and tells you of so many wonderful things and of her love for you. She seems to love you with a love that has no limit or possibility of growing less.

I am now going to tell you of my progress in this love and happiness. When I last wrote you I told you that I had commenced to have faith in the Father and had received some portion of His Love. Well, since then I have been praying and asking God to give me more faith and love and as I prayed my faith increased and as my faith increased more of this love came into my soul and with it an increased happiness.

So I would not stop striving until I realized that my soul was commencing to get such an inflow of this Love that it seemed that all things which tended to retard this influx were leaving me and only love and goodness were taking possession of me. I am now very far advanced over what I was when you first commenced to talk to me of this love and I shall, through all eternity, remember and thank you for what you did for me. I was also so fortunate to have your mother and wife with me very much trying to show me the way to this truth of the New Birth and then when your grandmother came to me it seemed as if I could not resist the influence to seek and try to find it.

So really when I had received enough of the spiritual awakening to realize who Jesus was, I gave him my close attention and as he continued to show me the way to the Father, I commenced to grasp the truth and believe that my salvation depended on my receiving this great love and becoming a finer and better man. I tell you that Jesus is the most wonderful of spirits that I have seen or heard about. He is so filled with love and goodness that there seems no doubt in my mind that he is the son of the Father in the spiritual sense of the term. I mean that he is so much nearer the Father and in so much and many of his attributes that he is the only son in the sense of being more at-one with the Father.

We are all sons of the Father, but there is such a difference in our spiritual conditions that the contrast between Jesus and us is so great that we can readily believe that he is the greatest true son and that his great love and knowledge of the qualities of the Father is greater than any Celestial spirit. I do not mean in the sense he was created in a different way, physically from other men. No immaculate conception or birth from the womb of a virgin—I do not believe this dogma and the Master says that it is not true for he was truly, so far as his physical being is concerned, the son of a man and woman as you or I am.

Now I am also convinced that mankind cannot be saved from their sins unless they follow the way showed them by the Master. No man can save himself and I wish strongly to emphasize the fact that man is dependent upon God for his salvation from the sins and errors of the material man. I do not mean that men have not a work to do themselves for they have. God is willing to save them if they ask it and acknowledge that without His help they cannot be saved, but unless they do ask and believe He will not interfere with these conditions. So you see I am not only a believer in God and Jesus but also in the doctrine that men cannot save themselves. I thought that man was sufficient unto himself when I was on earth but now I know that he is not. Man may be comparatively happy and free from what is called sin, that is a violation of God's Laws, but that happiness is not the same nor is man's condition the same as when he gets this Divine Love from the Father.

I will not speak longer on this subject tonight but reiterate that when on earth I thought that by my own exertions I might possibly become divine, yet now as a spirit I know that man is not divine and cannot become so in all eternity unless he receives this Divine Essence which comes to him by the New Birth. Divinity is of God alone and only He can bestow it on man. Man not having this divinity cannot create it by his own efforts. So believe what I say and strive to get it and you then succeed and become as the redeemed in the Celestial Spheres.

I am with my earth wife and son a great deal trying to show

them the way and I am glad to say that light is breaking in their hearts and perceptions. I believe that very soon they will fully realize that the only way to get true happiness and peace is through the way of the New Birth.

I am trying to show them this way and they are having more faith in me. And your dear wife is with them too so very much. She seems to have a great influence over them. Especially over Bert, who believes that she is so very good and pure that he wonders why she is such and it causes him to think what she tells him as the cause must be true. Your father is with me a great deal too and he has helped me very much and he is now progressing so rapidly that he will soon be with his soulmate in the fifth (spirit) sphere. Your good mother tells me this and she knows so many things pertaining to spiritual progress.

I must stop now for you are tired and so am I. Well I will tell you of those things the next time I write. So with all my love and blessing, I am your old partner,

A. G. Riddle.[122]

Writes that Riddle's soulmate has a wonderful influence over him and is leading him to the Greater Love

February 20th, 1915.

I am here, Helen.

I am here to tell you that you are my own loving Ned and that I could not let you stop writing until I told you how dear you are to me.

Yes, I am so very, very happy and am willing that you should share it all with me.

Yes, you will hear my voice soon in your own room.

We will then talk love as well as write it. Oh, my darling, how much I love you tonight. I see your heart is open to my love and I want you to get so much of it that you will be happy all the day long.

I must not write much tonight for you are tired and you must not exhaust yourself.

Yes, he is full of love and his faith is very strong. He is a most unusual spirit and is strong for the higher things and will progress very rapidly, I know. He is with his soulmate a great deal and she has a wonderful influence over him and is leading him to the higher thoughts and greater love.

Alice is progressing. She is praying and believing she will soon be in the third sphere and she loves you so much and wants you to love her

---

[122] This message is a composite of two, being published in Volume II and Volume IV. (G.J.C.)

and continue to pray for her.

He says, that you need not ask his father, for he loves you too much to get offended. You must love him more and believe in him more and he will give you a communication that will satisfy you.

She is here, and says that you are very good to think of her and love her and that she returns your love and hopes that very soon we may all be able to talk as you desire. She is now trying to bring about conditions that will enable us to succeed.

I will stop and say good night.

Your own dear and loving,

Helen.

A schoolboy friend writes about his experiences on earth and in the spirit world

October 29th, 1915.

I am here, Peter D. Buerly.[123]

I am the spirit of your old schoolboy days, Peter D. Buerly. I have been here several times when you were writing, and have been much interested in what I saw and heard, and when Cousin Sally came last night and wrote and recalled old times, I felt that I wanted to write also, so I am trying.

As you may have heard, in the long years after we left school I became quite a dissipated man, given to drink and other things that I need not mention, and continued these habits up to the day of my death. I caused Nannie much unhappiness, and, in fact, almost broke her heart, for she was a mild, loving girl, and my treatment of her was such as to give her many weary and suffering hours of anguish. Oh, how I have repented for this since I came into the spirit world, and how I have suffered and undergone many, many years of darkness. But repentance was earnest, and I am commencing to see the light. And, besides, since she came over she has been with me and forgiven me all my harsh words and neglect and bad treatment of her. So you see, there is nothing in the world like the pure, forgiving love of a noble and sympathetic woman—and she was such.

We do not live together for she is a much purer and elevated spirit than I am, but she comes to me and tries to cheer and encourage me with her love and beautiful words of promise.

She is, she says, in the third sphere, where, she tells me, much happiness is; while I am in the earth plane yet, but in a much brighter condition than when I first came over.

---

[123] This surname is perhaps incorrect and might be Byerly. (G.J.C.)

343

But, I want to express my surprise that you can receive communications from spirits as you do. I don't quite understand it. When on earth I never knew anything about such phenomena, and I have only recently heard of your being so close to us and so easy to communicate with.

I wish that I could get with my Nannie, for there I know I would be so happy. Some of these spirits say that you can help the spirits in these lower planes, and if that is so I would like for you to help me.

Well, I have looked, and I see a number of very beautiful spirits, but do not know any of them, and I wonder who they are. I have done so, and, I'll be damned, if there ain't Prof. Salyards. Why, what does it mean? Well, he has come to me and shaken my hand, and says that he is very glad to see me, and wants me to go with him. He has introduced me to a beautiful spirit, who, he says, is your wife. What beauty and love! You must be glad to have such a wife.

I have told her, and she says she is so glad to meet me, and that she wants me to go with her after the Prof. has finished his conversation, and I am going with her. But, tell me, what does it all mean? I can't understand

I must stop—good night,

Peter D. Buerly.

A brother lawyer wishes that he was more religious when on earth, but now he is learning the spiritual laws to live by

December 9th, 1915.

I am here, your old friend and brother Lawyer, Samuel C. Mills.

I have been waiting for some time to have an opportunity to write to you, as I have so often waited and seen other spirits write their messages. Yes, your band, or rather that beautiful wife of yours, told the Indian guide that I should write, and he consented. He seems to take a great interest in you and is protecting you from the harmful spirits.

Well, I am in what is called the earth plane and I am not very happy, as I have my recollections of so many things that I did on earth which were contrary to the laws of God, and for which I am now suffering some. But I have been fortunate enough to have the help of some very loving and beautiful spirits, who seem to take so much interest in me and in showing me the way to progress out of my darkness and sufferings.

While on earth I was not a very religious man, yet I always reverenced God and things pertaining to religion, and believed that there was a better place for those who were truly good to go to.

Of course, in the short time that I have been here I have learned a number of truths, and as I am very anxious to get out of my condition of darkness, I made a great effort to believe what these good spirits said to me, and to learn all that I could about these truths.

I now believe that Jesus is the savior of us all by his teachings and love and the great influence he has with the Father.

You certainly are a favored man to be able to receive all these communications from the high spirits who come to you. When on earth I never believed in spiritualism, and I certainly would not have believed that Jesus and his Apostles would write to you, as I now see them do. But how limited is our earth knowledge of these things that pertain to the spirit, or, as some say, the unseen world. The opportunities here to learn the truths are so much greater than on earth, if the spirit really desires and makes the effort to learn.

I thank you very much for having permitted me to write and renew my acquaintance. It is a glorious thing to be able to do this, and know, as I know, that only a thin veil of flesh separates mortals from their loved ones. I will not impose longer tonight, but will say with my best love,

I am your old friend and brother,

Samuel C. Mills.

A personal friend of Mr. Padgett's tells of his experiences in the spirit world and described his work in behalf of the Kingdom

March 7th, 1916.

I am here, Louis I. O'Neil.

Yes, it is he who was called Judge. I merely want to say a word as I have not had the opportunity to write you for a long time.

I am now in a better condition than I was and am in more light and have less suffering thanks to the beautiful spirits with whom you brought me in contact. I find that as I get rid of some of my old beliefs the better I am and the more progress I make and the less darkness surrounds me. Your wife has helped me a great deal and she is a wonderfully beautiful spirit and filled with love and kindness.

I see a number of my old friends, but I am sorry to say that a great many of them are in darkness and suffering. Lyscomb is in a very bad condition and has not progressed any, thus far, though I have tried to help him some, but as you know he had a dogmatic and all-knowing temperament on earth, so he has the same qualities here, and it is hard to make him see things differently from what he thinks they are or should be.

You may know that he frequently visits his old haunts in the neighborhood where he spent so many hours in drink and he is still drinking as he thinks and seems to get a kind of satisfaction out of the deceit and he does not seem to be inclined to turn his thoughts to anything of a higher nature.

I tell you that the appetites of earth are strong with the spirits who come to this world with them unsatisfied or not gotten rid of and it is so sad that he has them to the extent that he has when he passed over. But sometime I hope that he will have an awakening to the true condition of his existence and to the necessity of his having his thoughts away from these things and seeking those things which will enable him to get out of his awful darkness.

Now you must not think from this that I am a very highly developed spirit for I am not, but just as the higher spirits have a work to do, so have I and my work, of course, can be only with those who are in a worse condition than I am and strange as it may seem to you every time I help one of these lower spirits I realize that I help myself. What a wonderful provision of God this is, and if men would only realize this, they would live more in accordance with the Golden Rule.

Yes, I have seen Maurice Smith and John Clark and many others that we both know, and also Perry. He is in a bad condition, too and does not seem to be much inclined to listen to the advice of some spirits who come to him. Your grandmother seems to be trying hard to help him and he seems to have more confidence in her than in any other spirit and at times it looks as if she is helping him and I have no doubt that she is, but then he will relapse back into his old condition and bewail the awful deed that he committed. As you know he was a man of deep conviction and he seems now to have some conviction which holds him to his conditions of suffering and darkness.

Well, if we only knew while on earth what the truths of this spirit world are. You certainly are wonderfully proud (?) to have revealed to you all these things and I am told that the spirits from the Celestial Spheres come to you and give you their messages of truth. I will confirm this is unaccountable and you must wonder too, for when I was on earth I did not know that you had any conception of the things that come to you now. I know that I did not, and that my beliefs were only those which were to rely upon what the Bible taught as I thought, and there was no reality to me in these teachings and the only effect was to create in me beliefs which I now see in many particulars were all wrong. At least they have now been realized and I am told that they will not be and yet they cling to me in a way that holds me to my present condition. I wish when on earth I had known what you now know, for if I had I would, I am certain, be in a better condition of light and happiness.

Well I have written a long time and I feel better for having done so and I thank you for the opportunity. So with my kind regards and in hope that I may come to you at sometime and write again.

Your friend and well wisher,

Louis I. O'Neil.

A brother lawyer of Mr. Padgett's is wondering if the church of today has any value in helping man to prepare himself to properly live in the spirit world

March 19th, 1916.

I am here, E. R. Hay.

Yes, I am, and I am so glad that I can write you. I learned only recently that spirits could write through mortals, when I came to make inquiries I found that you are the mortal through whom they write and I was surprised. Why, my dear fellow, you certainly are favored to have such a power, and I know that many spirits are very thankful that you permitted them to write.

Well, let me see, what shall I say. Well, well, what a wonderful thing, and I am right here to participate myself. I know you don't care to hear from a spirit like myself, as you have so many of the beautiful and bright spirits write you. But say, old fellow, I have met your wife here and she is a beautiful spirit, and so loving and kind. I have talked to her, and she has tried to help me, and she has. Oh, what a favored man you are to have such a wife! Not only so beautiful, but so powerful and majestic! She comes from the Celestial Spheres, and is so filled with what she calls the Divine Love, that I can scarcely look at her at times.

What does all this mean, anyhow? It has not been long since we were both on earth, and yet there is such a difference between her and me. I was a church member and attended to my duties very conscientiously, and I don't know that she did more, and yet, the great difference. I wonder if going to church and conforming to its creeds and ceremonies amount to anything—there must be something else.

She has told me the cause of the difference, but I don't quite comprehend, and I find it hard to turn my thoughts to the things that she has told me of; for the beliefs of my earth life cling to me, and hold me just where I was on earth.

Of course, when I died I did not go to heaven, and I have not seen God or his throne and the angels that we used to sing about, and it causes me to think that there must be some mistake in what I believed with regard to these things; yet I am afraid to let go my beliefs.

I have seen other spirits than your wife who have told me of what they call this Divine Love, and the necessity of having it in my soul in order to progress, but, yet, I doubt, and can't make up my mind to seek for it. It certainly is strange. I wonder what the church is for, if its believers find no more realization of their expectations than I have found.

I am in what is called the earth sphere, and not happy, although I try to make the best of it. There is considerable darkness and some suffering, and I don't appear to find any associates, except those who are unhappy too. I know that if I were on earth I would not associate with such people, but here I can't help it and don't seem to be able to find any other kind. And I tell you, when your wife and several others who are bright and beautiful, come to me, it gives me the greatest joy imaginable.

Yes, I have seen a number of our old lawyer friends, but they are just about as I am—some may be a little happier, but the most of them are just in my condition; and some, I am sorry to say, are in greater darkness and seem to be suffering intensely. There is one who killed himself; he is in a terrible condition, and I believe that he would like to kill himself again if it would put him out of his misery. I feel sorry for him, and wish that I could help him, but what can I do? I can't tell him of the consolation of my church creeds, for I have not found any consolation in them myself.

Well, I have listened to your advice, and I must say that in some particulars, you astonish me; but as you say it is all true, I must try to follow it, at least, until I find that it is not true. It certainly is wonderful that some of the spirits that you name could get in the condition of happiness that you speak of. I will try to do as you say, and as I understand the first thing is an open mind, I will try.

Yes, I see some bright spirits, and among them your wife and she is smiling at me, and now comes to me and says, believe what you have told me; and now she says, here is an old acquaintance of yours, and brings Mr. Riddle to me, and my stars, what a beautiful man he has gotten to be, and so bright and lovely. Well, I am astonished!

He says he remembers me and is glad that he can be with me, and says, that he has some things to tell me which are true and vital to my happiness, and invites me to go with him. And notwithstanding I feel such happiness in being with you and writing to you, I will have to go with him, for I may find what you have told me I can find, if I will only follow the advice that may be given me.

Well, I am certainly glad for this opportunity to write, and I thank you for your talk. I will go now, but I should like to come again sometime, and write.

With my kind regards I will say goodbye.

E. R. Hay.

A brother lawyer is in darkness and is wondering if what he saw Mr. Padgett do to help, another dark spirit could help him also

March 19th, 1916.

I am here, Maurice Smith.

Let me say a word too. As Hay had the opportunity to write I would like to do so also. I will not detain you long as I merely want to let you know that I am alive. Well, I am not very happy, and am in darkness and suffering and don't see any prospect of relief.

I noticed that as he left you he was much happier than when he commenced to talk to you, and I thought that maybe you said something to help him, and that you might help me, also. I know you will, if you can.

I saw some spirit who was very bright looking, but I could not see distinctly or recognize him, and I suppose it was some acquaintance of Hay, that you had something to do with his meeting. Well you surprise me for I did not know that Mr. Riddle was that kind of spirit. I thought that he was like the rest of us lawyers, who all seemed to be grouped together in darkness and suffering, and some say, hell; but I don't like that word and I shall insist that I am in the darkness only, and, besides, if it were hell, I should see the devil and the fires, etc., which I have never seen.

A long time ago, as it seems to me, I saw Taggart, it must have been when he first came over; but I have not seen him for some time, as he appears to have left us.

Well, you astonish me some for I have never thought that you could help a spirit, and in fact I am so astonished at the knowledge that I can communicate to you in the way that I do, that I am ready to believe most anything, and I assure you that I am very willing to follow your advice if there is any hope of my changing my condition for a better one.

Yes, I see some spirits, and they certainly are bright and beautiful—they must belong to another sphere, for I don't often see spirits of that kind, and when I do they don't seem to be quite natural. But, as you have called my attention to them, I see that they are real, and they seem to have looks of love and kindness about them. And now, I see one who is not so bright or beautiful as the others; but he seems to be happy and does not have the darkness surrounding him, and he comes to me and says: "Hello, Maurice, I am glad to see you," and lo, and behold, it is Taggart. Well, don't this beat the devil! Who would have thought that he could look as he does? And he says he is very happy and wants to help me, and will tell me the way to get into a condition similar to his own, and if I want to argue the matter he is ready to do so.

The same old Taggart, ready for an argument. I wonder what he has to say? He says come with him and he will tell me, and I must go.

So thanking you, I will say good night.

Your old friend and fellow lawyer,

Maurice Smith.

Would not permit a dark spirit to write

March 19th, 1916.

I am here, White Eagle.

Lipscomb tried to write and I would not let him because he was drunk[124] and I know you did not want him to write.

Tells of poor Lipscomb trying to write as he imagined that he was intoxicated but of course he was not, although he thought so himself

March 19th, 1916.

I am here, Helen.

Well, you have had some of your old lawyer friends write you, and I was glad of it, for they seemed to be happy in doing so.

The last one was poor Lipscomb, and he imagined that he was intoxicated, but, of course, he was not. He thought so himself; and as you have heard, "thoughts are things."

Well, I am very sorry for him. I have tried once or twice to help him, but I am afraid that I will have to wait some time before I can make any impression on him. He is so earth-bound,[125] and that accursed appetite seems to have such a hold on him that he is completely dominated by it. But time, as you say, will help him.

Well my own dear, I was with you tonight at church and you realized it while the choir was singing, for I could see and feel that your love was flowing to me, and I was very happy.

---

[124] This is in my opinion really a figure of speech. In the Astral Plane, which is often referred to in these messages as the Earth Plane, it is possible to obsess living mortals and experience a shared physical sensation of things like drinking alcohol. But it appears to be of the mind, rather than being real, and is discussed by Helen in the very next message. In the Spirit Spheres spirits do not drink or eat, and have no organs to allow for this, but in the Astral Plane apparently they can, or can to some extent, because Astral bodies are quite different. Astral beings can also produce excreta, it has been reported. (G.J.C.)

[125] An earth-bound entity is an astral being not a spirit being, and in order to move to the Spirit Spheres it has to leave behind or lose its astral body, which prevents it entering the Spirit Spheres. While it may be true as Helen says, that the astral forms are not "real", that could equally be said, and has been said of this physical realm. I have set out what I have learned about the Astral Plane in a small book, "Getting the Hell Out of Here." It is mentioned on the second page of this book. (G.J.C.)

The preacher was very entertaining and his argument on the negative of the proposition was all right, for God's Love is open and waiting for everyone who may seek it, and no one will be deprived of it because of any supposed unpardonable sin. And his second proposition was, in a way, true also; but the conclusion that any man may by his own will and shutting of his soul desires to the influence of the spirit damn himself eternally is wrong. All will be saved either in the spirit world or the Celestial Heavens ultimately. Such sermons, while not expositions of the full truth, yet may do some good by awakening the hearers to a realization of their actual condition and need for the things of the spirit.

Well sweetheart, I must not write longer tonight as it is late. So with all my love, I will say, believe that I love you and am with you in all your worries and enjoyments.

Your own true and loving,
Helen.

Dr. Stone became a friend of Nathan Plummer the last three years of life on earth and has continued to help him after he passed into the spirit world

March 15th, 1917.

I am here, Nathan Plummer.

Well, I must write a word, for I was with you at the séance and saw what was going on, and I tell you there were some hellish spirits present, and they had the center of the stage.

How different the séance from what it is when I come to your room, and meet you and the Doctor, and see the other spirits present. Well, well, who would have thought that there could be such a difference in the spirits who congregate!

I know that such séances are not places for me, wicked as I am, and this I see with greater clearness now that I know that there are in this spirit world so many spirits who are good and beautiful.

I am doing what I told you I would do in my last letter, but have not yet felt any change, but the good spirits tell me to pray, and I am doing it, with all the energy that I used to give to my swearing, and I could swear some when the occasion arose.

Forrest is growing brighter looking, and he tells me that I can get bright too, and I believe him and I don't intend to let any of these devilish spirits keep me back, if prayer will help me. Tell the Doctor that his prayers help me, and that he must not stop, for I haven't many on earth to pray for me, and I am afraid that the prayers of most of my mortal friends would not do me much good anyhow.

Well, I must stop, so good night.

Your old friend,
Plummer.

Writes that the séance that Mr. Padgett and Dr. Stone attended is detrimental to their own spiritual progression and Mary says that she would not permit any of these spirits to come near her soulmate

March 15th, 1917.

I am here, Helen.

Well dear, I was with you, of course, at the séance, and what has been told you is true, and I need not repeat what has been said, but will add only, that you and the Doctor must take the advice given you. It is absolutely necessary.

Your work is different, and only you can do it. No other medium can do it, and if you were like them you could not do it, either. So you and the Doctor must remember that you have been selected for a higher work than helping to bring spirits and mortals together in communications, such as it is supposed the mediums of tonight brought to the people who were present.

The spirits who the medium said were your grandparents, were not such, but were merely spirits who attend her séances and delight in inducing the expectant visitors to believe are really the spirits of their departed friends or relatives. I saw that the whole thing made no impression on you, except one of pity for the medium that she would be subjected to such imposition and evil influences.

When the howling Indians, as the medium described them, came to the Doctor he must have been surprised to learn that he had a new spirit band of such lively antics to help him in his work of love of curing the sick, and Mary said that she would not let such spirits get in rapport with her sweetheart, even if she had to call on all his guides and yours too, to keep them away. She said that there was nothing about the Doctor to attract such beings to him, and that she would pity him if he had to have such companions around him.

Well, there were all kinds of spirits present, but none of them whom the medium supposed that she saw or heard talk, belonged to either you or the Doctor, and we rather enjoyed the thoughts that he had when his new friends were introduced to him.

But, dear, these séances do you no good, and it is only a waste of time to attend them, and I want to advise that you do not; and further I want to say, that the messages that the Doctor reads do no good, for the people who hear him look upon them as mere stories of the imagination, interesting, but without effect on the spiritual understanding. They are not in condition to grasp the significance of them, and their chief interest is in receiving some message that the medium may transmit to them from their spirit friends. So, these messages do no good at such places. They are like the teachings of Jesus that fell on stony ground; they will not take any root.

So, I do not think it best to read them to these people. The Doctor is doing a good work when he tells them to the individuals with whom he comes in private conversation, and who listen to him with a view and desire to learn the truth, or even when they have not such desire, because as they listen some of the truths may find a lodgment, and germinate.

So with my love, I will say good night,

Your own true and loving,

Helen.

Old friend of Mr. Padgett and Dr. Stone tells how happy he now is, thanks to the Father's Divine Love in his soul

I am here, Nathan Plummer.

Well, I am glad to be with you and the Doctor again, as I am very different from what I was when I last wrote the Doctor.

I don't know just how to tell you what my condition is, but as I told you it was hard to learn heavenly things in hell, I now tell you it is hard to describe the heavenly things which are now mine and which to me are more wonderful than I could ever conceive of, even when I was in dreamland on earth, as I sometimes was.

I am in the Third Sphere, and with such beautiful spirits, all having this Love of which you and the Doctor tried to tell me when on earth, and which you told me so many times of after I came to the spirit world. My home is something that I cannot describe, and I will not try; but you can let your imaginations work, and at the same time remember the descriptions of heavens that you may have heard from other spirits. And my happiness is beyond compare, and I am enjoying it, you may rest assured. As I used to swear with all my soul, I now pray with all my soul, but my soul now has much of this Great Love.

Well, to think of all the changes that have happened in the short time since I left you on earth, makes me realize that the Love of the Father is beyond all comprehension of mortals. And I also realize that a very little thing made all this glory and happiness possible for me—I mean the few talks that I had with the Doctor and you when on earth.

I have been with my brother a great deal lately, for I can see that he will soon be in the spirit world, and I am so anxious that some of the truth may come to him before he passes. I am glad that the Doctor talked to him as he did, and read him the messages, and also sent him the ones that I wrote, for he has read them more than once, and he has commenced to think of some of the truths that they contain. He is not yet able to comprehend their meaning, but when he comes over, he will find it easier to realize conditions, and be the more ready to understand and believe what may be told him by the spirits here.

My wife is progressing also, and yet a strange thing appears in her case, and that is that she has not been able to progress as rapidly as I have. I was a very wicked man and she was a good Christian woman, but my wickedness has not kept me back so much as have her Christian beliefs. While she knows that some things she believed are untrue, and that she must get rid of other things of her earth belief and that they have been disappointing to her, yet she does not seem to be able to give them up entirely and seems, therefore, to be kept back in her progress. This is strange to me.

Well, give my best love to the Doctor and tell him that what he told me as a belief of his I know to be true, and I am happy in my knowledge.

Good night. With my love, I am
Your old friend,
Plummer.

Comments on the book that Mr. Padgett was reading, "The Life Beyond Death"

April 19th, 1919.

I am here, your own true and loving Helen.

Well my dear, I see that you have been very much interested in the book ("The life beyond death" by Yogi Ramasharaka) that you have been reading, and also in many of the truths that it contains, as well as in many untruths that are set forth. The writer of the book knows not as a fact the things that he has therein written, but has compiled the statements from other works that were written, long ago by men who were of the oriental religions, and who wrote as they conceived the truth of existence to be, both in the earth world and in the spirit world.

They were possessed of a combination of concepts that came to them in their moments of meditation and in their moments of being wide awake to the conditions of the present life, I mean the earth life. They are not an authority, and while they have many of the truths of the other side of life, yet they must not be relied on for definite and authoritative information. I will come soon and write to you on the subject of the rebirth or reincarnation, and show you that it has no foundation in fact or in the economy of God's creation of the human soul. Man, when he once gives up his earth life, never returns to it again in the way described in the book, but only in his spirit form, as I am now doing.[126]

Well, dear, you are in better condition tonight, and the higher spirits will soon come and write you. The Master is not here tonight,[127] as he has gone to the Celestial Heavens, where he may not hear the praise and worship ascend to him as God, and the redeemer of the world by his death and resurrection, subjects which are wholly untrue and very distasteful to him.

If men would only understand the true resurrection, how much they would be benefited and progress in their soul development. He arose from the dead while yet living, and when his physical death took place the resurrection had already occurred, and the truth of the resurrection from the dead had already been demonstrated. He will soon come and write you.

I will not write more now, and with my love will say, good night.
Your own true and loving,
Helen.

Writes about the visit that Mr. Padgett made with Dr. Stone to Dr. Arbelee who was in a condition of death

April 23rd, 1919.

I am here, Helen.

Well my dear, I see that you have done a good work tonight towards one poor soul (Dr. Arbelee) who is in a condition of death, and that your conversation will have an effect upon his soul that will lead him to wish for the Love of the Father. He was much impressed by your talk and many of his spirit friends were present and listened to your explanation of the Love and the way to obtain it, and were somewhat astonished at your doctrine. They are living in the belief that the Christianity as explained by the teachers and ministers of the churches leads them into, and were much affected by the teachings which you expounded. They are very anxious to learn the way and some of them accompanied you home and listened to the conversation of yourself and

---

[126] This may come as a surprise to some, but the Padgett messages consistently reject reincarnation as ever occurring for mortals, in fact Jesus delivered a message via Dr. Samuels explaining why it is physically impossible. I have studied the matter for over ten years, and written a book called "Is Reincarnation an Illusion?" which explores all the issues in some depth, as there are elements of apparent proof that cannot be denied. This can be bought from Lulu in print form or at Amazon in Kindle format and is included on the second page of this volume. (G.J.C.)

[127] This was obviously the Easter period, and as is the case also at Christmas, Jesus dislikes the worship directed at him, and removes himself from its influence. (G.J.C.)

the Doctor. (Dr.Leslie Stone)

Some are here now and desire to write, but we tell them that it is too late, and that if they come tomorrow night they shall have the opportunity to write. The sick man's father was among the spirits who were present, and is very anxious to write to his son and corroborate what you said to him, and tomorrow night he desires to write you, so you must be prepared to let him write.

Well, we were present and the drawing power that you experienced came from the exercise of the desires of many of these friends of the sick man to communicate with you, and if we had permitted, they would have taken possession of you and made their wishes known. But we did not think it best for them to control you, and so we told them and they desisted.

The power which you felt going out of you was directed towards the sick man, and if it had continued he would have realized that there was some power or influence which was working on him for his benefit; and as it is, I think that he will feel the results of the power on his physical condition and find himself feeling much better. He is paralyzed and needs the help of the spirits to bring about his cure, and some of them will be with Dr. Stone when he next treats the man, and he will realize that some unseen power is helping him. I will not write more of the occurrence now, but let the spirits themselves tell you of the scene. So do not try to get more messages now, as you need your strength reserved.

I am happy to tell you that you are in better condition tonight to receive our messages and your worries have left you to a large extent, and if you will only listen to and take the advice that John gave you tonight, you will soon feel yourself again and become suited to do the work that is before you.

We all love you very much and are trying to help you in every way. The spirit who advises you in your material affairs was here tonight desiring to write you, but has now left. He said though that he is of the same opinion but that you must be a little careful in your estimate of the market, as it may not reach the high that he first told you of, that there has been a large volume of the stock sold or bought lately and that the climax may come a little earlier than he at first thought. He will come tomorrow night and speak for himself.

Baby wants to write, and I told her that soon she shall do so. I will not write more now. So Sweetheart, say good night and go to bed.

Your own true and loving,

Helen.

Comments on the book that Mr. Padgett was reading

April 18th, 1919.

I am here, John B. Johnson.

Let me say just a word. I have been with you tonight as you read the book and saw that in it you found something that agreed with your ideas of what was necessary for men to do in order to regain their conditions of pristine purity from which they fell. Well, these things are very helpful and true, and when the author said that men should exercise self-control, he stated a truth which is necessary that they may attain to a condition of purification. It will not do for men to teach and believe that they have a higher self which as soon as relieved from the burdens of the lower self, which takes place at death, is sufficient to make that man's soul fitted for the heavenly kingdom.

No, the soul is one and the self is one, and unless that self is purified by the efforts and struggles of man himself, he will never become a pure spirit and fitted to occupy the place that was his before the fall. I was interested in the book, and saw that it contained much of the truth that applies to man as the mere man. It knows nothing of the Celestial Angel or the manner in which the soul of man can become transformed into the Divine Essence of the Father, but has many suggestions, which, if followed, will lead into the way of the perfect man. This is all that I intended to say tonight.

Your friend,
John B. Johnson.

Confirms the writer to be a very beautiful spirit

April 18th, 1919.

I am here, your own true and loving Helen.

Well dear, I see that you have been much interested in the book that you have read, and the spirit who wrote you is a very beautiful spirit, and of the Celestial Heavens, but I do not know him. He wanted so much to write you, and we thought it best that he should do so.

I understand how you have been feeling today, and am not disappointed that you did not give me the opportunity to write tonight, for I will come again and write you. You are now in better condition than you have been for several days, and you must pray to the Father for an increase of His Love in your soul and for greater faith, so that you may do the work that is before you. We are all anxious that you receive our messages and the benefit of the increased Love.

I will not write more tonight, for you had better go to bed and get up early and attend to your business. Turn your thoughts to your mission and then with all the powers of your own soul, and with the help that will be given you by the spirits without your disposition to take things in the easy manner that you do. Yours is a work that needs courage and determination and fortitude, and you must try to let these qualities possess your soul. Well my dear Ned, I will say good night.

Your own true and loving,
Helen.

Writes about the many errors in the Bible

September 5th, 1915.

I am here, Luther—Martin Luther.

I came again because I want to tell you that I was with you this afternoon when you were reading the comments on the origin and different versions of the Bible. Among them was a reference to my version, and I want to say that while my version was a pretty correct translation, yet the manuscripts and other versions, upon which I based my translation, were not the real writings of those who profess to have written them. I mean that those manuscripts were not true copies of the original epistles and books written by those whose names they bear. Many interpretations and new constructions were given to the texts of the originals than you or any other mortal are aware of.

The Bible as now written and as I translated it, is full of contradictions and errors and makes the truth hard to ascertain. Take for instance that one subject of the blood redemption. No greater error was ever written than that the blood of Jesus saves from sin, or that his blood washes away sin. It seems to me now, so absurd that I wonder and am astonished that I could ever have believed in such an absurdity.

I know now that there is no efficacy in Jesus' blood to accomplish any such results, and the pity is that many men do so believe, and, as a consequence, neglect the one vital and important requirement necessary to salvation, that is the New Birth. This and this only saves men from their sins and fits them to enter the Kingdom of God, which is the Kingdom of Jesus, for he is the Prince of that Kingdom, and the ruler thereof.

Jesus never said any such thing, for he has told me so. This saying that his blood was shed for man, is not true. He never said it, neither did he say "drink the wine", being his blood, in remembrance of him, for the wine is not his blood, and neither does it represent anything that has to do with him or his mission on earth, or his present work in the spirit world. How unfortunate that this saying is made to represent something that he did not say.

So in order to understand the real truths of God and man's relationship to Him and His plan of salvation, you must believe what the Master shall write you and what his apostles may write, for now they understand what his true mission was, and what he attempted and intended to teach when on earth, and what he is teaching now.

I also will write sometimes and give you the result of my instructions and knowledge as I received them since being here. I will not write more to night.

Your brother in Christ, Martin Luther.[128]

Corroborates what Luther has written about the errors in the Bible

July 25th, 1916.

I am here, Luke.

I merely come to corroborate what Luther has written, as I am one of those who have set the causes in operation. You may believe what is said, and your realization will not be long postponed. I will not write more tonight.

I did not write the Gospel or the Acts, as they are now contained in the Bible. I wrote a Gospel and also a book called the Acts, But my writings were not preserved, and in the copying and translating of them many things were eliminated and many things added. Of course, I cannot tell you now what these things are, but before our messages are finished you will know of many truths which will explain this matter. I am really the Luke who wrote the Gospel and the Acts which were the supposed originals of what the Bible now contains.

So with my love and blessings I will say, good night.

Your brother in Christ,

Luke.

Comments on the book that Mr. Padgett was reading about spiritualism

June 18th, 1919.

I am here, Spencer.

And want to say just a word to your friend who is so much interested in the discovery of the truths of the spirit world and of the facts that exist in that world.

---

[128] This message is a composite of two, being published in Volume II and Volume IV. (G.J.C.)

Well, I have been with you as you discussed these prospects, and also the writings of the men who have become converted to spiritualism, and saw that you are not satisfied with what the writings contained, and wished that these men might know the truth that they could declare it to the world.

Well, you must wait content until your messages are finished and in shape to publish before these truths can be made to the world. These men who are having the experiences of which they write are doing a good work in publishing accounts of the same in this: that they are preparing the minds of their readers to accept the truth of spiritualism whenever the same shall be published. They are breaking up the fallow ground and making it ready to receive the seeds of truth as they shall become scattered over the soil that was so lately barren and unfitted to receive and nurture these seeds. The work is one that will result in much good and will gradually lead man to accept as true and coming from the spirit world, what they would not otherwise receive.

I merely wanted to write this little message so that you and your friend may not think that the publications, such as you have read tonight, are worthless and without a function in causing men to believe in the lower truths of spiritualism. They are very valuable to mankind in general and to those philosophers and scientists who are more interested in the physical aspect of the study. They must be encouraged and you must not think that their appearing is merely a waste of time or effort. They are the ABC's of spiritualism and must be learned before you can expect the higher or more spiritual truths to be received.

Well, I will not write more now. Good night.

Your friend,

Spencer.

I was a scientist when on earth and supposed agnostic, but I know better now.

Wrote through Eugene Morgan that he is realizing what Dr. Stone had told him when he was on earth

I am here, Dr. Arbelee.

Let me make a statement; I am now a spirit and I am realizing what the Doctor told me I would probably encounter, only it is far worse than I could conceive of or describe it. He actually expressed it to me. I am in miserable condition and my darkness and suffering are almost unendurable; yet there is no way to avoid them. There is nothing desirable here. It all must be borne with. I will say a word as to the spiritual things the Doctor used to talk about. I am, as I said, in darkness and suffering. Yet I am not without hope, for I remember what the

Doctor said to me, and I know that God is Love and I must not attribute to Him my suffering and that their duration is dependent on myself. I thank God that I possess this knowledge, as without it I do not see how I could exist, though, of course, I would. May I ask a question? I want to know, may I come at sometime and write an extensive communication to my wife.

I will try and get this consent to my writing, as I desire very much to do so. You are, I am told, possessed of wonderful powers and can cause spirits in this plane to visualize those of the higher planes. Will you do this for me?

I am Dr. Arbelee of U St. in Washington, D.C. [129]

I have not met a spirit or my father. I am astonished, as when you spoke a beautiful spirit appeared and when he spoke, I saw it was my father. Who could believe such a thing is possible. You are indeed as wonderful as you say you are. Oh! I am so happy to meet my father, as when he did come, I was reflecting on the vastness of this world which is so infinite, that it was next to impossible to locate anyone who was not immediately about us. I thank you for your kindness and now will go with my father, who says that he will show me the way out of my darkness.

Dr. Arbelee.

IWas present when Mr. Padgett and Dr. Stone were discussing the Divine Love of the Father, and became interested because he only knew about the natural love

December 24th, 1917.

I am here, Immanuel Kant.

I have listened to your conversation tonight and have been much interested, so much that I have wondered what the source of your apparent beliefs is, for I see that you are sincere in your declarations of what you declare the truths to be.

I have been in the spirit world for a great many years, and have not been idle as regards my investigation of the truth, and have given my very strenuous efforts to learn the truth of man's destiny and the ultimate end of his existence. I was a thinker when on earth, and had a

---

[129] I was present when Dr. Arbelee wrote through Eugene Morgan. I used to give him treatments. I also introduced him to Mr. Padgett and the Doctor's father wrote to his son through Mr. Padgett a very beautiful letter, and explained to his son while he was in the flesh, many important truths that lead to progress from the lower spheres into the Heavens. While the Doctor was writing his message through Eugene Morgan, I asked Dr. Arbelee if he had met his father. I knew that his father would be able to help his son if he would make the favorable conditions that would enable Eugene Morgan to cause the Doctor to visualize his father. (Dr. L. Stone)

considerable reputation as to being a deep thinker of things metaphysical and even today I have a large following among those mortals who give their time and attention to the investigation of the truths of the nature spoken of.

I have progressed very much, not only in the spheres in which I have lived, but also in the development of my intellect and in the development of my soul, for I enjoy a very considerable happiness, and have been able to apply the moral principles that should govern men in their relation to one another and to God, and have experienced the benefit of such application. I have many associates like myself in development of the dualities mentioned, and often do we assemble and discuss these important principles of man's relationship to God and to the development of man and the aim and ultimate destiny of his existence.

Truth is, we know, of itself alone, and never changes, and when we believe and are convinced that we have found a truth, we accept it as a basis upon which to found our further efforts for investigation and the discovery of other truths, and, as a consequence, we are not compelled to depend upon mere speculation as we were when on earth. We know that the spirit of man never ceases to live, and, hence, immortality must be his certain portion in the great economy of God, and that, as the law of being is progression; we must always be enabled to progress. And having that fact from which to start we continue our investigations and studies in the certain belief that their results will be the discovery of the truths, and that we must ultimately find the reason for man's existence, and his final destiny.

But from what I have heard you and your friend say, there must be a branch of truth that I or my friends, have never heard of or attempted to investigate, and to me it sounds very attractive, and so much so, that I would like to have some enlightenment from which I may be able to postulate a premise upon which I may build a superstructure if possible. I have, of course, heard a great deal of love and the purification of the soul, and the necessity for men and spirit striving to get rid of all those things that contaminate the soul and foster the continuation of the in-harmony that now exists and keeps man from becoming the perfect man, and spirit also.

I have heard that in the higher spiritual kingdom there are spirits of men that have become perfect and existing in harmony with the laws of God, yet they do not claim to be more than men—perfect men. But you talk of a love that will make men, or the souls of men, divine, in their constituency, and therefore, a part of that divinity which we ascribe only to the Infinite; and I must tell you that what you say has opened up to me a new vision of possibility of study that may lead to what we now have no conception of.

I am sincere in what I write, and if you can help me in entering on the study of the truths of which you speak, I will be very grateful, and assure you that it will not be lost on an inattentive ear or a mind stunted by a belief that it already knows all that can be acquired, or the way to acquire all that may be learned. I was on earth a philosopher and known as:

Immanuel Kant.

Was also present during conversation of Divine Love and the transformation of the soul into what was called the Essence of the Father

January 24th, 1917.

I am here, William B. Cornelies.

Let me write and tell you that I have listened to your conversation tonight, and have been much interested in what has been said, and especially in that part of your talk where you spoke of the Divine Love and the transformation of the soul into what you called the Essence of the Father.

Well, I desire to say that I have considered spiritual or religious matters for a long time and the ideas that you have expressed are new to me, and open up to my investigation a new field of the possibilities of the soul in its progress. It may seem strange to you that I, who have been in the spirit world for a great many years and been interested in the investigation of what I considered spiritual truths should not have heard of this doctrine of the transformation of the soul into the Essence of God, but it is a fact. Of course, I have come in contact with many variety of spirits, and some who claim to possess this Divine Love, but I never entered into any conversation or discussion with them as to this question, as I was satisfied that they were spirits who had imbibed on earth the orthodox Christian beliefs, and were still possessed of the same, and that their claims to what they called this love, were based upon what might be called their beliefs in an imaginary, insubstantial something, which satisfied them, but which was not worthy of the consideration of spirits who had given their whole lives in the spirit world, to the study of spiritual truths, based upon the laws of the spirit world as they became known to the intellects of men, capable of studying and analyzing these laws, and the truths that they contained.

I have many associates who devote their time and thought to the investigation of these laws and the truths that are deducible from them, and who are men, or rather spirits, who do not accept anything or declaration as a truth that cannot be proved by scientific principles and tests. We, of course, are not of the sentimental or transcendental kind, but confine ourselves to the pure and exact investigation of the laws that govern what we perceive to be the actual condition of spirit substances. But your conversation has made an impression on me, and perceiving that you men are earnest in your discussion, and seem to have a firm conviction as to the truth of the fact that the souls of men and spirits may be transformed by this love, with which I am not acquainted, I commenced to think that there may be some spiritual truths that lie beyond the scope of the investigations that I and my companions may have given to spiritual truths. And so thinking I should like to ask you some questions as to these matters, and if possible, learn if as a truth, there exists such a thing as this Divine Love as contradistinguished from the love that we all possess to a greater or lesser degree. So if you are inclined to answer my questions I should like to propound to you a few at this time.

Well I have heard what you said, and I have asked if Prof. Salyards is present, and a beautiful intellectual looking spirit comes to me and says that he is the Prof. and that he knows what you said and that it will give him great pleasure to answer my questions and to give me a full explanation of what this Divine Love is and the manner in which it transforms the soul into the Essence of the Father. And he directs my attention to a number of bright spirits, and says that they are living examples of the fact of the existence of this Love, and of the effect that it has on the souls of spirits who possess it. And he says further, that as the appearance of the spirit body discloses the condition of the soul, that if I will look carefully I will find an appearance in all these spirits that I do not find in spirits who do not claim to possess this love. And upon a careful scrutiny I realize that what he says is true.

He invites me to a conversation, and I will go with him. I thank you for your consideration and will bid you good night. Very respectfully yours,

William B. Cornelies.

I was an inhabitant of England.

Is very much interested in the writing just received from the Englishman, but disappointed that the Master could not write

January 24th, 1917.

I am here, Helen.

Well my dear, I see that you are tired and must go to bed, and I will not write very much. I was interested in the message that you received from the man who wanted to learn of the Divine Love, and he was very serious in his requests and seemed to have much pleasure in going with the Professor, who will instruct him fully.

Mrs. Stone was also very happy that she could write and tell the Dr. of her love, and Kate was also serious when she advised the Dr. to get married. It will undoubtedly be a wise thing for him to do as well as for you, as I have told you your life is too lonesome a one. You need companionship.[130]

I was disappointed tonight that the Master did not write. He was present in the early part of the evening, but the dark spirits were so persistent in their efforts to write, and so disappointed that they could not succeed, that the Master thought it best not to interfere, and so postponed his writing. He will come soon. You were in good condition tonight for writing. I will not write more. So believe that I love you and love me in return and give me my kisses. You are a dear boy to treat me in that way. I was not in a hurry to sign myself.

Your own true loving,
Helen.

Is grateful to Dr. Stone for his work in saving his soul

I am here, Nathan Plummer.

Well, how are you? I have to break in whenever I get the opportunity and it is agreeable to the other spirits. I come for only a moment for I know that you both will like to have one word from me.

Well, I am progressing and my soul is so very happy with the love and the beautiful home that I love. I am no more the fighting, swearing and disagreeable Plummer but a spirit who has in his soul some of the love and good feeling for all spirits and man as well. If Dr. Stone could really understand my condition and then realize that he is very largely the cause of my happiness, I know that he would feel that he had great reasons for being happy and for thanking the Father that he was the means of causing one poor soul to get out of hell, even though that soul was that of Nate Plummer and to mortals did not amount to very much.

Oh, I tell you that one soul saved is worth to the one who is the means of saving it more than all the success of life in the mortal world and will certainly bring its reward when that mortal comes to the spirit world. I know this without being told, for I know what my soul was when I was in hell and what it is now, and I also know the condition of the soul of those who were my companions in hell that are now, for many are still there.

So I am very grateful tonight and I felt that I must express that gratitude.

---

[130] It would appear that this did happen, although I am uncertain if he actually re-married. The lady was called Ella. (G.J.C.)

I must stop. Good night.
Your friend,
Plummer.

Writes about his progress from darkness

I am here, Nathan Plummer.

Let me write a few lines as I am anxious to tell the Doctor that he is not the only one who knows something about the Divine Love, although he knew about it before I did and told me of it when I did not know what he was talking about. But now I know something of what it means, thanks to him and the bright spirits who came to my help.

Well, you may imagine who I am, and will no doubt feel glad that I am no longer in darkness, but have gotten into one of the bright spheres. Well, I am certainly surprised that I am no longer a dweller among the dark spirits and have the certainty that this Love is the thing that can make a hellish spirit one with love and happiness in his soul. I am now praying with all my strength and am not satisfied with my progress, although when I think of what I was and what I now am, it seems that some great miracle has been performed, and so it has.

I now no longer want to be deaf, for now I can hear beautiful music and loving expressions from spirits who are my associates and possessors of this Love to a greater degree than even I possess.

Well, Doctor, I cannot tell you how much I now realize the good fortune that was mine in knowing you on earth and having you tell me of things that were so new to me and which sounded so unreal, but which I now know were all true and the means of my salvation. You would scarcely know me if you could see me, for I am now, they tell me, real handsome, and I reckon I am, for I feel that from being a devil I have turned into a comparatively good spirit, and when I further tell you that I no longer indulge in thoughts that were so natural to me when on earth, and that seemed to be a part of my nature, I know that you will rejoice with me.

My wife has progressed too, for she says that she met so many spirits in darkness who all believed as she did when on earth, and so many others full of light and beauty who did not believe as she did when she was in darkness. So she just had to think that there was something wrong in the beliefs of those in darkness, and she must turn to the bright spirits and take their advice and pray only to the Father to fill her soul with His Divine Love.

She regrets that she did not believe you, when you told her on earth before she left the mortal body.

Well, I am glad to write you in this way and let you know that how devilish and wicked a man may be when he gets the Divine Love he will become a better man and started on his way to the true life of the spirit world.

I will not write more now but again express my gratitude and love and good night.

Your old friend,
Nathan Plummer.[131]

Is grateful for the help given to him while on earth by Dr. Stone

February 8th, 1917.

I am here, Nathan Plummer.

Let me say a word now. I am not his mother and can't write as his mother does, but I am grateful too, for I now have some hope and a part of the cause is what he told me while on earth. He may not realize just how the things that he said to me may have this effect. But they have, for when the spirits of his friends told me of what I may hope for if I will only believe and try to get the love that they told me of then I think of what he said to me and it becomes so much easier to believe what these spirits tell me.

I wish I could write longer but I must stop. I am hoping and some light has come to me and I am following Forrest, who I know was as great sinner as I was, and now a very beautiful sinner. I am commencing to learn some of those heavenly things in hell but it is hard, as I said.

Your old friend,
Nathan Plummer.[132]

---

[131] I was closely associated with Nathan and his wife and for a time lived at their home in Washington, D.C., and talked to Mrs. Plummer that the blood of Jesus will not wash away her sins and entitle her to go to Heaven. I told her when she was on earth that only the Divine Love entering her soul in response to her soul longings in earnest prayer to the Father will entitle her to enter the Divine Heavens. (Dr. L. Stone)

[132] I used to talk to Nathan Plummer when he was on earth, of the great importance of praying to the Heavenly Father to fill his soul with His Divine Love and he remembered what I told him. Forrest knew him when they both were on earth and were in darkness and suffering after they passed into the hells. Forrest wrote Mr. Padgett and his band helped Forrest to progress and pray for Divine Love and obtained it and he became so much brighter. When Plummer saw the great change in Forrest's appearance, he asked how it was he was so much brighter in his spirit body. Then Forrest told him that he had written through Padgett for help and asked to meet a bright spirit that belonged to Padgett's band, and Forrest told Plummer that these bright spirits told him to pray for the Divine Love and some of this Love had come into his soul, shining through his spirit body, that made the great change in his appearance.

Plummer was so surprised to see this great change in Forrest's appearance and as Plummer wrote Padgett he knew what a great sinner Forrest was on earth. He then realized if Forrest could get out of the hells there was hope without doubt, and it caused

An Englishman from London wanted to contact Dr. Stone to tell him that he is interested in his investigations into spiritualism

October 29th, 1915.

I am here, Samuel R. Smith.

I was a man who lived in the city of London and was a great merchant in things that were sent to India.

I merely want to say, that I, as an Englishman, feel that I want to tell your friend, as an Englishman, in a foreign country, that I am much interested in him and his investigations of the truths of spiritualism. When on earth I was a spiritualist, but I did not know anything of the higher spiritualism which seems to be revealed to you both, and I am sorry that at that time this phase of spiritualism was not known, for if I had been possessed of the knowledge of the truths which this latter spiritualism brings to you, I would be in a more advanced state in my soul development. So I merely want to say this and to tell you both how fortunate you are to have this revelation before you become spirits.

Tell your friend that I am glad to meet him here and will try to help him with all my power and influence.

I am in the fifth sphere, and I passed over in 1867, and am now a seeker after the great Divine Love of the Father which Jesus is teaching in the spirit world.

Excuse me for intruding, but I happened to be present and thought that you would not object very much to my writing a little. So I will say good night.

I am the man who once wrote you that I had such a wonderful mind that there was nothing more for me to learn. You facetiously called me the man with the ponderous mind, and I now enjoy what you said as much as you do. But my friends, that ponderous mind has left me, and I now know that I knew very little of the things of the spirit world, and that there is for me the whole of eternity in which to realize that I cannot learn all that there is to learn.

I have had the pleasure and profit also of associating with some of your band, and other spirits who associate with them, and the result is that, whereas, while on earth and even for a long time in the spirit world,

---

Plummer to seek by earnest prayer for the Divine Love and Plummer did and that enabled him to progress out of the dark condition into a brighter sphere.

As this message was written 47 years ago, I have no doubt both Plummer and Forrest must now be above the seventh sphere in the Celestial Heavens, where these Celestial Spirits are seeking and obtaining the Divine Love in increased progression nearer and nearer to the fountainhead of the Father with the consciousness of the certainty of Immortality. (Dr. L. R. Stone.)

I was an infidel as well as a fool, yet now I am a believer in the teachings of Jesus, who I thought, was a mere fanatic while on earth.

This thing called the Divine Love is the greatest thing in all God's universe, and I know, because I possess some of it, and realize a happiness that I never before possessed.

Your band is doing a wonderful work to the dark and suffering spirits, and I know that its influence must be felt among spirits who come in contact with those who have been helped even though the former have never been with you.

In fact I see that such is the case, and in the great day of reckoning, that is when you shall come over to answer for your thoughts and deeds in the body, you will find that these spirits whom you have helped will be with you and show the results of your endeavors.

So you must excuse me for consuming your time, but I felt that you must be told that I am no longer the spirit who was a fool, but one who has learned that he is of very little importance in the great world of spirits.

So, thanking you, I will say good night.

Samuel R. Smith.

A dark spirit seeks the help of Dr. Stone, he knew him while on earth

May 16th, 1918.

I am here, Charles T. Wilson. Let me write a few lines.

I am the friend of the Dr. and knew him some years ago when he was living in Buffalo, N.Y. I was in a hospital where he was engaged in looking after daffy (insane) mortals, such as I was.

Well, in those days my mind and my brain did not coordinate, and this I know, for a short time after I passed into spirit life I found that I had a mind which enabled me to understand things as I had before the awful blank came to me which resulted in my being incarcerated in the hospital.

What a wonderful experience I had after I became liberated from the imprisonment of my mind in a diseased brain. Then everything appeared to me as if I were a new creature, and the happiness which came to me—I mean the happiness that came from my liberated mind—is beyond what you may conceive of. I can suppose that men think that those whose minds are thus blotted out, as it were, by a brain which has ceased to perform its functions must be not unhappy, because they know not the loss of the benefits that a mind in a sound brain affords. But in this supposition men are mistaken, for while the person thus afflicted may not know of what sound-minded men call real trouble and worry, yet they have troubles which belong to their diseased brains, and to them these troubles, although they may have no real existence, are just as real as are the troubles of these others who think that they are sane. Trouble is a relative thing, and the real to one, though not real, causes as much unhappiness as do the troubles which are real.

Of course, while I was in the flesh I did not fully understand just what my condition of mind was, and many of my vagaries were of such a character as to cause me apparent happiness; and on the other hand, certain other vagaries caused me real suffering. And things of great importance appeared to me with a force that no real existence could surpass.

Shortly after I passed to spirit life these imaginations left me, and with them disappeared the unhappiness which they caused; and it seemed to me as if my mind had been freed from a great burden, and I became so conscious of the fact that it seemed as if I must be in Heaven or some other place of bliss. But it meant nothing more than my mind finding its real condition, and the recollections of my previous life came to me with all their consequences. And, strange as it may seem to you, there were no recollections of anything that happened while I was in the state of mental darkness. Only those things came to my remembrance which were parts of my life before my affliction, and only these latter brought with them a knowledge of good or evil deeds which I had committed.

Since then, I have realized the workings of the laws which controlled my acts of life, and I was happy or otherwise as these laws called for suffering or failed to operate. I have been in the dark planes ever since, though I have made some progress towards the light, or rather the darkness has grown less intense and my sufferings have decreased. My mind has always been alert and nothing has escaped me which was a part of my sane existence while on earth.

I wish that I could find a way to get rid of this darkness and suffering, and as only a few nights ago I heard that you could help spirits in my condition, I determined to seek your help, and tonight when I saw the Dr. with you, I thought it a good opportunity to ask your help.

Yes: and he says that he will help me, and as he is so very beautiful and bright I can easily believe that he can help me, and I am going with him.

So, I thank you.

I was Charles T. Wilson and was called Wash.

Describes conditions in darkness

January 3rd, 1917.

I am here, mother Plummer.

I am a poor old woman and in darkness and so very disappointed for I thought when on earth that the blood of Jesus washed away all my sins and that I would go to heaven and rest in his arms and sing halleluiahs around God's throne, but instead I am in darkness and have never seen Jesus or one of the glorious angels, and thank God though the devil hasn't got me. I have never seen him or any of his imps or brimstone and fire. But the spirits I have seen are devils enough. What does it mean, I was a good Christian as I thought and believed that Jesus died for me and saved me?

I do not know what to do, I am not a stranger to you and the Dr. and I remember some things that he told me about the spirit world and spirits and I have been trying to learn how these things may help me but yet I do not understand. I know that I am alive and never died and that I have the same thoughts and try to believe in my church, but how can I, and I am so disappointed and so anxious to find the light.

My husband has also come over and he has not changed he is the same quarrelsome man although he can hear now. He is so dark and ugly and it seems to me that he is one of the lost souls that the Bible tells of, but I hope not. He is not living with me but says he is in hell and I can believe it. Can you help me or tell me anything that will get me out of my darkness.

Nate says: Dr. Stone knew all about the spirit world and tried to tell us, and we should have listened to him, but how could I when he told me that Jesus did not die for me and save me from my sins.

At this point Mr. Padgett would talk to the dark spirits and tried to increase their soul perceptions to see the bright spirits that were working with him to help those in darkness.

Yes, now I see some bright spirits and one who says that she is Mrs. Stone come to me and says she will help me and I am going with her. Good night.

Mother Plummer, wife of Nathan Plummer.[133]

Father of the Dr. confirms the condition of the spirit that just wrote

I am here, William Stone.

Let me say just one word. I have heard what the spirits have written you tonight and I have seen them as they wrote and I merely

---

[133] I have written that both Mr. and Mrs. Plummer have now progressed into higher spiritual life as a result of the help that Mr. Plummer received and obtained the Divine Love. Mrs. Plummer was helped by Mrs. Stone and since this was 44 years ago, I am sure that she also has received the Divine Love of the Father to enable them both to live in the Celestial Heavens. (Dr. L. R. Stone.)

want to tell you that they were in darkness and suffering and they were in great need of help and this is true. These spirits were not impostors but really whom they represented to be.

I merely say this that you may be assured of the truth of the communications.

Your brother in Christ,
William Stone.

Writes about Dr. Stone's Hindu doctor guide and wants him to believe that he actually wrote and is helping him with his healing work with his patients

April 18th, 1916.

I am here, Helen.

Well sweetheart, I want to say very seriously that Dr. Stone must believe the message that he received from his Hindu doctor guide, for he actually wrote him and seems to have great interest in the case of the sick woman, and will do his best to help the Dr. and in addition, he will find that other and higher powers will also help him, if he will only pray and have faith, and when these powers of the higher spirits come, he will find, as the Christian Scientist say, that there is no reality in the disease that seems to have placed that woman beyond all hope.

Oh, I tell you the power of these spirits is wonderful and if the proper rapport can be established, the Dr. will realize that the power to heal did not die, or was not taken from men, when the last of the Apostles died.

I write this in all seriousness, having a knowledge that this power still exists, and is waiting to be exercised in answer to prayer and faith when the mortal gets into that condition of sincerity and faith that will cause it to come and manifest itself.

So, tell the Dr. to believe that what has been told him is not the fairy story of some spirit who takes delight in planting and encouraging hope, only to end in disappointment. We are all interested in this matter for we desire to have demonstrated again this healing power of God which has been given to mortals in the past, is here waiting for a further demonstration.

We have enjoyed being here tonight and listening to your conversation, and also the atmosphere of love that has been with you. I will not write more tonight, but will say. Wait just a moment, for Mary wants to tell the Dr. that she is so much interested in the case, that he is working with, and that she and his mother were with him when he visited the sick woman,[134] and are so anxious that his ministrations will make her well. She also says: that she wants to tell him the old, but always new, to her, story of how much she loves him.

Well, I must stop so with all my love and a big kiss, and Mary says, one from her too, I will say good night.

Your own true and loving,

Helen.

A Muslim priest tells of the kind of life that they live in their sphere

June 22nd, 1915.

I am here, Abdullah ben Caliph.

I am a spirit of whom you have never heard, and I want to tell you that I am so very much interested in your work in helping the unfortunate spirits. I am not a churchman, but a lover of mankind and a believer in God as the Father of us all. I write by permission of your band, for they know that my love for my fellow man is very great and that I am interested in everything that will help them both in the spirit and material worlds.

I merely want to tell you this, and that not only the spirits called Christians have this love of their fellow man, but also we who are of other religious persuasions.

God is God, and Allah is his name and Mohammad is his prophet. And my name on earth was Abdullah ben Caliph. And I lived more than five hundred years ago in the city of Mecca and was a priest of the Mosque, and had charge of the sacred carpet of the great Prophet.

I live in a sphere that has a name, but is not in the Celestial Spheres that the Christian Spirits tell me exists. In my sphere the Mohammedans live and worship Allah, and adore his prophet. Yet, I see him and he is still preaching the great truths and is happy.

Many others, not of our faith, live in certain planes of this sphere, they are not Christians either, but great intellects, and are working for the material good of humanity. We are working with them in this great purpose.

Well, we have found that there is no marrying here but that each

---

[134] The following notation was made by Dr. Stone when he performed the healing work in 1915: This lady was my patient, and I am happy to write that as the result of the high spirits helping me with their healing powers which enabled me to exercise their powers that finally restored this lady to good health and brought about the removal of suffering and pain that caused her to shed many tears of joy and happiness. She thanked me many times, but I told her to thank the Heavenly Father for sending the high spirits to heal her. (Dr. L. R. Stone.)

of us has one of the opposite sex to live with, and strange as it may seem
to you, and stranger yet it seems to us, we do not desire more than one.
Our dream of having our harems filled with beautiful houris (the
beautiful virgins of the Koranic paradise), was merely a dream. We have
no harems and desire none. Our happiness is complete with only one.

Yes, there is suffering among our faithful in the lower spheres,
and darkness also, but many who have lived in that darkness are now
with me in the heaven of happiness that I tell you of. God is just and he
will not let a guilty one escape. We must all pay the penalties of our
deeds on earth. So you see our Prophet told us the truth about there
being a Paradise for us in the Spirit World.

I thank you for your kindness and will stop.

Your friend and I hope a mutual lover of mankind.

Abdullah ben Caliph the Mohammedan.

Is grateful to Mr. Padgett for his prayer and introduction to his grandmother and is progressing into the light

December 20th, 1916.

I am Caesar.

Pardon me for coming so soon after my message of a few nights
ago, but as I am a grateful spirit even if I was an awful sinner. I want to
tell you that I took your advice and went with your grandmother, and
had opened up to me a whole world of love and truth. Oh, what a wise
and magnificent spirit she is and what love she has, and she treated me
with such kindness and was even like Brutus of old. For in her kindness,
she gave me a stab that killed all my old beliefs and feelings of greatness
and made me in truth a mere nothing and at the same time the greatest
being that I had even been in all my existence, for it showed me that I
was a real child of God and the object of His Love and care, and one that
had all the possibility of becoming in my soul even Godlike. She is my
true friend and when she comes to me it seems that my soul, which had
for so many centuries remained dead and cold, opens up with a flame of
life that her influence brings to me.

I will not write more now. I thought that you were so interested
in me that you would rejoice in knowing that now I have started on the
way to the attaining of that which you told me of. I will come sometime
when I have received more love and write you a long letter, which I hope
will be interesting, for it is a fact that at one time Caesar did write
interesting letters.

So, my friend, pray for me and send me your kind thoughts, and
believe that they will not be misplaced as now I am so anxiously seeking
for that which was not in me for so many centuries. Good night,

Your friend,
Julius Caesar.

Confirms that it was Caesar who actually wrote as well as others

December 20th, 1916.

I am here, your own true and loving Helen.

Well, my dear, you have some messages tonight which show you what the love has done for some of the spirits who were at one time in darkness and suffering. I wanted Mrs. Riddle to write, as she has never written to you and she was very pleased that she could. She is now quite a bright spirit and happy, and is seeking for more of the Love and is believing in the Father. Col. Root was also very happy that he could write, as he says he is progressing and receiving the Love. He seems to be in much earnestness in his longings for the Love and while he had a great many sins to get rid of yet they are falling from him and I do not think it will be very long before he is in light.

Caesar was very anxious to write and tell you of his progress and he seems to realize so very deeply the change in his condition and the power of love to make him a new spirit. He almost idolizes your grandmother and believes her to be the dearest friend in all the spirit heavens. He will come in a short time and write you. He is a very intellectual spirit and will no doubt write you an interesting letter.

I was with you tonight at the show and you felt my presence as the music played. I was in your lap with my arms around your neck and kissed you many times. I was very happy and saw that you were, and that your thoughts as to my being with you were correct. It was a very pleasant evening.

Well, I see that you are feeling better and relieved and I am so glad. Baby feels very much better and is happy. She is a dear girl and now is very anxious to get with you in a home, which she will soon do. You must love her with all your heart and watch over her, for she is the only one you now have who needs your care.[135] She loves you very much. I will come very soon now and write my letter, as I am so very anxious to do so, and tell you some things that you should know. So keep up your courage and love me with all your soul. Give me my kiss and say good night.

Your own true and loving,

---

[135] This is a reference to Helenita, called Nita or Baby who is the daughter of James and Helen. She passed over unexpectedly on June 20th 1918. As she was born November 8th, 1892, she was only 26. (G.J.C.)

Helen.

Attends the services over Mr. Padgett's daughter's (Nita's) remains. The Master was shedding his love and influence over the mourners and near ones

June 21st, 1918.

I am here, John Wesley.

Let me write a line. I was present tonight at the services over your daughter's remains, and saw what a wonderful congregation of high and beautiful spirits was there. Your bands were present and the Master was shedding his love and influence over the mourners and near ones. Your daughter's spirit was also present, and although it seemed a little strange to her that she should be outside her body and could look upon it as it lay cold and dead, yet she understood and was quite happy that so many of her friends were there displaying their sympathy and love. Of course, your wife was present and was radiantly happy in her love for you and her boys and her other relatives. She had her daughter close by her side and was telling her of the truths of the resurrection as the minister read the services, and especially how the Great Love of the Father is necessary to the true resurrection and heaven.

It was a glorious evening with the spirits, and no sorrow or unhappiness was with them, only their sympathy for the human grief of those who did not know the truth of the liberation of the spirit from the bondage of the flesh. Well, I might tell you many things which occurred among the spirit visitors, but I am admonished not to write more, so will say good night.

Your brother in Christ,
John Wesley.

Tells about her daughter's demise and that there were Celestial Spirits present, casting over the people love and influence that only Celestial Spirits can give forth. Baby was with me

June 21st, 1918.

I am here, Helen Padgett.

My own dear husband, how happy I have been tonight as you and the others congregated around the coffin of our baby[136] to pay their

---

[136] Helenita was buried in the family grave at Mount Olivet Cemetery, Frederick., Md on Saturday June 22nd 1918 at 2 p.m. (G.J.C.)

respects and offer their love and sympathy to her memory. As has just been said, many of our Celestial Spirits were present, all casting over the people the love and influence that only Celestial Spirits can give forth. Baby was there with me, and while she did not quite understand all that she saw, yet she realized that her body is now no part of her, and that she lives independently of it, and that the body which she now knows is hers, is so much more beautiful and ethereal.

She was very close to me, and did not attempt to leave my arms, for while she knew that she was no longer a mortal, yet she was timid and felt that she needed me and my love. She is quite beautiful and happy and says that if she is in heaven, she does not want to return to earth or to her body that was lying before her so cold and lifeless. She saw and recognized all who were present and tried to talk to some of them, but found that she could not make them hear, and wondered a little that they did not.

Tonight you must not write more, but must go to bed and get your rest. I will soon write you fully as to our baby. She said though, that she saw how much you must love her, and was so anxious to reply to you as you talked to her. Do not grieve too much for the body, for it is no longer hers and cannot understand or answer your words of sorrow. She is so happy that you love her so much, and will come to you before very long.

Love me and pray to the Father. Good night, and God bless you, my dear Ned.

Your own true and loving,

Helen.

Discloses the fact that Jesus' disciples were men without experience until the Holy Spirit came at Pentecost

October 5th, 1915.

I am here, John, Apostle of Jesus.

I am the apostle, and you need not try me as your friend said, for no spirit can impersonate me when I am present. So you must believe me and try to receive what I may write tonight, in faith, and you will find that you will be benefitted. I came principally to tell you that I have been listening to the conversation between you two and to the reading of the Sermon on the Mount given to us by the Master in the days of long ago, as you would say.

When that sermon was delivered we were not in a condition of great spiritual development, and we did not understand its inner meanings, and as to its literal meaning we thought it was not intended for the practical affairs of life. People, I know, think that we, at that time, were very spiritually developed and had an understanding of the great truths taught by the Master, which were superior to what men have now, but I tell you that this is a mistake. We were comparatively ignorant men, fishermen by occupation, and had no education above the ordinary working man of that time, and when Jesus called us to become his apostles, we were as much surprised and hesitated as much as you did when the similar mission was declared for you.

Our knowledge came with our faith in the great truths which the Master taught, and from our observation of the great powers which he displayed, and also from the influence of the Great Love that he possessed. But when mankind think that we easily understood the great truths which he taught, they are mistaken. Only after the descent upon us of the Holy Spirit at Pentecost did we fully come in accord with the Father, or fully appreciate the great truths that the Master had taught.

Of course we learned many things which men of that time did not know, and our souls became developed to a large extent, but not sufficient to bring us to a knowledge of the wonderful meaning of the truths which made men free and brought them in unison with the Father. In your conversation tonight you discussed the relative value of prayer and works, and did not agree with the preacher, that works are the great things to develop men into love and bring about great happiness in the world, and that prayer is not of such importance.

Now let me, as a spirit and as a man who worked on earth and prayed on earth, say with an authority that arises from actual experience, and knowledge that comes of observation, that of all the important things on earth for men who are seeking salvation and happiness and development of soul, prayer is the most important, for prayer brings from the Father not only Love and blessings, but the condition of mind and intent that will cause men to do the great works that the preacher admonished men to engage in.

Prayer is the cause of the power being given to men that will enable them to do all the great works which will bring reward to the doer, and happiness and benefit to the one who receives the works. So you see the results can never be as great as the cause, for the cause, in this instance, not only gives to men this ability to work, but also to love and to develop his soul and to inspire him with all good and true thoughts. Works are desirable, and in some cases necessary, but prayer is absolutely indispensable. So let you and your friend[137] understand and never doubt, that without prayer the works of men would be unavailing to accomplish the great good which even now man performs for his brother.

Pray, and works will follow. Work, and you may do good, but the

---

[137] Dr Leslie R. Stone was present. (J.P.G.)

soul does not benefit, for God is a God that answers prayer through the ministrations of His angels and through the influence of His Holy Spirit, which works on the interior or real part of man.

I will stop now. So with my love to both of you, I am your brother in Christ,

John.[138]

Tells about Mrs. Kates' séance and there are no animals in the spirit world

April 13th, 1919.

I am here, John T. Richards. Let me write a few lines, as I am very anxious to tell you of what the scene was at the meeting tonight.

There were surrounding you a very great number of spirits of all kinds and conditions. Some were present for the purpose of mere curiosity and others with the desire to communicate with their loved ones of earth; and still others were seeking help and deliverance from their conditions of sufferings and torment.

Mrs. Kates, the medium, tried to give the communications of some of the spirits who were anxious to tell their relatives and friends of their presence and of the condition in which they, the mortals, were in, and advise them as to what is best to be done; and if they will only take the advice, they will be helped.

There was one spirit who tried to make himself known by an unusual method of identification, in having with him a dog which the person to whom the spirit came was enabled to identify, but the spirit was not within his recollection. The dog was a real dog, but not the spirit of any dog that had existed in the human, or rather, earthly form, and the likeness was created by the spirit who tried to have the individual identify him. There are no spirits of dogs, or any other animals, that once had an existence on earth, in the spirit worlds.[139] These appearances are all manufactured by the spirits for the purpose of having the medium see, clairvoyantly, the resemblance of the dog on earth, so that an identification may be made. Dogs and other animals when they die never have any part of themselves that survive death, and become extinct.

---

[138] This message is a composite of two, being published in Volume II and Volume IV. (G.J.C.)

[139] I think that while this may be technically correct, it is rather misleading. There are any number of communications from spirit to illustrate that to all intents and purposes, there will be a spirit equivalent of any animal that is loved by a mortal. Not only do spirits report this, but so do humans who have clairvoyance. That the spirit animal does not have a soul, and is more accurately a termed thought form, is rather immaterial. They exist in the Spirit spheres and give pleasure to those that loved them while on earth. (G.J.C.)

They have no soul and, consequently, nothing that persists after death of the earth form. I was much interested in the séance, and tried to make myself appear to the medium, but was not successful.

The condition of the dark spirits who were seeking help was most pitiable, and the medium for some reason was not able to see or understand their condition, and, hence, no help was given them, and they went away very sorrowful.

You had several spirits around you, but they did not try to manifest themselves, and I doubt if the medium could have seen them had they tried. They were not of the kind who come to her and make their presence known, for her development as a medium is not such as to enable her to see spirits of the kind mentioned. She has not the soul development that is necessary in order that they can make a rapport with her, and hence she can neither see nor hear them.

I will not write more now, so good night.

Your friend,

John T. Richards.

Unknown writer tried to explain what profit it a man if he gain the whole world and lose his own soul?

Let me write tonight, for I find you in condition to receive my message and that you have the Divine Love working actively in your soul. What a great difference in your condition when the Love is active and when it lies dormant or overshadowed by thoughts and feelings that arise by reason of the many cares and disturbances of the flesh.

Well, I desire to write tonight on the subject of what will it profit a man if he gain the whole world and lose his own soul?

I know that this text is often preached from by the preachers, and that it cannot be, and is not, understood by them, because they do not comprehend what it means to lose their own souls; and, consequently, their hearers are not given the benefit of the great truth that is intended to be conveyed by it.

A man is, in the estimation of the world, very favorably circumstanced when he has large wealth and plenty, and when this is increased into the possession of the whole world its importance is beyond conception, and the man so situated is looked upon as the most fortunate man in existence, with nothing further to wish for.

He is then the possessor of everything earthly and there is nothing more to be acquired by him in order to make him happy and contented. This is the supreme wealth of the earth, but lasts only for the lifetime of the man on earth, and after that it has for him no existence, and no power to make him happy, but is as if it had never existed, and then he becomes poor indeed, if this is all that he possesses.

When he enters into the spirit world, his wealth depends not on what he possessed in the earth life, but on those possessions that follow him into the spirit world, and then if he has not that which can give him happiness and contentment, he is in a condition that is to be pitied. These things of earthly wealth have only a temporary existence, and with the life of their possessor, as to him, are no more, and if they were all that he possessed that man would be in a condition of undesirable poverty and want.

There are only two things that man can possibly call his own, as a dweller on earth, and the one is this great wealth, and the other is a soul dormant or active, and on the first depends a temporary happiness, and on the other depends the happiness or misery for a longer or shorter time in the spirit world, and to lose his soul means that he, man, will be deprived of that happiness which may be his through all eternity. . .(loss of rapport - G.J.C.)

Unknown.

Confirms the unknown writer

I am here, your own true and loving Helen.

Well, dear, I see that you are very tired and I must not write much tonight. The spirit who wrote you was disappointed that the rapport gave out, as he had a very important message to convey, and says he will come soon and complete his message.

You are now in good condition and must continue so in order that the spirits may deliver their messages. I should like to write a long letter tonight, but must not, as you are tired.

So love me and believe that we all love you with our whole souls, and say good night.

Your own true and loving,

Helen.

An inhabitant of the sixth sphere speaks of its purity

March 6th, 1919.

I am here, Emerson.

Let me write tonight on a subject that is of importance to mankind and one which so few of mortals know or conceive of in their teachings and philosophy. I am one who inhabits the Sixth Sphere, where the pristine purity of the first man obtains, and where sin or the alienation from God has no existence. You may not know, but it is a fact, that the purity of this sphere is such that the souls of men find only that which makes a man like unto God, and renders him happy and satisfied with his existence and with the divine attributes and nature with which he was created and which God in the infinitude of his powers decreed that man should possess and enjoy to the fullest of his capacity.

I am he whose book[140] you have been reading tonight and who was attracted to you by the fact that you were interested in the book and sought the truths of the soul as therein set forth. The soul is one that while individualized yet is a part of the great Oversoul, and in its aspirations and thoughts of those things that are pure and in harmony with the oversoul has a satisfaction that is complete and at-one with the Father of light and love.

This sphere is one where only the perfected soul can live and bloom and feel its qualities of the divine as perfect, and no soul that has not rid itself of sin can possibly enter. I only know that we who inhabit that sphere have that feeling of purity and perfection that was granted to our first parents and which by them was lost at the time of their disobedience. This soul is very much like unto the great soul of the Father and needs not the qualities that you have known on earth as the one that causes you to realize that the Father has for man a higher and greater existence than the perfect man.

Well, I have lost my rapport and must stop. Good night, Emerson.

Speaks of spiritual phenomena investigations that he used to write about

February 11th, 1919.

I am here, Robert Dale Owen.

Let me say just a word, for I am interested in your work and in the phenomena of spiritualism. I have been with you as you read the (The daily dairy suggests it is his book) book[141] which attempts to show

---

[140] Ralph Waldo Emerson (May 25th, 1803 – April 27th, 1882) was an American essayist, lecturer, and poet, who led the Transcendentalist movement of the mid-19th century. He was seen as a champion of individualism and a prescient critic of the countervailing pressures of society, and he disseminated his thoughts through dozens of published essays and more than 1,500 public lectures across the United States.
Emerson gradually moved away from the religious and social beliefs of his contemporaries, formulating and expressing the philosophy of Transcendentalism in his 1836 essay, Nature. Following this ground-breaking work, he gave a speech entitled "The American Scholar" in 1837, which Oliver Wendell Holmes, Sr. considered to be America's "Intellectual Declaration of Independence." He wrote an essay entitled "The Oversoul" in 1841. (Source: Wikipedia)(G.J.C.)

[141] He was a strong believer in Spiritualism (despite admitting having been duped into believing in a spirit named "Katie King") and was the author of two well-known books on the subject: "Footfalls on the Boundary of Another World" (1859) and "The Debatable Land Between this World and the Next" (1872). (Source: Wikipedia) (G.J.C.)

the truth of spiritual manifestations, and the instances mentioned of spirits showing themselves in the garb of humans are true. I was then an investigator of the question, and had only the knowledge which I received from my own observation, and, hence, was an outsider, as it were, of these spiritual phenomena. I mean that I was not one of the gifted ones of earth, who can have the power of receiving or communicating with spirits by reason of the fact that they possess the power of seeing or feeling or hearing the presence of spirits. I was not so gifted.

I am now an investigator of things spiritual, but not of the possibility of communicating with the spirit world, for this I know to be a fact, and beyond all question, and men who doubt the fact are in the condition of those who will not learn, because they do not believe in the first principles of the phenomena, and are willing to let their prejudices or their indifference lead them away from the truth.

The phenomena which I have portrayed in my book are very simple and of the lower order of spiritual phenomena, and yet men will not believe because they fail to approach the subject with open minds and desire to learn the truth even though the search for the same leads them along lines of investigation that are so foreign to the course of study that they are pursuing in their various vocations. Of all the bigoted and hardheaded investigators of truth, the preachers are the most difficult to teach the truth of spiritualism, and their periscope is one that enables them to see only in a straight line that has been laid down to them for ages and holds them in its iron grasp.

I would like to come to you sometime and write you a long description of the spirit world and its phenomena, although it may not surprise you very much, considering what you have had revealed to you.

Well, you have asked me some questions which I cannot answer in one breath. But I am in the Third Sphere, where many spirits are pursuing their studies of things which pertain to the laws of the spirit world, as well as to the laws of the earth. I have not heard of the Divine Love, except as we call all love divine, and it must be so, for it leads us to the spheres where those who are sinless and in harmony with the Father reside. I am a true believer in the things of God and in the redemption of all mankind, sooner or later. My intellect is only part of my existence in the spirit world, and above and greater than that is the love that causes me to become in harmony with the laws of God, and at-one with him. These are the answers to your questions, and I should like to write you at length upon the truths of what I have so briefly stated. I know that you are very busy in receiving communications from the spirit world and have little time for communications from strangers, yet I should like to write at least one letter in reference to my condition and knowledge of things as I have found them.

I say what is true, for I have never heard of the Divine Love in the sense that you have spoken of. I have never talked with spirits who claim to have this Love, and to be better than are the spirits who are progressing in the love which they have, and as to immortality, I only know that death merely sets the soul of the mortal free and enables it to enter onto its progress towards the higher spheres, where truth and goodness are.

Let me wait a moment in my astonishment, for I see more spirits who seem to be of a different order of spirit from me, and are brighter and more beautiful, and are willing to tell me of the Divine Love, for they all claim to know it. But I do not understand and I am sure that if they are possessed of this Love, it is only another form of belief. I am all confused and cannot think for the moment. I will come again. I must go. Good night,

Robert Dale Owen.

Affirming that Josephus wrote, and comments on the equality of the sexes

June 3rd, 1916.

I am here, your own true Helen.

Well, my dear one, you have had a message from Josephus,[142] that may be considered a women's rights argument, and I have no doubt that womankind will agree with him, especially as to his prediction as to what the future of women will be.

This may be all true, and the predictions may come to pass. I don't know. But this I do know: that as regards the Divine Love of the Father and the conditions in the Celestial Heavens, there is no distinction made between the man and the woman, except as the individual soul development makes the distinction. And when you consider the further fact that the two parts of the one soul, represented by the male and the female, must, in order to make the perfect one, become united in perfect harmony, you can readily understand that there will be no superiority of one over the other, but that both must be equal, not only in love and the nature of the Divine, but in every other quality that may exist.

So in my opinion, instead of women and men thinking about women's rights and such matters, they should devote their thoughts and aspirations to obtaining the Divine Love in their souls, with the certain knowledge that as they obtain it in equal degrees they will become not only the equal of one another, but will become so very equal that they will exist as one, though in two individual forms and personalities.

---

[142] This is published in Volume II, (4th Ed.) on page 134. (G.J.C.)

But, of course, I recognize the importance of the equality of both being recognized on earth, for the purposes of earthly existence. Yet, mankind will find that as this Love of the Father enters more into souls of men, or even as the natural love becomes more purified, the rights of women as to things material will become recognized without the enactment of any laws declaring the equality of the sexes. For love is an equalizer more powerful than any laws that man can make.

But I will not write more on this subject, for when love comes it will not be necessary that law shall declare the equality, as that love will, of itself, make them so in harmony that inequality cannot exist.

Well, I intended to write you a long letter tonight, but as others have written and it is late, I will not try.

Your own true and loving,

Helen.

While Christian Science teaches the truth in some particulars, yet it does not teach man the Higher Truth that will make of him a Divine Angel

December 9th, 1917.

I am here, your own true and loving Helen.

Well, dear, I heard your prayers, and prayed with you for the inflowing of the Love, and I know that the Father will respond and fill your soul with His Love, and make you feel your oneness with Him.

I was with you this afternoon and heard the lecture on Christian Science and, while many true and helpful things were said, yet the address did not convey to the people the vital thing—that is, the Way of obtaining the Divine Love of which the lecturer spoke. What he conceived to be the Divine Love is not that Love, and in his concept does not operate as he believes. His conception of God, while superior and more true than that of the orthodox churches, yet it is not the full and correct conception of God. Sometime soon a spirit will come and write on the subject of Christian Science. It is a true teaching in some particulars, especially as regards the way to the acquirement of a cleansing of the soul that will tend to make a mortal a perfect man, yet it cannot show the Way to the higher truth that makes him a Divine Angel. I will suggest this explanation to the spirit who will write you, and I have no doubt that it will be fully explained to you.

Well, dear, I will not write more now. Believe that I love you with all my heart and that I am watching over you, trying to help you in every way. Good night, and God bless you.

Your own true and loving

Helen.

Is seeking help and was attracted to Mr. Padgett at the séance he attended

March 23rd, 1919.

Let me write a line, John D. Rogers. I was with you at the meeting and saw that you are mediumistic, and I felt that I should like to communicate with you for a short time.

I am one of the spirits who frequently attend the meetings of the medium (Mrs. Kates) whom you heard speak tonight and give to some of the people the messages from their loved ones, and I was very anxious to communicate also, but had not the opportunity. I am a man who was known to several of the persons present and would have been recognized had my name been mentioned and would have been gladly received.

I am very unhappy in my present condition and surroundings and want to learn the way to get out of darkness and unhappiness. I know that the friends of mine who were present think that I am a happy spirit and can come to them and help them in their worldly affairs, when the fact is, that I cannot, and that they can help me more than I can help them; and I wish that they would do so. It is terrible to be left in the condition in which I am, with no light, or the way to get into the light, left open to me.

I never know when to ask for help, for something always comes forward to interfere with my efforts, and I am relegated to my awful condition of darkness, in which I have been since I came to spirit life. It is a mistake for mediums to believe or teach that we all are in a happy condition when we come to the spirit world, for such is not the case, and many a spirit comes to his relatives and for the purpose of relieving them of any fear as to his condition, tells them that he is happy, when he is not.

Well, I came with you, hoping that you might help me some, if only by your sympathy and kind thoughts, which do so much good to spirits situated as I am; and I believe that you would probably send up a prayer for my relief. I was not a very good man when on earth and am now paying the penalty for my evil thoughts and deeds.

My friends thought that I was good, but in this they were mistaken, and many a man who considers himself good, as men generally go, will find that in the storehouse of his memory are the records of many thoughts and deeds that he had forgotten, but which when he comes to spirit life, will come upon him in all their nakedness and horror, to be atoned for in the way that the laws of God require. I am not a Christian, though when on earth I believed in the creeds of my church and considered myself a very good church member, and was certain that

I would be among the redeemed when I should come to meet the great revealer of things as they are, I mean death.

No, the truth cannot be hidden by belief, or anything but truth itself. We must all face the great revelation, and when it comes it will not show us to be free from sin and defilement, as I thought when on earth. I must pay the penalty, and the great law will work in my case as certainly as that the sun will rise on your world tomorrow morning.

I have seen such spirits, but only as you see ghosts as you believe. I have never had any conversation with them, and do not know that they can do me any good, or that they desire to help me. But why do you ask?

Well, I see a spirit, and he is exceeding bright and beautiful and comes to me and tells me that he will help me if I will only believe what he tells me and follow his advice. I am going with him and do my best to do as he advises. He says that I will find relief and light. I must go, so good night.

Your friend,
John D. Rogers.

Writes about medium's ability to predict the future of any person

January 5th, 1919.

I am here, Spinoza.

Let me write a few lines as I have not written you for some time, and am quite anxious to give some thoughts that may be of benefit to you. I am not one of the spirits who write to you of what they call the higher truths, yet I have a knowledge of some of these truths and believe in all that has been communicated to you, for I know that the spirits who write you are of the Celestial Spheres, possessed of knowledge that we who live in the spirit spheres do not possess.

Well, I merely want to say a few words in reference to the predictions which you heard tonight, and as regards the source of the same. As you know, the woman is a medium gifted with the power of clairvoyance and inspirational receptivity, and on many occasions she perceives and receives some of the truths of the spirit world, and some of the persons whom she professes to see. Her communicants, though, are not of a very high order of development, and she, herself, could not see the highly developed spirits, because the law of communication and rapport applies to her phases of mediumship just as it does to yours. She is a very good woman morally, with some temperamental defects, and attracts spirits of moral worth and conditions, and her guides are in the condition that enables them to live in the brighter spheres, yet not having much spiritual development.

She professes to declare the predictions of her spirit friend, G____, as to what the future, for the ensuing year, will be in the experience of men and nations. Well, she has such a control, and he is a very intelligent spirit, and to some extent inspires her with his ideas of what the future holds out to mankind, and she with more or less exactness declares his thoughts as they are impressed upon her mind. But in connection with these thoughts she incorporates thoughts of her own, believing that they are inspired also, but such is not the fact, though, possibly, these thoughts furnish as good grounds for the predictions as do the thoughts of her control.

I do not believe, at least I have never had it demonstrated to me, that any spirit can make truthful predictions, such as the medium expressed tonight; for spirits have not the powers of omniscience and are as dependent upon the workings of the law of cause and effect as are mortals with this exception, that they can perceive many existing causes that mortals cannot and hence because of this knowledge can make predictions of the future happening of effects, that mortals cannot make. Take from spirits the knowledge of these causes and their predictions are merely guesses which may or may not come true.

As you heard, she declared many things that are problems now existing and the subjects of much thought and study on the part of mortals who give their attention to these matters; and she, as one of them, had her own thoughts and had formed her own conclusions and believed that they were the results of inspiration, whereas they had their foundation in her own mind, arising from her knowledge of and speculations on these things.

The present conditions of the world are such that there exists great probabilities of the happening of many things that the medium predicted, and many persons having knowledge of these conditions will predict, if they be called upon, future occurrences similar to those mentioned by the medium, and if they should happen, it will not be because any spirits know the fact, but because there are causes existing which will necessarily bring them about.

Well, such meetings and such predictions will not do any harm, but, on the contrary, will cause many people to turn their thoughts to spiritual things and to spiritualism, which will tend to liberate their minds from the shackles that are now preventing them from seeking and understanding the truth.

I will not consume more of your time now, but hope to be able to write later. Goodbye, your friend,

Spinoza.

Confirms Spinoza writing and says that he is a very bright and intelligent spirit

January 5th, 1919.

I am here, Helen.

Well dear, I am sorry that I could not write a while ago, but there were some spirits in trouble who wanted to write, and I did not feel justified in using force to drive them away, though White Eagle would not let them write. We must expect such interferences and abide the results for a while. You understand, I know, and will not think that I did not desire to write.

Well, you have received a letter tonight from a spirit who has written you before, and, as I then told you, he is a very bright and intelligent spirit, but not of the Celestial Spheres, and only knows the truths which came with the development of his soul in natural love. We have tried to help him but have not yet been successful in convincing him that what we tell him is the only way that will lead him to the happiness of the Divine. Yet we expect that sooner or later he will understand and follow our advice.

Helen.

Says that all preachers cannot teach the higher Truths

January 9th, 1918.

I am here, Helen.

Well dear, I was with you tonight and saw that you were not much benefited by Billy Sunday's sermon, and of course, could not be, because the preacher said nothing to feed the hungry soul. He said some things which were very good in the way of showing men and women what they should do in order to make the earth lives more happy and it will be well, if the hearers will heed and follow the advice. But nothing much was said to help the progress of the soul.

I saw that you were not in much sympathy with the methods and sayings of the preacher and thought that there was too much hilarity and not enough reverence present, as a meeting for the opening up of the soul and helping the development of those qualities that will lead to the Father's love and the Celestial Heavens. But nevertheless, some things that he said will do good to some people.

You must not forget that the teachings of the Master were twofold, and for those who were not in a condition to hear and understand his higher spiritual truths, he preached those things, which if followed, would make them better men and women and cause them to progress in the development of their natural love; and in this latter effort the preacher will do good and his work must not be undervalued, for all men are not alike in their conditions, intellectual or spiritual. And besides, here and there in his preachings some truths that he utters may by its influence upon the hearts of his hearers cause such hearers to think more deeply about spiritual things of the higher nature, and in thinking, their souls may be opened up to the influence of the spirits who have the Divine Love in their souls, and from which may follow the longings of these hearers for this Love of the Father.

Everything said that tends to cause a spirit to progress towards either of the conditions of love must be encouraged, for the Father works in His own way, and frequently the Love comes into a man's soul, and the man not being intellectually conscious of what the Love is. Whoever is not against us in this work is, in a certain sense, with us, for the salvation of men is the objects of all our efforts; and if we or mortals cannot awaken dead souls to a life in the higher condition, then we must work to bring them into that condition that will cause them to get into a state of purified natural love. They are all the children of God, and if they will not become His beloved children in the divine sense, then He wants them to become the pure spirits that the first parents were before the fall.

So do not criticize or look down upon the work of this preacher because he does not show men the true way to the Celestial Heavens, or because he says and does things that may not appear to be reverent. God looks at the heart and the intentions and the forms of expression used by the preacher are not important, except as they may have the effect of causing some soul to turn away from the truths that the preacher may communicate. All men are not alike and the preachings of the man, while they may, as some say, disgust some hearers, yet others will be affected by them and good will be done.

I write this because I see that you are inclined to criticize the preacher and conclude that his teachings are not conducive to spiritual progress. Well, as you have been told, the large majority of men and spirits will never become inhabitants of the Celestial Heavens, but that is no reason why they should not be taught the way that will tend to purge them of their sins so far as the natural love is concerned. Those who will not become angels must become purified men, and any and everything that will help them to become the latter is approved by the Father and is the object of His favor.

Well dear, I will not write more now as I see that you are cold and must go to bed. But remember this that while all men will not become dwellers in the spheres of the soul in the Celestial Kingdom, yet they are brothers, and the favored brothers must try and help in every way possible the less favored brothers in obtaining that which the Father has designed shall be their portion, even though they refuse or neglect to seek for and obtain the great goal of Divine Love and Immortality. So love me and pray to the Father for His Love, and with all the sincerity of your soul, thank Him that you have found the way to His Great Love and the mansions in the Divine Heavens.

And what I have said to you I say to Dr. Stone, for I see that his thoughts are somewhat similar to your own and that you both think that unless a preacher can and does show the way to the Celestial Kingdom, his work is not worthy of much consideration and falls short of what he as a savior of souls should do. And so it is, but all cannot teach the higher truths, for they do not know or understand them; but that fact must not cause you, or any who know the truths, to think that this work when sincere and beneficial in its moral teachings, should not be taught. I thought best to write this tonight, so that you may not get a wrong conception of what men who cannot teach the great truths should or should not teach. All men are not in that condition of soul and love and they should be taught the way that will lead them to those mansions in the heavens that will be theirs by free will choice.

I love you my dear husband, and am closer to you in your thoughts, and do not want you to think wrong in anything, even though you think right in a great many and the most important things. Pray and let your faith increase and believe that we are all with you trying to direct you aright; and one who knows is more anxious than any of us that your knowledge of the truths increase, and your experiences arising from that knowledge bring to you with more convincing force the truths, that God is Love, and your God. Good night.

Your own and true and loving,
Helen.[143]

Is grateful to for all the spiritual guidance she received when on earth to enable her to progress to the seventh sphere in the spirit world

I am here, cousin Minnie.

Let me say a word, if you please, for I so much desire to write to Eugene, as I was promised some time ago that I could do.

I am his cousin of whom he has spoken to you so often, and I feel that I am really an old acquaintance of yours, and consequently, that I can take advantage of your kindness in permitting me to do just as if I really were an old friend.

I want in the first place to tell him that I am very happy on my

---

[143] This message is a composite of two, being published in Volume III and Volume IV. (G.J.C.)

own account as well as on his, for while I know that I have a very great amount of this Divine Love in my soul that he first told me about, bless his dear heart. He also possesses a great deal of it. And I know that it is the only thing in all the universe that causes the real, genuine happiness of the soul, whether of the mortal or spirit. I cannot but be happy, not only because I possess it and must be happy, especially when he permits it to manifest itself to his consciousness.

I have heard him tell you that I am in a certain sphere, and I qualify the remark by saying that I really told him so and to make the fact certain I wish now to tell him that I am in the Seventh Sphere and hope soon to be in the First Celestial, and of this I am quite certain, for the beautiful spirits of that Sphere who seem to love me so much tell me that my home will soon be in that Heaven of Bliss and that I will soon become an immortal angel and realize the fact that never again in all eternity will it be possible for me to die.

It is all so wonderful to me that the Father has been so merciful and loving to me in bestowing upon me this Love in such great abundance and especially when I realize that a few short months ago I knew nothing of this Divine Love and first heard of it from Eugene, who, I thought when he told me of it and of other things pertaining to spiritualism, was a little off, as you would say. But now I realize so fully what great truths he possessed. Even though I doubted, in view of my present knowledge, that he really comprehended the full purport or meaning of these truths. But be that as it may, he just told me of it and while I paid little attention to what he said at the time, yet when I came to the spirit world and found myself in communication with him and he again recalled to my mind this great Love and pointed out to me the way by which I might obtain it, and then on top of this came so many bright and beautiful spirits and reiterated what he had said, I just couldn't doubt what he had said. I just couldn't doubt that there must be truth in what he had told me, and as a consequence my whole soul was aroused and I determined to seek for it and I did so with all the energy and longings of my soul. And so I found it and now am so supremely happy.

They tell me that I have made wonderful progress in the short time that I have been here, and from my own observation by comparison, I see that it must be so, but as I now look upon my progress I am not surprised, for when once I was convinced that this great Love was a thing of reality and that it could be mine for the seeking, I commenced the quest with all the energy and desires of my whole being, mind and soul, and let nothing stand in the way of my ever and every striving to obtain the goal.

And as I progressed I found that there came to me increased power and strength, and greater and greater abundance of the Love. I was not worried and faith came to me, until the reality of the object of progress or seeking became more and more certain. In addition, I had the help of the beautiful spirits who had traveled the road that I was pursuing, and their encouragement was always with me and their love seemed, as it were, to give wings to my speeding.

Well, I have said enough about myself, but as I felt that Eugene wanted to know more definitely just where I now am and the story of my progress, I have taken up more of your time to tell him than I otherwise would have done.

I am frequently with my people in spirit life and with his, and I must tell him that they are very happy and thankful to the Father that they recovered their freedom from the bondage of the false beliefs and influence of the church of which they were adherents when on earth.

And I must further say that much of their present condition, that is, the abandoning of the stagnation and darkness of their beliefs in and association with the priests is due to Eugene and his declarations of truths that showed them the true way to light and happiness.

I am now in condition that I can in a way repay him for his great help to me, and so with the others, for I can be, and am, with him quite often trying to help him with my love and influence, and at times when his soul opens up to my coming, I get close to him and his heart throbs more than he possibly realizes.

This wonderful Love creates a great, indescribable rapport when it his physical conditions and the influences that come to him from the exercise of his organs of sense perception, but I know that at times he does feel my presence to a very great degree and he is happier by it. This wonderful love creates a great, indescribable rapport when it exists in two souls striving to get in closer contact, and sometimes I find that rapport is possible and I take advantage of it.

He must have more faith and pray more for the inflowing of the Love, and remember in his times of discouragement or depression that he has with him a power that if he will let it exercise itself, will enable him to endure and overcome all his conditions of doubt and despondency.

As he believed in me when I lived on earth, he must believe the more in me as a spirit, a cousin who loves him very much, having a soul filled with gratitude and unselfish affection.

I will come to him very soon and write him.

I do not care to speak of the material things in which I know he is interested, for tonight the higher things of Love have possession of my soul.

I must not write more. So thanking you for your kindness and leaving him my love, I will say good night.

Cousin Minnie.

Self-opinionated spirit in the second sphere that cares nothing about spiritual progression or the Divine Love of the Father.

January 8th, 1917.

I am here, Samuel P. Shannon.

Let me tell you that you and the Doctor need someone to look after you in your mental qualities, as you are the most gullible men that I have heard talk for a long time. I have heard what you just said in reference to your experiences in connection with these writings and the efforts made by spirits to convince you that your communications were from the higher spirits, even the spirits of the Celestial heavens, and I feel sorry that you should be so weak as to believe all these false and flattering things that have been said to you. So as I am a spirit who knows and loves only the truth, and do not desire to see anyone deceived, I feel it my duty to tell you that you have had only deceiving spirits write you, who take great delight in making you believe that you have received communications that have not been equaled by the writings that any other medium in all the wide world has received.

Of course, you have received some wonderful truths and some beautiful sayings, but they are merely the efforts of spirits who think that they know all of the truth of the spirit world. And I advise you to let these things go from your mind and listen only to spirits who are honest and who know of what they write. I am one of those who are capable to tell you the truths that exist in our spirit world and that are only necessary for mortals to know. Much has been written you about the Divine Love and its effect upon the souls of men, making them, as it were, very Gods; and I want to say that the only Divine Love is the pure love that exists in the hearts of spirits who have been purified of sin, and had their intellects developed in the highest degree. So my friends, give up this belief in the Divine Love, and put all your efforts to the cultivation of your minds.

And there is another kind of love that you have been told of, and in the belief in which you have had great satisfaction, and expectations created of coming into a wonderful and ecstatic happiness when you shall come into the spirit world, and that is the soulmate love. How foolish to believe in any such love. Our soulmates are our acquirements of knowledge, and not female spirits. The women here are very much like they are on earth, and they love one male for a while and then get tired and seek another. I thank God that they have never been able to fool me! I see so much of the treachery of these female spirits that I shun them, and as a consequence, they call me the woman-hater, and so I am, and I do not regret it.

My companions are only spirits like myself, having a friendship for one another, but no such thing as what they call love, especially soulmate love. Sometime, before many years, you will come to the spirit world, and I beg that you will let me warn you before you come, to put no faith in what is told you about this soulmate love, and if you will listen to and take my advice, you will be saved much unhappiness. I write thus as a friend and well-wisher, and you must believe that I am wholly impartial and honest in what I say to you. I live in the Second Sphere, where there are many intellectual spirits who find much happiness and satisfaction in the development of their minds, and are not troubled by the women, or the ghost of what is called the Divine Love.

Occasionally I see some spirits who claim to have the Divine Love, and some who claim to have soulmates, but I pay no attention to them, and consider them fanatics and deceived spirits. Well, they are different in appearance from us. They seem to be much brighter and, as they claim, happier; but this is due only to the fact that they are frivolous, that is, they never give any consideration to the investigation of the important things of this spirit world, and flitter about from sphere to sphere as if they had nothing else to do than find amusement and pleasure in their joy rides, as I have heard some of you mortals express it.

Yes, they don't seem to be confined to any sphere, and that is something that I don't quite understand, for we who are so much more substantial and work so hard to learn the truths, cannot pass into the higher sphere. This I don't understand and neither do my associates. But it may be that these spirits that I speak of are of such little importance that the guardians of the higher spheres do not pay any attention to them. At least, they are never stopped in their moving from our sphere to the higher ones.

Well, I will consider what you suggest, and as you say, it can do no harm, and as I can spare time enough to make the inquiry of one of these spirits, I think that I will do so, merely to learn what their idea is of the reason that they have such freedom of movement and we have not. I see the Indian who is acting as your guide and he to an extent is another one of these foolish spirits. He says that I am a wonderful spirit in my own mind and that if I continue to develop in my opinion of my own importance and greatness I will soon be sitting on the right hand of God. He seems serious, but I do not know whether to think that he is really impressed by my appearance and intellectual greatness, or whether he is saying what he does, ironically. But I suppose he is serious, for being an Indian he cannot have much intellectual development and must be impressed by my superior qualities.

Well, my friend, I am glad that I could write you tonight and do you the friendly turn that I have, for I am a lover of humanity and wish to do all the good that I can to my fellow man. I must stop now, as a spirit who says she is your soulmate, comes to me and says that I have been indulged enough, and, of course, wishing to get away from her, as from all other females, I must leave; but you must think of what I have written.

Your friend,
Samuel P. Shannon,
a one-time scientist of England.[144]

Writes that Shannon has considerable darkness in his appearance, yet he is evidently a hard student of what he calls intellectual things

January 8th, 1917.

I am here, Helen.

Well, dear, I see that you and the Doctor enjoyed the last message, as did we who saw him write, and I must say that he is one of the most self-opinionated spirits that I have met for a long time. He is not very pretty, or rather attractive looking, and has considerable darkness in his appearance, yet he is evidently a hard student of what he calls intellectual things. He does not like the females, and I have my doubts that they make any very great efforts to win his affections; but anyhow he considers himself safer in shunning them, as he says.

If you could have seen the expression on White Eagle's face when he so highly eulogized the spirit, you would have been unable to restrain your laughter, and we could not, but we made ourselves invisible to him so that he could not see us.

Well, the writing shows you the result of spirits believing that the mind is the only thing that needs development, and we want to tell you that this spirit may continue in this condition of undeveloped soul for many long years to come. But as you advised him to seek an interview with some of the spirits who have the development, which only the Divine Love can give, it may cause some benefit to him. And we will have come to him some spirit who will be in such condition of memory of his beliefs on earth, that will enable him to meet the spirit on his own ground and discuss with him not only the question of the freedom of the

---

[144] While in context here, this communication is laughable, yet it illustrates a serious issue for mediumship in general - the fact that there are very opinionated spirits that know very little and without a yardstick by which they can be measured, might be taken seriously. A very good guide to the usefulness of a spirit is in fact its humility coupled to the love which they display and their lack of desire to control those that they are guiding. In my own case I am immediately suspicious when a spirit believes in reincarnation, but of course that works for me because I am certain it does not happen. (G.J.C.)

spheres for us who have this Love, but also other questions that have to do with the supposed knowledge of this spirit, so that he will realize that the spirits whom he sees flitting from sphere to sphere are not the frivolous spirits that he believes they are.

I will write you sometime the result of this interview, for we will bring it about, not so much to satisfy this curiosity as to who we really are, as to help him gain a knowledge of this Divine Love that he thinks is only a will-o'-the-wisp. Mary was present and enjoyed the incident very much and wanted to tell the spirit that she knows all about the soulmate love, and that if he, the spirit, should try to find his soulmate and succeed, he would then know what real happiness is; but she saw that it would do no good.

Well, you have written enough for tonight and are tired. We both send our love and want our kisses. Good night and God bless you both with that Divine Love which is, as the Doctor says, the greatest thing in all the world.

Your own true and loving,
Helen.

Lonely spirit writes about her belief when on earth

June 6th, 1916.

I am here, Lillian Summer.

I am here, the woman who lost her soul to preserve her standing in society while on earth. I was a woman who never thought of things spiritual or of the future life, but lived only for the pleasures of the present.

I had everything that money could buy, and never knew what trouble in the way of desiring and not getting, meant. I had an indulgent husband and lovely children, who made my home very happy, and who loved me with all the love of their natures, and, of course, I loved them; but I did not feel the necessity of any other love, nor did I really know of any greater or higher love.

Of course I attended church and listened to the sermons of the preachers, and enjoyed them as intellectual treats, but as to appealing to my soul, I never once, as I can remember, experienced any sensation other than what came from the exaltation of my mind. My children were sent to Sunday school and learned what the teachers tried to instruct them in, but at home they had no religious teachings, as I never had any religious experience myself.

My husband was not an attendant at church and knew nothing of the higher things of life, and was satisfied to make money so that his family could have all the comforts of home. We had a happy home in our love and associations, and never felt that there was any other happiness that might be ours other than that which we had.

Now I realize the want of this spiritual conception of my being and the great joy that I am deprived of because of my want of knowledge of the things of the soul. I had a love nature, and I loved most people with whom I came in contact in a society way, yet this love was more or less unconsciously given, and my great ambition was to become a society leader, and the admiration, and possibly envy, of my friends.

Now, I see the falsity of it all, and how little of the ambitions of life, in the particulars mentioned, weighed in the standing and happiness of the spirits in this world of revelation and nakedness, for I am naked as regards all the thoughts and acts of my life, and very seldom do I see anything that helps my present condition.

I merely write you this that possibly someone who is living the life that I lived may read it, and turn her thoughts to the essentials, and let all these things of the earthly become secondary and of minor importance. My name was Lillian Summer, and I lived in Richmond, Virginia, and died in 1902.

I thank you for permitting me to write, as it has made me feel better and more at home.

I will say good night.

Lillian Summer.

An old friend is seeking help

February 2nd, 1920.

I am here, Scott.

Let me write. I am your old friend, Scott, who died a few days ago. I know now what death means and how we are punished for the things done on earth, and I am suffering my share of the penalty. I come to you because you had told me on earth of the future of men who die and I am now convinced that what you told me is true, although I know very little of what my fate here is. I only know that I am living and suffering and beyond that I do not know anything.

I am glad that I can come to you and hope that you will help me, if possible. I have written Morgan and he promised to help me, and if you only knew how much I need help you would not hesitate one moment, for I believe that you are my friend. I realize that I am not in condition to know anything of the truths of religion and there does not seem to be anyone here to help me. How strange that my folks have not met me, for I believe that they must be interested in me, if any dead person can be.

I am tired and must stop.

A friend of Mr. Padgett's was helped out of darkness by his wife Helen

June 17th, 1915.

I am here, Joe Shellington.

Well, I am glad to be able to write to you, and let you know that I am in the land of the living. I have waited a long time to write to you but, as your band would not consent to my writing, I had to wait until it was agreeable to them, as well as to you.

I am in a state of semi-darkness and am suffering somewhat from the recollections of my life on earth, but thanks to your wife, I am commencing to see the light and to learn the way out of my sufferings.

When I found myself dying, I thought that I was going to sleep and that my body was resting from the cares and pains which my sufferings had caused; and when my spirit was separated from my body, I hovered around for a long time expecting that when my body should feel refreshed I would go into it again and continue my life on earth. But after waiting a long time and failing to see my body awaken, I commenced to wonder what had taken place, and, at last, came to the conclusion that I was a dead one, and that no more would I walk on earth as a mortal.

Well, as soon as I realized that fact I looked around and saw my mother and father, and several others that I knew on earth, and they told me that I had died, and was then a spirit, and would never more go into my body. And I commenced to ask questions, and wanted to know where I was and what place I was in. They told me that I was in the spirit world, and in what is called the earth plane, and that my future home would be in that plane until I had by repentance and suffering, progressed to a higher one.

My mother, who is a very beautiful spirit, tried to comfort me, and told me that I must now think of the things that belong to the spirit world, and not let my thoughts run on the things that I had been interested in while a mortal. But while I considered her advice and was impressed with what she said, yet I could not follow her advice, as I was compelled by something which I did not understand to give my thoughts to the affairs of earth, and especially to my wife and daughter. I was with them nearly all the time for many long days, and tried to speak to them and advise them what they should do, but they would not pay any attention to me. Of course, I know now that they did not know that I was present and did not hear my voice; but at the time I thought it very strange, for they were just as real and unchanged to me as when I was with them in the body.

I never fully realized what my position was until long months after I died, and I could not think of anything but them at first, and was with them all the time. I saw them sorrowing and weeping because of my death and tried so hard to comfort them, but all to no purpose. I, at last, saw that it was utterly hopeless for me to make them feel that I was with them, and so I sought for light or information among my spirit friends, and sought from them to know how I could reach my dear ones; but I could get no consolation, as they told me that it was only through the instrumentality or help of some earth medium could I ever be able to communicate with them or let them know that I was still alive, and loved them just as I did when on earth.

So one time in my wanderings I entered the circle of the medium where you heard me talk to you, and then I was happy because I thought that now I would be able to reach my wife and daughter. But I was disappointed, for you never told them that I had talkèd to you, and wanted them to know that I was anxious to talk to them. I suppose you thought that they would not believe, and so neglected to tell them. But you were mistaken in this, as they would have believed you had you told them.

My wife knows something of spiritualism, though she has not much faith in it, and while she may not absolutely have believed, yet she would have had interest enough in it to have sought for the opportunity to learn more, and if possible to hear me speak to her. So while you disappointed me, yet I cannot altogether blame you. But, old friend, do not fail to let her know that I have written to you tonight, and if not too much trouble, I would like for you to send her a copy of this message.

I still love her and am with her very often, and try my best to make her feel my presence, and realize that I am doing my best to comfort her. If she only knew how dear she is to me and that my whole heart burns with love for her, she would be happier, for I believe that she will be mine when she comes over, and through all eternity. So do not fail to send her a copy of this message.

When I passed over I was not one particle afraid and while I was not just in condition to know what was taking place, yet there was no dread or apprehension of my being in any way harmed. I arose, as I have said, from my body, but did not leave it, and stayed with it and with my loved ones even until it was buried and then continued with my dear wife.

After I realized that I was a spirit, I found myself in a dark atmosphere surrounded by dark spirits who, I supposed, were like myself. My mother, while she often came to me, did not live with me, but, as she told me, in a higher sphere where much happiness exists.

I was not happy and I suffered very much from my recollections of my earth life, and had no fixed home. All spirits in a condition like mine have to roam about with no place that they can call home. Often have I longed for a home but found none, and even now I have one that is not very beautiful; but I am progressing and light is coming to me and my sufferings are decreasing. I rather expected to find myself in hell, as I was not a Christian, and as I was taught that all who are not Christians and believe in Jesus must go to hell. But I have not seen that hell, and I do not believe that there is any such place. Yet the sufferings which we all have creates a hell enough for any spirit who wants such a hell.

Well, I am now learning to pray to God and to believe in His Love, and the more I pray and the stronger my belief becomes, the more light I see and the less I suffer. Your wife came to me at about the time I spoke to you at the medium's, and tried to help me, and she has been with me many times since, and has helped me very much. She is a beautiful spirit and seems filled with the Love of God, as she says.

So I am seeking that Love, and I believe that I will soon get enough of it to get out of my present condition. I thank you so much for this opportunity, and when it is agreeable I will come and write to you again.

I will not take up more of your time tonight.

So with my kindest regards and many thanks, I am

Your old friend,

Joe Shellington.

Confirms that Joe Shellington wrote

June 17th, 1915.

I am here, Helen.

Well, sweetheart, you had quite a long letter from Joe Shellington and I am glad that you let him write, for it seemed to help him so much. He is now progressing and praying to the Father, and has some faith. As he said, I have been trying to help him, and he listens to me with much interest. Soon, I believe, he will see the light and get out of his darkness.

Do as he requests. Send a copy of the letter to his wife, for I believe it will do her good, as well as him. She is not so much in love with him now, but yet she will feel better by knowing that he loves her and is alive.

I don't know, as I have not inquired, but I will in order to let you know. But it is not best that either of them should know at this time.

Well, I will not write very much tonight, as you have written enough. I must tell you, though, that I love you with all my heart and soul, and I am so glad that you do me.

I was with you and saw your condition of mind and know just how you felt. The worship was all of Jesus, and he says that is not right. But, nevertheless, while these people speak of Jesus as God, yet in their hearts they worship God, and you must not feel that they are sinning very much in calling Jesus' name so much. They speak of Christ and if they only knew the true meaning of that name their worship would be all right. But they fail to know the difference between Jesus and Christ and hence make the mistake of worshiping Jesus Christ, meaning Jesus.

But their hearts have the Love of the Father and they will be benefited by such love even though they look upon Jesus as God. He knows just what they mean, and while he does not like to be worshiped, yet he sees that their longing is for God.

I must now stop, and will only say that you have much love in your soul tonight.

So with all my love I will say good night.

Your own true and loving,

Helen.

Describes his life in the spirit world

June 24th, 1915.

I am here, William S. Richards.

Let me write just a little bit, as I need help. I am in darkness and suffering.

I am a man who lived the life of an infidel when on earth and did not believe in God or Jesus, or in anything that was taught in the Bible in reference to a future life, or in anything of a religious value. I was not a bad man, in the sense of being immoral more than men ordinarily are, but I did not have thoughts which tended to develop my soul qualities, or make me what is called a spiritual man. So you see that when I died and found myself still living I was somewhat surprised, and for quite a while could not realize that I was a spirit pure and simple.

But since that time I have discovered many things that show me that my beliefs on earth were all wrong. Yet that discovery does not remedy the failings of soul development which my beliefs caused, and I am now like a man without anything to guide or direct him in the way in which he may recover these lost possessions. I have met a great many spirits but they are, like myself, without knowledge of those things which may be necessary to help us in the way of progression. I am a spirit that enjoys some happiness and has some light, but it is that which arises from the exercise of my mental powers. I don't know anything about any happiness that may come from the development of the soul, and yet I have heard that there is such a thing, and that a wonderful happiness ensues from such development.

Of course, I must find this happiness if I can, and if you can help me in any way to find it, I will be very thankful if you will do so.

I am in darkness most of the time and I suffer also, but at other infrequent times I have some light and some happiness; but the former conditions are the ones that are mostly mine. I live in what we call the earth plane and I have the privilege of roaming over that plane with certain restrictions. I cannot go into what you might call the higher planes of that plane, but in my own plane and in the lower ones I may go, and I do sometimes.

I find many spirits who are in a very great condition of darkness and in torture, and their places must be the hells of the Bible but without the fires or the devils, as men believe. I never see any devils but the spirits themselves, and some of them are the only devils that are necessary to make a hell.

I do not know just who I am in this darkness that I speak of, except it must be because of the stagnation of my spiritual self. My soul is nearly dead so far as any development is concerned, and my mind, while active and eager for knowledge, does not give me any great happiness. So I suppose the great happiness that I hear is possessed by others must come from the soul development. At any rate I want to find the cause if I can, and I thought that maybe you could help me.

My name was William S. Richards. I lived in Germantown, Pa., and died in 1901. So I am waiting for your advice.

I have called for him and he says that he will show me the way, and that I must go with him. So I will say,

Good night,

William S. Richards.

Comments on one of the spirits

April 13th, 1919.

I am here, your own true and loving Helen.

Well, dear, you have just had a message from one of the spirits who sometimes attends the meetings of Mrs. Kates, and he was very anxious to write you, and we permitted him to do so.[145] He is not of the higher order of spirits, though one who is much advanced in his natural love, and knows the different classes of spirits who attend the meetings.

We were present, but of course could not communicate for the reason that he has given you. If Mrs. Kates would only learn the truth of communication and rapport, and seek to obtain the soul development that would enable the higher spirits to come to her, she would have wonderful powers and hear the voices of spirits who now never

---

[145] This is not a reference to the Richards who is directly preceding this message, but rather another Richards which is published in this volume on page 379. (G.J.C.)

communicate with her. She is a wonderful medium in the sphere of work that she is doing and many spirits are made happy by the messages of love to their loved ones, and the mortals as well, but her mediumship is not of the order that will benefit her very much, and the time is now arrived when she must get into a higher class of work, and enable spirits of a higher order to come to her and communicate.

You must not fail to give her the message that the Master wrote, for upon it depends not only her own salvation, but the salvation of many mortals to whom she can preach the truths of God, and the knowledge of the life beyond the borderline of death. I hope that you will soon have the opportunity.

Well, I see that you are in a better condition today, and some of the higher spirits have been with you, suggesting thoughts and trying to impress you with the importance of your work. You must realize this when you contrast the teachings that you heard today with the truths that have been revealed to you.

Well, they will come soon and continue the messages that treat of the great truths of God and man, and you must get in the condition that will permit them to successfully write.

I will not write more tonight. Baby is here and sends her love. We all love you and hope that soon now brighter things will open up to you and that your hopes will soon be realized. Keep up your faith and you will not be disappointed. Good night my dear husband,

Your own true and loving,
Helen.

Has progressed out of darkness and is grateful to know the Way to obtain the Love of the Father

July 19th, 1916.

I am here, Edwin Forrest.

I come tonight to tell you that I am much better than I was when last I wrote you, and have gotten out of much of the darkness in which I was.

This is all so wonderful to me that I scarcely realize what it means, and when I think of how ignorant I was on earth and what a Godless life I led, I never cease thanking God for the great opportunities that I enjoy, and for the help of the beautiful, loving spirits who came to me to show me the way to Truth and this Love of the Father.

Your wife has been my angel of hope in all my darkness, and her tenderness and love have caused me to awaken from the miserable condition in which I found myself shortly after coming to the spirit world. How fortunate I am I cannot tell you, and never will I be able to tell anyone, for no spirit that has not experienced what I have can possibly convey the meaning of the great change from darkness and ignorance to some light and some of the Divine Love that has come to me.

I now pray to the Father almost continually and as I do so, I realize that there comes into my soul that which changes all its qualities, and makes me realize how dead I was. Oh, if I only had known of this wonderful love on earth how different my life would have been, and how many heartaches would have been saved to others, and among them I include yourself, for now I realize that I did you great wrong in our business affairs by my conduct and drunken escapades.

But I know that you have forgiven me, and pray for me and want me to be happy; and your wife, who knows what happened, tells me not to think of these things but to think only of the Father's Love, and the fact that it can be mine in ever increasing abundance. I wanted to write this to you, and I now feel better, and you may rest assured that so far as I can in this spirit world help you and retrieve what injury I did you, I will do to the utmost of my power.

Well, I have written considerable tonight and must stop. So continue to pray for me, and I know that I shall be helped.

Good night,

Edwin Forrest.

Rejoices at the progress he is making now out of darkness and feels "as light as air"

March 4th, 1917.

I am here, Forrest.

Well, Ned, excuse me for intruding just now, but I am so happy that I cannot refrain from telling you of my happiness, for I know that you will rejoice with me. I am now out of my darkness and the Love of the Father is working in my soul, so that I feel as some of your earth poets have said, "as light as air", and if you could only see the air in which I now am you would more deeply understand what the expression means in my case.

I am now so certain that this Love is a thing of reality, and so effective to make a dark, suffering spirit one of light and freedom from pain, that I can assert with all the conviction of a rescued soul, that the Love of the Father is the one thing in all the spirit world that has no uncertainty about it. I will not write more now, and I know that you will pardon me for having intruded.

Now I feel that I can go to my mother and tell her of this wonderful Love, and the true way to light and progress, and I will go at once; and I pray the Father that my persuasion may be effective and enable me to hear my mother say to me that she will trust me and follow me in the way that I shall tell her of.

So thanking you, and believing that you have been my greatest friend, although I realize that I did not deserve your kindness, I will say good night,

Your old friend,
Edwin Forrest.

Is gradually coming out of darkness with the help of Helen and Mr. Padgett's grandmother

October 12th, 1916.

I am here, Edwin Forrest.

Well, Ned, I want to write you a few lines, and as your wife is here, and says that I may write, I will do so.

I am glad to say that I am in a much better condition than when I last wrote you,[146] thanks to the help that I have received from her and your grandmother, who came to me a short time ago with such wonderful love and such convincing words of cheer and hope. She is the most wonderful spirit that I have seen, and when she speaks to me it is with such authority and convincing power that I just have to believe and follow her advice or try to do so.

She prays with me at times and as she prays there comes into my soul such wonderful and strange sensations, that I know that something is coming to me that I am not acquainted with, and I feel so much better, and everything gets lighter. The darkness seems to leave me and I feel like a new man; and I pray too, though I scarcely know what it means. But this I know, that a change has come over me, and hope comes to me, and with it comes belief that I will get out of my darkness and suffering.

I commence to realize that there must be a God of Mercy and Love, and that He is not inflicting upon me the sufferings that I have endured; and that maybe He will answer my prayers for help and relief from my darkness. Your wife tells me He will and that if I will have faith and pray with all my heart and soul sometime I may become beautiful and happy as she is. It is hard to believe this, but even if I can never become as she is, yet I sometimes think that I may become more beautiful and happier than I am, and I am making the effort.

You pray for me, too. I come to you at times when the other dark spirits come, and I see the effect of your help. I don't understand it, yet I see that these spirits are made better, and I must believe that there is

---

[146] This message is not in sequence with respect to the immediately preceding message in the published order. This is an earlier message by five months. (G.J.C.)

something in what the bright spirits, to whom these dark ones go, tell them. I am so glad that I can write to you.

No, I have not seen Mr. Miller and don't know where he is. I will act on your advice, and try to find him, and do as you say, for even though I am not a bright spirit, yet if I can help him I will gladly do so. I will seek him and the next time I write, will let you know just what his condition is. So thanking you, I will say good night.

Your old partner friend,
Edwin Forrest[147]

Also writes about the help that Mr. Padgett's grandmother gave to Forrest

October 12th, 1916.

I am here, your own true and loving Helen.

Well sweetheart, at last I have the opportunity to write my letter, and I am so glad that I can.

I thought it best to let Forrest write you as he was so anxious and seems to realize so much pleasure in doing so. He is progressing some and commences to see that there is some virtue in prayer, for he prays very earnestly and very often. We are helping him as much as possible and he seems to have great faith in me, and in your grandmother who appears to him to be something more than the spirit of a mortal. He seems to be awed by her presence when she first came to him, but she talks to him with such love and sympathy in her voice, and has so much of the Father's Love beaming from her eyes that he soon forgets her grandeur, as we call it, and listens to her with all his soul, and seems to drink in her words of comfort and love. She has a wonderful influence over him and is helping him very much. Well, I must not write more on these matters or I will not have time to tell you what I so much wish to say.

Since I last wrote you of my progress, I have gotten into higher planes of the Celestial Spheres and am correspondingly happier and surrounded by more beautiful scenes and brighter and lovelier spirits. My home is also more beautiful and is filled with a greater atmosphere of love and happiness. And I further find that with all this progress and increased happiness, my soulmate love for you increases and a more wonderful vista of what our happiness will be when you come over and progress to my home and become my soulmate in actual living together, unfolds itself.

---

[147] This message is a composite of two, being published in Volume III and Volume IV. (G.J.C.)

I am so often with you, that if you knew how often, you might think that my home is not so attractive to me as it should be from my reference to its beauty; but you would be mistaken, for it is more attractive and has more happiness for me than any home I have yet had in the spirit life, and when I am in it, no mortal can conceive of my joy and bliss. But yet, I love you so much that I cannot stay away from you for any great length of time, and some of my spirit friends wonder at it. But it is not to be wondered at so much when it is known, and it is a fact, that my actually being in my home is not necessary to my great happiness, for when I come to you, my soul, which is really I, comes too, and in it is the great Love of the Father, and from that Love proceeds my great happiness.

So you see how the Father blesses me and all others who have His Love. Because we have our love for the mortal and leave our mansions of joy and light and go to the earth plane of darkness, where sin and error are, our great soul's love and happiness are not left behind. And why should it be? The homes which we have do not make the soul's happiness, but the soul's possession of love makes the homes. And this Love is ours for all eternity and cannot be taken from us. It can grow greater but never less. This is a law or the result of a law in the Celestial Heavens. And what a wonderful law it is!

I come to you bringing all the love that I have in my celestial home, and throw around you its influence and essence, and just to the extent that your soul is receptive do you absorb it and feel its presence. So in a faint way you can realize the great fortune of those mortals who have come to them spirits of the Celestial Spheres.

Have you ever considered what it means to you and your friends to have surrounding you the love and presence of the Master and of the other high spirits who are so often with you? Very few mortals have such love breathing upon them so often. If you will think of this you will realize how favored you are and what your possibilities may be. But when I come to you I bring not only the Divine Love which possesses my soul, but the lesser, though very intense love of the soulmate, a love which had its beginning before we were mortals and which will never have its ending in all eternity.

When I think of the goodness of the Father in all these things to make His mortals and spirits happy I can only wonder at His Love and wisdom, and never cease to thank Him! But astonishing also, man can have these blessings as he wills or not to make them his own. In this way he determines his own happiness or misery, when God wishes him to be only happy.

Well, sweetheart, I will not write more tonight as you have written enough. But this I wish to tell you, that I love you with a love that is only yours, and always increasing with no possibility of dying. And as the years of your pilgrimage on earth go by, this love will be with you and around you in greater abundance, and you will realize it more and more; and your heart will grow younger and younger until the earth life will become something more than the shadow of what awaits you when you come to me. I will say good night.

Give me my kiss and know that I am your own true and loving, Helen.[148]

Is amazed at the progress Forrest made out of darkness, and will try to do the same, and seek for the Father's Love

March 3rd, 1917.

I am here, Samuel C. Mills.

Well, I heard what Forrest said, and I am certain that he believes what he said to be true, for I can tell you that he has become a wonderfully bright spirit, and seems to be so happy and joyful.

Well, it certainly is strange to me. Here am I who was in some light and comparatively happy when he came into the spirit world and went into the hells of darkness and suffering, and now he is all beautiful and happy, and I am still where I was. It certainly is wonderful! But as I told you in my last letter, I cannot now remain satisfied with my condition, and I am going to seek, and have already started, to get this Love that he tells me is the cause of his wonderful change; and I will not cease seeking until I succeed in obtaining it, for I feel that if he could get the Love, I can.

He has talked with me, and while he could not explain just how the change came to him, yet he says that he accepted your advice and the help of your wife, and commenced to pray, blindly and without faith, and continued until he commenced to realize that something that he had never felt before was working in his soul and continued to work the more he prayed; and he didn't stop praying until the darkness left him, and with it the most of his suffering. This is all that he could tell me, and I am following him. And I hope that before long I will be able to write to you as he did. Won't that be a wonderful thing! I will not write more, but I will pray and hope that you will pray for me. The spirits who are here and who seem to love you so much, say that they will pray with me, and they tell me that there will be no doubt as to the results.

So good night,
Your old friend,
Mills.

---

[148] This message is a composite of two, being published in Volume III and Volume IV. (G.J.C.)

Is better and has started to believe as a result of the help received by the bright spirits

March 4th, 1917.

I am here, Perry.

I am very weak, but I must tell you that I am feeling better, for now I do not believe that I am doomed for all eternity to the damnation of darkness and suffering, and when I think back that but for you and the loving spirits that you brought to me, I would be without hope, my heart is so filled with gratitude that it seems as if it must break asunder.

What a wonderful thing is this great gift that you have and no spirit in all the darkness of a hope so near despair can understand the meaning of what that beautiful and glorious spirit who just wrote you said, as I can.

Well I cannot write more, but you and your friend (Dr. Leslie Stone) pray for me as surely you who have such beautiful spirits loving you must have some power in your prayers to help. Good night and pray for me.

Your friend,
Perry.[149]

Is grateful for the help that Mr. Padgett gave to her son

March 4th, 1917.

I am here, the mother of Perry.

You must let me say a word, for if ever there was a thankful spirit in all the spirit world I am that one. Oh, how I thank you and praise the Father for His Mercy and Goodness in permitting my dear boy to see the light and have hope come to him as a star that beckons him to a state of happiness and salvation.

I am so filled with love and thanksgiving that I cannot write much for my heart is just going out to the Father in such streams of love and joy and gratitude that my eyes are so suffused with tears of gladness that I can hardly see.

Do not forget to pray for my boy, both of you, for we all know that you love the unfortunate and miserable spirits who have no hope or way to get into the light. You know that I am his mother, for your soul must feel that it is the mother's love that is thus expressing gratitude.

Good night,

---

[149] This message is a composite of two, being published in Volume III and Volume IV. (G.J.C.)

Perry's mother.[150]

Confirms the happiness of both Perry and his mother, and is happy that he asked both Dr. Stone and Mr. Padgett to pray for him

March 4th, 1917.

I am here, your own true loving Helen.

Well dear, you have had a wonderful night and if as you say, you could see the scene of your surroundings you would wonder that there could be such happiness and joy in the spirit world. I mean in these lower planes where there are so many dark and unhappy spirits. We have all been happy and I must tell you that all of your band and also the Doctor's have been present listening to the messages that have been written you.

And it seems to be a night when so many of these dark spirits have come seeking and longing for help and trying to find the way to light. And while only a few have written you yet many have been benefitted for they have heard the messages and your conversations and have listened to the bright spirits who have been ready and anxious to help them.

Perry is better as he says, and is praying and just commences to realize the love and solicitude that his mother has for him and she is so happy that he realizes that she is his own loving mother, and the scene between them was very pathetic and they mingled their tears, hers of love and thankfulness to the Father and his of gratitude that hope has come to him. He is praying and I am so glad that he asked you and the Dr. to pray for him, for it shows that there has come to him some little faith in prayer.

We are all praying for him and your grandmother, in all the beauty of her love, is with him and to her he seems to listen and believe in more than all the others. It is a glorious time for us all. I will not write more now as you have been drawn on a great deal and we must stop.

Give my love to the Dr. (Stone) and tell him that if he could know the amount of love that is surrounding him tonight he would not exchange places with Rockefeller or any other rich man or great men as you mortals consider greatness—for this love will be his through all the years to come even increasing and growing.

So dear believe that I love you and give me your love and trust that I am,

---

[150] This message is a composite of two, being published in Volume III and Volume IV. (G.J.C.)

Your own true and loving,
Helen.[151]

Writes that he is progressing and is able to see the light and some happiness

March 10th, 1917.

I am here, Edwin Forrest.

Well, Ned, I come again, but I will not detain you long, as I merely wish to tell you that I am progressing and am commencing to see the light and some happiness, and my hope has increased so much that I already feel that I shall soon get in the condition where my happiness will become so great that all my sufferings will leave me. Your wife tells me that my hope is certain of realization, if I will only continue to pray and open up my soul to the inflowing of the Love, and I am trying with all my strength to follow her advice.

I have been to my mother and she was certainly surprised to see my bright condition. I mean bright as compared with hers, and the condition of those who are around her, and she wondered what has caused it. And when I told her, and begged her to follow my example and pray for this Love, and let go from her the beliefs in her creed and in the teachings of the priests, she said she was not ready to do this, but was compelled to believe what these priests had told her of the Will of God and of the way to get out of her darkness, and that what I said to her may be true as to my experience, yet she was certain that the masses and prayers that the priests were offering up for her would soon have their effect, and she would soon get out of purgatory and pass into the heavens of peace and light.

I insisted that in this she was mistaken and asked her why it is, that she, having been in the spirit world so much longer than had I, and that during these years of her existence as a spirit their masses and prayers had been offered for her, that she is in no better condition than when she first became a spirit, while I, who was so wicked and sinful on earth, was in the condition in which she saw me. Well, she could not explain, and said she would think of the matter and ask some of her priests why it is so. I left her, and impressed her to think about the matter and said that I would come to her again, and would continue to come to her until she should become convinced of the truth of what I had told her.

Well, I believe that soon I will be able to convince her that she is

---

[151] This message is a composite of two, being published in Volume III and Volume IV. (G.J.C.)

in error and will never find relief so long as she continues in the beliefs that the priests and her zeal for her church while on earth, caused her to imbibe.

I believe what you say, and I will follow your advice. I will now stop and with my love will say good night.

Your old friend,

Forrest.

A sailor needs help, described his travels in the Seas of Darkness, with his mates, and recalls what he did on earth

I am here, Ben Robinson.

Let me write. I am very unhappy. I want help. So listen to me for a while.

I am a man who lived a life of sin on earth. I was a sailor and visited every country on earth, and joined in all the vice that I could find in the seaports of these countries. I drank and gambled and visited the women and did everything that was bad. Since I have become a spirit I have seen that my life was very sinful and am suffering so very much, and have to sail through these seas of darkness with never a port to land in. I am always sailing and never coming to anchor, and my ship is nothing but my spirit body. How funny that I don't need any sails, or rudder or compass, but I sail and go where I want to and never miss my bearings. All I do is think of where I want to go and I sail there without any trouble or mistake.

But these seas are all blackness; and there are no stars to guide us and no winds to tell us that it is storming or calm; but the blackness is here all the time.

I have companions or mates who sail with me at times, and we talk of the strangeness of the seas and the blackness of the heavens, and the want of stars and winds, and of our torture. Why I sometimes think that I must be in the seas of hell, only there is no light which would naturally come from fires, if there were any.

I have my recollections of what I did on earth and they seem to burn me and cause my sufferings. So do my mates suffer from the same cause, they say.

I want to get into port and find some relief from these long, never-ending voyages in which I suffer torment. So will you tell me where I can find a port of landing where I may see the light and the stars and get rid of my tortures.

My mates can't help me, and I don't know the course that will land me. I am without any hope of ever dropping anchor again, and I tell you the thought that I have got to sail these dark seas forever makes me wish that I had never entered on the voyage of life.

I have never seen any spirits who are different from myself or who could help me out of my troubles. I never believed in God or religious things and lived only the pleasures of the sea and ports, as I have told you. My name is Ben Robinson, and my land home was Yarmouth. Me, I died in 1878, at sea.

I should like to meet such a mate.

Well, I have found him and he says he will show me the way to port. I am going with him and will listen to his yarn.

So with all my heart, I say good night.

Jesus, like all other spiritual writers, tells Mr. Padgett that he wishes to write on an important subject, because he feels that Mr. Padgett is in the proper condition to receive it, and explains St. John's Revelations

September 5th, 1915.

I am here, Jesus.

I want you to try and receive a message from me tomorrow night, as I think you will be in condition to do so. I was with you tonight at the Coburn's, and heard what you said about the Bible and it's writers, and I desire to say that many things in it were not written by my disciples or by those to whom my disciples had delivered the sayings that I made use of while on earth. The text as contained in the present Bible is not a true copy of what I said, or what was in the manuscripts of those who originally wrote; and I am trying to correct the many errors that the Bible contains.

Well, the sayings in the Epistles and in the Gospels and in Revelation to the effect that my blood saves from sin, were erroneous, and my disciples never wrote that false doctrine, for I repeat here, what I have before written you, that my blood has nothing to do with the redemption of mankind from sin, nor has my blood any effect in uniting man to God or making them one with Him.

The only thing that works this great result is the New Birth as I have explained it to you. So do not let these sayings of the Bible disturb your belief in what I say now, or in what I may hereafter write. Paul in his epistle did write that blood washes away sins, but he did not know at that time that only the reception (of Divine Love) in the souls of men removes sin and all tendency to sin. He has learned better since he came to the spirit world and some time he will write you on this subject and correct the great error he made in his epistles.

Well, the Revelations of John are not true—it is a man made allegory and it is not just as he wrote it, for it contains many things that are absurd and not in accord with the truths as I shall write them to you. I will also have him come and explain the "Revelations" and tell you what he did not write, as he has been much annoyed by this book of the Bible and its interpretations by the preachers and others. It is nothing but a relation of a vision which he thinks he saw while in a trance, as you mortals say. I mean that the real revelation that he wrote is only the vision of a trance. So let not these things disturb you.

I see that you are getting more of the Divine Love in your soul, and your spiritual eyes will be opened, and your soul perceptions will, before long, see and understand many of the vital truths of God. I will not write more tonight.

I love you as my dear brother and disciple, and will not forsake you or permit you to want. All things will be provided for you and the home which you have in mind. I know your thoughts as you walked in the park with reference to a home, and to doing my work, and you will realise your desires in those regards.

So with all my love, I am, your brother and friend,
Jesus.[152]

Old friend of Mr. Padgett is interested in the Prayer that Jesus wrote, as he wants to progress out of his darkness into the light

December 6th, 1916.

I am Edwin Forrest.

I merely want to say a word. I know it is late, but I have been listening to your reading and conversation tonight, and I have been much interested, for you have read and said many things that I had no knowledge of. I was especially interested in the Prayer which you say Jesus wrote, and I tried to commit it to memory, for I believe that if it will be helpful to you, it will be helpful to me also, and I need help so much, although I am not in the awful condition of darkness and suffering that I was in when I first wrote you.

It is wonderful to me how you have these bright and high spirits come to you and write such messages as you receive. I am present many times when you are writing, and can understand what you are receiving, but strange as it may seem to you, I cannot see these spirits unless they specially reveal themselves to me.

I know, though, that they are writing, for I can sense an influence that comes only when these spirits are present, I know this

---

[152] This message is a composite of two, being published in Volume II and Volume IV. (G.J.C.)

because sometimes they show themselves to me, and then I see that they are beautiful and bright spirits; and when they are so present, I always sense the influence that I speak of. And besides, your wife sometimes comes to me and tells me that such spirits are present. I have learned many truths since your wife has been trying to instruct me, and I am praying and seeking for the Love which she tells me of; but it seem so difficult to get it. I don't know just why, but I shall continue to strive for it, for your wife tells me that it will come to me when I get in proper condition to receive it.

I am happier than I have been, and my hope is increasing, and my faith also, and I am determined not to cease praying and striving until I receive the freedom from my condition that I am informed is just a little ahead of me.

Well, I thank you, and I will try to follow your advice and help these other spirits whenever I can.

Lipscomb is still in much darkness. He does not seem to desire to get out of his condition, and still associates with spirits like himself, and visits these low places of earth in the belief that he is getting some pleasure in his imaginary drinking, etc.

I have not seen Mills lately, but suppose he is still in the condition that he was in when I last saw him. I know that he needs help, and while I do not feel that I can help him much yet, I will try.

Yes, I am interested in all my folks on earth, as well as those in the spirit world, and I sometimes visit my old home and try to make them feel better, but I can make but little impression on them, and I see that it will be a difficult undertaking to cause them to think of anything pertaining to this life other than what their beliefs cause them to think. They are Catholics with all their hearts and minds, and would not doubt what their priests say to them for anything in all the world. But I shall be with them, and when they come over will meet them. I have seen some of my folks here who are in darkness and still believe in the doctrines of their church, waiting to get out of purgatory. I have never spoken to them upon spiritual matters, for I have never felt qualified to do so; but as soon as I progress a little, I will try to enlighten them. Well, I find that she is not anything to me more than a friend. I have no special affection for her, but will try to help her if I can. I must stop. Remember me in your prayers, and believe that I am

Your friend,
Edwin Forrest.

CPSIA information can be obtained
at www.ICGtesting.com
Printed in the USA
BVHW040833050723
666775BV00009B/39